"PARISH-FED BASTARDS"

Recent Titles in
Contributions in Labor Studies

Social Workers and Labor Unions
Howard Jacob Karger

Capitalist Development and Class Capacities: Marxist Theory and Union Organization
Jerry Lembcke

Occupation and Class Consciousness in America
Douglas M. Eichar

Our Own Time: A History of American Labor and the Working Day
David R. Roediger and Philip S. Foner

Women, Minorities, and Unions in the Public Sector
Norma M. Riccucci

Labor Relations in Europe: A History of Issues and Developments
Hans Slomp

The Fictitious Commodity: A Study of the U.S. Labor Market, 1880-1940
Ton Korver

The Re-education of the American Working Class
Steven H. London, Elvira R. Tarr, and Joseph F. Wilson, editors

New Trends in Employment Practices
Walter Galenson

Order Against Chaos: Business Culture and Labor Ideology in America, 1880-1915
Sarah Lyons Watts

The Emancipation of Labor: A History of the First International
Kenryk Katz

The Unsettled Relationship: Labor Migration and Economic Development
Demetrios G. Papademetriou and Philip L. Martin, editors

Workers' Participative Schemes: The Experience of Capitalist and Plan-based Societies
Helen A. Tsiganou

"PARISH-FED BASTARDS"

A History of the Politics of the Unemployed in Britain, 1884–1939

RICHARD FLANAGAN

Contributions in Labor Studies, Number 37

GREENWOOD PRESS
New York • Westport, Connecticut • London

Library of Congress Cataloging-in-Publication Data

Flanagan, Richard.
"Parish-fed bastards" : a history of the unemployed in Britain, 1884-1939 / Richard Flanagan.
p. cm.—(Contributions in labor studies, ISSN 0886-8239 ; no. 37)
Includes bibliographical references and index.
ISBN 0-313-27439-8 (alk. paper)
1. Unemployed—Great Britain—Political activity—History.
I. Title. II. Series.
HD8395.F53 1991
322'.2'0941—dc20 91-47

British Library Cataloguing in Publication Data is available.

Library of Congress Catalog Card Number: 91-47
ISBN: 0-313-27439-8
ISSN: 0886-8239

First published in 1991

Greenwood Press, 88 Post Road West, Westport, CT 06881
An imprint of Greenwood Publishing Group, Inc.

Printed in the United States of America

The paper used in this book complies with the Permanent Paper Standard issued by the National Information Standards Organization (Z39-48-1984).

10 9 8 7 6 5 4 3 2 1

Copyright Acknowledgments

The author and publisher gratefully acknowledge the following:

History Workshop Journal, for permission to quote "The Workers Front," reprinted in Tom Thomas, "Their Theatre and Ours," *History Workshop Journal*, No. 4 (Autumn 1977).

The Bodleian Library, Oxford University, for permission to extract from anon., "Disabled Through Service" (c. 1919-20), Unemployment, Box 8, John Johnson Collection, Bodleian Library.

Ebenezer Morris, the copyright holder for Idris Davies, "Gwalia Deserta," reprinted in Gwyn Alf Williams, *When Was Wales?* (Penguin Books, Harmondsworth, U.K., 1985).

Every reasonable effort has been made to trace the owners of copyright materials in this book, but in some instances this has proven impossible. The author and publisher will be glad to receive information leading to more complete acknowledgments in subsequent printings of the book and in the meantime extend their apologies for any omissions.

Wisdom cries out in the streets
and yet no man regards it.

Proverbs 1:20
Henry IV, Part I

In memory of
Geoff Clarke
Drago Mance

But the worst night of all was Sunday night, about 1:30 . . . . We were all wakened at the sound of heavy motor vehicles, which turned out to be Black Marias. Lights in the houses were lit, windows opened to see what was going on. Policemen bawled out "Lights out!" and "Pull up those ——— windows!"

Hordes of police came rushing up the stairs, doors commenced to be smashed in, the screams of women and children were terrible. We could hear the thuds of the blows from batons. Presently our doors were bashed by heavy instruments. My husband got out of bed without waiting to put his trousers on, and unlocked the door. As he did so, 12 police rushed into the room, knocking him to the floor, his poor head being split open, kicking him as he lay. We were all in our night clothes. The language of the police was terrible. I tried to prevent them hitting my husband. Then they commenced to baton me all over the arms and body. As they hit me and my Jim, the children and I were screaming, and the police shouted "Shut up, you parish-fed bastards!"

—*Statement by Mrs. Davin, on a police raid following Birkenhead unemployed riots, 18 September 1932, quoted Allen Hutt,* The Post-War History of the British Working Class *(1937), p. 224.*

Contents

List of Tables

List of Abbreviations

The following abbreviations have been used throughout the text:

Organizations

AEU	Amalgamated Engineering Union
BEU	British Empire Union
BSP	British Socialist Party
BUF	British Union of Fascists
COR	Court of Referees
CPGB	Communist Party of Great Britain
CUWC	Coventry Unemployed Workers' Committee (1920-1923)
CWC	London Central Workers' Committee (1905-1906)
FUBW	Fascist Union of British Workers (1933)
ILP	Independent Labour Party
IUX	International Union of Ex-Servicemen (1919-1920)
IWW	Industrial Workers of the World
KPD	Communist Party of Germany
LCC	London County Council
LDC	London District Council of Unemployed Organisations
LRC	Labour Representation Committee
NAC	National Administrative Council -of unemployed organizations (1921) -of NUWCM / NUWM (1921-1939)
NCSS	National Council of Social Service
NFDDSS	National Federation of Discharged and Demobilised Sailors and Soldiers (1917-1921)
NUPPO	National Union of Police and Prison Officers
NUWCM	National Unemployed Workers' Committee Movement (1921-1929)

NUWM	National Unemployed Workers' Movement (1929-1939)
NUX	National Union of Ex-Servicemen (1919-1920)
NWCM	National Workers' Committee Movement
PAC	Public Assistance Committee
RILU	Red International of Labour Unions
SLP	Socialist Labour Party
SDF	Social Democratic Federation
SDFUC	SDF Unemployed Committee (1893-1894)
SDP	Social Democratic Party
SS&WCM	Shop Stewards' & Workers' Committee Movement
SWMF	South Wales Miners Federation
TUUOC	Trade Union Unemployed Organisation Committee (1890-1891)
UAB	Unemployment Assistance Board
UOC	Unemployed Organisation Committee (1892-1893)
UWC	Unemployed Workers' Committee (1920-1921)
UWO	Unemployed Workers Organisation (1923-1924)
WSF	Workers' Socialist Federation
WSPU	Women's Social and Political Union
YCL	Young Communist League

Introduction

This book is about the politics of the unemployed, a crude rubric that is used for want of a better one. Unemployment in its various campaigning guises, "Work or Maintenance", "The Right to Work", "March For Jobs", is one of the great and central themes of British working class history, and there is little in the vast corpus written upon that subject that does not make mention of the unemployed. And yet much of the experience of the unemployed remains outside of the collective memory that nourishes and sustains the British working class. While its great victories and even its great defeats, such as the General Strike of 1926, are the marrow of its consciousness, the battles of the unemployed have been largely forgotten. This book is no more than an exploratory essay seeking both to recover this marginalized past, and to understand why it was marginalized in the first place. Its scope is wide, the years between 1884 and 1939, and therefore there are, no doubt, innumerable omissions, and it is, no doubt, guilty of generalizations about historic themes about which some may feel uncomfortable. But this book is also written against the stultifying orthodoxy that has emerged in the last two decades of writing highly detailed monographs about highly specific events or themes. These black holes of knowledge take pride in concentrating all knowledge about a minuscule moment but never making connections between such knowledge and the larger world as it was and is. It is not simply that this approach is fundamentally ahistorical in its refusal to seek a relationship between its findings and the past and the present. It is not just that this approach is arrogant in refusing to ally its scholarship with the experience of the everyday world. It is that it is an approach that offers only despair to those who would seek to learn from it. If history is not about hope, then it has failed.

This book is about the way the unemployed engaged politically with the society in which they lived; it is about how they tried to wrest and retain some control over their lives as unemployed workers. It is about how the people most disadvantaged in a society can, under certain circumstances, manifest power, albeit of an ephemeral and transitory kind. It is therefore about assertion and not submission, about activity and not passivity. It is not about the everyday, somewhat better documented ways in which people battled from one day to the next, substituting lard for margarine, dripping for lard. It is not about token acts of rebellion such as the incident in Hunslet in 1932 when Ernie Benson and his fellow unemployed test workers locked their two supervisors in the mess room, and then pissed through a hole onto the glowing wood stove inside, leaving their overseers staggering about in a cloud of misty urine.[1]

At the beginning of a recently published book on unemployment by D. N. Ashton we find the following passage: "In public discussions it is often assumed that one of the political costs of mass unemployment is a threat to the social fabric, a threat which sooner or later will manifest itself as evil unrest. In fact, in neither the 1930s nor the 1980s have such forms of mass action emerged. . . . In the 1930s the Unemployed Workers' Association [*sic*] was formed by the unemployed in Britain but it never achieved mass support."[2] Implicit in this mishmash of assertion and historical distortion, is the belief that the unemployed are helpless victims, dolts who have suffered much, and yet are incapable of affecting their destiny. It is as political cripples, their bodies deformed by the thalidomide of unemployment, that they are deserving of our sympathy and help. Ashton's view of the unemployed is at once patronizing and class based. It is also widely held by historians writing upon the subject, who while ever ready to discuss the unemployed as symptoms of economic decline, symbols of injustice, objects of administrative development, statistics, and examples of stoic fortitude, rarely consider the unemployed as active agents. Were it not for the central importance of the lies that these historians' work echo for our age their dissembling scholarship would long ago have been exposed for the fiction that it is.

What little has been written upon the political activity of the unemployed, a small handful of articles, and a book upon the inter-war hunger marchers,[3] focuses solely upon the National Unemployed Workers' Movement (NUWM), the inter war unemployed organization. All of these works stand indebted and in the shadow of *Unemployed Struggles*, an account of the NUWM written by its leader, Wal Hannington. Chapters Five and Six of this book show that Hannington's work contains certain inaccuracies and is misleading, particularly upon the origins of the NUWM. This is not to cast doubts upon the general veracity of *Unemployed Struggles*, but to suggest that as a historical document it needs to be used with greater sensitivity to the circumstances of its production than has been the case. Written in 1936, the year, if ever there was one, of the Popular Front, it is in some ways an argument for a mass working class politics different from that of the Communist Party, and very much at odds with that of the Popular Front. The Labour Party leaders are paraded only as poltroons, the Communist Party is given but a bit part, the insurgent proletariat is the hero, the bourgeoisie the enemy. This is far more than an account of the NUWM: it is a working class narrative of almost mythical proportions. In its telling of the seemingly spontaneous uprisings of the workers, the "tremendous" demonstrations, and the ceaseless, unremitting struggle of the unemployed (there is no sense of ebb and flow in the book), Hannington presents us with an idealized version of the working class and of working class activity. Hannington's book is deservedly a working class classic, but its full greatness will not be appreciated until it is read not so much as a straightforward history, but as a high point of autodidact culture, an idealized fiction about a mythical working class as it ought to be, and not how it was.[4]

Unemployed Struggles is nowhere more misleading than in the impression it imparts of the politics of the unemployed beginning with the founding of the NUWM in 1921. This book seeks to break with the tradition begun by Hannington of looking at the political activity of the unemployed only in the inter-war period, and seeks to place the NUWM in a tradition of unemployed struggle by tracing the history of the unemployed from 1884, when they first emerge as an entity with political aims, through to 1939 when the NUWM effectively came to an end. In doing so this book labors under the numerous limitations produced by the constraints of space, the breadth of time covered, and the incessant activity of the unemployed themselves. It is a general outline that has had to sacrifice considerable detail to make its major points. In summary, these are that the politics of the unemployed are essentially about conflict, because only through conflict were the unemployed ever able to win concessions. This book shows that such concessions were invariably double-edged, as the state sought to twist them to their own advantage and impose new forms of control upon the unemployed. In following this crazed dialectical dance between the state and the unemployed, it is evident that the growth of what is sometimes termed a "social conscience" about that unemployed was not the product of humanism and altruism, but rather of a fear of the political activity of the unemployed. This book shows that while only socialists ever succeeded in organizing the unemployed in Britain, their relation with the unemployed they sought to lead was always highly problematic. This is not then a history that sits easily in any existing historiographical tradition: for those on the right it is a condemnation of an entire system that they serve to defend; for Labour historians it is a history that brings the Labour vision up against the narrow walls of its limitations; and for Communist historians it is a mixed story that reflects credit upon Marxist militants, but brings little glory to Marxist organizations. No one ever felt very comfortable becoming involved with the unemployed on equal terms; today historians are no different.

While it is undoubtedly true that the unemployed were generally inactive, apathetic, and uninterested in the socialists' visions, this in itself is not particularly interesting: their narrowly circumscribed worlds were far more obvious to them than they are to us; pointedly, and constantly, they had the police, the charity workers, and the poor law officials to reinforce the bitter knowledge of their own profound weakness. The unemployed were not a constant and given group in the way say center lathe operators were, possessing a common experience and shared sense of solidarity. They were a group as diverse as the entire working class, some out of work between jobs, some because of a trade downturn, some because their industry was in decline, some for days, some for weeks, some for months, some for years. Their individual experiences of unemployment varied enormously and were an unpromising foundation upon which to build a collective political practice that was viable. What is interesting, and what this book explores, is why at certain moments of economic and social rupture these shackles weaken to the extent that they can be momentarily cast aside.

The assumption that the unemployed were dispirited and destroyed by unemployment is based on the belief that unemployment was a rare event for working-class people that they were unaccustomed to, rather than a structural part of their existence (being regularly in and out of work) that they were familiar with and had evolved techniques to deal with, and against which they had a history of struggle. In the masses of information generated about the unemployed it is altogether too easy to forget that people did not experience unemployment as a sociological or statistical phenomenon, but as the arrogance of a relieving officer, the long cold wait in a queue to pick up a dole check, the terror and humiliation of the visit of the means test man. Their lives as unemployed lacked the the coherence and structure of their employed counterparts; but where there was a structure—*a social relationship*—they were able to exert pressure, that is, at the local and immediate level. By refusing to play the game here they could disrupt the system, and if that system was experiencing a moment of crisis, changes were possible. At such times organization mattered, and the longest lived and most coherent unemployed organization, the NUWM, is of considerable importance in the history of the politics of the unemployed. Paradoxically even in the case of the NUWM its successes occurred not at times of best and most efficient organization, but at the times when the organization was often at its most ineffectual. At such times the NUWM and its predecessors, rather than being hidebound by ideology, were able to seize hold of a prevalent mood, and use it to generate a consensus capable of manifesting considerable, if transitory, power. At such times the unemployed, who had previously seemed so fragmented and inert, could transcend themselves, and become united and active on a mass scale.

The politics of the unemployed does not lend itself to easy demarcations: the leadership was generally more committed, more political, and more militant than the unemployed. On the rare occasions when they were not they were genuinely shocked. Reliant as the leadership was upon mass consent and the mass involvement of the unemployed to be effective, they also had to be responsive to both the torporific and cathartic desires of the unemployed, and conscious of the levels of activity that the unemployed desired and deemed possible at different times. Both leaders and led shaped each other.

This book shows how the unemployed to some extent made themselves; how their political activity led to reformulations of what it meant to be unemployed, and how these new concepts, themselves the product of conflict, in turn became new arenas for conflict. The general arguments of the book are that while unemployment is an inevitable product of industrial society, the unemployed are only specifically defined through their relation with the state, and that this relation is to some extent shaped in reaction to the activity of the unemployed. Second, while there exists a fluid relationship between welfare and popular protest, any welfare system, from the old poor law onwards, is but a temporary, and hence impermanent, resolution of the class antagonisms extant in society.

Finally, the book is an attempt to break the tyranny of those who look at the unemployed only in terms of their suffering. It is not concerned to compare domestic expenditure with domestic income, to make spurious calculations about the number of weeks a child could live on margarine and bread before it would suffer from malnutrition, to explain exactly why a race of stunted people—the "wee folk"—in their sixties and seventies can today be found in such industrial centers as Glasgow. This is not because I wish to deny the intolerable yet tolerated suffering, or to minimize the enormity of the misery that was and is unemployment. It is because no account, no statistics, no literature can bear adequate witness to the monstrosity of unemployment. From the "Swing" rural laborers of the 1830s who died behind hedges with only sour sorrel in their protruding bellies, to the London rent boys of today who die with only heroin in their protruding veins, unemployment has always been one of the great indictments of capitalist society.

1

A Procession of a Most Grotesque Character: The Origins of the Unemployed

The feudal world was not a pleasant place in which to be poor. To be poor though was not, as it was to become, something reprehensible in itself. Poverty was seen as a social phenomenon, rather than as evidence of personal failure. The medieval church taught that poverty could be spiritually enriching. Ascetism was equated with poverty, a state pleasing to God (if not his more materially minded representatives upon earth), and this view was to reach its apotheosis in the life and teachings of St. Francis of Assissi. Certainly poverty was not seen as a vice for which an individual was culpable and ought to be punished, as it was to become in later times. "Poverty", wrote Joannes Andrae in the twelfth century, "is not a kind of crime."[1]

Too much should not be made of this: the poor did not meet with constant beneficence in the feudal world. But what is important is that nor were the poor part of the demonology of this world. Widows and orphans in particular, and the poor in general were defined in canonical law as "*miserables personae*"—wretched persons—and to these, in theory at least, the church extended its protection. Parishes were required to take care of their own poor, and the rich were extolled by the church to help the poor, such good deeds easing the journey of the rich to heaven. Wealth was seen to have a social rather than an individual character; and to withold alms when there was necessity was a mortal sin. As late as the sixteenth century Latimer preached "The poor man hath title to a rich man's goods", and Thomas Cromwell, adviser to Henry VIII, observed the ancient custom of feeding the poor, 200 people being fed twice daily at his gate.[2]

Yet people do not act upon ethereal promises alone, and charity has also always been a reflex of fear. In the medieval world charity had a magic value, reflecting fear of turning away empty-handed a beggar who might then resort to witchcraft for retribution. From the beginning of the modern period the poor came to be relieved not only out of fear of such individual revenge, but also out of fear of the social consequences of the poor's rebellious activities if they were not given some relief. The history of the relief of the poor is inextricably bound up with the history of the modern state and the methods it used to ensure its own survival. More fundamentally, both are bound up with the overarching emergence of capitalism. As Christopher Hill has reminded us, permanent wage labor, the precondition of capitalist production, and the poor law arose together.[3]

Poverty Becomes a Crime

The first crisis of feudalism had already begun prior to the arrival of the Black Death in 1348, but the plague dramatically exacerbated existing tensions. Because of the Black Death the population of Britain was reduced, labor became scarce, and wages rose quickly, leading to a weakening of feudal ties. The first national attempt to control the relief of the poor came in 1349 in an ordinance which tried to ensure a cheap supply of labor at pre-Plague rates by pegging wages at the old levels. This was to be enforced partly by forbidding individuals to give charity to able-bodied beggars on the grounds that they ought to "be compelled to labour for their living". In this way the first attempt to compel the poor on a national scale to become waged laborers was bound up with the first attempt to impose some national control on the relief of the poor. This process of creation of a mass of waged laborers was given momentum by changes taking place elsewhere.[4]

A rapid growth in the manufacture of wool in Flanders led to a rapid rise in the price of wool, which had the effect of stimulating the transformation of arable land into pastoral land. As the agrarian revolution began, enclosure (the stealing of commons land), engrossing (the turning of villages and small farms into sheep runs) and other new practices employed by the nobility combined to render small-scale tenant farming by the peasantry unviable, and to destroy remaining manorial ties. Their land taken from them, without the means to produce their own subsistence, many peasants were forced to leave the land or die. Sheep, wrote Sir Thomas More in *Utopia*, had "turned into maneaters."[5]

A new mass of wandering poor people, without masters, without landholdings, and without loyalties, forced into a life of beggary, robbery, and vagabondage, began to appear throughout Britain. Elements of this mass have since been characterized as unemployed by many historians,[6] and here we founder upon a fundamental problem. It is reasonable to use the word "unemployed" as a descriptive shorthand when talking exclusively of the early modern era. But in the context of this book, which is concerned with the unemployed of the last 100 years, we need to ask if it is possible to regard the vagrants and vagabonds of the sixteenth and seventeenth centuries as being "unemployed" in the twentieth century sense of the word?

First, we need to remember that the modern idea of full waged employment, of working a set number of hours, days and weeks in return only for a sum of cash, was totally alien to the medieval mind. Dr. J. F. Pound has erroneously argued that for many vagrants in Tudor England the "idea of a fair day's work was anathema . . . and they would go to any lengths to avoid it." Far from being anathema to vagrants, the idea of "a fair day's labor" was wholly anachronistic to them and their period. Dr. Pound may as well admonish the vagrants for choosing to wander upon forest tracks instead of advancing along career paths. The vagrants belonged to a society where waged labor was seen as a loss of freedom, and in an era of falling wages, at best an unattractive economic prospect. Unlike today when we must all engage in waged labor, waged labor then was only one of many economic options available to people. We cannot then assume that a life of waged work was preferable to a life of vagrancy. Many vagrants did not want waged work, and saw beggary as a better and more profitable alternative, which their historian, A. L. Beier, has agreed it was.[7]

Second, vagrants and vagabonds were not so much unemployed workers astride their metaphorical bikes in search of a permanent job, as they were dispossessed people on the road pursuing an eclectic variety of beggary, thievery and occasional work as and when it could be had. A Wiltshire vagrant arrested in 1605 declared that he was "sometimes a weaver, sometimes a surgeon, sometimes a minstrel, sometimes a dyer, and now a bullard." Not all the dispossessed poor chose to wander and many eked out a living in forests, erecting shelters and setting up small farms. Self-sufficient, they had no desire to work as wage laborers. Declared an Elizabethan surveyor of dwellers in Rockingham Forest "So long as they may be permitted to live in such idleness upon their stock of cattle, they will bend themselves to no kind of labor." This leads to the third and most important point: the vagrants and paupers neither constituted nor acted like a modern reserve army of labor, by, for example, keeping wages down. Even on the land where the majority of people still worked, the supply of surplus labor was so small that employers had to be prevented from paying higher wages. As Professor Elton has rightly observed "This is not the sort of thing that happens when many landless men press on a glutted labor market."[8]

Even if the sixteenth century vagrants had, to use Dr. Pound's fatuous formula, desired "a fair day's work" it generally wasn't available. While feudalism in its final stages was setting masses of laborers free, they were laborers to whom embryonic capitalism was by and large unable to offer work. "Nobody will give them a job", wrote Thomas More, "however much they want one." Not until the mid-seventeenth century were the structural factors inhibiting the development of industrial capitalism to be sufficiently eroded for this mass of masterless people to be absorbed into the new relationships of work. The vagrants and vagabonds of Tudor England were people who no longer possessed status in the declining feudal order or, as yet, utility in the rising capitalist order. As such they were a potent threat to the social order of the sixteeenth century.[9]

Tudor society was far from stable, and always, everywhere, in ever increasing numbers were the vagrants, who became identified with disorder. In consequence the concept of poverty was redefined. Along with the "new" crimes of treason and witchcraft, vagrancy came to be seen as threatening to the state. Poverty became a crime, and to counter its political dangers the Tudors expanded the role of the state. Powers of summary justice were given to parish officials throughout the kingdom.

If arrested, vagrants ran the new risks of the pillory (from 1520), whippings (from 1531), ear borings an inch in diameter made with a hot iron (from 1572), and being branded "R" for rogue (from 1604). The state's response was not wholly punitive, but a mix of punishment and relief given on qualified terms. In this respect the Tudors' most important innovation was the houses of corrections, also known as bridewells, the forerunner of the workhouses in their attempt to reform vagabonds through work, and their penal-like discipline. Within the bridewells relief and punishment combined: floggings were common, conditions terrible, and overseers often corrupt. The bridewells degenerated into general lock-ups, but the idea of them was to be revived in the eighteenth century.[10]

The problem of the maintenance of public order took on a particular urgency in the final years of Elizabeth's reign. The prosperous years of 1575 to 1590 had been succeeded by a string of disastrous harvests from 1592 to 1596, a financially crippling war, the return of the plague and conditions of near famine. Combined these factors created conditions pregnant with unrest, and led the earl of Bath in 1596 to write to the Privy Council of the need for the gentry to now return to their estates "to be at hand to stay the fury of the inferior multitude if they should happen to break out in sudden outcry for want of relief, as without good circumspection many suspect they may and will do." The Tudor ruling class responded to this threat with charity (a response that was to become a reflex action in the succeeding centuries) and with legislative action. In 1597 two acts were passed that codified the practice of the Tudors with regard to the poor. The first act, for the relief of the poor (39 Eliz., c. 3), was re-enacted in 1601 and formed the basis of the poor law up until 1834. This act made it a legal obligation for parishes to provide poor relief to those who had "no ordinary and dayly Trade of life to gett there lyvinge by." The second act, (39 Eliz., c. 4) provided for the punishment by whipping of vagabonds, who were, for the first time, defined as including those "refusing to worcke for such reasonable Wages as is taxed or commonly gyven."[11]

"Thus", wrote Marx in an acute summary of these processes, "were the agricultural folk first forcibly expropriated from the soil, driven from their homes, turned into vagabonds, and then whipped, branded, and tortured by grotesquely terroristic laws into accepting the discipline necessary for the system of wage labor."[12]

The Related Rise of Wage Labor, Poor Relief, and the Unemployed

The masterless men and women of the sixteenth and seventeenth centuries with their mutilated faces and branded bodies were the parents of the industrial working class. They were not a reserve army of labor, but a precondition for the development of industrial capitalism, which would require the reproduction of their misery in the form of waged labor to prosper. In this the poor law was to pay an important role.

For capital to increase its value it needed to be able to purchase labor power, which alone could enrich it: without labor power capital could only petrify. For this enrichment to take place it was necessary that masses of wage laborers be brought into existence. In 1696 John Bellers asked, "if one had a hundred thousand acres of land as many pounds in money, and as many cattle, without a labourer, what would the rich man be but a labourer?" Bellers added, "And as the labourers make men rich, so the more labourers there will be, the more rich men . . . the labour of the poor being the mines of the rich." But it was not sufficient to have only the labor necessary for a particular job. To maximize profits it proved helpful to have a large surplus pool of labor always ready to work for less than those in employment, so as to keep wages low. This principle was understood as early as 1680, the year in which it was declared in the *Brittanica Languens*: "plenty of people must also produce the like odds in Manufacture: plenty of people also cause cheapnesse of wages: which will cause the cheapnesse of Manufacture."[13]

Part of the way of both ensuring the existence of a surplus pool of labor and of guaranteeing low wages lay in building an infrastructure of state support for the general principle of wage laboring (but not the individual wage laborer) in the form of the poor law. Wages were fixed by the justices of the peace, who were encouraged by the existence of poor relief (which they also administered) to fix wages at the lowest possible levels. Poor relief thus became a subsidy to wages. "Were it not for what they receive out of the tax", observed Lord Townshend in 1730, "they would not knit or spin for so small wages as they receive for that work because they would starve by it." "Everyone but an idiot knows that the lower classes must be kept poor," wrote Arthur Young four decades later, "or they will never be industrious."[14]

Poor relief did more than provide an allowance to the employed wage laborers sufficient to maintain them in a state only marginally better than utter wretchedness. It also helped in the creation of work discipline at the time of industrialisation. For a long time many people found the concept of waged labor, so acceptable to the twentieth century mind as to be unquestioned, utterly repugnant. The seventeenth century digger Gerrard Winstanley, called for the abolition of waged labor, which he saw as a source of exploitation. Both wage labor and its colleague of later years, factory discipline, were not readily accepted by the lower orders. The industrialist Richard Arkwright admitted he had difficulty "in training human beings to denounce their desultory habits of work, and identify themselves with the unvarying regularity of an automaton." It was important that not only those in work, but those out of work, be so trained and here, from the 1600s, workhouses began to play a small role. The Tudor idea of the house of correction was revived in the late seventeenth century with the Bristol "Mint", a huge workhouse established by the merchants of the city, which became adopted throughout England as a model.[15]

The workhouses were partly intended to deter the poor from applying for relief, which was given conditionally upon them going into the workhouse. This became known as indoor relief. Within the workhouse the poor would be put to work on jobs that would offset some of the cost of their relief. More importantly the workhouses were intended to discipline the poor, to give the externally masterless people a new internal master of rigid self control and belief in work discipline. Not for nothing were many factory works modelled on workhouses, a similarity that would not have escaped the notice of the working people nor have endeared them to either type of institution. Many who viewed wage labor as being as great an evil as slavery saw pauperism not as a natural state, but as part of the system of wage labor. A file hewer of the eighteenth century lamented:

As negroes in Virginia,
In Maryland or Guinea,
Like them I must continue
To be both bought and sold.
While negro ships are filling
I ne'er can save one shilling,
And must, which is more killing,
A pauper die when old.[16]

Poor relief was not wholly framed from above, but was also, to an unknown degree, fashioned from below. The early workhouses, to give an extreme example, were often attacked by armed bands, and in 1768 one was burnt to the ground. Institutionalized relief within the workhouse was not popular and was presumably resisted in other less dramatic ways. Certainly it did not catch on, and Gilbert's Act of 1782 recognized what had become practice: workhouses became poorhouses reserved for the old, and the sick and infirm, while parishes became legally able to pay outdoor relief to underpaid and unemployed able bodied workers. This policy was contradictory in its effects: it both assisted in keeping wages down, and reinforced a new and growing belief of the poor that relief was a right, and not a privilege.[17]

Prior to the industrial revolution work was a very different matter from what it is today. It was irregular, determined largely by the forces of nature, which could freeze a watermill into inaction, and the rules of custom which could lead to the abandonment of a workshop for a wake or a fair. The concept of full employment in a modern sense, of one job assiduously pursued for a set number of days per week, weeks per month, and months per year, for a regular fixed salary, would be far more alien to the pre-industrial mind than many of the much lauded technical marvels of modern society. Manufacture in Britain before the industrial revolution rested not upon a system of factories and wage laborers but upon a system of small workshops and artisans who sold and bartered their goods rather than their labor. When demand for their goods was down, they might turn to other forms of work to support themselves. A farming weaver on the eve of the industrial revolution would, in addition to his weaving, have spent his days harvesting, threshing, churning, calving, ditching, and gardening. Alternatively they might take to the road heading to where work was plentiful. There existed the universal system of tramping, whereby jobless artisans were given a card by their craft society that guaranteed that similar societies in other towns would provide them with work if it was available, or relieve them until they set off for the next town where work might be got.[18]

The industrial revolution not only ended such patterns of labor by putting people in factories to work at a regulated pace upon a single job, but also brought about a fundamentally new economic relationship between men solely contingent on profit. Work came to be determined not by bad weather or festivals, but by an employer's willingness to buy or not buy the labor of the worker. We only find unemployment in the modern sense when we find its concomitant, employment, existing in its modern sense of regular work for wages. When there was no demand by the early capitalists for labor, and the wage laborer could turn his hand to no alternative work with which to survive, then there was, for the first time, unemployment, and we have, for the first time, the unemployed. Prior to the industrial revolution under-employment had been a major feature of the British economy; its human expression was paupers. After the industrial revolution unemployment took its place; its human expression was the unemployed. Use of the word "unemployed" in something like its modern sense of being without waged work has been found as early as the late seventeenth century. But it is significant that the words "unemployed", and (though less frequently) "unemployment" in their modern sense first enter common usage in the years between 1818 and 1830 being used by trade unionists, Radicals and Owenites to describe an aspect of the new relations of work then becoming commonplace. In Chapter Two we will see how it took another sixty years and considerable activity by the unemployed before political economists would deign to use such words.[19]

In the troubled early decades of the nineteenth century unemployment was often the immediate catalyst for the threatening political activity of the working class, but it would be wrong to label such activity as unemployed protest. Rather, it was a major attempt by the working class to end the suffering and oppression, of which unemployment was only one aspect, that the new system was bringing to them. In the end the old poor law stood condemned upon the grounds it had originally been designed to meet: if the old poor law was, in E. M. Leonard's words, "partly police measures" it had failed. The continued unrest culminating in the Swing riots showed that the old poor law was no longer capable of mediating class conflict and, in this respect, had broken down. As well as failing to bring social stability, the cost of the poor law had continued to rise. And like a gloss upon these failures were the criticisms of the political economists. They argued that by supplementing laborers' wages and thereby interfering with the naturally determined level of market wages, the old poor law acted as the last major restraint upon the workings of a free market in labor. In this and other criticisms the political economists were influenced by the writings of the Reverend Thomas Malthus.[20]

Malthus had first come to prominence in the atmosphere of ruling-class fear which prevailed in the final years of the eighteenth century. In 1798 he published his famous *Essay on the Principle of Population,* in which he propounded a theory that remains influential to this day. In a manner more timely than original, Malthus argued that population would increase at a rate far in excess of the means of subsistence unless naturally checked by moral restraint, vice, or misery. The poor law, by relieving destitution encouraged poverty by destroying the natural check of misery. This in turn led the poor to breed in greater numbers, which only served to impoverish even more members of society. Poor relief, in short, created poor people, which in turn increased the bill for poor relief. If this theory was accepted, as it widely was, the consequences seemed dire indeed. David Ricardo, the greatest of all the nineteenth century political economists, put it bluntly when in 1817 he wrote, "whilst the present laws are in force, it is quite in the natural order of things that the fund for the maintenance of the poor should progressively increase till it has absorbed all the net revenues of the country." This, for Malthus, answered "the question as to the natural right of the poor to full support in a state of society where the law of property is recognised . . . . The concession of such a right, and a right of property, are absolutely incompatible and cannot exist together."[21]

These arguments reverberate throughout the subsequent history of the unemployed. Unemployment, according to the political economists who followed Malthus, was not a social problem produced by particular kinds of societies, but a natural problem that arose from the naturally occurring surplus of population. In 1834 the Poor Law Amendment Act was passed. This radically restructured the practice of poor relief, and became known as the new poor law. It was to remain the basis of social welfare in Britain until 1946. The new poor law was based upon the Malthusian theory of "less eligibility" which, suggesting that laborers up until 1834 had been made into paupers because relief had been at least as attractive as wages earned by working, proposed that relief should always be less than the lowest returns that could be obtained through working. The method adopted to this end was brutal: the ending of outdoor relief. All who needed relief would now have to enter the workhouse, which, wrote the Reverend H. H. Milman to one of the framers of the new poor law, Edwin Chadwick, in 1832, "should be a place of hardship, of coarse fare, of degradation and humility; it should be administered with strictness—with severity; it should be as repulsive as is consistent with humanity." Rather than acting as an instrument of relief, it was intended to act as a deterrent, and for those desperate enough to seek its shelter, as punishment. Little wonder then, that they became popularly known as "Bastilles".[22]

To "make such machines of men as cannot err", as the early industrialist Josiah Wedgewood desired, the defective worker had like a machine to be repaired, or better still, fearful of the workhouse, to repair himself. The new poor law, argued the poor law commissioners in 1834, "restored and improved" the industry of laborers, "created or strengthened" their "frugal habits", and led to an abatement of "discontent". The worker was held up for comparison with the image of bourgeois rationality: if he was employed he was successful, if he was unemployed he was unsuccessful and found wanting in the bourgeois values of hard work and self-discipline. The new poor law made no pretense of caring for the unemployed worker: he lay outside the narrow realm of economic relations as understood by the political economists. What this meant to working men and women is summed up by a rural laborer who experienced the new poor law as a child in the nineteenth century. "They thought", he recalled as an old man, "every mother's son of them, that when a laborer could no longer work, he had lost the right to live."[23]

For in all truth the new poor law was a violent attack upon the working class. At a personal level the old poor law, whatever its failings, had played a vital role in providing some relief in working-class lives against utter destitution. This was now to largely disappear. On an ideological level the new poor law represented the extension of the disturbing new morality of capitalism from the industrial sphere into the domestic. Politically, the new poor law was an attempt to try and halt the burgeoning political activity of the working class. In general its proponents believed, as we have seen, that it would allay discontent. In particular it sought to weaken the indirect and sometimes direct influence of working-class people upon poor relief policy by establishing a new administrative structure for poor relief. This was to be run by boards of guardians elected by the rate payers, and it had the power to employ full time officials. For the first time there was to be a central authority to ensure among local bodies a uniformity of practice and an adherence to legislative principles hitherto unknown. All these changes strengthened the hand of those seeking a successful application of the principles of political economy, but other measures were included to ensure a complete win. Country magistrates were made ex-officio members of the new boards of guardians with full voting rights, the Poor Law Commission in London was permitted to challenge the expenditure of any local board lest it became frivolous in the execution of its duties, and election to the boards was to be by secret ballot, denying working-class militants the use of intimidation to ensure the return of sympathetic candidates.[24]

Yet too little remains known about the operation of the old poor law, particularly about the relationship between those who dispensed relief and those who received it, for us to fully recognize the magnitude of the attack that the new poor law represented. If the old poor law was by 1834 part of what has been termed the moral economy, it certainly wasn't at its inception in 1597. It is difficult, if not impossible, to see the original act as containing the notion of paternalism later attributed to it. The "laboring people of England", wrote William Cobbett in 1830, inherited from their fathers "the habit of regarding parish relief as their right." So strongly held was this belief that sections of the ruling class echoed it. All those, wrote the poet William Wordsworth in 1836, "who cannot find employment or procure wages sufficient to support the body in health and strength, are entitled to a maintenance by law." This was, he added, "one of the most precious rights of the English people."[25]

When did relief come to be seen as right? How did relief come to be seen as right? Most importantly, what part did the laboring population play in redefining the "police measure" of 1597 into what was popularly known as "the beloved 43rd of Queen Bess"? Until we have a study that shows how the working class and its precursors were able to appropriate at least something of both the ideology and practice of the old poor law and turn it to their advantage, we are not going to fully understand the subtle historical processes whereby attempts at ruling-class hegemony are subverted, nor completely appreciate how class based was the attack that the new poor law encapsulated.

We can, however, crudely gauge what much of the working class felt about the new poor law by the extent of their opposition. So strong was this that it was to be some decades before the new poor law was implemented on a national basis. In some areas it was resisted with such ferocity that troops had to be sent in. It was opposed not simply because it proposed changes in relief practices, but because it was seen as an expression of the new, pitiless class basis of modern capitalist society. The Chartist, Bronterre O'Brien, spoke for many when he said that the new poor law placed "the whole of the laboring population at the utter mercy and disposal of the monied or propertied classes". The new poor law became the focus of popular discontent (not only of the working class, but some elements of the middle class) with the nature of the new capitalism; and it is not surprising that much of the strength and energy of the Chartist movement derived from opposition to the new poor law.[26]

When in the 1840s capitalism produced the most catastrophic slump ever known up until that time, the unemployed became a distinct and highly visible feature of British cities. Frederick Engels, then a young businessman in Manchester, described how they "stood in the streets in all directions, besieged the sidewalks in armies, and appealed to the passer-by for help; they begged, not cringing like ordinary beggars, but threatening by their numbers, their gestures and their words." But beyond such personal intimidation they did nothing. No organization of the unemployed arose, and no attempt was made by the Chartist movement to organize the unemployed during what was the worst depression of the century. While we can only speculate why this is so, it is telling proof that suffering alone is never sufficient explanation of the political activity of the unemployed.[27]

The new phenomenon of mass unemployment that emerged in the "hungry forties" brought to an end many of the older ways of coping with joblessness. In the new large cities where the workers were being concentrated, alternatives to waged employment were both minimal, and increasingly irrelevant. Cash displaced barter, and those without cash were unable to procure the necessities of life: shelter, food, and warmth. The system of tramping collapsed, unable to cope with an economy that could put such large numbers out of work not only locally but nationally, and thus nearly bankrupt the trade societies in relief payments. By the mid nineteenth century the artisans' societies were looking at new ways of dealing with unemployment: friendly societies, emigration, and, most importantly, an unemployment benefit paid at home. A large part of the story of the nineteenth century labor movement is the story of the working class striving desperately to develop new ways of coping with the new, chronic insecurity of unemployment; vainly attempting to fashion a life raft out of the wreckage of an old way and concept of life that had been destroyed by the most elemental force. But whether through savings banks or through gambling, whether through the temperance movement or through the bottle, the many and varied solutions people resorted to were patently all inadequate to the gargantuan problem they sought to address.

Mass unemployment also illustrated the absurdity of the workhouse system, for what workhouse, asked "A Renfrewshire Heritor" in 1843, "could contain 10,000 to 15,000 human beings?" In an attempt to retain the principles of the new poor law while at the same time acknowledging what was common local practice, the Poor Law Commissioners in 1842 issued a general order permitting outdoor relief to be given to able-bodied men if they performed a task of work to be set by the board of guardians. Such task work was intended to help maintain the principle of less eligibility by substituting monotonous and unpleasant work such as stone breaking and oakum picking (separating the fibers of old rope) for the workhouse. Though experiencing such setbacks, and although transforming poor relief slowly and incompletely, the new poor law still transformed it. While statistics for the nineteenth century are crude and incomplete, it is clear that the new poor law did succeed in driving the unemployed off outdoor relief.[28]

There were, of course, numerous minor exceptions and two major exceptions to this process: the Irish potato famine of 1845-49 and the Lancashire cotton famine of 1862-63. But far from proving the failure of the new poor law system, the occasional resort to large scale outdoor relief showed that the system could be temporarily and successfully buttressed against the rare gale of adversity. The unemployed were sometimes restive as in London in 1860 and 1866-67 when semi-violent demonstrations took place, but they seem never to have been organized. The unemployed remained not only outside of the realm of voting, but of organization, and politics. Prior to 1884 the one time that the unemployed appear not as sporadic and spontaneous groupings intent on immediate gain though little else, but as an organized body with authorized spokesmen and a definite program (as opposed to immediate threats), is in 1870. This one attempt to organise the unemployed of London prior to 1884 was made by the republican Land and Labour League (closely allied with Marx's First International). They called a public meeting in Trafalgar Square on the afternoon of Good Friday to discuss "the state of unemployed workmen in London". A procession, like so many to follow, assembled at Clerkenwell Green that day and marched behind two bands to Trafalgar Square. The banner bearers and some of the other demonstrators wore broad scarlet sashes around their waists in, for some, an unsettling reminder of the fashion popular among the sans-culottes of the French Revolution. To underline the point caps of liberty were borne aloft poles. It was, said *The Times,* a procession "of a most grotesque character".[29]

Although the meeting attracted considerable publicity, the Land and Labour League does not seem to have made any further attempt to organize the unemployed.[30] Various speakers at the meeting called for the nationalization of land upon which the unemployed would be hired to work. In this way all who wanted work would be able to obtain it, and, said one speaker, "all who will not should be punished as rogues and vagabonds", thereby introducing the poor law distinction between deserving and undeserving poor into left-wing discourse upon the unemployed, a theme that was to recur frequently in years to come.

Mr. Hennessy, president of the meeting, told the crowd that "there was no reason why whatever for any one man being out of employment in this country". To this he linked a rudimentary class analysis: "The people were kept on the verge of starvation that the classes above might indulge in luxury."[31] The solution of land nationalization proposed by the League may well have been anachronistic and impracticable, but in their challenging of one of the central tenets of political economy—the natural inevitability of unemployment—through the actions of the unemployed themselves, they bequeathed a radical dynamic to the politics of the unemployed that was to remain with it until 1939. And it is for this reason that the demonstrators who assembled on Clerkenwell Green that Good Friday afternoon in 1870, with their sans-culottic scarlet sashes and caps of liberty, stand at the head of the history of the politics of the unemployed.

2

Black Banners To Red Flags: The Unemployed and the Socialists, 1884–1904

In October 1887 the unemployed began to hold meetings in Trafalgar Square. In spite of harassment by the police, meetings being banned and violently broken, the unemployed came to the square in growing numbers. Processions began to be organized, marching from the square through the West End beneath a large black banner inscribed "WE WILL HAVE WORK OR BREAD". The black banner, according to James Allman, an unemployed Socialist League member who, along with a few other unemployed League and Social Democratic Federation (SDF) members, had become involved with the Trafalgar Square meetings, was seen by the unemployed as symbolizing "the dark prospects of unemployed workmen, and borne in our parades as an appeal to the commiseration of the wealthy and symbol of despair." During a baton charge dispersal of an unemployed meeting on 14 October 1887 the police seized and destroyed the black banner. The following day the unemployed reappeared at the square with a red flag surmounted by the cap of liberty. The change of symbols, wrote Allman, was seen by the unemployed as "a significant incident", the red flag being regarded by the unemployed as "the emblem of sturdy revolt".[1]

The change from black banner to red flag did not mean (nor did Allman claim it did) that the unemployed had become revolutionary. But this change of symbols does capture the essential point of this chapter: how between 1884 and 1895 there was a fundamental change in the outlook of the unemployed which manifested itself in their changing from a passive role of beggary and supplication, to an active role of political struggle. Black flags had been a symbol of the London unemployed since at least the 1860s,[2] and although they continued to be used as such well into the 1920s, Allman's story suggests the influence of socialism upon the unemployed. It is between 1884 and 1895 that the unemployed first emerge as an articulate grouping. And when they speak politically, no matter how muddled the words, they do so with a socialist voice. This was not because the unemployed were somehow innately predisposed to socialism, but because in the absence of organization by anybody else, they followed those who were prepared to lead them, who could give them an intelligible explanation of their plight, and who offered them the hope of some amelioration of their condition. This did not mean the unemployed all became socialists; on the contrary, the continuing Tory electoral dominance of many London working-class areas in this period would suggest that the socialists failed to persuade the unemployed to make the all-important connection between their immediate struggles and the general world. But it did mean that when the unemployed acted politically, they did so within a socialist paradigm. And that meant, for the socialists, that their politics were from the beginning, for better or worse, inextricably linked with the politics of the unemployed.

British capitalism experienced its golden age between 1851 and 1873. Globally it was triumphant, and nationally, following the collapse of Chartism in 1848, it was unchallenged. The final quarter of the nineteenth century saw this position change rapidly. The years 1873-1896, known as the Great Depression, were a period of momentous transition in which Britain took on more or less the shape it has had ever since. It lost its international industrial supremacy to the exploding economies of Germany and the United States of America, which overtook it in key areas of production, both in terms of technology and total output. British industry met the challenge in a typically British fashion, by ignoring it. With renascent imperialism it found new markets to monopolize; and as an alternative to modernizing (and thus investing in) an already aging industrial infrastructure it relied upon a vast reserve army of labor (and its corollary, the consistently high levels of unemployment characteristic of Britain both this and last century) to service its industries, to keep its labor and hence production costs down, and to enable the rapid expansion of industry in times of prosperity. British ironmasters did not need to "give encouragement to inventive talent to devise labour saving machinery" because they enjoyed "pauper labour", commented the American journal *Iron Age* in 1874. The enormous growth of the British coal industry in this era was achieved without either a large influx of capital or the introduction of new technology, but by a continuous addition of new untrained workers, many from the ranks of the unemployed, the number of coal miners increasing from 485,000 in 1880 to 1,128,000 in 1913. It therefore remained cheaper to have most coal cut by hand rather than by machinery, and most British coal continued to be extracted by hand up until World War I. That in consequence the British coal industry was grossly inefficient (although its failings were not to become obvious until the 1920s) worried few. Despite the development of mass forms of production, small-scale industry, out work, and domestic production remained major but unstable forms of employment in Britain during this period. In these varied ways British industry relied on the unemployed, and in so doing, on the ongoing impoverishment of much of the British working class to remain antiquated yet profitable.[3]

The final quarter of the nineteenth century is remarkable politically for the rediscovery of socialism and the related rise of a political labor movement. It is remarkable socially as the era in which what is now regarded as the traditional

British class system solidified into its modern shape. Part of this process of solidification was the way in which the scraps and pieces at the bottom end of British society came to develop a shared sense of culture that defined them in terms of other classes as being working class, yet, at the same time, largely avoided an overtly political definition. The working class prior to 1914 was a balkanized grouping: at the bottom were the poor and even among them were myriad divisions based on gender, locality, age, and preferred forms of labor (when it could be had), who shared little beyond their poverty and discontent. The politics of the unemployed both in the nineteenth and twentieth centuries illustrates that not the least part of the class struggle was the struggle to create a class, that the ideal (or more accurately the various ideals) which the labor and socialist movements had of the working class was sometimes so discordant with reality that reality was best ignored. As SDF member William White put it in 1893, on the one hand you had "an aristocracy of labour... and facing them in opposition, an ignorant, unemployed blackleg class on the other. Both are distasteful to Socialists, and both must be swept away."[4] The politics of the unemployed, which is to be an occasional, discordant feature of working class life from 1884 until 1939, is the troubled nexus where working-class culture, as it is manifested in an apolitical class consciousness, meets with socialist ambition and vision. It is the nether world of British history, in which the hope of the socialists intermittently meets with the despair of the unemployed for brief desperate forays into a larger world, that is sometimes shocked, sometimes moved, and sometimes desperate to destroy this fragile connection.

"Better a Sudden Death than a Pauper's Grave"

The unemployed were organized through various bodies between 1884 and 1895, nearly all of which were SDF inspired, and SDF dominated, the unemployed having representatives upon none of them. The story of the SDF, Britain's first Marxist party, is well known; but less well-known is the story of its strange, symbiotic relationship with the politics of the unemployed. "The Social Democrats have devoted more attention to the question of the unemployed than to any other matter whatever," wrote H. M. Hyndman in 1911. "Nearly all our principal agitations, demonstrations, and collisions with the 'authorities' have arisen from our efforts in this direction." He added, "No more disheartening task can possibly be undertaken." But at the beginning it had not seemed so; and the relationship between the SDF and the unemployed was to alter considerably between 1884 and 1904. At first the unemployed offered the SDF the mass support it so desperately craved. The Democratic Federation, as the SDF was at first known, shifted from the Radical program adopted at its inception in 1881 to a Marxist program in 1883. This indicated the long-term direction of the SDF, in the short term causing the loss of much of its radical support. Hyndman, who soon established himself as the leader of the SDF was, wrote William Morris in late 1884, "always on the look out for anything which could advertise the party he is supposed to lead: his aim has been to make the movement seem big; to frighten the powers that be with a turnip bogie which perhaps he almost believes in himself."[5]

The story of the politics of the unemployed in the years from 1884 to 1904 is very largely a London-based tale, for although the unemployed were sporadically active elsewhere in Britain, only in London was the SDF strong enough to organize the unemployed on a long-term basis with national goals. It does not follow from this that the SDF's organization actually succeeded in organizing the unemployed as a cohesive force: rather, as the subsequent events of 1886 were to show, it introduced into the chaos of the casual labor market an occasional focus for feelings of rage and impotence. London, often thought of as atypical of nineteenth-century Britain, perhaps more closely resembles the true nature of the nineteenth-century economy and society than is often thought. Certainly it did not contain the starkly new features and the new proletariat of the pit villages and the mill towns, but then these received so much contemporary and subsequent interest precisely because they were so new and different. Late nineteenth-century London was not a modern industrial city; but then late nineteenth-century Britain was, in many ways, not a modern industrial nation in the way the United States of America and Germany were becoming. London's small scale manufacturers relied not upon new forms of production, but upon a massive reservoir of casual labor to remain profitable. Pre-industrial divisions between artisans and the casual poor prevailed. London was a city not of the factory proletariat, but of street hawkers, prostitutes, paupers, pimps, artisans, servants, journeymen, sweated out-workers, and everywhere swarming hordes of casual laborers. Late nineteenth-century London may not have been typical of what Britain was becoming. But it did possess many features of what Britain had been: not least a fragmented working class whose lives were shaped by, and revolved around, not the union or the co-op or any of the other of the labor movement's varied manifestations, but around the street and the daily battle to find enough of anything to live upon, be that by legal or illegal means. It was a world shaped not by class but by poverty: not work but the lack of it was the dominant shaping influence of their lives. Paul de Rousiers was wrong when in 1896 he wrote that the problem of unemployment was largely a problem of London, but he was right in so far as unemployment and London were popularly perceived of as synonymous. The unemployed of London were at once an investigative genre, a journalistic cliche, and the basis upon which major middle-class careers could be built; the period produced a seemingly endless series of tracts and reports, which if serving little to solve the problem of unemployment, at least kept some sections of the middle class assidiuously employed in their production. In part this chapter seeks to explore the role the politics of the unemployed played in shaping this perception.[6]

The social basis of the politics of the London unemployed in this period was not the experience of mass stand downs and sackings from vast factories consequent upon a downturn of trade; but of the casual labor market, where unemployment was experienced not as a tragic change in life's circumstances, but as an everyday event. Work might be got today, but not tomorrow. The transitory nature of work had its corollary in a transitory population. Each year it was estimated that a third of the population of working-class London suburbs moved. Accordingly, unlike towns in the new industrial centers in the north, there was little sense of community in many of the working-class areas, and what little there was diminished further as the artisans, those who normally led the working class, retreated into the suburbs, leaving the inner city to the casual poor, who, when they were not eternally moving in search of work, were being displaced as large residential areas of inner London were transformed into a maze of offices, warehouses, workshops, and vast new works such as the railway lines and yards. Politically, writes their historian Gareth Stedman Jones, they adhered neither to the right or left, but were characterised only by a "rootless volatility". It was upon these unpropitious, shifting sands that the SDF would attempt to build its unemployed organization. Most powerful of all images of the London casual labor market of this era is that of masses of men scrabbling for work at the docks: and it is wholly appropriate that the most important of the leaders of the unemployed before World War I, Jack Williams, was himself a London dock laborer.[7]

In the one known photograph of him, Jack Williams' weather-beaten, shaggy bearded face glares at the camera, eyes finely balanced between contempt and dignity. This remarkable photograph shows Williams as a wild, unkempt man, who looks both querying and pugnacious, as though he cannot make up his mind whether to question the photographer or to punch him out. His clothes are poor and rough, his countenance signalling barely suppressed anger. It is an image much at variance with the photographs of late Victorian and Edwardian trade union leaders, whose fine suits, stiff collars, and neat and composed demeanor suggest a reassuring combination of respectability, conformity, and authority. He seems to have been held in high regard by all who knew him: George Bernard Shaw, many years after he ceased to be involved with far left politics, publicly supported Williams when he stood as an SDF candidate in the 1906 general election; while the SDF newspaper *Justice* thought: "no-one has had more imprisonment, more kicks and cuffs from the police, or has done more for his class by teaching, organization and agitation than has indefatigable and plucky little John E. Williams."[8]

Like some later leaders of the unemployed—such as NUWM activists Fred Copeman and Tommy James—Williams' hatred of the poor law system was based on bitter childhood experience. The son of a Crimean war veteran who died the day he was born in 1854, Williams and his mother, terminally ill with cancer, were forced to enter the Edmonton workhouse. There his mother died and Williams was then shuffled between workhouses until, at the age of ten, he climbed over the wall of the Hornsey workhouse and ran away to live with an uncle and aunt. Both were Irish nationalists, and from them Williams gained his Fenian sympathies. When he was thirteen he walked from London to Manchester to join with the praying and crying crowds to witness the public hanging of the Fenian martyrs, Allen, Larkin and O'Brien. Williams was converted to socialism by the events of the Paris Commune of 1871 and he was from that time politically active. The end of the 1870s saw him a member of both the Rose Street Communist Club and the Commons

Preservation League, taking part in pulling down and burning fences on Plumstead Common and the Hackney Marshes. By the end of 1880 Williams was organizing demonstrations for the Anti-Coercion Association, and in 1881 he became a founding member of the Democratic Federation.

The publication in October 1883 of the pamphlet *The Bitter Cry of Outcast London* had an enormous impact upon contemporary opinion, and it seems no coincidence that a month later the Democratic Federation issued a manifesto addressed to the unemployed. While declaring that the problem of the unemployed could only be solved by the socialization of the means of production and exchange, the manifesto went on to say that there were ways in which the plight of the unemployed could be ameliorated under the existing system. It should not be concluded from this only that the unemployed had become the SDF's "turnip bogie": at the outset, as the manifesto indicates, the SDF Marxists were ready to organize the unemployed in the belief that concessions could be wrenched from the state. This showed a belief in the ability of the working class to affect its own destiny, which, however much grounded in the immediate political opportunism of the SDF, has important ramifications in the history of the unemployed. It should not be forgotten that a more obvious approach, and one that was to be taken by the Socialist League but a few short years hence, would have been to ignore the unemployed completely and retreat into revolutionary purism. In its manifesto the SDF called for the eight-hour day for all government employees, and for the setting of the unemployed to work on farms and public works, which were to be funded on a fifty-fifty basis by local and central government. In essence it was a call not for bread, but for work. It was to be upon this basis that the SDF would be active in the politics of the unemployed for the next twenty five years, but it is not this that fundamentally separates the SDF's unemployed demonstrations during the 1880s and 1890s from its metropolitan predecessors, the London bread riots of 1855, 1861 and 1866. What is new is the desire to engage with the state as a distinct entity, rather than as a random assortment of authorities who are to be intimidated for short-term gain. The desire for bread manifested itself socially in riot: the desire for work manifested itself politically in ongoing strategies and attempts at mobilization and (though with noticeably less success) organization. But among the unemployed the two goals were not readily or easily distinguished, and as 1886 was to show, riot could be consequent upon organization.[9]

The SDF's first attempt to organize the unemployed was made in September 1884, when it formed an "Agitation Committee", solely composed of SDF members, to give backing to its manifesto for the unemployed. The campaign they mounted in the winter of 1884-1845 was small in extent, and seems to have focused upon the East End of London, in particular Stepney, Limehouse, and Poplar—areas notorious for the chronic underemployment of their large casual labor populations. The campaign began in October 1884 and ended in pouring rain six months later, when a bedraggled procession of 5,000 unemployed dock laborers followed H. M. Hyndman, John Burns, Jack Williams, and James MacDonald to Whitehall, where Burns and MacDonald met with the under secretary of the Local Government

Board, (forerunner of the Ministry of Health), calling upon the government to find work for the unemployed. The government took no notice, but for the first time the organization of the unemployed had been advocated, and however ineffectively, also practiced. For the first time a strategy was articulated for improving the unemployed's lot, and for the first time an attempt was made to mobilize the unemployed as unemployed, to act in their own interest. However insignificant the agitation was in every other respect, these were innovations that were to have important consequences. The SDF did not again during the 1880s try and organize the unemployed through a special committee. Instead it relied upon its branches implementing the leads given by the SDF General Council upon the unemployed, and the ability of its principal agitators to mobilize crowds of unemployed in central London.[10]

Through its involvement with the unemployed, the SDF's ideas about the working class had altered rapidly by 1885. It came to view the unskilled and the unemployed (in *Justice* the terms are used interchangeably during this period) sections of the working class, and not the labor aristocracy, as the progressive element of the working class who would bring about the revolution. One *Justice* correspondent noted of the labor aristocracy: "a clerk or skilled artisan finds his chief delight in considering himself to be a superior mortal to his unfortunate brother, the exigencies of whose position has compelled him to do the unskilled or dirty, distasteful work of society." A consequence of this contempt for the labor aristocracy was a contempt for the organized expression of the labor aristocracy, the trade unions. In 1888 only 10 percent or so of the working class was organized in trade unions, the large bulk of the skilled and unskilled working class remaining unorganized and deemed unorganizable. Tied to Liberalism or Toryism, composed almost entirely of skilled artisans, the trade unions had almost nothing to offer the semi- and un-skilled worker who regarded them as "aristocratic corporations with which he had as little in common as the House of Lords."[11]

The trade unions not only reflected divisions within the working class, but also reproduced and reinforced such profound divisions as those of hierarchy, craft, and gender. Unions served not only to create and defend a craft status against capitalists, but also against the teeming hordes of the poor who threatened their status, security, and salary. To this extent labor aristocrats, though part of the working class, were antagonistic to the general interests of the working class. They were invariably concerned with the problem of unemployment as it affected the members of their own particular trade societies and not as a blight upon the working class as a whole. Much has been made of the anti-trade union outlook of the SDF, yet what was to become a crippling dogma within the SDF had its foundations in a realistic assessment of the labor aristocracy of the 1880s, and a romantic conception of the cathartic potential of the unemployed lumpenproletariat. In the mid-1880s the SDF looked to the unemployed not just for immediate support but also to fulfill its faith in the revolutionary millennium. "As Socialists succeed in making their object clear, and in convincing the unemployed that they can afford them immediate relief, it will be strange indeed if they do not rally round and demand the Social Revolution

Table 2.1. *Unemployment, 1870-1939**
Percentage registered unemployed in certain trade unions 1870-1922; percentage of insured workers unemployed 1923-1939

1870	3.9	1880	5.5	1890	2.1	1900	2.5	1910	4.7	1920	2.4	1930	14.6
1871	1.6	1881	3.5	1891	3.5	1901	3.3	1911	3.0	1921	14.2	1931	21.5
1872	0.9	1882	2.3	1892	6.3	1902	4.0	1912	3.2	1922	15.2	1932	22.5
1873	1.2	1883	2.6	1893	7.5	1903	4.7	1913	2.1	1923	11.6	1933	21.3
1874	1.7	1884	8.1	1894	6.9	1904	6.0	1914	3.3	1924	10.9	1934	17.7
1875	2.4	1885	9.3	1895	5.8	1905	5.0	1915	1.1	1925	11.2	1935	16.4
1876	3.7	1886	10.2	1896	3.3	1906	3.6	1916	0.4	1926	12.7	1936	14.3
1877	4.7	1887	7.6	1897	3.3	1907	3.7	1917	0.7	1927	10.6	1937	11.0
1878	6.8	1888	4.9	1898	2.8	1908	7.8	1918	0.8	1928	11.2	1938	13.3
1879	11.4	1889	2.1	1899	2.0	1909	7.7	1919	2.4	1929	11.0	1939	11.7

Sources: B. R. Mitchell and P. Deane, *Abstract of British Historical Statistics* (Cambridge 1971), pp. 64-65, 67.

*Unemployment statistics are notoriously unreliable; like everything else to do with discussion about the unemployed, it is necessary to remember always that they are more telling as insights as to how the notions of "unemployment" and "unemployed" are historically constructed to place a particular interpretation on reality, than as a guide to what that reality actually was. At best they are crude approximations of employment patterns, and it is only as rough indicators that they are used in this book. A useful introduction to some of their deficiencies is W. R. Garside, *The Measure of Unemployment. Methods and Sources in Great Britain 1850-1979* (Oxford 1980).

. . . . It will never be commenced by the trade unionists" wrote A. P. Hazell in an editorial in *Justice* of 7 November 1885. "Better a sudden death", John Burns (ironically, himself a labor aristocrat) told a meeting of unemployed, "than a paupers grave."[12]

It is sometimes assumed that the strategy and tactics of the unemployed rarely rose above crude intimidation. This both implies that crude intimidation is ineffectual, and belies the subtlety and the sophistication of the politics of the unemployed in which intimidation was but one aspect of often complex strategies. It is clear, for example, that the Trafalgar Square riot of 1886 was not an unpremeditated foray into insurrectionary politics by the SDF. Rather it was one unforeseen, though partly encouraged, consequence of an unfolding unemployed campaign with an involved political strategy that was casting the activity of the unemployed into entirely new forms. The year1886 was the trough of the Great Depression. Unemployment savaged not only the casual workforce but the labor aristocracy, as Table 2.1 shows.

Unionized engineers, metal workers, and shipbuilders experienced what was to be their worst year for unemployment between 1880 and 1921. The authorities responded to a huge increase in demand for poor law relief by applying the restrictions upon the giving of outdoor relief more harshly, forcing many unemployed into workhouses. By February 1886 these were reported to be "filled to overflowing". The SDF had meanwhile made a brief and disastrous foray into electoral politics in the general election of 1885, its two candidates polling fifty- nine votes altogether. When it became known that Hyndman had accepted Tory money to finance the election campaign, what had seemed a futile waste of time looked like becoming a death blow to the SDF, still reeling from the Socialist League split less than a year earlier. With its support in tatters, and its continued existence uncertain, the SDF turned to the unemployed as its last chance to rehabilitate itself.[13]

On 19 December 1885 the SDF called for "simultaneous and concerted activity throughout our industrial centres" to organize the unemployed, but for a time these big words from a little party met with no response. Then, in early January 1886, a few hundred Sunderland unemployed gathered outside the Sunderland town council and threatened "bread riots" if work was not found for them. The authorities hastily found them work at stone breaking and road building. Touting Sunderland as an example of what could be won, the SDF argued that the unemployed's only hope lay "in protesting in so menacing a manner that it will be easier for the local bodies to grant their demands." While the SDF advocated the simple efficacy of intimidation, this was but the nature and not the form that the SDF envisaged for its campaign. The SDF unveiled a complex strategy that sought to combine extra-parliamentary agitation at a local level, centered on boards of guardians and local members of Parliament (MPs)(to whom the unemployed were to adopt a tone of "uncompromising hostility"), with parliamentary pressure, the SDF pressing the twelve "labour" MPs to speak up for the unemployed in the Commons. Sophisticated it might have been, but it was also over-ambitious for a party near death, lacking any parliamentary influence and with only a declining number of minuscule, demoralized branches to launch the scores of local campaigns necessary for the strategy to have any chance of success. The SDF's campaign would have been stillborn had it not been for an unemployed agitation begun at Clerkenwell by the local SDF branch.[14]

Clerkenwell had a long tradition of radical politics, and the SDF had early on established a strong branch there with able leaders such as H. H. Champion and George Bateman, ex-soldier and compositor. The Clerkenwell SDF seems to have drawn most of its membership not from the artisans who worked at watchmaking, jewellery and printing in the area, but from the ranks of the casual laborers, one witness describing the branch as "a poor lot . . . a sort of gathering of down and outs." Long after the 1886 unemployed agitation had died out in the rest of London it continued in Clerkenwell. In January 1886 the Clerkenwell SDF undertook a survey which revealed 40 percent of their area's inhabitants were unemployed, started a fund for an unemployed campaign, and began to organize the unemployed. In many respects their campaign, from the survey on, was a blueprint for innumerable others to follow. The SDF rapidly gained the support of the unemployed, and meetings were held, MPs were lobbied, and a deputation to the local guardians was backed by a large crowd of unemployed, angry that in spite of the distress in the district the Clerkenwell guardians would not give outdoor relief.[15]

It was the Clerkenwell unemployed who, on 31 January 1886, beneath a black banner and behind George Bateman, inaugurated the tactic of the West End unemployed march, which was to be repeated many times over the next fifty years. Throughout this time it remained a powerful way of expressing not only suffering, but of highlighting the injustice of unemployment against the background of commercial opulence and individual indulgence provided by the West End. It was a powerful piece of street theater and in it the unemployed exhibited a strong dramatic sense; marches through the West End in the 1890s being silent affairs without bands, banners, or talking, so as "to accentuate the effect produced by the dull thud and heavy tread upon the wooden pavement." But the marches went beyond being latter-day morality plays, being also a deliberate flouting of certain social conventions, the most important of which was that the working class did not and should not wander en masse through the West End, province of the upper class. In breaking this convention the marches mounted an unspoken challenge to bourgeois notions of order and place. As Bateman led the unemployed down Pall Mall he heard his challenge answered with cheering and derision by members of the Reform Club. Stung by this contempt the Clerkenwell unemployed ominously vowed vengeance.[16]

As a result of the Clerkenwell census the Holborn Board of Guardians granted the SDF use of the Holborn town hall for a meeting of the unemployed. Over 1,000 unemployed crowded into the hall on the cold evening of 3 February 1886 to hear speeches full of revolutionary fervor from Hyndman, Burns, and Williams, the latter suggesting to cheering that they go and raze the Holborn workhouse to the ground. John Fielding gave a further portentous focus to the feeling of revolt by saying that "The loafers in the clubs at Pall Mall laughed at you the other day. Maybe they will laugh on the other side of their faces before long.[17]

What is clear from the activity of the Clerkenwell unemployed is that far from being a spontaneous outburst of anger, their actions were part of a premeditated, coordinated pattern of events, from the survey through to the lobbying of local authorities to the Holborn town hall meeting. In this process SDF agitators attempted to imbue the unemployed with quasi-revolutionary ideas, the nub of which was that while something could be got with physical force nothing could be gained through inactivity. "Nothing but fear", wrote Harry Quelch at the outset of the campaign, "will ever induce our 'governing classes' to take any steps for the benefit of the unemployed". This had a resonance among the starving, freezing hordes of poor not only in Clerkenwell, but in the districts of Marylebone, St. Pancras, Battersea, Hackney, Shoreditch and Limehouse, where, by early February

1886, SDF branches were following Clerkenwell's lead. Acting as a leaven was a general desire for vengeance, focused particularly upon the West End clubs. What was not clear until 8 February 1886 was that in this seething mixture the subtler points of SDF strategy were quickly disappearing.[18]

On that day SDF speakers succeeded in winning the attention of a crowd of 30,000 unemployed at a meeting called by the Tory Fair Trade League in Trafalgar Square. At the end of the meeting John Burns was raised on some shoulders and carried off down Pall Mall waving a red flag, a large crowd following behind. The procession was brought to a halt outside the Reform Club, site of the humiliation of the Clerkenwell unemployed. In front of this and the social headquarters of the Tory Party, the Carlton Club next door, Burns and another SDFer, A. A. Watts, began to address the unemployed. Behind them, through the club's windows, the club members once more jeered and mocked. Some Carlton Club members threw crusts of bread at the unemployed. The response to this insult was immediate. The unemployed began to stone the clubs, and the mocking faces disappeared in a welter of shattering glass. The SDF leaders had lost control, and the unemployed ran down St. James Street smashing all the windows of the clubs that lined the street. Because the police had mistakenly gone to guard Buckingham Palace and the Mall, the unemployed were able to roam the West End unhindered, smashing shop windows; looting; halting; smashing, and sometimes overturning carriages; and ripping jewelry from the necks of upper-class women riding within them. The response to the riot was out of all proportion to the riot itself. It left London for some days in a state approaching terror, as crowds of the poor drifted together and then drifted apart, and as rumors of sans-culottic uprisings swept back and forth across the capital. As far away as Peckham workshops prepared barricades, and in barrack rooms throughout London troops were confined with nervous magistrates ready to read the Riot Act.[19]

From the point of view of the politics of the unemployed the riot had three important effects. First, it rescued the SDF from probable oblivion: credibility was restored, new branches were opened, and the SDF received considerable, and previously unobtainable, publicity in the press. Hyndman, Williams, Burns, and Champion were arrested, charged and tried for sedition, and to great surprise all round, were acquitted in April 1886, thus lending support to the belief that the transition to socialism could be effected peacefully and constitutionally. The prisoners believed that the trial "did much to restore confidence in the administration of justice . . . In the centre of capitalism therefore the Social Revolution may yet be accomplished by the peaceable demonstration of armed force." These comments were echoed and may well have provided the inspiration for Engels' famous observation, written only a few months later in his preface to the English edition of Marx's *Capital*, and so beloved of social democrats ever since: "in Europe, England is the only country where the inevitable social revolution might be effected entirely by peaceful and legal means".[20]

A second and in this light somewhat ironic effect was to render the renascent SDF's attitude towards the unemployed ambivalent. While the riot confirmed that the unemployed had a cathartic disposition, it also revealed the weakness of the SDF's influence over the unemployed at the moment of catharsis. The point at which the demonstration turned into a riot was also the point at which the SDF leaders lost control of the crowd and became superfluous to the activity and the aims of the unemployed. Karl Kautsky, German revolutionary, spoke for the SDF leadership as well as himself when he later told Engels, "the meeting proper was over, the brawling broke out, and so I made off." The SDF leaders had as little hold over the unemployed rioters as did the terrified bourgeoisie, and were accordingly as antagonistic towards the rioters as a West End shopkeeper. "If I had a revolver", Champion said immediately after the riot, "and I saw a mob looting a shop I would shoot the fellows down right and left with my own hand."[21]

Prior to the riot the SDF orators had talked of the unemployed as a violent revolutionary force and had addressed them as such. Burns told an unemployed meeting how as an unemployed workman he felt it to be "infinitely preferable to die fighting than to die starving." "What have you got to hope from the future", Hyndman asked of the same meeting, "unless there is a revolution?" The riot only too clearly demonstrated that a disposition to volatility did not equate with a revolutionary temperament. George Bernard Shaw, then doing propaganda work for the Socialist League, summed up some of the contradictions within the politics of the unemployed that the riot forced the SDF to confront. "The sullen fury of the man who has been tramping through the mud all day in bitter weather, vainly seeking a master is not—unfortunately—'revolution in the making'. The unemployed are as great a nuisance to the Socialists as to themselves. Angry as they are, they do not want a revolution: they want a job." After the riot the SDF leaders quickly distanced themselves from their pre-riot fantasies of insurrection by the unemployed. "I say no mere shooting, no mere looting of shops, can alter a great economic problem", Hyndman told an unemployed demonstration less than a fortnight after the riot. "You can only solve this great economic difficulty by educating and organising yourselves for victory in the future."[22]

Third, while the press denounced the rioters as "a few fanatics, a great amount of loafers, and a huge contingent of professional thieves" who were "not ill clad, not suffering", the response of the ruling class indicates that because of the riot the unemployed were recognised as a distinct group with legitimate grievances. "The unemployed are showing their teeth", wrote George Bernard Shaw, posing the question no one else dared publicly ask: "What are the cheapest sops that will quiten them?" At first these were deemed to be the charities that flourished in the humid post-riot climate of fear. The Mansion House Fund for relieving distress soared from £3,000 to £42,000 in the week following the riot, and would finally reach the considerable total of £78,629. The Liberal government worried that charity alone would not be sufficient to assuage the anger of the unemployed and a little over four weeks after the riot, on 15 March 1886, Joseph Chamberlain, president of the Local Government Board, issued his famous circular calling upon local authorities to provide work for the unemployed.[23]

The day after the riot Chamberlain had announced a relaxation on the distribution of outdoor relief. This was a tangible and important victory for the unemployed. However, it made administration of the poor law in line with principles of the 1834 new poor law difficult, and so four weeks later Chamberlain issued his circular. In a letter to Beatrice Potter (later Beatrice Webb) Chamberlain wrote that the provision of relief works would "remove one great danger, viz. that public sentiment should go over to the unemployed, and render impossible that state sternness to which you and I equally attach importance. By offering reasonable works at low wages we may secure the power of being very strict with the loafer and the confirmed pauper." While in one sense the thin end of a very important wedge, state provision of work for the unemployed, the circular paradoxically was drafted by its author as a return to the principles of the new poor law—state sternness—and as a way of negating public sympathy for the unemployed. Chamberlain was not concerned to alleviate the plight of the unemployed as an end in itself but as a means of ensuring control over the casual poor, and of maintaining the notion of respectability in other sections of the working class. The leading Radical of the day, Chamberlain was acutely aware of the need to maintain and strengthen the alliance between the Liberal middle class and the labor aristocracy, a large proportion of whom had been enfranchised in the reform act of 1884. "The spirit of independence", wrote Chamberlain in his circular, "which leads so many of the working class to make great personal sacrifices rather than incur the stigma of pauperism is one which deserves the greatest sympathy and respect, and which it is the duty and interest of the community to maintain by all the means at its disposal." The circular, which was to be reissued in 1887, 1891, 1892, and 1895, also then represented an attempt to maintain the divisions between the "respectable" and the "unrespectable" sections of the working class, so as to ensure the ongoing support of labor aristocrats for the Liberal Party, precisely at the moment when unemployment was threatening to begin dissolving such divisions.[24]

José Harris has attempted to belittle the significance of the Chamberlain circular by demonstrating how ineffectual it proved in practice, only being half-heartedly applied by a few local authorities. But her approach is ahistorical, concentrating on the immediate administrative shortcomings of the circular and myopically ignoring its long term importance. "What ransom will property pay?" Chamberlain had asked in 1885. His answer was embodied in the Radicals' Unauthorised Programme of the same year, which although making no direct mention of the unemployed, proposed reforms in local government, taxation, education, and landholding. Chamberlain argued that "the interests of rich and poor were not hostile but that the duties of property must be more strictly observed." But it was to be the state and not property itself who was expected to observe these duties, who would act to neutralize working class hostility: as it was put at the time by its proponents the Programme stood for "the intervention, in other words, of the State on behalf of the weak against the strong, in the interests of labour against capital, of want and suffering against luxury and ease." Only in this light is it possible to appreciate the importance of the circular, however much its implementation was to be frustrated by the Charity Organisation Society sympathizers who dominated the Local Government Board. First, the circular represented a crucial turning away from the old individualist idea of the state, although it was to be some time before the full implications of this were to be recognized on all sides. Second, it established an administrative relationship between the state and the unemployed that existed outside and separate of the new poor law; and third, it opened up a new arena in which the unemployed had a recognized place to fight, and a prize-relief works-to fight for. As the Webbs noted, many local authorities "responding to the perpetual pleadings and threatenings of deputations of unemployed workmen, availed themselves freely of this opportunity for demonstrating their usefulness to distressed citizens."[25]

Having produced and having need of the unemployed, British industrial society had not produced a mechanism able to adequately control and discipline the unemployed. The events of 1886 revealed the new poor law as inadequate to the task, and it is only in the light of this that we can grasp the fundamental historical significance of the Chamberlain circular. Certainly it proved inadequate to the problem it had attempted to solve, leading the state, as we shall see, in the short term to have resort to the old fashioned tactic of repression to silence the unemployed. But the circular was the basis of a fundamentally new and different approach to the relation of a capitalist state to its unemployed, an approach that sought not only to assist but also to control the unemployed, an approach that was to develop not through a gradual process of constitutional evolution, but by the barbed and jagged interaction of the state and the activity of the unemployed in each economic crisis succeeding the 1880s.

The considerable response to the riot imparted to the unemployed a belief in the necessity of their own activity to improve their lot, and illustrated to them the related worth of street politics and the importance of conflict as a motor of change. Over the next year and a half there was to be a surge of unemployed activity, not always organized by the SDF nor always in London. Unemployed demonstrations took place in the following weeks at Birmingham, Norwich, Nottingham, and other centers, while rioting broke out in Leicester, and in the following month in Manchester and Glasgow.[26]

In the short term the riot raised serious tactical problems for the SDF. As Harry Lee pointed out, "once an agitation gains impetus through sensational incidents, more sensational incidents are needed to keep it going." Having brought into being a movement of considerable momentum but no direction, lacking the branch strength to take it anywhere, the SDF for a time was unable to do anything other than mount largely symbolic demonstrations in central London. These were normally preceded by an intensive propaganda barrage, and met with some small success. The SDF tried to broaden its unemployed campaign in early 1887. Though the SDF was simply too small in 1887 to be very effective in its desire to pressure local authorities, there were some attempts made, such as in Clerkenwell, where the unemployed took to "visiting" the homes of vestry members in large crowds: among one such group in January 1887 was Paul Lafargue, Marx's French son in law. It hit upon the novel tactic, to be much repeated, of church parades, whereby a procession of unemployed would march to and attend a Sunday service in a church. The nineteenth-century London working class was, as is well known, little inclined toward religion. Far from assuaging middle and upper-class fears by an outward display of reverence, church parades cleverly played upon post-riot fears of sans-culottic risings. To appreciate the impact of a church parade it is necessary to imagine the successive feelings of astonishment, horror, and profound discomfort experienced by the well-to-do congregation of the Paddington church of January 1887 into which, during the service, Jack Williams led a gaggle of badly clad, under-fed unemployed whistling the "Marseillaise".[27]

The Politics of the Street

We have seen how the state met the political activity of the unemployed with a mixture of qualified concessions and attempts to increase control over the casual poor. But the state also acted to prevent the unemployed again using the streets and public places as arenas for organization and demonstration. The streets of the city had long been the one and only political forum where the poor of the city could articulate their grievances. Following the Trafalgar Square unemployed riot of 8 February 1886 bourgeois opinion became firmly set against the continuation of street politics by the unemployed. The police commissioner was forced to resign, and was replaced by General Sir Charles Warren, it being felt "that discipline could only be maintained by men of military training."[28] "Open air meetings, street crowds, processions of East-enders through the West-end must no longer be treated as trivial outbursts of harmless feeling, political or otherwise", said the *Daily Telegraph* four days after the riot."The people have better ways of informing Parliament than by tramping through the streets, and thereby giving a perilous opportunity to Socialists and roughs."

The police seem to have almost reveled in the license they were given to harass and break up unemployed meetings. According to *The Times* of 22 February 1886, a demonstrator ridden down during a baton charge of an unemployed meeting at Hyde Park "received shocking injuries to his face, but it is probable that rioters will not seek medical assistance . . . for fear of detection." The state's over-reaction to any activity by the unemployed through the 1880s was symptomatic of the grave tensions and worries about the stability of London society that had arisen in the wake of the Trafalgar Square riot. There was a near-obsessive fear of the unemployed organizing and demonstrating. One manifestation of this was the decision of Sir Charles Warren, following the SDF's call for the unemployed to follow the procession of the Lord Mayor's Show, to ban all marches on the route of the procession. At one stage Warren contemplated bringing artillery in. Although this idea was abandoned, on 9 December 1886, the day of the show, all troops in London were confined to barracks, Life Guards were brought up from Windsor, and a regiment of Hussars held in readiness should the ban be broken. As the show passed Trafalgar Square, a dozen unemployed led by George Bateman rushed and seized Nelson's column, from where they waved red flags and made speeches. Tom Mann was half way through Shelley's "Mask of Anarchy" when the cry went up that the guards were coming. Mann hastily put the SDF resolution on the unemployed and it was carried by the crowd before the police, with the aid of the guards, had time to clear the square.[29]

The event was a propaganda coup. The children sang ribald songs about the police commissioner in the streets, and Hyndman's old adversary Engels was forced to admit that "the Social Democratic Federation is beginning to become a power". But the SDF's committment to street politics was ambivalent, and was creating destructive tensions within the SDF. The Trafalgar Square riot, while an exceedingly fortuitous event as far as the fortunes of the SDF went, placed the SDF leadership in the position where they had to publicly declare themselves against a policy of riot to ensure their acquittal at a subsequent trial for sedition. Accordingly the leadership was not keen to commemorate the riot, which, for them, was best publicly forgotten. At the same time the riot seems to have reinforced the insurrectionary fantasies nursed by other sections of the SDF. Lee later admitted that by the end of 1886 "There were certainly a few wild 'comrades' knocking about . . . . and some of them did not hesitate to suggest violent, if largely impossible methods". In Harry Quelch's Bermondsey backyard some SDF members took to practicing elementary drill under the instruction of a couple of army reservists. These two contrary tendencies came into conflict over the first anniversary of the Trafalgar Square riot. The SDF General Council refused to sanction a torchlight procession which was to be held on 8 February 1886 to commemorate the riot. This injunction was disobeyed by the Clerkenwell SDF who, assisted by the Marylebone SDF, held a mass meeting at Clerkenwell Green. When the gathering unemployed were prevented by police from following the meeting with a torchlight procession, a riot broke out, the unemployed streaming through Clerkenwell, smashing windows and looting.[30]

Less than three weeks later the SDF withdrew from the organization of the unemployed. The SDF by this time seems to have become more intent upon building a national organization than upon leading the London unemployed: between 1 August 1886 and 30 July 1887 it spent 89 pounds, 3 shillings, and 10 pence on "Provincial Propaganda", while only 26 pounds, 14 shillings, and sixpence went on "Demonstrations, Bands, etc." It was becoming obvious that the general policy of spectacular demonstrations in central London that it had pursued throughout 1886 could only be milked for so much before the middle class public grew unimpressed and the unemployed uninterested. The Clerkenwell riot would appear to have been the decisive factor, demonstrating only too clearly that while the volatility of the unemployed could on occasion benefit the socialists, it could at other times discredit and divide the SDF. Through the Trafalgar Square riot the unemployed had ensured the survival of the SDF, but their undisciplined street politics were too unsteady a platform for the SDF to build a party upon.[31]

From March 1887 the unemployed were—with the exception of individual socialists—left leaderless. It might have been expected that the Socialist League, who had split from the SDF in 1884, would have stepped into this vacuum, but the League reacted strongly against the idea of palliatives, arguing that there could be "no half way house" on the way to revolution. The League, believing "There is no salvation for the unemployed but in the general organisation of the workers . . . for the REVOLUTION . . . We hold that there is no *direct* way in *which* we Socialists as Socialists can help them . . . the unemployed are not organised and cannot be organised", took no action. Not only did the League not support any agitation, but in at least one case, that of Norwich in early 1887, it sought to undermine what support there was for an unemployed agitation.[32]

In October 1887, as we have seen, the unemployed began to hold meetings in Trafalgar Square. By early November 1887 the unemployed had taken to sleeping in the square, while the police took every opportunity to discourage their presence. Regularly they would disperse any unemployed meeting with great violence, pairs and groups of policemen shoving and punching individuals to the ground, kicking them as they lay there. In spite of this violence the unemployed meetings and demonstrations continued to grow in size. On 9 November 1887 Warren, the police commissioner, banned all further public meetings in the square. The Metropolitan Radical Federation, an umbrella group for the capital's Radical bodies, had proposed a meeting in the square on Sunday, 13 November 1887, to protest the treatment of an imprisoned Irish Nationalist MP, William O'Brien. With Warren's decision to ban all meetings in the square, the meeting took on a new meaning, and the particular issues of O'Brien and the unemployed disappeared under the general (and for the Radicals more attractive) issues of the rights of free speech and assembly. Between 75,000 and 100,000 people tried to march on Trafalgar Square on 13 March 1887. By attacking the various processions before they were anywhere near the square the police prevented them from reaching their destination. By the end of the day seventy five arrests had been made, two hundred demonstrators had been hospitalized and three people had sustained fatal injuries. As dusk approached, Warren made a symbolic showing of the force he was prepared to resort to if the preceding brutality had failed him. With bayonets fixed and each with two hundred rounds of ball cartridge, three hundred Grenadiers made a token cleanup of the square.[33]

"Bloody Sunday", as the events of that day became known, can only be understood in the context of the political activity of the unemployed that had taken place over the previous three years. It was the final installment in a running battle between the police and the unemployed that had commenced with the police's humiliating mistake of having left the West End unguarded on the day of the Trafalgar Square riot in 1886. The police had been further humiliated on the day of the Lord Mayor's Show when the unemployed succeeded in defying their ban, and a year later in their remorseless baton charge clearings of Trafalgar Square they succeeded not in crushing the unemployed, but in giving the unemployed's cause an enhanced vigor.

And here we come to the fundamental issue at stake on Bloody Sunday. Were, or were not, the unemployed to be allowed to continue using the public areas and streets of London for their political activity? If we brush away the hyperbole we can see this is what *The Times* meant when the morning after Bloody Sunday it announced, "What Sir Charles Warren did yesterday was to crush a deliberate attempt to set aside the elementary safeguards of civilised society and to terrorize London by placing the control of the streets in the hands of the criminal classes." Given that *The Times* normally referred to unemployed demonstrations as being comprised of "the criminal classes" we can see that Bloody Sunday was not primarily an anti-democratic attack upon the right of free speech, but a class-based attack upon the use to which the unemployed were putting the streets. As such, Bloody Sunday dealt a devastating blow to the politics of the unemployed. Central London was the heart of the capital's casual labor market, and Trafalgar Square for a brief few years had been the political focus of the casual poor who crowded into the central environs of the city. As the SDF were aware, "It is all very well to talk about the inequity of prohibiting bona fide meetings, but the right of meeting in the open air is of far more importance to the unemployed who cannot afford to meet anywhere else, than it is for politicians who can pay for halls."[34]

The full effect of Bloody Sunday upon the politics of the unemployed was driven home the following winter, when an SDF-inspired agitation met with dismal failure. While a revival in trade meant unemployment had fallen considerably in 1888 (see Table 2.1), there remained considerable structural unemployment, compounded in the East End by the failure of the 1888 autumn's hop and fruit crops, the seasonal earnings from the picking of which so many families relied upon to survive winter. A slight agitation among the unemployed, which seems not to have been SDF-inspired took place in central London during the autumn of 1888. However, it had died out by December 1888 when the SDF announced its intention of returning to organize the unemployed. Their campaign met from the beginning with police repression. Meetings were constantly broken up with baton charges, lingering doubts as to the police's intention being dispelled by Superintendent Forster telling Jack Williams, appointed by the SDF as the campaign organizer, that any attempt to hold a meeting in London would be suppressed by the police. The small and impotent campaign battled on until February 1889 when it was effectively brought to an end with the arrest of Williams, to whom the magistrate offered the choice of taking a job or going to prison. Williams took the job, and the campaign collapsed.[35]

From their involvement with the unemployed in the 1880s socialist agitators gained a belief in a mass working class that encompassed the lumpenproletarian as well as the labor aristocrat. The great importance of the unemployed agitations of the 1880s lies in the impetus they gave to widening perceptions of what the working class was, of enabling the development of a class consciousness sufficiently broad so as to encompass both unskilled dock laborers and skilled engineers. The tangible expression of this fundamental change is the outburst of new unionism between 1889 and 1891. Long seen as "a colourful and baffling phenomena", new unionism's true antecedents can be found not in any union or strike of the 1880s, nor even in a similar outburst of general unionism in the early 1870s, but in the unemployed agitations of the 1880s. Here we find not only the same leaders, but the same ideas, the same mass following, and the same animating spirit of aggression, which Tom Mann had felt to be so lacking in the unions in 1886.[36]

It is well known that many of the leaders of the new unionism—H. H. Champion, Will Thorne, Eleanor Marx, John Burns, and Tom Mann—had worked with the unemployed during the 1880s. But it is forgotten how critical these struggles of the unemployed were to some of these leaders in forging their commitment to socialism, the most potent element of which for them was the importance placed upon the active role of the unskilled workers in a mass working-class movement committed to ending unemployment and its social corollary, poverty. New unionism's great legacy to the labor movement was to place the problem of the unemployed at the center of its concerns. Personifying this is Tom Mann, who throughout a life of agitation continued to stress "what is to me the chief concern—the CURING OF UNEMPLOYMENT". Harry Pollitt, who knew Mann intimately for the last twenty years of Mann's life, wrote of how "at the very centre of his thoughts was always those workers who were the worst paid, and suffered from unemployment most. It was this that made him at the very outset of his long career of service, rebel against the craft prejudices and sectionalism that characterised the trade union movement of the '80s." It is not coincidental that Mann began and ended his life of socialist agitation as a leader of the unemployed, being in his final years national treasurer of the National Unemployed Workers' Movement. It may well be, as H. H. Champion argued, that the socialists were accepted as leaders of the unskilled "not on account of their speculative opinions, but for the sake of their personal ability to help", but this point obscures more important truths. The socialist's "ability to help" was a consequence of their experience in organizing the unemployed, while their desire to help derived from their strongly held belief in a mass working class of both skilled and unskilled, which was another consequence of their experience with the unemployed. Their "speculative opinions" were grounded in a political practice that saw socialists willing to help the unskilled organize, and the better-known leaders of the new unions were but reaping the rewards of years of agitation by SDF rank and file members, a point upon which Annie Besant, leader of the match girls strike, was quaintly emphatic: "Burns, Champion and Mann . . . are gathering the fruits of the hard work done at the dock gates in the dark of morning by Burrows and Williams and other members of the SDF ere yet public credit was to be gained in working for them despised dockers."[37]

New unionism entwined with the politics of the unemployed in fundamental ways. In the late nineteenth-century world of casual labor the distinction between the membership and aims of both an unemployed agitation and a casual laborers union was very blurred, a point well illustrated by the fact that most of the limited support that the SDF unemployed campaign of 1888-89 received came from unemployed dock laborers. For this reason many of the dockers, prior to the dockers' strike, were SDF members. The demands for the eight-hour day and the public organization of the labor market were appropriated by new unionism from the unemployed and keenly fought for, while the push by the new unions for municipal workshops was eagerly picked up by the unemployed, and for a period was one of their main demands. One of Keir Hardie's earliest remedies for unemployment, made in 1893, was for the public employment of the unemployed at sixpence an hour or the "dockers' tanner". No better example of the continuity between unemployed agitation and new unionism can be found than Jack Williams, who only a few months after organizing the unemployed in the winter of 1888-89 was active in the dockers' strike, and was also active in recruiting for a National Federation of Labour Unions.[38]

New unionism also changed the way in which the middle class observed and reacted to the politics of the unemployed. With its emphasis on order, restraint, and discipline, particularly at the time of the dock strike, it established in middle class eyes a belief that not all the working class of London was degenerate, but only a small hopeless residuum. The dock strike reinforced what the politics of the unemployed during the 1880s had threatened to dissolve: the distinction between respectable and non-respectable. It is no longer possible, wrote one commentator, to mix up the problem of the "dregs of London . . . with the radically different question of the claims of labour." These dregs did not represent the same political threat that the fiction of the mid-1880s, the insurrectionary mob, had, and accordingly the politics of the unemployed during the 1890s were viewed in a much calmer light than in the 1880s. For this reason the 1890s were not to witness the same measure of police repression. While the activity of the unemployed became more extensive, the aims of the unemployed were no longer perceived of as revolutionary, or even menacing the stability of society: "they talk as they have always talked any time these past twenty years", Sir Evelyn Bradford, the police commissioner, wrote in 1894, "stark rebellion and riot but they don't mean to do anything."[39]

From Street to Vestry

It is then unsurprising that the 1890s brought attempts to link the politics of the unemployed with the resurgent labor movement, and that these attempts failed. The winter of 1890-91 saw the SDF make an imaginative, though ultimately doomed attempt to harness the energy of the new unionism to the cause of the unemployed. It started as an initiative of the London unemployed, who in early October 1890 were holding meetings at which trade unions, particularly the dockers' union, were called upon to take action to force local authorities to provide employment for the workless. The SDF gave substance to the call by convening a meeting in late October 1890 of forty delegates from London trade unions and SDF branches, at which the Trade Union Unemployed Organisation Committee (TUUOC) was formed. The TUUOC drew its support not from organizations of the labor aristocrats, but from the organizations of the unskilled and semi-skilled: the unions of the dockers, the navvies and the furriers, the boot finishers and the printers' warehousemen, the chair makers and the shop assistants, to name but some. The

TUUOC solicited funds from trade unions, issued a manifesto, appointed W. White, an SDF member, as organizer, and commenced unemployed meetings on Tower Hill. This TUUOC inspired agitation gained a measure of moderate support and success for a few months, but by February 1891 it was dead, and we hear no more of the TUUOC. Trade remained good, unemployment low, and *Justice* ruefully admitted to there being "times and seasons even for unemployed agitations".[40]

Although there was to be a minor resurgence of unemployed activity led by SDF activists the following winter, the SDF was to wait until the downturn in trade in late 1892 before it again felt the season for unemployed agitation had returned. In late October 1892 the newly elected Liberal government, under pressure from the Metropolitan Radical Federation and the Trafalgar Square Defence Committee, re-opened Trafalgar Square for public meetings on a limited basis. The latter body was an SDF-inspired umbrella organization, composed of representatives of some of the new unions, the socialist societies, a large number of Radical clubs, and SDF branches. In early October 1892 Hyndman called for an immediate unemployed agitation. The organizational hub was to be the Trafalgar Square Defence Committee, with its broad base of support and potential for raising funds. After the re-opening of the square the committee decided to continue its existence as an unemployed committee, and in late 1892 reconstituted itself as the Unemployed Organisation Committee (UOC).[41]

The change was more than one of name: the Radical clubs absented themselves entirely. The Fabians, after failing in their attempt to moderate the behavior and language of the UOC's paid organizers, Waite, Herbert Burrows, and Alf Oldland (a veteran imprisoned for a year for his part in the 1887 demonstrations) also departed, and in their place came an influx of union representatives. The UOC was a bold experiment: building on the experience of the TUUOC, it developed a strategy based on activity in local rather than central areas. This met with a great breadth of success and a much wider response than previously experienced. But it remained an organization from above, dependent upon the continued funding of the unions and the political will of the SDF, both commodities that were to be in increasingly short supply. Within a fortnight of its existence the UOC was already five pounds in debt, and promises of funds made by some unions were not to be honored. By mid January 1893 the UOC was in decline. Attendance at its weekly meetings were diminishing, the trade unions were increasingly unwilling to support it, and the SDF was growing disenchanted with the whole idea of unemployed agitation. By February 1893 the UOC was only meeting occasionally, and after March it is heard of no more.[42]

Given the transitory existences of the TUUOC and the UOC, it is unsurprising that the SDF's final attempt in the 1890s to organize the unemployed was made not through a semi-independent organization, but through a special Unemployed Committee of the SDF (SDFUC). The SDFUC owed its inception not to a renewed commitment to the politics of the unemployed, but to pique. Stimulated by the electoral successes of labor in 1892 and the formation of the Independent Labour Party (ILP) in 1893, the SDF by late 1893 seems to have had an eye on a future electoral strategy, and was ignoring the unemployed and concentrating upon a campaign for universal suffrage. Keir Hardie chided the SDF for its fecklessness, and in a letter to the SDF General Council in which he accused them of "desertion of the cause of socialism", Hardie asked, "Is the cause of three million voteless workers—whose hard lot you are so eager to champion—worse than that of the four million—including dependents—workless workers?" Stung into action, the SDF formed the SDFUC within a week of receiving Hardie's letter. J. E. Dobson was made secretary and Jack Williams organizer, the body relying not upon the fickle promises of trade unionists to pay Williams, but upon the voluntary contributions of the SDF members. The campaign failed to break out of central London, its pivot being Jack Williams' regular meetings on Tower Hill.[43]

A corollary of the SDF's growing uninterest in organizing the unemployed was a growing scepticism as to the value of the unemployed in any revolutionary strategy. The SDF became keen to sing the praises of the labor aristocracy it had once damned, and to portray itself as the party of the artisan. *Justice*'s columnist Tattler argued "the unemployed are not revolutionists—I wish they were . . . the most ardent revolutionists and most active Social Democrats are to be found among those who are in steady employment at good wages." The SDF began to retreat into the revolutionary purism that had crippled the Socialist League. The unemployed will have to be told, wrote Harry Quelch in late 1893, "that nothing short of a social revolution will abolish the misery from which they suffer". By this time the SDF's antipathy was grounded not only in its lack of faith in the unemployed's revolutionary potential, but also in its feeling that the unemployed were not even particularly active, and that nothing constructive, far less revolutionary, would come of working with them. "Unfortunately the unemployed want such a deal of stirring before they will do anything", moaned *Justice* of 16 December 1893, ". . . it may be possible to do something *for* the unemployed, but it is impossible to do anything *with* them!" The distinction between acting *for* and acting *with* the unemployed was, from that time on, to be a strong determinant of how the SDF behaved toward the unemployed.[44]

As the party of the respectable artisan the SDF tried to emphasise the essential respectability of those taking part in unemployed demonstrations, but this found little corollary in reality. Unemployment was the very essence of the casual labor market and in consequence the casual laborers were far more prone to unemployment than were the labor aristocrats. On the less frequent occasions when the labor aristocrats might be out of work, they tended to be bound by the constraints of some small savings, the trade union unemployment pay (small as it was), and, underlying these, the all-powerful notions of thrift and respectability. To take part in a demonstration was to join publicly the ranks of the unemployed, an open admission of the failure to maintain respectability. Consequently they were rarely seen in unemployed demonstrations. It was the unrespectable, the unskilled laborers and not the labor aristocrats, who formed the mass of demonstrations and meetings, and their desperate plight did not always find sufficient outlet in "orderly" demonstrations. An unemployed demonstration held by Jack Williams outside St. Paul's at the end of 1893 appeared, according to *Justice* "to be—as usual—mainly made up of

Scotchmen and whiskey." After police prevented George Lansbury from speaking, violence broke out. "The whole thing to my mind demonstrated once more the advantage of discipline and organization over mere numbers", noted the *Justice* correspondent glumly. To a party trying to build a solid, effective organization, unemployed agitation was no foundation.[45]

These ideas were used by the SDF to distance itself from the SDFUC's unemployed campaign. While praising Jack Williams' "zeal and self sacrifice" the SDF delivered a damning verdict of the campaign that concluded "we are still face to face with . . . the great initial problem of doing anything with the unemployed themselves." The only way in which local authorities might be forced to do something would be if others acted "for the unemployed, not with them." In February 1894 the London Trades Council held a conference on unemployment where the SDF was able to carry a resolution declaring that the only solution to the unemployed's problem was socialism. This marked the final stage of the SDF's retreat from a belief in the worth of the activity of the unemployed in altering society, to a belief in a kind of socialist nirvana, to which, however, it now offered no route maps. In nine years the SDF had gone from the position of believing the unemployed were a revolutionary force, to a position not that dissimilar to that of the Charity Organisation Society, acting for and on behalf of the perceived interests of the unemployed. The SDF's 1894 position was as paternalistic as their 1885 position had been improbable. Both were founded in faulty assessments of the nature of the working class, and characterised by a search for a revolutionary element within the working class—in 1885 the unemployed lumpenproletariat, in 1894 the employed labor aristocrat—that would alone clear the path to socialism. There was no strategy for the working class as a whole. The SDF's commitment to the SDFUC, at best luke warm, cooled into disinterest and the SDF in the early months of 1894 distanced itself from the SDFUC agitation, which by April 1894 had collapsed.[46]

In line with the new precept of acting for, and not with the unemployed, the SDF in late 1894, following the passing by the Liberals of the Local Government Act which abolished nominated guardians and allowed for guardians to be elected, turned to a policy of using the poor law from within: seeking not to destroy it, but rather to subvert it in aid of the working class. This move from extra-constitutional to constitutional methods complemented the SDF's internal growth through the 1890s and a string of limited though significant victories by SDF candidates in local elections. By 1895 there were eight SDF guardians and nineteen SDF vestry members in London. Constitutional politics seemed to offer the rewards extra-constitutional politics had not yielded: the tarnished jewels of political power. At the SDF's New Year's gathering in early 1895 Hyndman summed up this change of spirit and approach from street to vestry, telling the gathered faithful that it was now "necessary for them to do some of the drudgery and practical work of this miserable world. They had got to carry on the movement not merely for an enthusiastic ideal [and here Hyndman seems to intend no irony] but as practical men of business." George Lansbury, one such practical man of business, and chairman of the Poplar board of guardians between January and April 1895, wrote at the beginning of his chairmanship how "many of us would prefer being at a barricade and making one mad rush for freedom. This is, however, not the way I think our Social Revolution will come. It will come by our showing that we are better administrators than those who went before." Acting for and not with the unemployed meant for Lansbury using the poor law "to help forward the great cause of the people", arguing that under the statutes of 1601 the poor law could be administered to the great benefit of the unemployed. This philosophy was to reach its apogee in Poplar in the 1920s where the strengths—and the ultimate failing—of this idea would be finally revealed.[47]

The SDF leadership in the 1880s and 1890s could give leads as to policy and campaigns, but it lacked a structure capable of creating and enforcing a party orthodoxy. For a long time the SDF was a mass of branches and members held together only by tenuous dint of common readership of *Justice*, issued by the SDF General Council; London, the SDF's stronghold, did not have an SDF district council until October 1895. The failure to coordinate organization was freely admitted, the SDF declaring in 1895 that as far as London was concerned, "we have absolutely failed to organise the body of feeling and opinion which we have developed". Accordingly the features of SDF activity in this period are not to be found in the orthodoxy of the SDF General Council, but in the heterodoxy of local initiative. This was often at odds with what the General Council desired, Hyndman later complaining that "suggestion and interference by the Executive have not infrequently been resented" by branches. If those at the top lacked the means to discipline those at the bottom, those at the bottom did not conceive of their role as being to follow the party line, except in a very general sense. "The work of a branch of the SDF can be summed up in one sentence", wrote George Lansbury in 1895, "propaganda for the purpose of making Social Democrats." Propaganda was a term of protean dimensions. For many SDF members the political activity of the unemployed came under its aegis. When the SDF as a body withdrew from organizing the unemployed, many SDF members remained involved.[48]

The strength of such heterodoxy was evident in the activity of the unemployed in the early months of 1895. Official SDF policy that winter was that its representatives on the vestries and boards of guardians would look after the unemployed. But this was to prove impossible: the scattering of SDF vestry members and guardians were flotsam upon a general sea of reaction, unable to determine the current of local government. Locally, SDF activists began to organize the unemployed to back up SDF guardians and vestry members with strong external pressure. George Lansbury, as chairman of the Poplar board of guardians, discovered that he was unable to work for the unemployed without, in part, working with them. He began to gather an unemployed agitation in the East End, centered in Bow, Hackney, and Mile End. Lansbury took to using deputations of the unemployed to the Poplar board of guardians to support his own proposals. At an emergency meeting on 15 February 1895, he succeeded in getting the Board to agree unanimously to the opening of three stoneyards. At these, men were able to obtain work for six hours a day; single men being paid 2 shillings and sixpence a day, married men 3 shillings and sixpence with a two pound loaf of bread for every child over three years of age-the best terms available in any London stoneyard. In Camberwell J. E. Dobson, along with three other SDF members, was now a vestry member; and at a meeting of the Camberwell vestry on 16 January 1895 at which a deputation of unemployed was present, it was successfully moved that the vestry employ as much unemployed labor as possible. In Battersea the local vestry, with SDF representatives sitting on it, came under pressure from the unemployed and resolved to spend £10,000 employing the unemployed channelling the streets of the parish. Unemployed activity was given a great stimulus by the weather of February 1895, the coldest on record for that month in fifty years. As well as in many areas of London, there were minor unemployed agitations in Glasgow, Dundee, Sheffield, and Reading run by either or both the SDF or the ILP.[49]

The idea of pressing local authorities not simply to gain a few days' work, but in order to demonstrate the total inadequacy of the poor law system and force the government to do something for the unemployed underpinned the SDF's unemployed strategy through the 1890s. So intent was the UOC on local pressure that it tried to take the heart out of the central London agitation by restricting the Tower Hill unemployed meetings to one a week, and by instructing its agitators to build up local committees, leading one of their organizers, Burrows, to resign in protest. This increasing emphasis upon localized unemployed activity meant that after 1887 there were no longer the same threatening hordes of unemployed gathering at the heart of the nation's capital. The UOC's tactics shrewdly recognised the growing local strength of the SDF in the suburbs, but they may have also been an attempt to find a new social base for the politics of the unemployed among the tradesmen of the suburbs, rather than the casual poor of the inner city. Whatever the reason, it did mean that unemployed agitation under the UOC occurred over a much wider area of London than before, and that this agitation proved much more effective than previously, relief works being undertaken by thirty three metropolitan authorities in the winter of 1892-93 because of unemployed pressure. We may take the example of the Camberwell unemployed in December 1893 as typical of their tone in dealing with local authorities: leading them was Jack Williams, who forced an entry into a meeting of the vestry and demanded that something be done for the unemployed, while his cohorts cried "Down with the vestry men" and "Down with the dirty dogs."[50]

But the TUUOC, the UOC, and the SDFUC never saw their role as limited to terrifying hapless members of local authorities. The SDFUC, for example, also pressured the government in more conventional ways, holding conferences with London MPs and writing to Gladstone. Nor did any of these bodies lack an awareness of the immediate political context in which they organized the unemployed. To use the SDFUC again as an example, it saw its agitation not in isolation, but as a factor that, when combined with Keir Hardie's work within Parliament, Tory desire to make capital out of the Liberal government, the industrial depression, and the financial crisis in the City, might force the government to take action over the unemployed. And, as in the 1880s, aggressive dealings with local authorities took place in a context of longer-term organization. In 1895 the picture becomes more complex, and foreshadows future developments: the unemployed, rather than simply confronting local authorities, instead enter into an alliance with some members of the local authorities willing to support them. For the socialist members of local authorities the support of the unemployed was essential in legitimizing themselves as something more than the spearheads of the electoral ambition of the SDF. They offered the unemployed the possibility of a little more relief and perhaps some work; in return the unemployed gave them substance and authority as representatives of the people.[51]

Without the activity of the unemployed little happened. Keir Hardie had been elected to Parliament as an independent labor candidate in 1892 upon an extensive anti-unemployment program that had particular appeal to his West Ham constituency of dockers and laborers. In February 1893 Hardie moved in the House of Commons that the government appoint a committee to investigate the problem of the unemployed. He hoped to make the unemployed a live political issue through a double-edged campaign, him "making it lively for the government in the House of Commons" while outside unemployed demonstrations backed him up. But the UOC, a Tower Hill meeting of which Hardie had addressed, was in decline, and there was little activity by the unemployed to underscore Hardie's call in Parliament. Gladstone told Hardie that it was not the business of government to deal with such matters, and Hardie's motion was lost.[52]

Hardie's chance to compel the government to make unemployment its business came in February 1895. This was a month of crisis, which saw many local authorities, who were under great pressure from the unemployed, in turn pressure the Local Government Board for more effective powers to enable them to grant some concessions to stem the discontent. With the SDF officially not involved with the 1895 unemployed agitation, the ILP, at the behest of Hardie, attempted to step into the vacuum and lead the unemployed. Hardie decreed 26 January 1895 as Unemployed Day (also known as Black Saturday), and unemployed meetings were held at Huddersfield, Bradford, Morely, Liverpool, Hammersmith, Chelsea, Clayton, Jarrow, Stocton, Kensal, Rochdale, and with the support of the SDF, in central London. In the Queen's Speech of 1895 there was no mention of the unemployed, and so, in mid February 1895, Hardie repeated his request of 1893 in the form of an amendment. This forced the government's hand by offering a rallying point to opportunist Unionists and disaffected Radicals. Most importantly Hardie's amendment—unlike his motion in 1893—coincided with and amplified the peak of unemployed activity. Under this intense combination of extra-parliamentary agitation by the unemployed, local authority pressure, and parliamentary attack, the government had to give way. On 13 February 1895 it announced the setting up of a Select Committee on Distress from Want of Employment. While the committee was a sop, it was in its implicit admission of state responsibility for unemployment a sop of some importance. The report registered the important changes in the relation between the state and the unemployed since 1886, endorsing the Chamberlain circular and the various local and voluntary experiments in providing employment that had sprung up since 1892. In its prescriptions for increased joint activity between charity and local government it gave its seal of approval to what was becoming an important method of mediating state control over the unemployed. The report was an important part of the ongoing reformulation of the relation between the state and the unemployed that was to reach one endpoint in the national unemployment insurance scheme of 1911.[53]

The unemployed agitations of 1892-95 were successful because of their local emphasis, pressuring the decentralized nineteenth century state where it was most susceptible to street politics, and forcing change upon the state as a whole through the sheer cumulative power of numerous particular local victories. The centralization of state welfare powers that was to take place over the next fifty years, culminating in the advent of the "Welfare State", owed as much to the desire to deny such working-class pressure the chance of success, as it did to the desire for efficiency. The politics of the unemployed in the period 1892-95 did acquire an entirely different nature to those of 1884-89, and had an enhanced effect because of the presence of Keir Hardie in the House of Commons. Similarly, Hardie was able to acquire his considerable prominence and his tag "member for the unemployed", because of his association with the unemployed agitations. As unemployment was coming to the fore as the great insoluble social issue of the day, Hardie had the political acumen to identify it as the great symbol of the failure of capitalism, and himself and the ILP as its prospective solution. Hardie is the beginning of the very important but highly problematic relationship between the unemployed and labor's parliamentary representatives. Hardie's approach to unemployment was given a theoretical underpinning by H. Russell Smart, an ILP member, who turned Marxist theory on its head and argued that the destruction of unemployment would inevitably mean the end of capitalism, and not, as Marxists had long argued, vice versa. "To my mind", wrote Smart, "the true story is this, the unemployed question must be solved before Socialism can be realised." To achieve this Smart proposed a "Right to Work" bill that would oblige local authorities to find work for any unemployed who applied for it. Smart's theory demonstrated the centrality of the unemployed to socialist thought and practice at this time, to the extent that the unemployed became a fetish whose problem usurped the more general socialist aims. Smart's theory was seized on by the ILP, for whom it offered a path to socialism that complimented rather than challenged the ILP's chosen parliamentary path, by leading to seats in the House of Commons rather than to the barricades. Later that year the ILP adopted "Right to Work" as part of their policy where it was to remain dormant until 1907, when, as we shall see in Chapter Three, it became the focus of the national "Right to Work" campaign.[54]

A cartoon in the *Labour Leader* in 1895 showed Keir Hardie carrying an emaciated figure titled "Unemployed" into the House of Commons. There is much truth in this image, yet it seems to miss the more fundamental truth that the socialists were only able to come to the political fore in this period because of their involvement with the politics of the unemployed. As we have seen, Hardie had been elected on a platform largely dealing with unemployment, while the SDF had been resurrected by the 1886 unemployed riot. Membership of the SDF soared in its years of involvement with the unemployed: from 1,926 in 1889, to 10,536 in 1896. As George Lansbury put it at the SDF gathering in 1894: "It might be hard for them to see the Burns, Shaws and Webbs applauded as the saviours of society—of the people, while they knew it was the agitation which the SDF was keeping up at the street corners that was compelling them to move forwards."[55]

Between 1884 and 1895 the unemployed through their own activity had succeeded in creating an awareness of their condition, which while contributing little to the immediate amelioration of their suffering, did lead to the establishment of a new relationship between the state and the unemployed. Prior to 1886 this relationship had been mediated through the new poor law, which acknowledged the unemployed only in an indirect way as the able bodied poor, the sick, the insane, and so on. Political economy, the ideology of the new poor law, as one of its contemporary critics pointed out, did not "recognise the unoccupied worker, the working man in so far as he is outside the working relationship. The swindler, the beggar, the unemployed, the starving, the destitute and the criminal working man are *figures* which exist not *for it,* but only for other eyes-for the eyes of the doctors, judges, gravediggers, beadles, etc. Nebulous figures which do not belong within the province of political economy."[56]

The word "unemployment", we are told by José Harris, was "introduced into the language of political economists" by Alfred Marshall in 1888. As we have seen the word "unemployment" had been about for at least sixty years prior to this; but the point here is that those responsible for forcing the averted eyes of political economy to focus upon the unemployed and recognize them as such were the unemployed themselves. What was it that had changed the cloud like image of the unemployed that had formerly occupied only a small part of the beadle's time into a concrete reality that had become the "sphinx of the age"?[57]

What had led the casualties of nineteenth-century capitalism—Marx's swindlers, cheats, beggars, unemployed, starving, destitute and criminals—to coalesce into what are by 1888 "the unemployed"? As we have seen, the final decades of the nineteenth century had seen major disturbances associated with the unemployed in London. The most thorough study of these events is that made by Gareth Stedman Jones in *Outcast London.* Jones argues that London experienced a major social crisis in the mid-1880s that was composed of four elements: a severe cyclical depression, the structural decline of some old industries, a shortage of housing, and the rise of socialism as a challenge to Liberalism.[58] What is not apparent in Jones' account is how this "social crisis" was also a political expression given to deep seated economic grievances through the activity of the unemployed. A social crisis thus occurred at this time and not at any other when the economic malaise was as bad because class conflict was made manifest through the activity of the unemployed. Jones' use of the term "social crisis" obscures the true significance of the unemployed riots by making them appear as *(i)* inevitable, a combination of bad conditions and worse weather, and as *(ii)* a transitory and not a pivotal event; that is, it ignores the possibilities and importance of working-class activity in determining such a social crisis.

The empirical investigations that were made into the condition of the working class and that did much to discredit some of the assumptions of political economy in the 1880s and 1890s were undertaken to disprove "the lurid statements of the sensationalists and Socialists". The most famous and influential of all the early surveys, Charles Booth's seventeen-volume *The Life and Labour of the People in London,* was directly inspired by a survey of the unemployed made by the SDF, which claimed that one in four Londoners lived in poverty. Booth believed this account to be grossly exaggerated, and undertook his survey to prove the SDF wrong. But upon publication of his initial investigation in 1889 Booth conceded that, if anything, the SDF figures had been an underestimate. Pointedly, less than a month after the Trafalgar Square riot of 1886, the House of Commons resolved upon a suggestion of Charles Bradlaugh to take immediate steps to ensure "the full and accurate collection and publication of labour statistics". Reminding MPs—if they needed any reminding—that "an orator more potent than any—the orator of hunger" was abroad, Bradlaugh argued that such statistics would be useful to oppose to the "extreme" statements of "those who were pretending to speak on behalf of labour." And in this way, though not always successfully nor always without subversive potential, statistics have been deployed ever since.[59]

It would be wrong to portray this period as one of advance for the unemployed. There were limitations to the politics of the unemployed in these years, and outright failures. Although there was considerable activity by the unemployed outside of London, no real attempt (apart from Keir Hardie's Black Saturday in 1895) was made to integrate and coordinate their activity with the big metropolitan campaigns. The focus throughout remained on and in London. The period bequeathed no permanent organization of the unemployed. With each downturn of trade the unemployed had to begin largely anew, repeating many of the mistakes of previous campaigns. Worse still, far from challenging the many divisions that kept the working class fragmented, the SDF through its unemployed campaigns of the 1890s sought to reinforce them, reproducing the divisions between respectable and non-respectable workers. Even Keir Hardie, who earned his title "member of the unemployed" in the period 1892-95, was not free from prejudice against sections of the unemployed, which in his case was unpleasantly tinged with a eugenicist flavor. "There are two classes of unemployed-the fit and the unfit", Hardie wrote in 1895: "The fit are those both able and willing to work, while the unfit may be divided as (a) those willing to work but not able, and (b) those able to work but not willing. I ask for no mercy to be shown to the (b) class. Treat them as you will, and, above all, see that it is made impossible for them to perpetuate the species."[60]

Yet something had fundamentally changed: if, as Keir Hardie claimed at the 1889 TUC "the problem of the age was how to dispose of its surplus labour", then the cause for the discovery of this problem must be considered in part to be the activity of the unemployed. The unemployed had become part of politics, and their salvation a principal part of the socialists' appeal and hope: "Poverty, in our opinion," wrote Tom Mann and Ben Tillett in 1890, "can be abolished, and we consider it is the work of the trade unionist to do this." The great panacea was, for a time, seen to be the eight-hour day; this trade unionists could fight for, this alone could achieve the ending of unemployment, the ending of the perennial insecurity of working class life. As Alexander Keyssar has commented of the eight-hour movement in Massachusetts in the same period, it was not the applicability of the eight-hour day but its immense appeal to the working class that is historically significant. For unions and socialists alike it offered a simple realizable remedy that, it was believed, would bring about a near utopian state. It was a sufficiently attractive and plausible vision to inspire working class people through Europe, America, and Australia. Within Britain it was an important element in the growing strength of the labor movement during the 1890s, the first May Day parade in London, for example, being organized principally around the demand for the eight-hour day.[61]

What the politics of the unemployed in this period demonstrated ultimately was not only or simply the centrality of class conflict in British society, but more fundamentally the fragmentation of the working class, and the intra-class conflict that flowed from it. What unemployed agitations showed to the socialists was that far from being a homogeneous unit the working class was fragmented and divided, and that these divisions were not easily overcome, nor necessarily worth the trouble of overcoming. From the 1890s onwards the strategy of socialists within both the ILP and the SDF was to identify with, and proselytize around, the vision of the working class as a totality, but to mobilize and organize only particular sections of it when deemed expedient. Following the 1886 riot, the young Ramsay MacDonald, who was to build a rich career out of the poverty of this particular line of thought, wrote of how "By pandering to all the desires of the very lowest class, we may soon gather round us a mob and just possibly make a revolution, but the social reconstruction of society will be further removed from us than ever." He went on to plead for a socialism that would stand forth "as a stage in the progress of intellectual development". With such a socialism "the discontented will still be at our command, and as explosive as ever. We may have to use them, or we may not; but should the worst befall their destructive power will be skilfully directed; it will not cause ruin, but will clear a way . . . it will be the tool, but not the designer." In this way socialism was remade in the late nineteenth century in the image of the British working class, and to this day it wears the stigmata of its resurrection: a belief in a ideal proletariat that never accords with reality, a strategy of mobilization but not involvement, and a concern for palliatives but not power.[62]

The Politics of Cynicism, 1903-1904

As if as a postscript to MacDonald's comments we have the brief outburst of activity by the unemployed in 1903-1904, which demonstrates the essential bankruptcy of the notions that he, and later the SDF, propagated. The years between

1895 and 1902 saw good trade, low unemployment, and no activity by the unemployed. The Boer War came to an end in May 1902, and in the following months unemployment began once again to rise, as war industries wound down and demobilized soldiers began to enter the labor market. Cunningham Grahame, Radical MP, called upon the unemployed to once again parade their plight to society in a letter to the press in December 1902. "The one thing the Empire cannot stand", he wrote at a time when many believed the Empire could stand almost anything, "is to hear again the chorus of the 'Starving Poor of Old England' in the squares and streets". The SDF, echoing the paternalistic stance it had first adopted towards the unemployed in the 1890s, commented "that it is necessary for others to help the unemployed help themselves, even in this elementary matter of demonstrating their need." Still, sighed the SDF, "however difficult we may have found this work in the past it is our duty to take it up once more." And so the SDF returned to the political organization of the unemployed after a hiatus of eight years, conceiving of its role as that of a parent behoven of a tiresome responsibility with a fractious child.[63]

The SDF's unemployed campaign developed an illusory momentum during the first six weeks of 1903. This campaign differed organizationally from those of the 1880s and 1890s, being run not by veteran agitators, but by a new group of SDF members. Although the SDF called for a strategy similar to that of 1895, having local unemployed agitation backing socialists on local authorities in the hope of evincing a national reaction, this did not occur. Instead, the campaign was very largely a matter of the unemployed marching through wealthy areas collecting money. The model for this form of agitation were the unemployed of the East End who were organized by two brothers, H. and C. Martin. Using the Mile End SDF hall as their base, the Martins had begun their campaign with a march of fifty men to the West End on New Year's Day, 1903. The West End march became a near daily event and quickly grew in size, the largest march in late January having 3,000 men taking part. The dynamic that ensured the participation of such large numbers was not political but financial. The Martins evolved a highly elaborate system whereby each man was paid for marching. The Martins elevated what had been common practice in previous unemployed campaigns, the sharing out of a collection after a march, into the raison d'etre for the entire campaign. Collecting boxes-some on poles to reach wealthy benefactors leaning out of upper-storey windows-were carried in the procession. Each man upon joining the march received a ticket which was exchanged at least once during the march to prevent "ca'canny"—the practice of going slow at work so as to deliberately limit output. In this instance ca'canny presumably meant to drop out of the march and rejoin it only near the end of its return journey. When the march concluded each marcher would receive his share of the collection upon presentation of his ticket. The highest amount paid out by the Martins in January 1903 was 4 shillings, the lowest nine pence.[64]

The payment system soon caught on throughout London. This craze for substituting collection for agitation was accompanied by a strong sense of financial self-importance: the organizers in every district took to using the local police to audit their collections, which were then published as fully audited accounts in the pages of *Justice*. Though there were some exceptions where the unemployed did take political action, it was more in the way of protest than truth that the SDF claimed in mid-February 1903 that the object of unemployed marches was to force the authorities to find work, not make collections.[65]

For a short time the payment system did achieve spectacular, if superficial, results. After years of quiescence the unemployed were mobilized in many areas of London. The campaign was at its height on 7 February 1903 when, on the eve of the assembly of Parliament, 3,500 unemployed marched through the West End to a meeting in Trafalgar Square. After this the campaign rapidly petered out. We do not have to search far to discover why. The unemployed took part in the marches simply in order to gain a payment at the end. For many unemployed the marches were only another poorly paid area of casual labor when nothing better was offering. Thus we find the Lambeth unemployed threatening to go on "strike" and no longer march when the organizer held back 7.5 percent of the collection for organizing expenses. When the payment was forthcoming in smaller and smaller amounts—as was bound to be the case after a few weeks, once bourgeois consciences petrified and purses closed—the unemployed, sick of marching up to fifteen to twenty miles a day, deserted. The Lambeth Unemployed Committee, for example, collected 99 pounds, 8 shillings, and twopence in the last week of January 1903. A fortnight later it was only able to collect only a little over 7 pounds in a week, which then had to be shared out among 134 men. By March 1903 the campaign was dead, and the SDF, for one, did not mourn its passing.[66]

Though a flash in the pan, the campaign momentarily gave off enough heat to singe the beard of the government. Between 1 January and 18 February 1903 a quarter of all the police in London were occupied in marshaling unemployed demonstrations. The government struck at the Achilles heel of the unemployed campaign by rushing through legislation that prevented the unemployed from collecting money easily. This came into effect on 7 November 1903, the same day the SDF chose to call for a new unemployed campaign. From that day anybody street-collecting in a group had to apply to Scotland Yard ten days in advance, stating the date, purpose, names of streets to be marched through, and numbers involved in the proposed march. Permits had to be produced on demand, collecting boxes upon poles were banned, and no collector was allowed to annoy a passerby. Any breach of these regulations was a punishable offence. The legislation broke the tactical backbone of the proposed unemployed campaign, and beyond an occasional wriggle the campaign was to remain throughout the winter of 1903-1904, the worst for unemployment since 1895, an inanimate cripple. But the failure of the SDF's 1903-1904 campaign cannot be attributed to the stringent new regulations alone. These merely—though cleverly—took advantage of the SDF's cynical vision of the unemployed, as expressed in the foolish tactic of basing a campaign's support solely upon the regular payment of the unemployed.[67]

The ambivalent attitude toward the lumpenproletariat in general, and the unemployed in particular, that the SDF had developed during the 1890s had been modified in practice by the way in which the SDF made a further distinction between deserving and undeserving unemployed. Many of the SDF's unemployed agitators continued to hold strongly to this distinction during the early 1900s. J. Hunter Watts, a SDF unemployed organizer, conceded in 1903 to a *Times* leader writer that many who took part in the marches were "unemployable". Once embarked upon an unemployed campaign, the SDF continued to make distinctions between those it deemed respectable working men temporarily out of a job, and those it deemed unemployable. In the same year, Leigh, SDF organizer of the Paddington unemployed, went so far as not to allow men he did not consider "bona fide" unemployed to take part in marches. On one day alone he turned away as unsuitable 100 of 400 prospective marchers. While the distinction between the respectable working man and the unemployable was a reactionary one, the unemployed were sometimes able to use it to subvert and reshape other reactionary ideas. For many, virtue and respectability equated, first and foremost, with steady employment. To be unemployed was an individual and not a social failing, proof in itself of the non-respectable and undeserving nature of those who were unemployed. When a Kingsland magistrate said he "never knew a respectable man who could not get work if he wanted it", he was echoing the thoughts of many. When 300 unemployed "respectable looking men" then took to chanting the Death March while slowly walking past the North London Police Court in which the magistrate was ensconced, they were indulging in more than a piece of mass intimidation. Their action was a telling argument against all those who believed that unemployment was the fault of the individual. They were demonstrating both their unemployment *and* their respectability, implying that to be out of work was not their fault, but society's.[68]

In the torrid jingoism excited by the Boer War the SDF's ambivalence curdled into a despair that was felt about all the unemployed, not just those whom it deemed unemployable. The great outburst of pro-imperialist feeling that occurred in Britain at this time expressed itself in such activity as the notorious saturnalia on the night of the Mafeking celebrations, and the often violent disruption of anti-war meetings by jingo mobs. While it remains a matter of scholastic dispute whether or not jingoism was a working class phenomenon, there was no doubt though in the minds of those anti-war socialists who were jeered, heckled, and beaten up by these mobs that they were composed of the lumpenproletariat, whom they took to castigating in the most vicious terms as "sappy headed idle youths . . . low street corner ruffians . . . male prostitutes and bullies". The experience of jingoism had a profound effect on many socialist agitators and served to heighten the tension which underlay the relation between them and the unemployed they sought to lead. When the ILP returned to the organization of the unemployed in 1904, one member, H. Snell, wrote bitterly about the unemployed who, he felt, "deserved their present suffering." Those who had "vomited the Kipling ode of death, 'Pay, Pay, Pay,' in the face of every advocate of peace, now turn like whipped hounds to the same advocate, asking for 'Work, Work, Work'." The socialist's reply to such simpering working-class curs was to be a mixture of condescension and retribution. "Our remedy", wrote Snell, "should be rammed down their throats until they accept it and insist upon its adoption."[69]

Snell's unequivocal prescription for the unemployed was endorsed by the SDF. Their experience at the hand of the jingo mob led them to an extreme cynicism about the political nature of the lumpenproletariat. From being hailed as the revolutionary vanguard in the 1880s, to being dismissed as politically indifferent in the 1890s, the lumpenproletariat was now reviled as being positively reactionary. Along with Snell, the SDF saw unemployment not as capitalism's curse upon the working class, but as divine retribution upon reaction. "The SDF, as of old, once more unfurls the red flag, and takes its place at the head of the British Imperial Unemployed", sneered *Justice* upon the SDF's 1903 campaign, "to champion the cause of deluded and misled Patriots of the past three years. Verily, they have their reward, for they are refused work." Such despair bred a contempt for the unemployed who were no longer seen as having the potential to be even a progressive force. As for the unemployed "constituting an 'army of reform' ", said an amnesiac *Justice*, "no one in the SDF has ever entertained so idle a notion." The unemployed were reduced to the level of a tool that the SDF used to perform its tiresome public duty of demonstrating the suffering of the working class.[70]

This contempt found its corollary in the use of money rather than fixed objectives, programs and ideas to motivate the unemployed. The backing of the unemployed was to be bought by the SDF with cash. The campaign of 1903 had been a tactical cul de sac for the politics of the unemployed, a throwback to the unemployed's pre-1884 role of supplication, which revealed more about the failings of the SDF than it did about the susceptibility of the state to public parades of poverty. The truth was that the Empire, with a small dose of restrictive regulations, could stand to hear again "The Starving Poor of Old England". It was the absence of political purpose from the singing that rendered it just another music hall refrain.

3

The Right to Work: The Unemployed and Labour, 1904–1910

The Chairman said that they had met to consider a problem of the utmost gravity. The problem of Unemployment was very old and was world-wide in extent. . . . What then was the remedy? . . . The right to vote was conferred by the State, and was only won after generations of agitation. The right to vote was as keenly contested as was the right to work today, but just as the right to vote had been won so too would the right to work be won by the organised agitation which our movement would carry forward in its defence. In claiming this right we were not asking for any special class privilege. He would not object to it on that score even if we were. If a man possessed property the State maintained his right to own that property and protected him in the possesssion of that right, and we claimed for our labour the same degree of protection as given to the property of the rich.

—*George Barnes, chairman, to the Special Labour Party Conference on Unemployment, 27 January 1909.*[1]

As Engels pointed out in 1886 the SDF had been able to take the initiative with the unemployed because no one else would, the Radical Clubs of the East End preferring to do nothing. Their failure was more than symptomatic of the dissolution of working-class liberalism, then in its earliest stages. Unable to embrace an issue outside of their traditional ideology (except where it intersected with their traditional goals, such as the right to free speech at Trafalgar Square), the Radicals closed off for themselves a very important political space that the socialists were then to occupy. When, in the first decade of the new century, the New Liberals and the social imperialists sought to win working-class support by formulating varied policies attacking unemployment, it was to be too late. The decline of Britain as an economic power relative to the new economies of the United States of America and Germany, which we noted in the previous chapter, continued during the Edwardian era, with the important difference that there was now a growing awareness about this decline that sometimes shaded into hysteria, and occasionally provided common ground for otherwise seemingly disparate forces. A theory of hereditary urban degeneration came to receive widespread support among the middle class from the 1890s onwards, and posited an alternative explanation to that of the SDF socialists as to the cause of the outbursts of the unemployed.[2]

The problem of the poor and the unemployed in the inner city was not just a cause for concern and sometimes panic from the 1880s onwards. It was also a metaphor rich in material manifestations for the growing sense of crisis that affected Britain. This hydra-headed crisis—racial, industrial, military, political, and urban—seemed to have as its common reducible element the dark world of English poverty. Unemployment policy became an area in which New Liberal concerns with physical efficiency, social imperialist concerns with the future cohesion of the imperial master race, eugenecist aims to eliminate the residuum of those unable to work, trade unionist desires to preserve craft status and wage levels by reducing competition by the poor, and socialist attempts to improve the lot of the poor, could, for a time, seem compatible, rather than as they were, entirely contradictory. The two previously unrelated issues of poverty and economic decline were to become inextricably entwined during the Boer War, when disclosures of the appalling physical standard of working class volunteers for the army were used to vest poverty with an economic and imperial importance it had never previously had. Only in this light is it possible to see why the politics of the unemployed were to prove more influential in this period than they had previously, and only in this light is it possible to understand why the seeds of the political activity of the unemployed, when sown upon such reactionary soil, were ultimately to bear bitter fruit in the form of national unemployment insurance.[3]

It is commonplace that British working-class politics changed fundamentally in both organization and ideology between 1895 and 1910. There was an increasing institutionalization of industrial conflict in Edwardian Britain, reflected in the growth of the collective bargaining and conciliation machinery, a process complemented by the institutionalization of political conflict in Parliament. The Labour Representation Committee (LRC), formed in 1900 as a movement of defense on the part of the trade unions (who provided the cash and credibility) and as the nucleus of independent working-class representation on the part of the socialists (who provided the energy and activists) was renamed the Labour Party in 1906, and had by 1910 established a small but significant presence in the House of Commons. The working class who had cheered when the houses of Parliament burnt down in 1832 were now expected to cheer when Labour Party men entered Parliament as members. Underpinning these changes was the ideology of laborism, that strange and surly combination of socialist hope and Liberal belief, which sought change within capitalist society, rather than change through the elimination of capitalism.[4]

But what is often overlooked is that these changes did not impose themselves gradually upon the working class, but grew out of conflict with other forms and theories of political action available to the working class. Prior to 1910 the growth of laborism was to be challenged primarily by SDF activists and ILP radicals through the politics of the unemployed, which in its practice demonstrated that there existed a political alternative to laborism. Far from being a retrospective judgment, this was a belief that was strongly held by many Labour leaders of the time. Paradoxically, the eventual triumph of laborism in the form of the parliamentary politics of the Labour Party, owed something to the extra-parliamentary politics of the unemployed, which buttressed the Labour Party at crucial moments of its existence, and which gave the Labour Party the legitimacy it so desperately craved among large sections of the working class. Such a contradiction could not be sustained indefinitely, and in late 1908 the politics of the unemployed precipitated a crisis in the Labour Party that ultimately led to the crushing of any hope of the creation of a mass socialist party, and ensured the emergence of a mass laborist party.

Table 3.1. *Unemployment, 1900-1911*
Percentage registered unemployed in trade unions by month, Jan. 1900-Dec. 1911

	Jan	Feb	Mar	Apr	May	Jun	Jul	Aug	Sept	Oct	Nov	Dec
1900	2.3	2.4	2.0	2.0	1.9	2.1	2.2	2.5	3.0	2.8	2.7	3.5
1901	3.5	3.4	3.1	3.4	3.0	3.0	2.9	3.4	3.2	3.2	3.3	4.2
1902	4.0	3.9	3.2	3.4	3.5	3.7	3.5	4.0	4.5	4.5	4.4	5.0
1903	4.9	4.3	3.9	4.6	3.5	3.9	4.4	5.0	5.2	5.6	5.5	6.3
1904	6.1	5.6	5.5	5.5	5.8	5.5	5.6	5.9	6.3	6.3	6.5	7.1
1905	6.3	5.7	5.2	5.2	4.7	4.8	4.7	4.9	4.8	4.6	4.3	4.5
1906	4.3	4.1	3.4	3.2	3.1	3.2	3.1	3.3	3.3	3.9	4.0	4.4
1907	3.9	3.5	3.2	2.8	3.0	3.1	3.2	3.6	4.1	4.2	4.5	5.6
1908	5.8	6.0	6.4	7.1	7.4	7.9	7.9	8.5	9.3	9.5	8.7	9.1
1909	8.7	8.4	8.2	8.2	7.9	7.9	7.9	7.7	7.4	7.1	6.5	6.6
1910	6.8	5.7	5.2	4.4	4.2	3.7	3.8	4.0	4.3	4.4	4.6	5.0
1911	3.9	3.3	3.0	2.8	2.5	3.0	2.9	3.3	2.9	2.8	2.6	3.1

Source: K. D. Brown, *Labour and Unemployment, 1900-1914* (Newton Abbot 1971), p. 190.

While, as we can see from Table 3.1, unemployment did occasionally rise to substantial levels in the Edwardian period, levels were never as bad as the worst of the 1880s or the 1920s and 1930s (see Tables 2.1, 5.1, and 6.1). This was the *belle époque*, the beautiful era, during which the world economy boomed. The discontent of the unemployed at this time can only be understood by reference to other economic and social factors. Like Victorian Britain, Edwardian Britain was characterized by great inequality. This in itself was hardly new, but what was new, and what was cause on the part of the poor for sullen reflection and bitterness, was the way in which the rich, with their new lifestyle of conspicuous, public consumption, now flaunted their wealth and power. Yet it was precisely at this time, while the total national income grew by 20 percent between 1900 and 1913, that the poor—estimated in 1900 to have been 40 percent of the working class—found their position growing daily more desperate. Wages fell an estimated 5 percent between

1900 and 1913, while food and clothing (upon which wage earners spent an estimated 70 percent of their income) rose in price. As an additional insult the working class was paying more out in tax than it was receiving back in benefits. Taken together these factors created conditions pregnant with unrest. There were various political forces, which we will look at later, that would for a short time build a national movement of protest upon the basis of this unrest, but underlying this national movement would be an economic change of fundamental importance, which we can only note in passing. During the 1890s and 1900s the British economy became, for the first time, truly national in operation and effect, and the state played a growing and increasingly important role in this process of integration and concentration. The first organized national labor conflicts took place in the 1890s, and the idea of a truly national economy, as opposed to that of loosely related local economies, dates from the same time. "Two points stand out with tolerable clearness", wrote W. F. Black of the ILP in 1904, "(1) That we have already entered a period of exceptional distress caused by lack of employment and (2) That the question is one of national and not merely local concern." Joblessness, which had primarily been conceived of as a feature of the metropolitan casual labor markets, was coming to be seen as a national economic problem.[5]

This had both political and strategic implications for the unemployed. If the problem was a national one, who ought to take responsibility for it? The answer was less obvious than it may seem to us, for such matters as unemployment were, as we have seen and as Gladstone had told Hardie, not the business of government. But at the same time the working class was becoming increasingly homogenized in social composition and outlook, and the state played an important role in this process. It is perhaps exaggerated to say, as one historian has, that the state "nationalized" the working class during this time, but it is true that the working class was being encouraged to identify its interests with those of the nation-state, a process that was to be accelerated by the post 1906 laws guaranteeing trade unionism security, and the advent of national insurance and old age pensions. When Keir Hardie wrote in 1904 that "The responsibility of providing work for the able bodied unemployed belongs to the nation, and should be systematically undertaken by the state", he was conceiving of unemployment in a way that would have been incomprehensible a few decades earlier, as a national problem demanding a national solution. Strategically this meant that the unemployed had to organize nationally, but there remained the problem of how to organize upon a national basis when the unemployed could only be mobilized upon immediate local issues that they had a chance of winning. The paradox was to be overcome by embracing it. When in 1904 the SDF organized a national campaign to call for a special autumn session of Parliament to discuss the unemployed, their strategy focused on locally based pressure to win relief. The SDF correctly believed that local authorities when "faced with the enigma of how to deal locally with a serious situation which is national in extent", would have no choice but to amplify the SDF's call for the special session of parliament; and this idea underlies all subsequent campaigns by the unemployed. Part of the challenge for the Labour Party at this time was to transform itself not simply into a mass working class party, but into a national mass working class party, and the politics of the unemployed, as a national phenomenon, were to prove of critical importance in the course of this transformation.[6]

The Unemployed Workmen Act of 1905

Prior to 1904 the politics of the unemployed had been primarily about the relation between a socialist sect, the SDF, and elements of the London unemployed. After 1905 unemployed campaigns unfold on a national stage as a supporting act to the varied performances of the Labour Party. Before 1904 unemployment was a fact of life for the working class, but only after 1905 did it become a major political issue for the Labour Party. Why did everything suddenly change? In 1904 the LRC, a minuscule and incoherent working-class party united only in its commitment to parliamentarianism, came into collision with the politics of the unemployed. The emasculated bastard that was the issue of their brief union was the Unemployed Workmen Act, and it is in the story of its genesis that we must seek the answer to our question.

In part the passing of the act is a record of vacillation by the government as it wavered between inaction and forced activity. What screwed the government's courage to the sticking place at each succeeding moment of crisis was the activity of the unemployed. "It is all forgotten now", Walter Long, at the time the president of the Local Government Board, some years later told the Royal Commission on the Poor Law, "but during the eighteen months that the pressure of the unemployed was growing, the methods adopted by the unemployed towards the authorities were violent in the extreme. There were crowds besieging the offices of the relieving officers . . . the boards of guardians could hardly sit in some places without safeguarding their doors." The government's intention in finally passing the act, designed as a feeble and ineffective piece of legislation, was to offset the blossoming demand for state action to help the unemployed. The paradox of the act was that while it was designed to stymie the call for state aid of the unemployed, its admission of the state interest in the unemployed gave an impetus and legitimacy to calls for state action that they otherwise lacked, and which meant in the long term that they could not be ignored.[7]

With the approach of summer in 1904 unemployment levels failed to drop as they had done for some years previously. On 1 October 1904 the SDF called for an unemployed campaign to demand a special autumn session of parliament to deal with the problem. The SDF hoped that beleaguered local authorities, prevented by government regulations from effectively helping the unemployed, yet strongly pressured by local unemployed activity, would be won over to the demand for national action on unemployment. The call quickly gathered momentum, and on 6 October 1904 Walter Long tried to defuse the situation by calling a conference of all London's guardians. Saddled with the invidious task of having to do something so as to take the heat off the government without doing anything that might relax the principles of the poor law, Long came up with an ingenious scheme which he revealed at the conference. Throughout London local unemployment committees composed of representatives of local government and local charities were to be established (although the scheme was voluntary and local authorities not obligated to take part), with the job of sorting out the "respectable temporary out of work men" from the "ordinary pauper". While the former were to be offered jobs (though at less than the going rate) on relief works funded by charity, the latter were only to be offered the workhouse. Long's scheme was based on a small East End scheme that Canon Barnett, head of Tonybee Hall, had come up with in response to the unemployed marches of 1903, as "a really sensible and non-philanthropic way of dealing with the problem and abolishing street processions". The scheme fittingly thus had its genesis in an anti-street politics measure. The SDF saw Long's scheme as both an attempt to divert attention from their call for an autumn session, and as an admission of the success of unemployed pressure. Suddenly it seemed possible that serious concessions might just be won. Theodore Rothstein called upon SDF branches to now put aside all other work and concentrate on forcing an autumn session. Within London the SDF's unemployment campaign came to life under the leadership of Jack Williams and W. J. Salmon. In the final months of 1904 the unemployed grew active in Hackney, Bethnal Green, Poplar, Stratford, Islington, and Shoreditch. By mid-November 1904 three rural district councils, twelve town and borough councils, forty urban district councils, and forty-five poor law unions were backing the SDF call for an autumn session of Parliament.[8]

The agitation spread beyond London to Glasgow, Leeds, Brighton, Liverpool, and most noticeably to Manchester. There the SDF was working with the ILP and the trades council to organize the unemployed, but it was the SDF whose influence predominated. The unemployed elected their own committee, and two SDF members, W. E. Skivington and J. B. Hitchen, both shopkeepers, were made secretary and chairman. A series of threatening marches and meetings led to the raising of relief from 4 shillings to 6 shillings, and the opening of a labour exchange where the unemployed took to holding their meetings. In spite of these concessions and pleas to desist, 2,000 unemployed chanting "Work not charity" marched on the Chorlton board of guardians in late November 1904 and compelled them to give immediate relief in kind. The next day the Chorlton guardians set 600 unemployed men to work clearing snow, some of whom were so weak from extended periods of unemployment that they collapsed as they worked in the street. The authorities then sought to defuse the agitation with charity. In excess of £7,000 was collected for a mayor's relief fund. An identical fund established nine months before had raised only £561. Shann, the mayor, who was later to admit that the fund undoubtedly "allayed for some time the serious agitation that had arisen", was astute enough not to rely on charity alone: he also incorporated the activists into a Lord Mayor's Unemployed Committee that he chaired and that was additionally composed of local dignitaries and city councillors. In return for this recognition the unemployed meekly agreed henceforth to meet in a police station yard. Activists believed "that the movement was being kept on hang by the mayor and his friends to tide over the critical period of winter".[9]

By November 1904 the TUC, along with the ILP and LRC, had picked up the SDF's call for a special session of Parliament and were presenting it as their own demand, the LRC using the issue to present itself as the "proper" voice of the working class, justifying itself in this role by deriding the worth of SDF street politics. Unemployment gave the LRC a cause of its own that was popular with the unions, and they seized upon it with fervor. It was Keir Hardie, building upon his achievements of the 1890s, who was both to precipitate and to personify the LRC's concern for the unemployed. Hardie was in 1904 a figure of diminished stature in the Labour world. He had been badly ill, and his relations with the other Labour leaders, Ramsay MacDonald and Philip Snowden, were strained. It was the issue of the unemployed that was to bring Hardie back to the prominence he had first acquired as the "member for the unemployed" in the 1890s. At his instigation the ILP, often in conjunction with the LRC, was by the end of 1904 holding meetings on unemployment throughout the country.[10]

This, and the SDF's street campaigning, were having an effect. The leaders of the Liberal Party began, in December 1904, to discuss seriously the formulation of new policies on unemployment, though their thinking upon the matter remained severely circumscribed. On 24 January 1905 the cabinet first discussed proposals by Long for legislation regarding the unemployed. The government was careful not to publicly intimate its possible intentions, leading the SDF to conclude that agitation had to be stepped up. The unemployed campaign grew stronger, and on 14 February 1905 it was announced in the King's Speech that an unemployed bill was to be introduced that session. Against strong opposition within the cabinet Long now argued for legislation that would make a permanent fixture of the experimental committees he had set up in October 1904, with the major alteration being funding the committees out of rates rather than by charity. Only if the scheme was rate-funded could it succeed, and if it were to fail, argued Long, the demand for state intervention to help the unemployed would become irresistible. Under pressure from Labour MPs and large unemployed demonstrations, Gerald Balfour, the prime minister's brother and Long's replacement as head of the Local Government Board, introduced the Unemployed Workmen Bill on 18 April 1905.[11]

The bill proposed the creation of borough distress committees in all major cities. These would be overseen by a central body responsible for providing work, funded out of the rates, to those passed on to it by the borough committees. In spite of the bill's many shortcomings—its distinction between deserving and undeserving unemployed, its concentration only on the major cities, its intention to pay less than the going rate of wages on relief works—the labor movement saw the bill as an admission by the state of its duty to help the unemployed, and gave it qualified approval. The ILP hoped that it could be improved by amendments.[12]

"Socialism Being the Theme of Each Discourse": The First Hunger Marches

Discontent among the unemployed did not subside with the introduction of the bill, and found one new outlet for its expression in the hunger march upon London. In this the unemployed were inspired by 115 striking shoe workers from Raunds, who in May 1905 marched to London to publicize their case and put it before the government. The march had SDF connections, being led by James Gribble, an SDF councillor and boot worker, and being looked after in London by Jack Williams. It was highly successful in generating publicity and led to a government enquiry that went some way to meeting the marchers' grievances. The first to awaken to the possibilities suggested by the shoe workers' march were the unemployed of Leicester. Trade in the two staple industries of their town, hosiery and shoemaking, was bad, and unemployment high. From March 1905 between 500 and 1,000 unemployed took to holding meetings and processions in Leicester. Inspired by the Raunds shoe workers, one of the unemployed leaders, Amos Sheriff, suggested that they march upon London, and the unemployed seized upon the idea with enthusiasm.[13]

Although it was now suspected that the government intended to let its unemployed bill drop, the LRC was aghast at the prospect of the unemployed marching en-masse on London: "these disorganised bodies of unemployed", wrote Ramsay MacDonald, ". . . would seriously damage the chances of securing a rational and sympathetic consideration of the Unemployed Problem." The SDF was temporarily inactive, concentrating its agitation upon the demand for the state feeding of necessitous school children, which it justified in terms of the utter pointlessness of organizing the "unemployables". "A glance along our streets will show that there is hope for the children," wrote Harry Lee, "though none for the adults". As in 1895 the ILP stepped in and took over the leadership of the unemployed. Keir Hardie envisaged an ongoing unemployed campaign relentlessly forcing the government to yield concession after concession, of which the Unemployed Workmen Bill was but the first. Under his influence the ILP decided that rather than opposing the Leicester and other more recently proposed marches, it would organize them on its own terms to help secure the passing of the bill. The marches, starting from several major cities, were to culminate in a national day of protest on their arrival in London, with great demonstrations throughout the country. The aim, wrote Hardie, was to make "such a protest on behalf of the Unemployed as this generation has not seen."[14]

The government remained impassive in the face of this threat, giving a number of Labour MPs the opportunity to declare their opposition to the marches. Hardie was forced to back down and had to call the marches off. He remained determined to save the bill, believing that whatever its faults it recognized important principles, and the plans for the national day of protest went ahead. The SDF taunted the LRC on the backdown, declaring that "Mr Hardie's own colleagues have no more love for a demonstration of popular force than Mr Balfour."[15]

Only the unemployed of Leicester could not be dissuaded from marching, and on 4 June 1905 the first ever hunger march began when 440 men walked out of Leicester. The Leicester march foreshadowed future hunger marches in a number of ways. First, it was an exclusively male event. Although the national hunger marches of 1930, 1932, and 1936 were to have small separate contingents of women, the hunger march remained to the end a predominately masculine affair. This goes some way in explaining the extreme martial nature of this and other marches that followed. The Leicester marchers were organized in a very military, and therefore hierarchical and authoritarian manner. They were divided into twenty-two "companies" of twenty men, each company under the command of a "sergeant". In addition to an "ambulance corps" there was a "flying squad" of cyclists who had been chosen to "move in front of the army, and arrange for the provision of forage and billets". At the apex of this structure stood Amos Sheriff called, perhaps predictably, the "general".[16]

It is easy to belittle the martial nature of the hunger marches. Yet it was a method of organization and external discipline that the men understood and took to with relative ease. Many of the marchers, in 1905 and later years, were unemployed ex-soldiers. Out of the 440 Leicester marchers 164—some 37 percent—were ex-soldiers. The proportions were even higher after World War I when, for example, 75 percent of the Manchester contingent on the 1922 national hunger march were ex-soldiers. More fundamentally, the marches' hierarchical and authoritarian nature was a mirror image of the hierarchical and authoritarian structure of everyday working-class life, both in its industrial and domestic spheres. Far from objecting to such features, the men scarcely discerned the presence of what for them were familiar facts of life. Most importantly, the martial nature of the marches enabled them to succeed. From the distance of many years, it is only too easy to be blind to how difficult the organization of the marches was, to fail to realise how much more likely they were to fail and disintegrate than to succeed. Organization upon military lines meant that no march was a debacle, and many marches that might otherwise not have occurred did take place. But it had its price: with hindsight it can be seen that it effectively excluded women from the most potent weapon the unemployed forged for themselves this century.[17]

Like later marches, the Leicester march was to be dependent on sections of the labor and socialist movement for support once it left its home town, without which any march was doomed to failure. But also like future marches, its relationship with its political patrons—be it the ILP for the Leicester march or the Communist Party for the inter war marches—was riddled with tensions. Ramsay MacDonald, an opponent of the marches, succeeded in first persuading the Leicester unemployed to postpone their march, and then later, when they were intent on marching, to take only "the most able and reliable" of the unemployed, thus considerably reducing the number of marchers threatening to descend on London. Before it aborted its other marches in 1905, the ILP circularized branches organizing marches, emphasizing the importance of recruiting as many of "the artisan class" as possible, and excluding all "vagabonds", to ensure maximum public support, but also thereby reproducing poor law distinctions between deserving and undeserving poor.[18]

The Leicester march had a strong sense of divine mission that was present to a greater or lesser degree in all subsequent marches. Stewart Gray, a leader of some pre-World War I marches was described as "almost a biblical figure.... the prophet of the submerged and the outcast." In the diary of Eddy Jones, a Welsh hunger marcher of 1936, we find the following entry: "We arrive at Bath after a good march and are put up at the Assembly Rooms a Building of Great Aristocratic Traditions .... Going through it one could imagine the revels and orgies that were indulged by the decadent aristocrats of those days. According to Lewis Jones [leader of the Welsh hunger marchers] the presence of the marchers has purified it." And, after all, the most famous hunger march of them all, that of Jarrow, pointedly took on the title of the Jarrow *Crusade*. The beginning of the Leicester march was a harbinger of such marches, as the following description bears witness: "The proceedings in the Market Place were of the nature of a religious ceremony. All the component parts were there, hymns, prayers, a surpliced priest with an inspiring message and attentive congregation."[19]

Finally, the Leicester march resembled its successors in its anti-climactic ending in London. All the major hunger marches raised great expectations that they could never fulfill. In Leicester 20,000 people lined the streets to bid farewell to the marchers. Comparisons were made with the peasants' march of 1381, yet when they arrived in London less than a thousand people gathered at a meeting in Trafalgar Square to greet them. This pattern of great expectations followed by failure in London and no immediate gains was to be repeated time after time. J. T. Murphy, a Communist Party leader, wrote of the beginning of the 1922 hunger march, "Such a revolutionary portent had never been seen in Britain". Yet the 1922 hunger march ended as a broken shambles. The nature of the hunger march was such that this could never be otherwise. They were a highly dramatic form of political action, enacted throughout the length and breadth of Britain by hundreds of unemployed, semi-starved men over a period of weeks. In some inter-war marches the emotional impact of the drama was deliberately accentuated by having the marches take place in midwinter. "The feeling was of tragedy and pride", wrote Wal Hannington some years later. "People used to weep at the sight of the men facing the rigours of such a march in wintertime in order to draw attention to the plight of the unemployed." But the tension built up during marches could never find a dramatic focus at the moment of climax, the entry into London. No government, however much its policies would be subsequently influenced by the marches, could let itself be seen to give in and grant immediate concessions to what they saw as a hungry rabble. No hunger march, on the other hand, ever saw itself as an insurrectionary force set to storm the House of Commons. Thus the cathartic ending demanded by the unfolding dramatic logic of the hunger march never took place.[20]

Less than a week after the Leicester marchers set off for London, the SDF returned to the fray and called for a renewed unemployed agitation. At the same time the ILP in conjunction with the LRC began a national program of mass meetings, many of which were organized by or with the SDF. In the following four weeks over 100 major meetings were held, many attracting very large audiences. The unemployed again grew active in London and Manchester. On 20 June 1905, three days after the first ILP mass meeting, the Unemployed Workmen Bill was read for a second time, and came under fire from government supporters, who were troubled by the way the labor movement was interpreting the bill as an admission of the state's responsibility for the unemployed. In the face of these opposing pressures the government vacillated, at first appearing to bow to its own supporters and making ready to drop the bill; then in mid July 1905 seeming to succumb to the growing external pressure when it had the Unemployed Workmen Bill read for a third time. But the bill had been fundamentally altered, the rate aid clause having been removed, leaving the funding of relief work to charity. The amended bill was probably read in the hope that Labour would at last abandon it as an impotent and useless measure. But the LRC, while criticizing the removal of the rate aid clause, chose not to drop the bill, and instead renewed its campaign for the bill's passing. Due to the combined efforts of Labour and socialist activists the meetings continued, and they continued to be successful; the demonstration at Mexboro in late July, for example, being the largest demonstration on record there. Allowing for understandable rhetoric, Hardie's claim that not since "the Chartist movement has there been such a genuine uprising of the common people" does make it clear that the socialists, through the unemployed, had for the first time touched a genuine vein of popular sentiment among the working class.[21]

On 31 July 1905, the same day as Balfour was preparing to drop the bill by not having it included on a list of bills to be put through the house that session, there came sensational reports of rioting by the unemployed in Manchester that had, said the *Manchester Evening News*, "no parallel in the history of the city since the dreadful days of Peterloo". Since mid-July 1905 the Manchester unemployed, under the leadership of W. E. Skivington and Arthur Smith, had, in contravention of police orders, taken to holding their meetings in Albert Square to demand the passing of the Unemployed Workmen Bill. On 31 July 1905 they marched through Manchester behind a banner carried aloft by Skivington and Smith that read, "We Demand the Unemployed Bill". A tram car was prevented from moving by the mass of the demonstrators. The police used this as a pretext for attacking the unemployed, brutally laying into the crowd with their batons and fists.[22]

It is difficult at first to see why this street fight should have had the impact it did. We need to remember that, unlike the 1880s and 1890s, the politics of the unemployed between 1903 and 1905 had been characterized by peaceful activity and not regular street brawling between the unemployed and the police. The unemployed between 1903 and 1905 avoided confrontation. Rather than challenge the government's regulations on street collecting in the winter of 1903-1904, as they would have done in the 1880s or the 1890s, the unemployed accepted them. The unemployed had been pliant in their relations with the police to the point of near obsequiousness, as, for instance, when the Manchester unemployed agreed in 1904 to meet in the yard of a police station. The events of 31 July 1905 were the first break in this pattern, and given the extent that unemployment had now become a major national issue rather than a minor metropolitan one, this in itself was a disturbing portent. But at a time when a general election was looming and the electoral support of working-class voters was increasingly important, it was also an event that could not be entirely ignored. So in a clever political move, the government had the bill rammed through the house by 7 August 1905 in a form so emasculated it no longer offended Conservatives. To appease the outraged labor movement Balfour threw in the sop of a Royal Commission on the Poor Law, which was, as K. D. Brown has shown, not the result of a considered long-term policy, but a knee jerk reaction to extricate the government from the position it now found itself in.[23]

While the unemployed campaign of 1904-1905 lacked the support of either major party, it did evince greater interest among the working class than any previous initiative made by the labor movement. The joint ILP/LRC mass meetings had for the first time widened the focus out from London, and in so doing made unemployment a national rather than a metropolitan issue, which, warned the *Manchester Guardian*, "had created a new labour sentiment among the people that will greatly affect the political history of the future." The LRC had found an issue of great moral power and working-class popularity with which it could define itself politically against the Liberals. Although by the end of 1905 Campbell Bannerman would be canvassing the issue of unemployment almost as much as Keir Hardie, the LRC had succeeded in appropriating the issue and making it its own. The impetus the issue gave the labor movement is reflected in the sudden growth of the ILP from 292 branches in 1905 to 426 in 1906, and confirmed by the way it restored the standing of Keir Hardie as the greatest socialist leader of his era. When in 1925 Stanley Baldwin admitted that he was "profoundly grateful" that the Labour Party had been in office for they "no more than any other government, have been able to produce a panacea for unemployment", he was also conceding just how successful the Labour Party had been for nearly two decades in identifying itself with the problem of the unemployed. In this respect the real beneficiaries of the Unemployed Workmen Act were not the unemployed, who gained little from the feeble legislation, but the parliamentary socialists.[24]

Radical Possibilities and the Radicalizing Effect of Women's Involvement

While the Unemployed Workman Act was a de facto acknowledgment of the principle that the state had a responsibility for the unemployed, as a practical measure it was useless. As a tactical response to the act the ILP in late August 1905 announced its intention of enrolling the unemployed in an organization pledged to securing the right to work. Keir Hardie, the architect of this plan, envisaged a national unemployed movement subordinate to, and run by, the labor movement. Hardie wanted such an unemployed movement to be effective, and recognized that its base of support had to be broader than the narrow, exclusive stratum of respectable working men whose support had been previously coveted. He argued that "the unemployed of both sexes and of all ages and conditions, must be organised", which meant that "all the unemployed should be brought in; not merely the respectable, but the loafers and the wastrels." He added, "Those who are burdened with a sense of respectability, or who are so enamoured of law and order that they will countenance nothing which transgresses its sacred limits, had better give it a wide berth. If there be not a snap of revolutionary spirit in it, it will fail of of its purpose." For the first time since the 1880s the socialist movement was actively encouraging the organization not only of the respectable working men, but of the unrespectable men; and not only of men, but also of women. Hardie was able to make this advance because he had come to believe that the unemployed could redeem their humanity through political activity. "The unemployed must be taught how to insist upon their rights as citizens, and as human beings", wrote Hardie. "Once they begin to feel their own power and the fighting spirit is reawakened within them, they will shake off the paralysing meddling of the fussy busy bodies". This idea of political activity as a force of personal redemption was later to permeate the very being of the inter-war unemployed movement. During late 1905 it was to lead the politics of the unemployed into its most radical phase prior to the inter-war years. Although enjoying only the shortest of lives, this radicalism briefly illuminated the possibilities of the politics of the unemployed if it could rid itself of its exclusive pretensions, and only base itself in the experience of all, and not just a few particular sections of the working class.[25]

The unemployed were organized in late 1905 on an entirely different basis than that of 1903, when the object had been only to demonstrate the existence of distress. The highly political aims of the East London Unemployed Committee, formed in late August 1905, make this clear: they stood for the socialization of the means of production and distribution as the means of eliminating unemployment, and aimed to "demonstrate the futility of all legislation while the present industrial system exists." The new spirit of radicalism found a London-wide expression in a new organization of the unemployed, the London Central Workers' Committee (CWC), established at the end of September 1905. Although supported by trade unions, the ILP, the LRC, and the Fabian Society, the CWC executive was dominated from its inception by the SDF. Harry Quelch was chairman, and among other members were Jack Williams and Fred Knee. The CWC aimed to organize the London unemployed to compel local authorities not only to fully implement the Unemployed Workmen Act, but also to concede the the right to work. To give itself organizational substance the CWC took to forming local committees along the same lines, composed of representatives of labour and socialist organizations. These had full autonomy, the role of the CWC being limited to initiating and coordinating agitation. Within three weeks of the CWC's formation unemployed committees had sprung into existence at Hackney, Islington, Shoreditch, Southwark, Westminster, Lewisham, Brentford, Dartford, and Tottenham.[26]

Similar coalitions were formed in Glasgow and Manchester, where an "Entente Cordiale" was said to prevail between the ILP and the SDF in organizing the unemployed, and in general, good relations prevailed between the ILP and the SDF. The ILP, in early November 1905, had established the National Right to Work Council upon whose executive the SDF had representation, and of which the SDF approved in spite of the council's general inactivity. Prominent ILP members, such as Keir Hardie, spoke at CWC demonstrations, and when the ever penurious CWC appealed for funds to employ Jack Williams as an unemployed organizer, both Keir Hardie and Frank Smith donated money.[27]

In the final months of 1905 the unemployed began to challenge and confront, rather than accept and reproduce, individualist distinctions between the deserving and undeserving poor. In Shoreditch a clergyman of a well-to-do church described the unemployed in a sermon as "a lazy, thriftless lot who spend their money in the public house". He repeated his accusation the following week at an open-air service. Girling, one of a number of unemployed present, got upon the platform with the clergyman and proceeded to berate him for his views and for his statement that "he as a Christian would not feed the children of the lazy". Girling criticised the clergyman for having voted on the Distress Committee against the feeding of the children of the unemployed, and concluded: "If that was Christianity then he would work for Socialism, which would solve the unemployed question and enable the workers to live as they should, free, happy and healthy lives." For the first time since the 1880s the notion of working class respectability was under attack. John Tamlyn, in an article in *Justice* of 30 December 1905 entitled "An Open Letter to That Strange Creature the Respectable Working Man" admonished those unemployed who starved in silence, rather than participate in "unrespectable" unemployed demonstrations.[28]

Of all the areas in London the unemployed agitation was at its most powerful in Poplar which, it was reported, "leads the van with its meeting of unemployed twice a week on municipal premises, its Dock Gate meetings, its marchings and rumours of marching." This was in no small way attributable to the presence of socialists such as George Lansbury, Will Crooks, and A. A. Watts on the Poplar board of guardians, and the short history of such socialist representatives working in concert with the unemployed to secure better conditions. But equally important were women, who were more active in the politics of the unemployed in Poplar than anywhere else in London.[29]

The right to work movement was in some ways a recognition of new trends in society, and nowhere is this more apparent than in the sudden prominence of women in the politics of the unemployed during late 1905. The wave of feminism that rose in Edwardian Britain was particularly influential within the ILP, who nurtured the organization of the suffragettes, the Women's Social and Political Union (WSPU), in its early stages. A spirited debate took place within the ILP during late 1904 about the right of women to work. There was considerable support in both the ILP and the SDF for the restriction of work by married women as a partial solution to unemployment, the SDF holding to the prevailing belief that "racial deterioration" was in part due to bad mothering caused by women working. A number of women within the ILP were critical of this attitude, and in November 1904 Margaret MacDonald called upon ILP members to consider "women as well as men in any agitations and schemes for the unemployed."[30]

In a particularly eloquent letter Theresa Billington put forward the case for women's right to work in tandem with a damning assessment of the attitude of the socialist movement toward women. "How long are we to rub shoulders with men who are only Socialists in respect of 'male' interests?" asked Billington:

> I feel that there are members of our party who are as prejudiced against the woman's demand for justice and freedom as the capitalists are against the demands of labour. . . The labour market is not a monopoly of man by right. In the past it has been forcibly turned into a closed corporation, but it is no more justifiable than the land monopoly. Give to the woman equality of opportunity therein, pay her an equal wage for the same work done, throw open to her every branch of industry, and accord her the political training her brother obtains, and let her freely find her level. The artificial restrictions imposed upon her . . . seem to be based upon the assumption that only by closing every other avenue to her but house drudgery and sex dependence can you force women into marriage and motherhood. . . . A divided humanity cannot reach Socialism.[31]

This remarkable letter (which reads more like a manifesto) conveys an impression of how much more radical the idea of the right to work was for women than it was for men, and of how much more radical the right to work movement could be if it included, rather than excluded, women. The subsequent historical emphasis upon women's fight for the right to vote, though to some extent modified in more recent times, has obscured the importance of the right to work movement as a radical women's movement, especially in its formative stages. Much of the strength and vitality of the right to work movement was to derive from women's involvement. What has also been obscured is just what the feminist movement lost after the WSPU sought to direct its energies away from such issues as the right to work, and toward chasing the vote.

The history of the WSPU and the politics of the unemployed were for some years entwined. It was as a result of an unemployed agitation taking place in Manchester that Emmeline Pankhurst was elected as the ILP candidate for the Chorlton board of guardians in December 1894, and thus began her political life. The high unemployment being experienced among women cotton operatives in 1903 led her to form the WSPU in the October of that year, as an organization to fight for working class women. Emmeline Pankhurst was to campaign actively for the unemployed up until March 1906, and the WSPU was involved during late 1904 with the Manchester unemployed, and later had representatives on the Manchester and Salford Unemployed Committee formed in September 1905 by the SDF and the ILP. The WSPU was directly influenced by the politics of the unemployed. The riot of the Manchester unemployed on 31 July 1905, which had led to the passing of the Unemployed Workmen Act, was the inspiration for the WSPU's historically significant switch to militant tactics.[32]

In early 1906 the WSPU moved its headquarters to London with the intention of using "the East London women of the unemployed movement" as the basis of its support. The WSPU had been active in London since mid-1905, and it seems probable that they, in conjunction with the SDF, were responsible for a meeting of unemployed women and the wives of unemployed men at Caxton Hall on 17 July 1905, after which a deputation of unemployed women and Jack Williams interviewed the prime minister Arthur Balfour and the leader of the Liberal opposition at the House of Commons. The first London branch of the WSPU was formed by the "Unemployed Women of West Ham" who reconstituted themselves as the Canning Town WSPU; and at the WSPU's first London mass meeting at Caxton Hall the East End women sang the "Red Flag". This alliance between unemployed women and the WSPU seems to have ended in mid-1906, when Emmeline Pankhurst's daughter Christabel set about disengaging the WSPU from working class politics, in order, wrote her sister Sylvia, to "attract especially the support of wealthy Conservatives".[33]

The most striking demonstration of the new prominence of women in the politics of the unemployed came on 6 November 1905 when between 3,000 and 6,000 working class women, unemployed or the wives of unemployed men, marched through the West End demanding work. Probably the most effective unemployed demonstration staged before 1919, it saw processions of shabbily dressed women of all ages from throughout London gathering at the Embankment and from there marching to Whitehall, many carrying babies in their arms and leading young children by the hand. Hundreds of eager women were held back by organizers for want of shoes in which to march. The ones with shoes marched behind banners inscribed with their urgent demands: "We demand the right to labour in order that we and ours might live"; "Women of London DEMAND the right to live"; and "Bread for our children". A deputation of seventeen women and thirteen men from the march went to an arranged interview with the prime minister Arthur Balfour and his brother Gerald, the head of the Local Government Board. Most of the men were CWC representatives, and included Jack Williams and George Lansbury. Nearly all the women, however, were unemployed or the wives of unemployed men, described as "women literally damned by poverty, made prematurely aged, pinched and haggard." They were dressed in "work-a-day" clothes and several carried babies in their arms. To try to ward off their smell Arthur Balfour protected himself with a scent spray.[34]

The women told of their destitution in "brief sentences, some of them unfinished and broken with sobs". One woman was a mother of six children who had been starving on parish relief for seventeen months; another, whose husband had only thirteen weeks' work in the previous twelve months, was taken from the prime minister's presence "in a fainting state and vomiting blood." Some pointed out that unemployment affected women even worse than men. Mrs. Wood of Poplar, whose husband and son were both unemployed, read out a memorial from the women of south and east London, both the "many thousands" of wives of unemployed men, and the "many thousands of unemployed women . . . who through sheer desperation were driven to shame on the streets of this great city." Thus did Mrs Wood raise the intimate and important connection between unemployment and prostitution, showing them to be cause and effect. Prostitution had never previously been mentioned by unemployed activists, who while always ready to stress the effect of unemployment upon men chose not to mention its effects upon women. Arthur Balfour replied expressing his sympathy for the unemployed, and his belief that charity would respond and make the Unemployed Workmen Act a success. George Lansbury later repeated Balfour's reply when the deputation reported back to a packed audience of 3,000 women in Westminster Chapel. "Were they going to take this quietly?" he asked. The women shouted back "No! No! Follow the Russians—give them St. Petersburg."[35]

The march of the London women was a bold example of what women could contribute to the political practice of the unemployed. For a short time it inspired the socialists who saw it as "a turning point in the unemployed agitation which is portentous of much", and it was propounded as a model for future action. A brief examination of the poetry of unemployment in the 1900s gives us some insight into why the involvement of women acted as such a radical stimulus. Common to nearly all the many poems written by socialists about unemployment in this period is the notion that unemployment is a *man's* problem, and one that meant much more than the loss of a job. It meant the breaking of the financial nexus which was the source of the man's power within the home. The destruction of the domestic structures of power are often symbolized in the suffering and even death of the family. We find in one poem that "pinched home faces that smiled before" now appear as accusations; while in another poem "Mother and child are starving unfed / And dead is the newly born." In another the reader enters the homes of the unemployed "Where bairns and mothers die of hunger."[36]

The values and traits of masculinity were acquired by men largely through the processes of production. Employment was masculinity and unemployment a negation of it. For this reason we have the endless dark hints of the sexual impotency of unemployed men. Keir Hardie wrote of how "manhood is destroyed by unemployment." This gender-based view of what to be unemployed meant to a man remained strong at least until World War II. In 1934 an unemployed miner, Walter Brierly, wrote one of the finest of the autodidact novels of his era, *Means Test Man.* The unemployed hero, Jack Cook, imagines that to his fellow miners "he would have become a woman, working in the home providing for it with money which came from a pool into which all the bread winners in the land threw a determined, compulsory amount". Being unable to work, Jack Cook believes that "his creative point had been removed, that point which was always ahead of him as a being, drawing him through existence, that point on which all his drive converged to reach out and clear a pleasant place in existence for him and his. Wives and children, as wives and children, were mere camp followers, all dependent on the man's creative point." Unemployment leaves Jack Cook impotent in every sense: he can no longer satisfy his wife physically or his family materially. Unemployment has altered the power structure in his family, because now that he lacks his "creative point", his wife and child—as prostitutes, "mere camp followers"—no longer depend upon him. To be unemployed was not then an experience that was simply knowable; rather, as with Jack Cook, it was an experience perceived through the filter of the values and ideas of an oppressive society. An unemployed person's perception of himself was shaped by what we could clumsily refer to as the ideological construct of unemployment, and this had important consequences for the nature of the politics of the unemployed.[37]

NUWM leader Wal Hannington believed that "militant action" by the unemployed was a "necessity" to save their "spirit of manhood". In this context a call for political action by the unemployed revolved not around the radical social aim of work for all, but rather the conservative individual aim of regaining masculinity and restoring the unequal domestic power structures. Because the best that can be got from political activity is only the retrieval of some manhood, we find that many of the poems about unemployment are marked by a grim resignation to the horrors of joblessness. In "The March of the Unemployed", participation in a West End march, referred to as "this beggars plan", is undertaken not for any political reason, but because it offers a lessening of the erosion of masculinity, for "it shames our manhood, this beggars plan, / Yet to do nothing would shame us more." But the London women had marched for different reasons, and their actions gave the politics of the unemployed a militancy it had lacked since the 1890s, and a radical edge it had never before possessed.[38]

The women who marched through the West End and who carried their babies into the presence of the prime minister did it not to assert their masculinity or to reestablish old domestic inequalities. Their demand was work for themselves and their men. This was no "beggars plan", but the demand of politically active and assertive people. As long as the politics of the unemployed remained a male domain, it was as much concerned with the preservation of patriarchy within the working-class home as it was with gaining "work or maintenance". The significance of the women's march was that it challenged this reactionary underside and threatened to wrench the politics of the unemployed away from its exclusively male concerns. But such threats remained threats, and the directions indicated by the womens march remained unexplored. Far from signaling the beginning of a major new phase in the politics of the unemployed, the march was an endpoint. Women remained involved, sometimes playing an important and occasionally prominent role. But the possibilities that appeared on 6 November 1905 were to have as lasting an existence as the transitory odor of poverty that had for a moment troubled the nostrils of the prime minister.

In spite of its financial difficulties, the broad support that the CWC enjoyed meant that it continued to be very active, holding meetings and demonstrations and organizing deputations. Large West End marches continued through December 1905, and a CWC deputation met with the new Liberal prime minister, Campbell Bannerman. The Unemployed Workmen Act, by creating numerous local distress committees, unwittingly gave a new focus for the political activity of the unemployed in most urban localities. Groups of unemployed now fought not just for immediate relief, but in political battles such as in Battersea, where the distress committee was forced to adopt the SDF's unemployment program, and in Shoreditch, where unemployed pressure led to two SDF members being placed on the local distress committee. Within London this strengthened the trend, apparent since the 1890s, away from central to local agitation. Paradoxically the strength of this locally based agitation was nowhere more in evidence than in the central London demonstrations. A fortnight after the women's march came the largest unemployed demonstration then ever seen in Britain. Called by the CWC less than a week before it was held, a procession of 15,000-25,000 unemployed men and women marched behind Jack Williams through the West End to Hyde Park, where their numbers swelled to 100,000. The demonstration was against the funding of the Unemployed Workmen Act by charity, and the profusion of charities in recent weeks in the face of the activity of the unemployed. Everywhere the banners carried the same message: "Curse their Charity!", and the message was given a political meaning by a resolution carried by the meeting declaring "unending war on the capitalist system and its upholders which condemns homes and willing workers to starvation".[39]

It was at this moment, when the politics of the unemployed had entered a phase of the broadest support and the most extensive activity that it had ever known, that the agitation fell apart. Not only did unemployment fall, from 6.3 percent in January 1905 to 4.5 percent in December 1905, the lowest level for that month since 1901 (see Table 3.1), but so too did the Balfour government. Campbell Bannerman formed a Liberal government in late 1905 that faced an election in early 1906. The Liberals were returned with a greatly increased majority, and with thirty LRC candidates hanging on to their tails, who after the election reconstituted the LRC as the Labour Party. During the election the SDF fell prey to its recurrent fantasies of electoral success, and diverted its activists away from the unemployed campaign into the election campaign. The CWC was thrown into disarray when Jack Williams was sent away from London to campaign in Raunds as an SDF candidate. Even more woundingly the election diverted attention yet again from street politics to parliamentary politics. The Liberal government had no real policy on unemployment, yet the aridity of its ideas was not immediately apparent, in part because of the euphoria and high expectations which accompanied the Liberals' return to office, in part because of the return of a number of new left wing Liberals, and in part because of the cunning appointment of John Burns, once champion of the unemployed, as president of the Local Government Board. Many activists believed that the Liberals would take some definite action for the unemployed and ought to be given a chance before returning to demonstrating. Such hopes were boosted, and support for the CWC further undermined, when it was announced in the King's Speech that the Unemployed Workmen Act would be amended.[40]

By late March 1906 the CWC was in crisis. Unable to mobilize the large numbers of but a few short months before, its demonstrations dwindled into poor copies of the massive protests of late 1905. An emergency conference of representatives from the SDF, the ILP, trade unions, and unemployed committees resolved to continue the existence of the CWC, but it was never again to experience the heady support of its first months of life. Unemployment fell to 3.1 percent in May 1906 (see Table 3.1), and the politics of the unemployed, which in late 1905 had briefly threatened to become a cohesive radical force of considerable importance, was reduced to a succession of fragmented, largely symbolic events.[41]

In February 1906 seventy unemployed men marched from Liverpool to London behind a red flag and a banner reading "We demand the Right to Work", to little effect. There were minor unemployed agitations at various times in Northampton,

Bournmouth, Fulham, and Poplar. There was the ultimately futile phenomenon of land grabbing. The idea of "returning" to the land as a solution to contemporary problems has a history as old as that of capitalism. As a specific solution to the problem of unemployment, returning to the land was being advocated from at least the 1820s, was given campaigning shape in the Chartist Land Plan of the 1840s, and subsequently reappeared in various guises, and with varying political aims, as the Land and Labour League's call for land nationalization in 1870, Chamberlain's slogan of three acres and a cow, farm colonies, and the cry of the 1890s, "Back to the Land". There were some attempts by socialists to establish farm colonies for the unemployed that, at best, met with limited success, and at worst, confirmed fears that they were little better than outdoor workhouses.[42]

While only one small unemployed campaign, a spate of land seizure by unemployed ex-service men on the northeast coast of Scotland and the island of Lewis in 1920, was ever mobilized around the nebulous virtues of returning to the land, the land continued to carry strong associations among working-class people of freedom, independence, and security known in a past golden age, which starkly contrasted with the chronic poverty and insecurity of contemporary unemployment. The special spade carried by the Manchester hunger marchers of 1907 symbolized not only their hope that they would once again labor, but the desire for a different world in which all were able to work, and where the wealth produced by a man remained his own. For many working-class people, the Industrial Revolution was still sufficiently close for them to correctly identify capitalist industry as the cause of unemployment, but to then falsely see an abandonment of industry and a return to agriculture as its solution. There was, wrote Keir Hardie about the unemployed in 1904, "a genuine and widespread desire among individuals in all sections of industrial life to escape from the overcrowded haunts of industry and to seek a more rational method of living in the peaceful tilling of the soil". Hardie believed that "one harmonious combined attempt to re-people the deserted idle land of England with an industrious peasant class, would in the course of a lifetime of one generation revolutionise the industrial situation." There did remain some limited support among the unemployed for the idea of returning to the land into the 1920s, nationalization of land being one aim of unemployed ex-servicemen after World War I, and a motion at the NUWCM's 1923 national conference calling for "Back to the Land" to be adopted as the unemployed's policy mustering twenty-seven votes in support out of ninety-seven votes overall.[43]

But for all the symbolic importance of the idea, few socialists by the 1900s would have concurred with what W. K. Hall had written in *The Clarion* of 22 October 1892, that the "land question" lay at the "root of the labour question". When in the summer of 1906 groups of unemployed began seizing land they did so not not then with the intention of re-peopling it, but in the hope of winning propaganda points. The purpose, said A. F. Dunkley, secretary of the Manchester and Salford Unemployed Committee, which organized the first land grab in July 1906, was to prove the willingness of the unemployed to work. Inspired by the Manchester example, the unemployed seized land at Leeds, West Ham, Finsbury, and most successfully of all at Bradford, where the unemployed, led by ILP councillor Albert Glyde, built a cookhouse, constructed rockeries, and erected a stone wall around their land. The National Right to Work Council called upon distress committees to provide the land grabbers with temporary use of the land rent free, and the SDF called for the establishment of "home colonies" on the commons at state expense. But neither the ILP nor the SDF was willing to organize the unemployed, particularly at a time of low unemployment, around the tactic of land grabbing, and the movement did not even see the summer out, the victim of evictions, low unemployment, and socialist indifference. In this way the attempt to move the politics of the unemployed from the street to the paddock came to an inglorious close.[44]

Parliamentarianism or "Political Hooliganism": The Dilemma of Labour, 1908

Amidst a general revival of unemployed activity in late 1907, some socialists formed the Unemployed Citizens' Association in Birmingham. Its efforts met with sufficient success for the authorities to take to using a heavy hand to end its activity. In early 1908 its leaders were arrested and its meetings and processions forcibly broken up by police. When sixty hunger marchers from Manchester on their way to petition the king arrived in Birmingham, they decided to stay for three days to help fight the police bans, leading to a number of violent clashes with the police. Fred Hughes, a Birmingham unemployed leader, found support in these violent events for the new theories of direct action then beginning to spread through Britain; they served, he wrote, "as a reminder that while we aim steadily at a political majority to control the forces of the crown, we shall do well to hold jealously every effective weapon of direct action." It was to be upon the horns of this dilemma, the coupling of parliamentary politics to direct action, that the politics of the unemployed would be tossed, gored, and finally at the end of 1908, impaled as a limp carcass.[45]

Between 1905 and 1907 the struggles of the unemployed revolved around the Unemployed Workmen Act, at first to have it passed, and later to have it amended in the hope of rendering it an effective measure. After 1907 the focus changed and the politics of the unemployed were to revolve largely around the Labour Party's Right to Work bill. In spite of promises, the Liberal government's only gesture to the unemployed was, in July 1906, to throw them the sop of £200,000 with which to fund the administration (though pointedly not the relief costs) of the Unemployed Workmen Act. Frustrated, the Labour Party, the TUC, and the GFTU drafted the Right to Work bill in the early months of 1907. The bill proposed the formation of unemployment authorities that would be required to provide work for all registered unemployed on public works.[46]

But the bill was not so much an attempt to help the unemployed as a method of wooing the support of the skilled trade unionist by playing upon the latter's fears of the unemployed. "Trade unionists!" asked a Labour Party pamphlet of the time,

What have you to say to this bill?
You know the unemployed man always threatens your wages.
He increases the power of the non-unionist.
He is constantly liable to become a blackleg.
He drains your funds.

Nor was the bill as radical as either its proponents or its critics claimed. The controversial Clause 7(3) provided local authorities with the power "to enforce control" over any unemployed person they deemed to have a "deliberate and habitual disinclination to work" for up to six months, which were to be spent working "under the supervision" of the local authority. This gave very substantial powers of discipline and punishment to the local authorities, which even the poor law in its most draconian aspects denied them. The loafer, wrote Ramsay MacDonald, "must not be allowed to damage the claims of the deserving temporarily unemployed. . . . He must be treated separately. He too must be educated. A sentence of six months will do him good." In this respect the bill served the important public function of highlighting the essentially conformist and respectable nature of the Labour Party: MacDonald told the House of Commons how he "hoped it would not again be said that the Labour Party had any sympathy with the loafer and shirker who tried to batten and fatten on public funds." "Under the Bill", wrote Keir Hardie, "the drunkard, the loafer, and the lazy will have short shrift."[47]

When Will Thorne attacked the penal clause at a special Labour Party conference on the unemployed in January 1908, MacDonald replied that it strengthened the Labour Party's hand in getting the measure through the House of Commons. Thorne argued, with little support, that unemployment could only be solved through the nationalization of the means of production, exchange, and distribution. But the conference, by an overwhelming vote of 210 to 13, voted for a resolution that declared that unemployment could be solved by legislation and administration along the lines of the Right to Work bill. Unemployment, said J. Bruce Glasier, could be eliminated under capitalism. Far from being a challenge to the prevailing social order, the bill was an accommodation and endorsement of it.[48]

The renewed emphasis upon the distinction between deserving and undeserving sounded a retreat from 1905 when women and lumpenproletariat had been briefly wooed. Once again the unemployed were viewed in a patriarchal light, and the Labour Party very much pushed their Right to Work bill as an attempt to gain the right to work for men only. It should be added that only the deserving unemployed were truly men; the undeserving unemployables were neutered by their very condition, a point coldly put in an ILP pamphlet by H. Russell Smart: "the unemployables", he wrote, are "creatures who were once men." This patriarchal bias is not simply attributable to the patriarchal vision of many socialists, but also to the direction feminism took after 1906, focusing its energies on the right to vote rather than the right to work. While the mainly working class radical suffragists continued to be concerned with issues other than the vote, including the right to work, their support remained largely confined to Lancashire. London remained the heart of the politics of the unemployed prior to the war, and, while some prominent

London feminists such as Dora Montefiore and Charlotte Despard continued to work with the unemployed, here feminist politics were dominated by the WSPU, who after mid-1906 had no interest in the unemployed.[49]

How was it that this bill, which contained the means of promoting and intensifying existing divisions within the working class, setting respectable apart from unrespectable, man from woman, became a nationally popular cause? As luck would have it, the campaign for the Right to Work bill unfolded against a background of deepening economic depression and growing discontent among the unemployed. Between April and December 1907 the number of trade unionists registered as out of work doubled to 5.6 percent (see Table 3.1). In these fortuitous circumstances the right to work campaign began to muster support. Unemployed agitation began to pick up not only in London but in Sheffield, Brighton, Reading, and, as we have seen, in Birmingham. The sedulous Jack Williams, assisted by Dick Greenwood, had run a ragged and ineffective unemployed campaign in early 1907 at the behest of the SDF (the CWC seems to have been now defunct) but largely out of his own pocket. His efforts met with more success at the end of 1907 when he and Greenwood resumed unemployed meetings at Tower Hill. This revival of activity was from the start marked by violent clashes between the police and the unemployed. The Right to Work bill had been introduced in the House of Commons in July 1907, and was read for a second time on 13 March 1908. The Labour Party had run a series of successful demonstrations up until this time in favor of their bill, and this combined with the violence of the unemployed agitation, began to concern the Liberal government. Yet it remained intransigent about unemployment, and this became a source of frustration both to the Labour Party and to many of the government's supporters. On its second reading the bill, although predictably defeated 267 votes to 118, did muster considerable support from left-wing Liberals and the Irish nationalists.[50]

But the emphasis on a parliamentary strategy implicit in the bill had for the time being failed. The Social Democratic Party (SDP), as the SDF now styled itself, who had initially supported the bill, now grew critical of it. The right to work campaign ground to a halt and discontent began to manifest itself in extra-parliamentary forms. Rather than express support for the bill, a large demonstration in Glasgow on 27 June 1908 chose to return to protesting about the working of the Unemployed Workmen Act. Similarly, a small unemployed campaign mounted during the summer by Jack Williams and a companion known only as "Docker" Waites, concentrated not on the bill but upon general agitation. The Labour Party was in no condition to restart the campaign. Within Parliament it had little fight left in it; outside its organization was in decline; and among the party's rank and file there was widespread disaffection. Keir Hardie, who had spent from July 1907 to April 1908 traveling for his health, returned to a dispirited party. The issue he chose to revitalize it with was again that of the unemployed. In early August 1908 the National Right to Work Council was reconvened to organize effective extra-parliamentary action.[51]

The council envisaged a campaign that would "stir the nation from centre to circumference". "The chief difficulty at the outset is with the unemployed themselves", said the council in a circular. "No effort must be spared to get the unemployed to shake off their apathy, and put themselves in evidence". Nobody seemed very hopeful that this would occur, and as in 1905 the campaign failed to garner the mass support of the trade unions, leaving the council no choice but to rely for its success upon the active support of socialists in mobilizing the unemployed. In essence, if not in desire, the council's strategy was to be built upon the shifting sands of continued good relations both between the SDP and the Labour Party, and between the ILP and its rank and file. This had to be achieved without alienating the SDP, and without radicalizing ILP members to the extent that they might begin to question the relevance of the Labour Party. As such, it was a strategy fraught with destructive tensions.[52]

The beginning of what was to be a short lived winter of discontent came in Glasgow in September 1908. The city had been harshly hit by the depression: unemployment by mid-1908 had risen to 25 percent in engineering and to 28.5 percent in shipbuilding, levels unknown on the Clyde for decades. The SDP and ILP began to hold weekly unemployed meetings in George Square; and on 2 September 1908 1,000 unemployed, demanding that they be heard, broke into the Glasgow council chambers while the council was sitting. Three days later the unemployed interrupted Prince Arthur as he inspected the Glasgow Boy's Brigade; afterward they gathered outside the town hall to sing the Red Flag and shout invective at the hapless prince stuck inside at a civic lunch. The next day the police twice baton-charged a surging unemployed church parade to prevent them entering the cathedral. At midnight of 9 September 1908 a large force of police was called out to prevent a big crowd of unemployed marching on the home of the lord provost. Four days later over 10,000 unemployed attended a Glasgow Green demonstration. In such fashion the demonstrations continued, marked occasionally by such pieces of audacity as Tom Kerr, unemployed leader, ILP member and future lord provost, threatening to reveal publicly freemason rites if nothing was done for the unemployed, thereby causing a sensation; and John MacLean, SDP member and later one of the more famous revolutionaries of post-war Europe, one afternoon leading a large procession of unemployed into the Glasgow stock exchange and there, to the astonishment and horror of the stockbrokers and investors, marching the unemployed right around the floor and then back out into the street. The worried authorities placed a ban on any further meetings in George Square, withdrew all leave of absence for a week for troops stationed in Glasgow, and on 9 September had the troops confined to barracks. Never had the unemployed been so politically active, and their agitation was countered with what was described as "a deluge of charity". The state was also suddenly generous. On 11 September 1908 the Local Government Board announced that Glasgow was to receive £25,000 instead of the budgeted £8,000, to be spent under the provisions of the Unemployed Workmen Act. The Glasgow corporation did what it had never before done, and started work schemes.[53]

Nationally the Glasgow unemployed agitation put the question of the unemployed back at the top of the socialist agenda. By October 1908 mass unemployment, officially at 9.5 percent (see Table 3.1), existed on a scale unknown since the mid-1880s. During September and October 1908 the unemployed became very active, holding meetings and demonstrations in Birmingham, Leicester, Coventry, and Manchester. In Sheffield 10,000 unemployed gathered silently outside the town council chambers in a manner so intimidating the council voted £10,000 for relief works. Hunger marches traversed Britain with no set goal beyond that of being roaming propaganda. A march led by "Docker" Waites, for example, saw men harnessed in ropes dragging a heavy truck laden with cooking utensils, food, and socialist literature, traveling all over, singing the "Marseillaise" or the "Red Flag" as they went, holding meetings—"Socialism being the theme of each discourse"—taking collections, losing some men who gained work, gaining some men who lost work. The *Labour Leader* of 2 October 1908 told of its office table covered with newspaper cuttings describing "the dramatic and always sorrowful marches and counter marches, mid-day meetings and mid-night gatherings of thousands of sufferers taking place." The unemployed who only a few months previous had seemed such an inert force, were now active on a scale so large that it had grown beyond the organization of the socialists.[54]

A tone of militant desperation appeared. "Get food immediately", Victor Grayson, elected in 1907 as the first ever socialist MP independent of the ILP or Labour Party, advised the unemployed "—get it honestly if they could, but get it". A meeting of 10,000 unemployed at Trafalgar Square in early October 1908 resolved that if the government would not help the unemployed "it will be left to hungry men to ignore the rules of a society that has not regard for them." The banner that headed a London demonstration put the onus for such threats squarely on the government's shoulders: "Work or Revolution: Which? The Government Must Decide!" The SDP was keen to capitalize upon this outburst, and in late September 1908 appointed an Unemployed Committee, with Jack Williams yet again in charge. Hamstrung by lack of money, they forsook a national campaign and concentrated all energies and funds upon London. On the eve of the assembly of Parliament, 11 October 1908, the National Right to Work Council organized a full day's program of unemployed agitation. By 6 P.M. there were thousands assembled around Parliament, and the MPs were told by the police that if they refused to see the deputations there would be a riot. When Parliament resumed the next day MPs had to find their way to the benches past long rows of policemen. Outside in Parliament Square 2,500 mounted and unmounted policemen fought running battles with the unemployed. There was now concern in official circles. Herbert Gladstone, home secretary, was informed by the police commissioner on 11 October 1908 "that the strain on the police caused by demonstrations of women, unemployed, etc, was heavy and was increasing. Yesterday or Thursday (I forget which) he had 'hunger marches' taking place in twenty divisions." This spate of unemployed activity coincided with the nadir of the Liberal government's existence: during 1908 it had lost seven seats with an average swing of more than 10 percent.

Liberal MPs from working class electorates felt threatened, and grew insistent that something be done about unemployment.[55]

On 14 October 1908 the cabinet discussed the unemployed. Tacit recognition of the strength of the unemployed campaign was given by inviting the Labour Party chairman, Arthur Henderson, to give advice. He was less than reassuring, and said that "unless prompt action was taken he would be unable to restrain his extremists". This was a threat both to the immediate alliance between Labour and the Liberals, and to the long-term parliamentary containment of working-class aspirations. The cabinet told Burns that something had to be done,Winston Churchill describing unemployment as "a burning question." Burns claimed that nothing was the matter, that nothing could be done; but his power was waning. A cabinet committee that effectively superseded his powers was appointed to draw up a list of proposals that could be implemented immediately to ease the unemployed problem. In December 1908 Churchill, now president of the Board of Trade, presented the cabinet with proposals for labor exchanges and unemployment insurance. The exchanges were seen not as interfering with the free enterprise system, but as a positive step that would ensure that the free labor market operated more efficiently, and legislation for labor exchanges was introduced in 1909.[56]

The Labour Party was also being badly rocked by the passions being unleashed by the unemployed agitation. The expulsion and violent removal of Frank Smith, ILP secretary of the National Right to Work Council, from a meeting of the London County Council (LCC) on 13 October 1908 following his pleading for work schemes for the unemployed, was symptomatic of the growing militancy of some ILP members. Smith refused to leave, and was dragged out of the meeting, leaving broken chairs and ripped collars in his wake. Above in the gallery unemployed shouted, "we want work, we want bread". Then on 15 and 16 October 1908 came the sensational action of Victor Grayson in the House of Commons. Grayson would rise while the house was discussing a licensing bill, and refuse to sit down until it discussed the unemployed. When told that he was obliged by the rules of the house to sit down and desist, Grayson replied, "I feel that the crisis of unemployment is so great—people are starving on the streets—that we must ignore these rules." On 15 October he was removed from the House, and on 16 October he was suspended, all the Labour members bar two voting for his suspension.[57]

For the Labour Party and the trade unions Grayson was a publicity-seeking poltroon, who refused to accept the tedium that had to be endured in Parliament to effect change. But for many socialists Grayson's action, occurring at a time of Labour Party supineness but great rank and file activity, illustrated the failure of the Labour Party and its chosen parliamentary path. For them Grayson was a hero, and they shared with him the belief that the horror of unemployment invalidated the legitimacy of Parliament, and, by implication, the legitimacy of the Labour Party, whose raison d'être was bound up in unequivocally accepting Parliament. The feeling in favor of him and against the Labour MPs ran high for some weeks. At an ILP mass meeting in Nottingham on 24 October 1908 a packed audience rose to its feet and sang the Red Flag at the end of Grayson's speech. At a public Labour Party meeting in Bradford the following day Grayson received an ovation upon saying that the House of Commons "could not solve the unemployed problem". The *Labour Leader* was flooded with resolutions from ILP branches congratulating Grayson on his stand. His popularity among the unemployed was enormous: a meeting of 5,000 unemployed carried him aloft in triumph from St Pancras Arches to Highbury corner; 12,000 unemployed gathered at Tower Hill to hear him speak alongside Jack Williams and Dora Montefiore.[58]

As Keir Hardie recognized, the socialists' support of Grayson and their criticisms of the Labour Party focused upon the party's actions over the unemployed. Its failure to prize concessions from the government with the crowbar of the Right to Work bill clinched the case, as far as the party's critics were concerned, against the parliamentarianism of the party. "There is a feeling fairly widely spread amongst our friends", wrote MacDonald, "that in view of the prevailing distress and the pressing needs of human beings out of employment, the House of Commons in discussing the Licensing Bill is merely wasting time, and that, in consequence the Labour members should obstruct its business or adopt other methods to bring Parliament to its senses. I do not take that view." Nor did the rest of the Labour Party, and for this reason it responded both by issuing defenses of parliamentarianism, and by arguing that the "political hooliganism" of the Grayson supporters would leave the cause of the unemployed "seriously discredited". What had been a tactical alliance, street protest plus parliamentary action, broke down when it became an strategic argument with ideological overtones: parliamentarianism versus the extra-parliamentary politics of the unemployed.[59]

So it was that Grayson's outburst became the issue over which a major crisis crystallized within the Labour Party. If the ILP socialists were to abandon parliamentarianism it would render the continued existence of the Labour Party meaningless. It would also create a vacuum of ideology and practice within the progressive elements of the working class that the new radical political philosophies such as anarcho-syndicalism might fill, a point upon which Hardie was worried. "Without meaning it in the least," he wrote, "they are heading straight to anarchy. In France and Italy the Trade Union movement is largely an anarchist movement, driven out from Socialism by tactics which the Socialist parties have pursued." It might then mean the end of the alliance between the socialists and the trade unions, so essential for any chance the Labour Party had of future success. J. Bruce Glasier asked what seems to have been the question of the moment: "But may not the unemployed themselves force matters? May they not take the law into their own hands and, heedless of Parliament or of the people, proceed to help themselves?" Glasier believed the answer was "No.... We cannot play at revolutionary politics". The reason why was as plaintive as it was obvious. Are we now, he asked, "when, as the result of years of advocacy, we have persuaded the Trade Unionists to join with us . . . to begin to speak of breaking faith with them."[60]

The short-term strategy for destroying this threat to the alliance was ironically, but perhaps inevitably, closer involvement with, and supervision of, the politics of the unemployed. Presumably it was hoped that in this way the politics of the unemployed would benefit the Labour Party as they had done in 1905, rather than threaten to destroy it. On 19 October 1908, three days after Grayson's suspension, the London Right to Work Council was formed at a meeting of delegates from the ILP, local Right to Work committees, the London Trades Council, the Clarion Scouts, and the SDP, as well as Keir Hardie and a small group of militant Labour MPs. The council was effectively a joint ILP-SDP committee.[61]

Meanwhile, after fierce debate in the cabinet, Burns announced a number of minor concessions for the unemployed, but made it clear that relief works would continue to be funded by charity and not out of the rates. This announcement only deepened the Labour Party's dilemma. While the trade unions were reported to be satisfied with the concessions, the socialists were deeply dissatisfied, and there was now open talk of the party splitting. On the streets Burns' announcement fueled the unemployed campaign. In Bradford the mayor arranged for armed troops to be present when Sydney Buxton, Liberal cabinet minister, spoke there on 23 October 1908, in fear of the meeting being disturbed by either the unemployed or the suffragists. Throughout London, local unemployment committees were formed, tending to be, as often before, a local alliance of SDP, ILP, and trade union activists. Although they had longer term political aims, their agitation was centered upon the demand for work or immediate relief, in Southwark, for example, £14,000 of work being put in hand by the borough council in response to unemployed pressure.[62]

There was now a bitter division between SDP and ILP activists on the one side, and Labour MPs on the other. Even militant Labour MPs found themselves defending conservative positions they did not approve of. "I grow weary", confessed Hardie in a letter to Bruce Glasier in late 1908, "of apologising for a state of things for which I am not responsible and with which I have scant sympathy". There was much vitriolic journalism, accusation, and counter-accusations as the cracks began to appear in public. Early in November, Peter Curran, an MP who had been active in the cause of the unemployed, was heckled at a Liverpool meeting by members of the ILP and the SDP, as well as Direct Actionists. Major ILP branches such as Woolwich and Stoke Newington seceded from the Labour Party, and others contemplated similar action. At Bradford on 15 November 1908 a pro-Labour Party speaker was prevented from addressing a public meeting by heckling from Grayson supporters. Labour's bad losses in the municipal elections of November 1908 were attributed by some MPs to the growing disunity.[63]

The turning point came on 17 November 1908 when Keir Hardie received a letter from the London Clarion Van Committee asking him *not* to speak at a large public meeting they were holding the following night. It had been intended to have Hardie, Hyndman, and Grayson appear together and speak from the same platform. But Grayson and Hyndman refused to appear on the same stand as Keir Hardie; Hyndman later wrote that "there was a distinct cleavage between myself and Keir Hardie as to his recent action and his timid behaviour in the House of Commons with reference to the unemployed". Robert Blatchford agreed with Grayson's and Hyndman's stand, and it was then decided to ask Keir Hardie not to come to the meeting. This was a foolish and highly insulting action, which, as the *Labour Leader* accurately predicted would "be felt as a personal insult by every man and woman in the ILP ranks". It aroused great indignation within the ILP and served to galvanize the membership behind Hardie and behind parliamentarianism. The stream of pro-Grayson resolutions from ILP branches dried up, and was replaced by a torrent of pro-Hardie and pro-Labour Party resolutions. The threat of the ILP abandoning its leadership, and splitting off to form a new party in alliance with the SDP and the Clarion Scouts, though it was to sputter on until the formation of the British Socialist Party (BSP) in 1911, had effectively been extinguished. Precipitated by Grayson's action, the ILP activists had been forced into a corner where they had to choose between seriously questioning parliamentarianism or abandoning the unemployed movement. They chose the latter course, and ILP support for the unemployed campaign came to an end in late November 1908. By 20 November 1908 the London Right to Work Council was appealing for funds, its work at a standstill for want of money.[64]

It seems only due to the selfless efforts of Jack Williams and Dick Greenwood that men did continue to march through the streets of London after November 1908. Regular marches were made through the West End, but the numbers declined from 2,000 early in December to 800 on 23 December 1908. To boost flagging participation Jack Williams hit upon the new tactic of holding unemployed meetings in fashionable West End residential squares, much to the horror of their upper-class inhabitants, but little to the interest of the unemployed. The numbers taking part in protests continued to decline. To revive activity the payment system of 1903 was reintroduced, though to little effect. Jack Williams fell ill in January 1909 and was declared bankrupt in February, the result of a failed court action against the *Daily Express*, which had accused Williams of being a drunk and a "chronic loafer". Dick Greenwood was left to continue organizing the unemployed with what little money could be gleaned from the increasingly desperate appeals for funds made by Fred Knee in *Justice*. By 12 January 1909 Greenwood was unable to gather enough unemployed at Tower Hill to stage a West End march. Eight days later he did succeed in mustering 200 unemployed, most of them from Lambeth, and getting them to Berkeley Square, around which they marched singing revolutionary songs. They were set upon by a large force of police, who bundled Greenwood up a side street and there beat him up. Although there was some further minor activity inside and outside of London, the debacle at Berkeley Square marked the end of the 1908 agitation and brought to a close the dreams of those who envisaged a mass socialist party.[65]

A final doomed attempt was made in February 1909 by the London Right to Work Council to revive the unemployed agitation with a series of great demonstrations culminating in a West End march on the day Parliament opened. The February campaign was remarkable only for the revival of the participation of working-class women. Women had been active in the 1908 agitation, but nowhere on the scale of 1905. What little agitation there was among women centered on demands for provision of more work and creches at the three women's workrooms established under the Unemployed Workmen Act. It says much about the 1908 agitation that rather than pick up and popularize these demands, it ignored them. The last unemployed march for the next ten years took place on 16 February 1909, the day of the opening of Parliament. Over 3,000 unemployed women accompanied by thousands of children marched through the West End.[66]

In the rear of the procession some children sang "We'll hang Johnny Burns on a Sour Apple Tree", but apart from this small jollity the march was a depressing sight. "Though here and there in the procession there were to be seen bright eyed Socialist women, happy in the glorious gospel of economic freedom, yet generally it was a drab mass of misery", commented *Justice*. And here we have an insight into the profound ambiguity felt by the socialists toward the unemployed since the 1880s: the unemployed never fitted the mold of the noble, strong, proud proletarian bursting out of a Walter Crane May Day illustration. The unemployed remained dirty, broken, dissolute, and unrespectable. The unemployed demonstrations seem sometimes even to have shocked the socialists as to the true extent of the degradation of sections of the working class. "Twas a woeful sight to see almost an incredible thing", reported the *Labour Leader*, ". . . . Many of the women seemed to be hardly fit to walk." Within the House of Commons George Barnes condemned the march of the women, and officially dissociated the Labour Party from it.[67]

The truth was that despite the considerable if vacillating involvement of the Labour Party with the unemployed, the great mass of the poor, while susceptible to mobilization, remained largely indifferent to organization. This was an important distinction: the ability to raise a mob, was not, as Ramsay MacDonald had realized back in 1886, the same thing as advancing the hopes of a reformist, parliamentary party, however useful it could prove in buttressing that project. Organization and discipline were central to the advance of the Labour Party: they were the antithesis of the spirit and form of the politics of the unemployed. Poverty ruthlessly defined the poor as impotent, but within their own immediate localities, with local knowledge of employers likely to give jobs and shops likely to give credit, they could to some small extent affect their destiny. To be shown a world outside and beyond this by the socialists was to be a shown a world they were unable to influence in any sustained and cohesive fashion, to be brought, in James Hinton's words, "up against the larger parameters of their deprivation", to be shown a world of total despair, rather than the one they knew of intermittent hope. Tactically this meant that unemployed agitations were most successful when they were locally based, pressuring local authorities to achieve specific demands. Strategically it meant that there were enormous problems in attempting to forge a significant lasting political force out of the unemployed. A socialist visiting North Kensington in 1906 was appalled by the chronic poverty, and wrote, "But not a revolt had they amongst them . . . . It is absolutely no use talking socialism to people who die at the rate of 40 per 1,000. What they want—and need—is Drink."[68]

The formidable organizational difficulties permitted the labor movement to remain entrenched in its ideological disdain for the mass of the unemployed: ultimately they were only interested in working with the unemployed insofar as they could protect the privileged status of the upper echelons of the working class, and enhance the electoral appeal of the Labour Party. Riots and demonstrations had their uses for conservative Labour leaders as well as radical militants. But in general they were too volatile to be trusted: a politics of riot and agitation was a politics of unknown risks, not the least being the threat to Labour's leadership. And, ultimately, the questions raised by the unemployed were ones to which the Labour Party was unequal. The Labour Party, unlike the unemployed, had no fundamental quarrel with the state: "our central grievance", as Philip Snowden put it in 1912, "is that we ourselves are not the Cabinet." As Stephen Yeo has eloquently argued, the Labour Party's major desire became to subsume itself within the state. The idea of joining with the unemployed so as to make a truly radical, truly working-class politics capable of transcending such limiting notions, remained the dream of a few socialists, and never the intent of the Labour Party.[69]

The same week as the demonstration, William Beveridge's seminal and highly influential *Unemployment. A Problem of Industry* was published, and the Royal Commission on the Poor Law—established to appease pressure by the unemployed—issued its reports. In mid-1909 the government had announced its intention to introduce compulsory insurance against unemployment, but it was not until 1911 that legislation was passed. The 1911 scheme was restricted to certain trades in which worker, employer, and state paid fixed amounts weekly into a national insurance fund. Workers in these trades, when unemployed, could apply for benefit from the fund, payable at the rate of seven shillings a week for a maximum of fifteen weeks, provided that they had paid five weeks contribution for every one week of benefit received. The scheme was not directly influenced by the politics of the unemployed in the way the Unemployed Workmen Act of 1905 had been. After 1910 unemployment subsided to extremely low levels from which it was not to rise until after the war. There were no further unemployed campaigns after February 1909 and in early 1912 a testimonial fund was raised to pension off Jack Williams. But the politics of the unemployed very much formed the background to the decision to introduce national insurance. Churchill argued in August 1909 that the idea of national insurance was to "increase the stability of our institutions". He believed that "With a 'stake in our country' in the form of insurance against evil days the workers will pay no attention to the vague promises of revolutionary socialists."[70]

National insurance was not so much about insuring the worker against joblessness as ensuring the continuing stability of capitalist society. In this regard national insurance was a product of general forces, of which the politics of the unemployed was simply one element, though not one lacking in import or influence. As Roy Hay has shown, an important element of the business community was advocating, alongside more repressive measures to control the working class, measures of social reform to divert the working class from potentially revolutionary solutions to their problems.[71]

Far from being a triumph of collectivism, national insurance was in many ways a powerful restatement of the old individualist creed. It perpetuated the poor law distinctions between deserving and undeserving poor, as it did the poor law principle of less eligibility, by ensuring that unemployment benefit was far lower than a laborer's income. In so far as it represented new ideas, these were not so much humanitarian as political, and not socialist but new liberal. National insurance was a system of what G. D. H. Cole termed "compulsory self help". It was a method of bolstering industrial efficiency, which, at the same time as it made workers shoulder a large part of a burden that was not of their making, sought to regulate the labor force through strengthening the forces of decasualization, and to develop a moral consensus between capital and labor to counter a class critique of society. Politically it was of considerable importance to the Liberals in their efforts to simultaneously, if somewhat disingenuously, counter the class based politics that the Labour Party represented, while presenting themselves as the party of the working class. As such it failed. Like the introduction of labor exchanges, the introduction of unemployment insurance was greeted by the working class with a mixture of suspicion, indifference, and sometimes hostility, and never aroused the support of the working class in the way the Right to Work bill had.[72]

But as an attempt to embed new Liberal ideology into the reality of working-class life, as a mechanism to reintegrate working-class demands that poverty be ended into a world view that saw tinkerings with state welfare as the area in which social justice (that most slippery of concepts) should be sought, national insurance was a successful way for the New Liberals to divert attention away from the fundamental economic causes of, and possible solutions, to poverty. It should not be forgotten that other proposals for combating unemployment, which did not involve the same sense of state responsibility, were fiercely promoted in this era. Joseph Chamberlain attempted to sell his Tariff Reform campaign to the working class on the basis that "tariff reform means work for all". Chamberlain's campaign failed, and the massive popular victory of the Liberals in 1906 was a victory for the free traders, a defeat for those like Chamberlain who argued—albeit from a reactionary viewpoint—that only by restructuring the economy could one attack unemployment. The socialists were right in expecting the state to do more for the unemployed, but were naive in believing that the state would unambiguously act to improve the lot of the unemployed. The fundamental issue of whether state welfare was about extending working-class power was lost in arguments over the minutiae of a bureaucratic system designed to deny any such power.[73]

Fittingly, it was to be the Labour Party's destiny, and its tragedy, to realize the New Liberals' dreams of social engineering in which the poor were simply objects for manipulation, rather than masters of their own destiny. Central to this process was the critical role national insurance played in redefining the problem of being without work. Up until 1911 this had been discussed as a problem of *the unemployed*. Even in its most reactionary forms this was then a political battle about people. After 1911 it is discussed as a problem of *unemployment*, as an economic conundrum. In this way the focus of the debate shifted from an area in which people (the unemployed) were its primary subject, to an entirely different area where an abstract concept (unemployment) was the subject. Unemployment was no longer a problem of individual failure but, as Beveridge made pointedly obvious in the title of his classic work, "A Problem of Industry", and hence a subject for proper concern and action on the part of the state. The unemployed, as Beveridge recognized, were as necessary to the British industrial system "as are capital and labour themselves" and accordingly, through national insurance unemployment became an issue for the administrators and not just the unemployed. From that time on bureaucrats who administered unemployment welfare were seen to have more public credibility than unemployed agitators, who were dismissed as ill informed and hysterical.[74]

National insurance was then of singular importance, for it was the crucial step in a process of recognition by the state of unemployment as a national problem for which it had some responsibility. Within ten years a national movement of the unemployed would spring into existence for the first time on the basis of this recognition and the contradictions that flowed from it; and through its political activity this movement would alter the insurance scheme out of all recognition to that introduced in 1911. The success of the Liberals had been not in attacking poverty, for their reforms had little substantial effect, but in seducing the socialists into believing that it actually lay in the power of the state to end poverty, an entirely different thing.

4

My Comrades Are Extremists: The Politics of The Unemployed Ex-Service Men, 1919–1920

I am a rebel, my comrades are rebels, I am an extremist, my comrades are extremists, because we have been driven to it by extremist conditions. Don't think we are anything to do with the Labour Party, we have had some of those bleeders, they dope us as the church dopes you. There is no Christianity, during the 1914-18 war the clergy was praying for you to kill Germans, is that Christianity?

—*Tom Dingley; former shop steward, former member of the National Union of Ex-Service Men, and a leader of the National Unemployed Workers' Committee Movement, to the 1922 hunger marchers.*[1]

After World War I the politics of the unemployed fundamentally altered, and many of the reasons for this change lie in the response of unemployed ex-service men to the bewildering circumstances in which they found themselves in the immediate post-war years. Prior to the ending of the post-war boom in the autumn of 1920 unemployment, though at its lowest levels for the entire inter-war period, was very largely concentrated among ex-service men. Their story forms an important, if now forgotten chapter of the history of the tumultuous years that followed the war. It gives us some better idea of the considerable social tensions that underlay the strike wave of 1919-1920 and that led the ruling class to vest the happenings of that era with such portentous gravity. And, for us, it helps explains much about the inter war unemployed movements that is otherwise inexplicable.

The Italians termed the two years that followed World War I the *biennio rosso*—the two red years. The spectre of revolution haunted Europe in a manner unknown since the revolutions of 1848. Following the failed German revolution of January 1919 came the successful but short-lived revolutionary governments of Hungary and Bavaria, as well as a failed revolution in Austria in the spring of 1919. By the late summer of 1920 the Red Army was triumphantly advancing into central Europe; and at the greatest meeting of world revolutionaries ever assembled, the Second Congress of the Communist International, the chairman Grigori Zinoviev declared that the whole of Europe would become a soviet republic within three years. The revolutionaries applauded and bourgeois commentators, far from dismissing Zinoviev's claims, echoed them. Throughout Europe what was immediately obvious to them was the perilous state the ruling class now found itself in. With hindsight what is evident about the ending of the war is how the world capitalist order (if not the British economy) emerged from the experience invigorated. But what contemporaries of both the left and the right saw was something completely different: a system so dehabilitated by war that it was now teetering upon the abyss. It is only against this background of bourgeois fear and working-class hope that we can begin to understand the potency that the politics of the unemployed ex-service men assumed. All working-class activity was viewed, and much of it mediated through red tinted spectacles. That is why when General Wilson peered out of 10 Downing Street on 8 January 1919 and saw an angry demonstration of 1,500 soldiers he chose to describe it as having borne "a dangerous resemblance to a Soviet."[2]

Within Britain in 1919 the ruling class confronted an aggressive working class more organized than ever before. If contemporary historians were wrong to view them as the revolutionary years, they still had a better understanding of the immediate post-war period than later historians who see it merely as a time of industrial militancy. If this had been the case it might explain the policies of appeasement toward the unions pursued at the time, and the growth of arbitration and conciliation machinery; but it would not tell us why the government felt driven on occasion to such crude acts of repression as the pouring of 10,000 fully armed troops into Glasgow to end the forty hours strike in January 1919, nor why thousands of troops, accompanied by tanks and armored cars, were similarly sent into Liverpool during the police strike of August 1919, while two destroyers and a battleship sent up the Mersey ominously trained their guns on the city center. The state was, if anything, better aware than the revolutionaries of the international context of dissolution and revolution in which domestic industrial conflicts were being enacted. The cabinet once a month received highly detailed, accurate reports of revolutionary developments around the globe, as well as numerous special reports on trouble spots. Once a fortnight it received a ten-to-twenty page report upon the activities of revolutionary organizations within Britain, from which some of the information in this chapter has been collected. That the British state, with a guileful mixture of concession, compromise, and occasional repression survived these years is not so much evidence of the *biennio rosso* being without threat or danger, as of the state being acutely aware of what was at stake and framing its response around this knowledge. As David Lloyd George put it to his cabinet in March 1919: "Russia had gone over almost completely to Bolshevism, and we had consoled ourselves with the thought that they were only a half civilized race; but now even Germany, whose people were without exception the best educated in Europe, prospects were very black . . . Great Britain could hold out, but only if the people were given a sense of confidence—only if they were made to believe that things were being done for them."[3]

Even before the end of the war the government had been concerned about the political consequences of the economic dislocation it expected to come in the wake of the war's ending. With memories still strong of the political difficulties generated by the activity of the unemployed in the relatively stable pre-war era, the government found itself less than a month before the armistice with no plans for assisting those soldiers and civilians it expected to be without work at the war's end. Although the Munition Workers' Insurance Act of 1916 had extended unemployment insurance to a further one and a quarter million workers, the vast bulk of the workforce and those in the forces remained outside of the scheme, and in the times of hardship that were expected they would have nothing but the poor law to support them. Accordingly, a scheme was prepared to give an out-of-work donation to ex-service men. On 19 October 1918 the Minister for Reconstruction, Christopher Addison, sent the cabinet a long memorandum urging that the out-of-work donation be extended to all workers who found themselves unemployed in the first months of peace. Addison warned that such a scheme, funded entirely out of the Exchequer and not the Insurance Fund, would create an awkward precedent and make a full return to the contributory basis of the 1911 insurance scheme difficult, but there seemed little alternative. The cabinet, far more concerned with the political and social cohesion of post war Britain than with the sanctity of actuarial principles, approved Addison's scheme. The initial rates were cynically upped just four days before the general election of December 1918, from 24 shillings to 29 shillings for men, and from 20 shillings to 25 shillings for women. When the government announced the scheme it stressed the purely emergency nature of the measure, hoping to soon find the economy in a position sufficiently buoyant, and itself in a position sufficiently strong to withdraw the measure. In the face of the possibility of widespread working-class discontent this was to prove an impossible desire to fulfill.[4]

The out-of-work donation was nowhere near enough to obviate the destitution that unemployed ex-service men experienced after the war. In order to survive many were forced into humiliating activities. Not only in Britain but throughout Europe it became commonplace to see unemployed and often starving ex-service men, without legs, without sight, without minds; parading the obscene effects of the cataclysm in the streets, begging and preying upon the guilt of those who had stayed at home. In the public square of the small port town of La Ciotat in the south of France, if a story of Bertolt Brecht's is to be believed, what appeared to be a bronze statue of a French soldier was in fact a living man, an unemployed ex-soldier coated in bronze paint. He stood immobile upon a plinth against which was propped a piece of cardboard that explained how as a result of being buried alive at Verdun he had acquired "the unusual faculty of remaining as motionless as a statue for any desired length of time. This skill of mine has been tested by many professors and described as an inexplicable disease. Please contribute a small donation to the unemployed father of a family." Many other ex-soldiers were afflicted by the same wasting disease of immobility and supreme passivity. In London some tried to pursue the chimera of commerce by selling single sheets upon which a piece of verse would be printed. Some, such as the sheet sold by crippled ex-rifle men titled "Disabled Through Service", were pathetic in their rude obsequiousness: "Dont be angry, my approaching you so; / And if you can't help please ask me to go. / . . . There's not half enough work for a fit man to do. / So what hope for the man who is lame?" Some of the ex-service men banded together and marched through the streets with collecting boxes, sharing the money out at the end. Often rival groups would come into conflict over the right to parade in the streets returning the biggest collections, and fighting would ensue.[5]

Others began to organize themselves into bodies with larger and more political aims than successfully begging in the streets. Ex-service men's organizations throughout Europe embodied and perpetuated many of the contradictions of war. The National Federation of Discharged and Demobilised Sailors and Soldiers as it was in Britain in 1918, the Croix de Feu in France, the Stahlhelm and Freikorp in Germany all shared many antipathies: a hatred of the rear, a contempt for the workers they felt had shirked, a hatred for the trade unions who along with the politicians were not to be trusted, and a strong resentment against women that bordered on pathological misogynism. We find one symbolic juncture of all these attitudes in the Freikorp members who found a "source of permanent pride" in their brutal murder in 1919 of Rosa Luxemburg, the principal leader of the failed German revolution. The Fascist potential of some of these bodies was to be realised in the years to come. The Croix de Feu evolved into a distinct and important Fascist body in the 1930s, while Hitler's stormtroopers were originally recruited from the ranks of the Freikorp. "The Third Reich", said Rudolf Hess, "comes from the trenches."[6]

The politics of unemployed ex-service men thus had an enormous potential for reaction. That British veterans' organizations avoided the Fascist trends evident on the Continent can be attributed to a number of related factors. First, however bad the economic and social situation got in Britain, it never reached the revolutionary levels of instability that obtained through much of Europe, particularly in Germany. Second, and following from this, the British state only saw unemployed ex-service men as a source of social instability that needed to be controlled, unlike in Germany, where the state had to resort to using and encouraging far right paramilitary organizations of ex-service men as the shock troops of the counter revolution. Rather than exploit their potential for violence, the British state, as we shall see, was keen to defuse this explosive mixture. This meant that in Britain there were effectively only two directions for ex-service men's organizations: toward the one that the state desired, a depoliticized centre, or, against and away from the state, toward an oppositional politics somewhere along the spectrum of the left. Unlike in Germany there was to be no external support for a far right organization of ex-service men.

Service men demobilized immediately at the end of the war could have joined one (or all) of three ex-service men's organizations: the National Association of Discharged Sailors and Soldiers (NADSS), the National Federation of Discharged and Demobilised Sailors and Soldiers (NFDDSS), and the Comrades of the Great War. The NADSS was the oldest of these groups, established in Blackburn in 1916.

At first it had strong Labour sympathies, but it soon divested itself of these and broke with the labor movement in 1918, moving to the political center and concentrating exclusively on ex-service men's questions. Largest and most powerful of these organizations was the NFDDSS, which had by May 1920 an estimated membership of 1,500,000. Formed in July 1917, the moving spirit behind the NFDDSS was the Scottish Liberal MP James Myle Hogge, and it had in consequence strong links with the Liberal Party, and was at first an intensely patriotic and pro-war body. Its jingoism was evident in its calls for the immediate internment of all enemy aliens, and manifest in its antagonism toward the labor movement. During the engineering workers' strike in the summer of 1918, the executive of the NFDDSS called upon its members to remain loyal to the troops at the front by staying at work. Many NFDDSS branches pledged to work in the strikers' place, and the Deptford branch went as far as offering to help the police round up unpatriotic strikers. A little over four weeks later members of the Royal Arsenal NFDDSS branch violently broke up an ILP meeting on Plumstead Common. Carrying banners inscribed "All patriots, so to hell with Ramsay MacDonald and his German Comrades!" they prevented the pacifist MacDonald from addressing the meeting, and badly beat up several ILP members.[7]

Let us pause and consider precisely what all this meant: wandering the streets of Britain at a time of great social tension were hundreds of thousands of men with experience of warfare, "four million trained and successful killers" as Churchill described them, many still with their weapons that they had kept in the confusion of rapid demobilization, but without work. The socialist William Allan, looking back from 1922, wrote, "In 1919-1920 we had exceptional destitution, soaring prices, a demobilized army which had been promised Heaven and granted Hell, and which also knew how to handle guns, the psychological effect of the Irish, and the military exploits of the Russian Red Army; all these resulted in the conception of a sudden and successful upheaval in this country". He added " 'mass action', 'physical force', 'secret armies', 'mob psychology', etc, etc, are phrases that arose, not from the overheated brains of agitators, but from actual social conditions."[8]

Patriotic as the NADSS and NFDDSS were, their existence outside the aegis of the state aroused a feeling of unease within the government, and led it on a number of occasions to try to wrest control of the ex-service men from them. The first of three attempts came in the summer of 1917. General B. E. Wyndham Childs, Director of Personnel Services, approached the imperial adventurer and Conservative MP Sir John "Empire Jack" Norton Griffiths to assist the War Office in creating an ex-service men's organization to counteract the possible politicization of ex-service men by socialists. Childs later confessed that he had been "very apprehensive of the fact that there was no scheme of a non-political nature for absorbing the discharged and demobilised soldiers." Griffiths first publicly broached the idea of a non-political ex-service men's body in a letter to the press in July 1917, and his proposal gathered enough support to establish the Comrades of the Great War the following month. Though launched with strong financial support, numbering among its backers Lord Rothermere, Lord Beaverbrook, and Sir Alfred Mond, and though enjoying the unofficial support of the state (the Secretary of State for War wrote an "unofficial" letter to the lord lieutenants of the counties asking them to back the new organization), the Comrades did not prosper as had been desired. In a foolish blunder that served only to antagonize ordinary ex-service men the first executive was composed entirely of ex-officers. Even worse for an avowedly apolitical organization, two-thirds of this executive were also politicians, the chairman, Colonel Wilfred Ashly being, for example, a Unionist MP. The Comrades became not the sole national organization of ex-service men as had been hoped, but one of a number of conservative, predominately ex-officers' associations.[9]

The origins and purpose of the Comrades were not forgotten: among members of the NADSS and the NFDDSS there was a "very bitter feeling" against them, reported one ex-service men's newspaper in July 1919, many ex-service men considering "that this organization had been started officially by officers to break up theirs". So great was this hostility that in some areas the NFDDSS waged an active and aggressive campaign against them. In Norfolk in May 1919 the local NFDDSS disrupted a meeting of the local branch of the Comrades with much shouting about army discipline and verbal attacks upon the "officer class".[10]

The NFDDSS leaders had a narrow conception of their body as a progressive group acting solely in the interests of its members. While the NFDDSS was in no sense a radical organization at the beginning of 1919, there was within it considerable heterodoxy because of its structure. Membership was restricted to ranking soldiers and sailors, and officers were admitted only if they had been promoted from the ranks. In this way the officers, who were largely drawn from the middle and upper classes and who tended to act as a moderating influence, were generally excluded from the NFDDSS. Branches of the NFDDSS enjoyed full local autonomy and thus ranged from the reactionary to the revolutionary and often a mixture of both. Within branches there was a great diversity of opinion, and given the size of some NFDDSS branches, this is scarcely surprising: in April 1919 the Camberwell NFDDSS had over 3,000 members, the Hull NFDDSS over 4,000, and the Birmingham NFDDSS over 12,000. Unemployment was to be the point where the NFDDSS would be forced to make the connections it tried so hard to avoid between its own struggles and the larger battles being fought out between the working class and the ruling class.[11]

Unemployment and Ex-Service Men

The low levels of unemployment experienced among insured workers during 1919 and 1920 give a falsely roseate view of the state of the labor market in the immediate post war period. As a result of a series of army mutinies of considerable magnitude in early 1919, a fearful government abandoned plans for a slow process of demobilization in which men were released as they were required for industry, and instead introduced the principle of "first in, first out" and set about demobilizing the army with almost obscene haste. In the peak month of February 1919 (following a strike of 14,000 soldiers at Calais in January 1919) soldiers were demobilized at the rate of 170,000 a week, and in the following month at the still stupendous rate of 106,000 a week. A slight recession took place immediately after the armistice and the tidal wave of demobilization threatened to swamp the labor market: by February 1919 unemployment was increasing at the rate of roughly 70,000 a week. The immediate onset of mass unemployment was averted by a boom that began in March 1919 and that was to last a little over a year. Many ex-service men were thus, at first, reabsorbed into industry. A considerable and rising number were not: by May 1919 408,000 ex-service men were out of work.[12]

One feature of the boom and a cause of the notable industrial militancy of this period was the rapid escalation of prices, an issue upon which many militants sought to gain support. The physical and psychological effects of all this upon the unemployed ex-service men are impossible to measure precisely: all that can be said with certainty is that the position of the unemployed was becoming increasingly desperate during the boom years of 1919 and 1920 as the value of already minimal state payments was significantly eroded by massive price rises. A contemporary study estimated that a week's food for an ordinary family that would have cost 1 pound, 5 shillings, and 9 pence in 1914, would, by June 1920, cost 4 pounds, 6 shillings, and 10 pence for the same items, an overall increase of 237 percent. While, as Table 4.1 shows, prices increased by over 200 percent between 1913 and 1920 the unemployment benefit remained frozen at its 1913 level of 7 shillings until December 1919 when it was raised to 11 shillings. The out-of-work donation, on the other hand, was reduced in May 1919 from 29 shillings to 20 shillings for men, and from 25 shillings to 15 shillings for women. The unemployed were caught in the paradoxical and tragic situation of finding their position steadily worsening with each passing day of the greatest boom Britain was to know for the next thirty years.[13]

In such circumstances discontent among ex-service men about unemployment began to arise almost as soon as the war had ended, the cabinet being told as early as January 1919 that there was strong feeling upon the issue in Nottingham and Coventry. Unemployed ex-service men played a prominent role in the Glasgow 40 hours strike (itself called over the issue of unemployment) of the same month, at one stage routing the police by unearthing a steel picket fence and charging baton-wielding constables. By April 1919 there were reports from almost every center of industry of mass demonstrations by ex-service men demanding the right to work. The radicalizing effect of such activity was reflected in the decision of some NFDDSS branches to affiliate with their local trades council, and led to the beginning of the all important connection between the unemployed and the shop stewards' movement; radical West London branches of the NFDDSS making contact with the West London Engineering Workers' Committee with whom they then organized some joint demonstrations.[14]

When the out-of-work donation scheme came to an end in May 1919, the government found itself unable to do away with the scheme without risking the wrath of the unemployed ex-service men. So instead it chose to emasculate the scheme through restrictions and reductions. The scheme was extended for a further

Table 4.1. *Comparison of Prices, Wages, Unemployment Benefits, and Out-of-Work Donation, 1913-1921*

Year	Quarter	Prices	Wages	Unemployment Insurance Benefit		Out-of work-Donation	
		1913=100	1913=100	1913=7/-		Men	Women
1919	1	249	228	7/-		29/-	25/- (Nov. 1918)
	2	242	230				
	3	258	238				
	4	288	244				
1920	1	309	255	11/- (Dec. 1919)		20/-	15/- (May 1919)
	2	324	276				
	3	314	294	Men	Women		
	4	284	301	15/-	12/- (Nov. 1921)		
1921	1	227	304				
	2	201	295	20/-	16/- (Mar. 1921)		
	3	190	269				
	4	174	251	15/-	21/- (July 1921)		

Notes: The out-of-work donation for civilians was ended in November 1919, for ex-service men in March 1921. The rate of unemployment benefit was to remain unchanged from July 1921 until August 1924, when the Labour government put it up to 18 shillings for men, and to 15 shillings for women.
Sources: W. Beveridge, *Unemployment* (1930), p. 460; Wal Hannington, *A Short History of the Unemployed* (1938), pp. 17, 20-22, 28-29.

six months from 25 May 1919, but the donation was, as we have seen, slashed from 29 shillings for men to 20 shillings, and from 25 shillings for women to 15 shillings. In addition, civilian applicants for the donation were now required to prove that they were "normally in employment, genuinely seeking employment and unable to obtain it." This provision was the origin of the "not genuinely seeking work" test, which was to become so notorious and so hated in the 1920s.[15]

In November 1918 the NFDDSS had organized several thousand ex-service men in a victory demonstration at Trafalgar Square. Behind banners such as "Down With Bolshevism" and "No Pacifist Government" the ex-service men afterwards marched to Buckingham Palace to cheer the royal family upon its return from a thanksgiving service. On 26 May 1919, the day after the new provisions were introduced, the NFDDSS held a day of national demonstration to protest the unemployment of ex-service men.[16] When on this day, following a peaceful meeting of 10,000 at Hyde Park, a large crowd of ex-service men again sought to march to Buckingham Palace, to lay their case before the king, and from there to the House of Commons, to see the prime minister and the minister of labour, beneath banners asking "NO WORK-WHY?", their intentions were considered sufficiently different and threatening that the state chose to array large numbers of police to forcibly prevent them from reaching their immediate destination.

The police were able to head them off from the palace, but were unable to prevent them reaching the vicinity of the houses of parliament. The demonstrators fought their way down Victoria Street, the police being forced to yield in a bloody battle that started at the street's top end and continued down into Parliament Square, which became the scene of a wild and confused melee. Some unemployed ex-service men stood in the roadway opposite St. Margaret's and hurled wooden blocks and pieces of concrete at the mounted police who, for their part, were intent on batoning to the ground the thousand or more demonstrators left in the square. The fighting was fierce and many on both sides were injured. Personifying the ultimate destination of the politics of the unemployed ex-service men on that day was Dennis Jennett, who was charged in connection with the battle that took place in Parliament Square. Then thirty-seven years old, an army mutineer suffering badly from shell shock, working as a shoe maker in Islington, Jennett was a member of the radical Soldiers', Seamen's and Airmen's Union and resurfaced in the early 1920s as one of the leaders of the NUWCM.[17]

This street battle marked the end of the short-lived era of polite relations between the state and ex-service men, and the beginning of an era in which the politics of the ex-service men was to take on the form of the politics of the unemployed and the nature of class conflict. While the leadership of the NFDDSS was attempting to pilot the organization back into the calmer, less agitated waters it had sailed on up to 1919, large sections of the rank and file were all for taking the NFDDSS into the eye of the maelstrom of radical working-class politics. These opposing tendencies came into open conflict at the NFDDSS national conference held at Manchester on 8-9 June 1919. It had long been feared by many within the NFDDSS that an influx of officers would act as a conservative influence upon the body and enable

Whitehall to eventually "obtain controlling power." While the decision of the conference to admit officers as members thus fundamentally altered the political outlook and social composition of the NFDDSS, a potential channel for radical political influence was closed off by the conference decision not to admit conscientious objectors as members. The socialists' attempt to formally ally the NFDDSS with the Labour Party was crushed by an overwhelming majority. The leadership's moderate line triumphed and within the NFDDSS the socialists were finished.[18]

Socialist Ex-Service Men's Organizations

The disappointment many ex-service men felt with the NFDDSS conference of 1919 gave a great impetus to some of the socialist ex-service men's organizations, of which there were three of significance in mid-1919: the Soldiers', Seamen's, and Airmen's Union (SSAU), the International Union of Ex-Service Men and Adult Dependents (IUX), and the National Union of Ex-Service Men (NUX).

The SSAU was the smallest and shortest lived of these bodies, as well as the first to have come into existence. An attempt to merge the SSAU with the NUX in June 1919 came to nothing, and by October 1919 the SSAU was £77 in debt and defunct in all but name. Of longer-term importance was the IUX which, more than any other organization of ex-service men, anticipated both the practice and the ideology of the NUWM. The IUX's passionate belief in a class struggle in which members of the working class beyond the factories played an important and active role prefigured much that was similarly distinctive about the NUWM. The IUX was never a national organization, its support largely restricted, at various times, to Glasgow, Dundee, Bristol, and west London, yet sporadically it was a dynamic and important body. Formed in May 1919 as a breakaway from the Glasgow NFDDSS by ex-service men who found their efforts within the NFDDSS constantly frustrated, and themselves continually berated for "trying to introduce politics into a non-political organization", the IUX had from the beginning strong organizational and ideological links with the Glasgow shop stewards' movement. In June 1919 the Scottish organization of the shop stewards recommended that all its members support and participate in IUX activity, and by early autumn of the same year the IUX was affiliated with the Clyde Workers' Committee.[19]

The IUX was thus, like the NUWM, greatly influenced by the shop stewards' movement, but the channels of influence were different in each organization. Many of the early leaders of the NUWM were shop stewards out of a job, who came direct from organizing the workers to organizing the workless. The IUX had no such organic link to the Shop Stewards and Workers' Committee Movement (SS&WCM). No SS&WCM activists were known to have been active in the IUX. While the IUX was inspired by, sympathetic to, and sometimes obsequious toward the SS&WCM, it was never a direct offshoot in the way the NUWM was. This meant that the NUWM was to be, among many other things, a collision between the direct experience of shop stewards and the ideology of the SS&WCM as mediated, enriched and in some ways distorted through the experience of the IUX.

The IUX is "an out and out revolutionary organization", wrote its secretary James Cox; and through the medium of *The Worker*, the weekly newspaper of the Scottish Workers' Committee in which it had its own regular page, the IUX argued that war could be ended only through the abolition of capitalism. Strategically it stood very much in the tradition of the soviet-influenced shop stewards' movement, aiming "to establish proper relationships with all Workers' Committees throughout the country with a view to forming Workers Sailors and Soldiers [*sic*] Councils with the express purpose of taking over the means of production, distribution and exchange", with the hope of "freeing the worker from wage slavery and exploitation." The IUX was the first ex-service men's organization to advocate the merging of the particular battles of the unemployed ex-service men with the general struggle of the working class. Yet in spite of its stance the IUX failed to generate much in the way of active support from socialist activists. With the exception of John Steele, who was later active in the NUWM, no IUX activists seem to have had any involvement with the socialist movement before or after the brief existence of the IUX. This does not mean that IUX activists had not been active socialists before the IUX, but there does seem to have been a suspicion held by socialist activists that the IUX was composed of nouveau socialists. Although the leading Scottish revolutionary John Maclean addressed some IUX meetings in Glasgow, and the anarchist Guy Aldred briefly assisted the IUX in Dundee, the industrial militants who formed the shop stewards' movement did nothing beyond providing passive support, ignoring the possibility of the organization of ex-service men up until late 1920. toward the end of its life the IUX complained, "We at least expected that we might have the moral support of all advanced organizations but have been doomed to disappointment-and serve us right. Instead of the I.U. receiving support they are looked on with suspicion."[20]

Revolutionary as the long-term aspirations of the IUX were, its immediate aim was simply to construct a strong ex-service men's organization and during 1919 it did succeed in becoming something of a force in Glasgow and Dundee by winning over disillusioned NFDDSS members. By September 1919 the IUX had 7,000 members and in the following months the organization grew rapidly. At least some of this expanding membership were women: the Partick and Whiteinch IUX branches were kept going for a time solely through the efforts of women; and a woman, Mrs. Masterson, was for a time national propaganda secretary of the IUX. In contrast to the misogynist calls of some of the other ex-service men's organizations, the IUX took a radical stance upon women's issues, calling at its 1920 congress for equal wages for women, and equal gratuities and pensions for women who had served in the forces.[21]

Up until 1920 the IUX did not indulge in any mass activity beyond the occasional public meeting. The crucial factors leading to the adoption of the methods of direct action by large groups of unemployed ex-service men seems to have been the problem of unemployment, which, as we have seen, was compounded by rising prices, coupled to the influence of the resurgent Irish revolutionary movement. It is difficult to ascertain how close the IUX was to the Irish revolutionary movement, though a secret intelligence report in August 1919 claimed that leading members of the IUX frequented "Sinn Fein resorts" in Glasgow. The psychological effect of the example of Ireland was enormous, and in comparison to the influence of Russia, much under rated by historians since. At its 1920 congress the IUX pledged to support the Irish in their struggles "by all the means at their disposal", but what forms, if any, this support took we have no knowledge of. What is known is that it is from the Irish that the IUX gained a belief in the efficacy of physical force, which for a period in 1920 threatened to become a major strand of IUX activity.[22]

Largest of the socialist ex-service men's organizations was the NUX, which by mid-1920 had a membership of 300,000. The NUX was formed in May 1919 as an NFDDSS breakaway by Ernest Mander, who was to be the NUX's secretary for the course of its existence, and John Beckett, who had previously been the organizer of the Acton and Shepherds Bush NFDDSS, and who was to be the NUX's first chairman. Beckett later became an ILP MP, and then, in the early 1930s, was to move to the extreme right of populist politics when he became a leading member of Sir Oswald Mosley's British Union of Fascists. From the beginning the NUX allied itself with the Labour Party. Its headquarters were at first based at Labour Hall, Ilford; it was helped in its organization by prominent ILP member Fenner Brockway; and by the end of 1919 the Labour Party was circularizing trades council recommending the NUX as a body worthy of the support of organized labor. At first the NUX was moderate in its approach so as not to frighten off prospective members whom they hoped to recruit from the trade unions. But it was still anti-militarist, still had as its aim "to help in the destruction of capitalism", and elaborated a political program that included the common "ownership of land and all the means of producing wealth for the people." Like the IUX the NUX stressed the essential unity of interests existing between ex-service men and the working class. When the NUX was first established Mander wrote that for "ex-service men to organize independently of Labour is for them to play into the hands of the Capitalist class. The discharged and demobilised are, essentially, above everything else, ordinary civilian *workers* once again; and their *general* interests are absolutely identical with those of their fellow workers."[23]

This remained for a long time little more than a theoretical construct. It was to take another year and the onset of a depression before a sizeable body of ex-service men would arrive at similar conclusions to Mander, and begin to organize and agitate upon the basis that their plight was shared with, and was part of the general plight of the working class. Until then the NUX continued to organize ex-service men upon the particular issues that affected them.

The Disillusionment and Growing Anger of Unemployed Ex-Service Men

As the war and its bandages of jingoism sloughed off into the past, the suppurating wounds of a class-divided society were once more revealed for all to see. This did not mean that all unemployed ex-service men became immediately class-conscious, but it did mean that many came to despise the myths of militarism and patriotism as insulting lies. A group of unemployed ex-service men in Manchester in July 1919 had grown offended by the army recruiting posters displayed at the Whitworth Institute, where they received their out-of-work donation. In particular they took umbrage at a poster that depicted a bronzed, well fed horse soldier who claimed to have "not a care in the world." After a mass meeting of unemployed ex-service men that protested against "the neglect of the community" that found them no work, 100 unemployed ex-service men entered the Whitworth Institute and, declaring that they were prepared to be arrested for their actions, tore down the posters. In the face of the poverty that unemployment brought, the myth of militarism (so seductively communicated in the image of the hale and hearty horse soldier) lost all credibility. To take another example, a soldier brandishing a revolver had, in 1916, entered the Edinburgh castle cell of the deported Glasgow shop steward David Kirkwood, and declared; "I would rather shoot you than any German." Three years later, in June 1919, at an outdoor ILP meeting in Stirlingshire, the soldier, now unemployed, publicly apologized to Kirkwood, the main speaker. "I have found out my mistake", he told Kirkwood. "I have been discharged and cannot get work after risking my life for my country. . . I am now with you in the fight against capitalism." It may be objected that these were isolated incidents, that such examples of disillusionment brought on by unemployment are only symbolic, and not representative. Any who held such notions in 1919 saw them perish in the flames of the rioting that accompanied the peace celebrations of 19 July 1919. Intended as a moment of national self-congratulation, it became instead a focus for the anger felt by many unemployed ex-service men, and it is chiefly remarkable for highlighting not a nation united in victory, but a society divided by class.[24]

A change of mood among ex-service men had been apparent since early summer. In June 1919 the Directorate of Intelligence warned the cabinet that "revolutionary sentiments" were increasing in some NFDDSS branches, and by July reported that feeling within the NFDDSS generally was "becoming bitter". The extent of this discontent was revealed in the wide opposition of ex-service men to the official peace celebrations, which for many symbolized the injustice of a society where public funds could be extravagantly spent on such an event, but largely denied to the men who had fought in the war and who were now starving in the streets. The NFDDSS advised its branches to abstain from participation in the peace celebrations, and many did so; the St. Pancras NFDDSS went further and successfully moved at a borough meeting that the borough not celebrate the signing in view of the unemployment among ex-service men.[25]

In other places opposition to the peace celebrations took on the day a violent, and for the government, more disturbing form. In Coventry the entire police force was called out to quell bad rioting that destroyed much of the city's business center, and left forty people injured. At Swindon a flagpole had been recently erected at considerable expense outside the town hall. In a town where unemployment was rising rapidly, the flagpole became for many a symbol of the extravagant misuse of council funds, and on the day of the peace celebrations it was burnt to the ground by an angry crowd who then attacked the police station. At Bilston a crowd of 2,000 attacked and attempted to burn down a police station. While battering rams with which to smash down the police station's doors were being improvised, a wall was torn down by the crowd, and the bricks from it used as missiles. Petrol was poured onto the police station, but police reinforcements arrived in time to beat the crowd off and put the fire out before the station burnt down.[26]

The worst incident took place at Luton, where a crowd succeeded in razing the town hall to the ground. Discontent among local ex-service men about unemployment was catalyzed into a ferocious outburst by the Luton Council's refusal to allow the Luton NFDDSS the use of a local park for a memorial service. A closer examination of this incident is warranted by the depth and extent of anti-state feeling it reveals as having been generated by unemployment. That such a feeling was widely held in Luton is suggested by the trouble later found in prosecuting the rioters because, as the Luton chief constable admitted in court, "the greatest difficulty was experienced in getting witnesses to come forward."[27]

A large crowd first began to collect outside the Luton town hall after the mayor had read the proclamation of peace on the afternoon of Saturday, 19 July 1919. A number of impromptu speeches were made dwelling on the condition of unemployed ex-service men. A manifesto later issued by the council claimed that the underlying cause of the riot was the "alleged unsatisfactory allowances" paid to unemployed ex-service men. Though the council would have been anxious to play down the significance of its blunder in refusing the park to the NFDDSS, it does seem undeniable that what lay at the heart of the wild events that were to follow was the miserable condition of unemployed ex-service men, brought into sharp contrast by the state's lavish expenditure upon the peace celebrations.

After the speeches the crowd rushed the town hall, broke through the police guard, and, once inside, tore down the decorative streamers and lights that had been put up in preparation for the peace banquet. Furniture was smashed, and the pieces thrown from the balcony to the crowd below. Police reinforcements at length arrived and managed to retake the hall. The crowd dispersed, but the tension remained. On the advice of the chief constable and the town clerk, the mayor fled the town, not to return for five days. When the pubs began to close around 10 pm a much larger crowd than before assembled outside the town hall. Fighting broke out between them and the police, and in spite of appeals to desist made by NFDDSS officials from the town hall steps, the crowd succeeded in taking the hall for a second time, with, it seems, the definite aim of razing it to the ground. Fires were started inside and the flames fed upon lighted boxes pushed through the crowd into the hall, and encouraged with petrol looted from a nearby garage and then thrown round the building. As the town hall began to blaze cheerily, something akin to a carnival atmosphere gripped the crowd. Surrounding shops were looted, and from one a piano was wheeled out into the middle of the street where it became the center of wild and exuberant dancing.

At 3.30 am on Sunday, as the town hall—the physical embodiment of the state in Luton—subsided into a pile of embers and ash, detachments of fully armed soldiers in battle dress arrived from Biscot and Bedford. They cleared the streets and by midday were controlling all movement in the center of the town. Strong police reinforcements were drafted in from St. Albans, Bedford, and Cambridge; upon arriving in Luton they ran amok in the streets. The final tally of civilian casualties from police charges was put at 100. The reinforcements were strong enough to prevent a second serious riot on Sunday night, when the police station was surrounded and a demand made for the release of an imprisoned soldier. As the crowd prepared to rush the police station the police baton charged and broke them up. Resentment ran high against the police. A further battle took place on the evening of 22 July 1919, when a crowd attacked the police with bricks.

The NFDDSS disclaimed any responsibility for the rioting, and was principal among those who helped to restore bourgeois order to Luton. Along with the local Labour Party, the trades council, and the Luton branch of the Comrades of the Great War, the NFDDSS issued a manifesto on Thursday, 24 July 1919, condemning the riots and promising support in the restoration of order. Of course the bourgeoisie did their bit too: Lady Wernher, "lady of the manor of Luton", arranged to entertain the 4,000 ex-service men of Luton to a day of tea and sports.

The razing of the Luton town hall had been symptomatic of a fundamental shift in the attitude of many unemployed ex-service men, which was not to disappear with the passing of the peace celebrations. Such demonstrations of mass discontent as a parade of 20,000 unemployed ex-service men in Sheffield on 26 July 1919 showed that many suffering men were not going to submit quietly to their fate. The Directorate of Intelligence, noting that it was "significant that such opposition as was offered to the Peace Celebrations came from demobilised soldiers", went on to tell the cabinet on 24 July 1919, that over "the past week there have been signs from every part of the country of serious discontent and unrest, that may break out with serious consequences at any moment". At a time of great working-class militancy there was a fear of the ex-service men making common cause with other working class groups leading to combinations with unknowable, and possibly unpreventable, consequences.[28]

The ex-service men had begun to make links with the radical National Union of Police and Prison Officers (NUPPO), who in August 1919 called a national police strike. Although the strike was unable to garner enough support nationally to succeed, it was strong enough in Liverpool to elicit a dramatic show of force from the state. At a mass meeting of the NUPPO in London on 1 June 1919 banners of the NFDDSS flanked the speakers' platform, and one non-police speaker declared that the demobilized men of Paddington were with the police union. In Manchester ex-service men attempted to bring the police there out on strike, and at an NUPPO mass meeting in Birmingham, a NUX activist called Blythe moved the resolution calling for a general strike in support of the police strike. The band of the radical Kensington NFDDSS headed a police strikers' procession on 10 August 1919, and several ex-service men spoke at a large meeting of police strikers at Hyde Park on 24 August 1919. These links were to find an echo in the involvement of victimized police strikers in the early days of the NUWCM, the Liverpool Unemployed Workers' Committee, for example, being led by Bob Tissyman, an ex-police striker.[29]

Such friendships and tendencies toward radical activity at a time of national crisis disturbed the ruling class. "In the uncertain state of national affairs that then existed there was considerable danger", Duff Cooper was later to write of the NFDDSS, "that these and similar powerful organizations might be tempted to play an important part in politics and seek by political pressure to obtain their private ends." Various attempts were made to draw the teeth of the politics of the unemployed ex-service men, of which the most important was that made by the government. In the wake of the disturbing behaviour of unemployed ex-service men in June and July 1919 it launched a third and ultimately successful bid to gain control of their organizations by bringing them into one body existing on the terms of the government. Six days after the Luton town hall had subsided into hot ash, the War Office announced the setting up of the United Services Fund, a body charged with the responsibility of dispersing some £7 million of profit accumulated from war-time service men's canteens. General Byng was brought out of the army to administer the fund, and he set about dangling the money in front of the various ex-service men's organizations as an incentive to amalgamation upon the government's terms and conditions.[30]

The existence of various ex-service men's organizations was viewed as class divisive and potentially revolutionary. Field Marshal Douglas Haig, speaking to a meeting of the Grand Council of the Officers' Association in late 1920, admitted how during 1919 he had become greatly disturbed by the revolutionary ideas that existed in some societies of ex-service men. "The only solution", said Haig "was to get these men back to their old leaders the officers, and consequently I urged union among all ex-service men." Haig began in early July 1919 to use his considerable prestige in a campaign for amalgamation. He told an audience in Liverpool on 5 July 1919 how "nothing could be more regrettable than the tendency of the ex-service men's organizations to develop a political aspect." He pleaded for a national organization of ex-service men. "We want above all things", he continued, "to keep this great national effort to help our soldiers . . . clear of all political connexions."[31]

Byng devised a scheme that offered a basis for realising the hopes of Haig and those who were similarly worried. Like Haig, Byng was above all else concerned to create a non-political organization. To achieve this he imposed three conditions upon amalgamation and the prize of the United Services Fund. First, membership was to be open to all ranks; second, there were to be no party politics; and third, no civilians were to be admitted to membership. Effectively, these conditions politically neutered any body that was to be born of them through specifically banning party politics, by opening the body up to the influence of officers, who, as we have seen, were feared by ex-service men as a conservative force, and by banning interested civilians who at the time tended to be socialists and who were in 1920 to act as a radical leaven when mixed in with unemployed ex-service men. With the backing of powerful allies such as Haig, and the temptation of £7 million and considerable semi-official status, Byng's proposals quickly gained ground. By October 1919 there was enough support for Byng to be able to hold a meeting of representatives from the Comrades, the NADSS, and the NFDDSS, the NUX being excluded because of its overt political stance. As a result of the meeting an executive committee chaired by Byng and composed of representatives from the three bodies was formed. The one remaining stumbling block to unity on Byng's terms was the official opposition of the NFDDSS to amalgamation. But as the militant left-wing organizations of ex-service men came to the fore in 1920 the NFDDSS was to be gutted of its radical heart. The shift rightwards was confirmed at the NFDDSS national conference in 1920, when the NFDDSS finally decided to seek amalgamation with other ex-service men's bodies. A number of amalgamation conferences followed, culminating in the inauguration conference held on 14 May 1921, at which the Officers' Association, the Comrades of the Great War, the NADSS, and the NFDDSS formally joined together in a new organization called the British Legion. They made the Prince of Wales its patron and Haig its president and were rewarded for their loyal efforts with recognition by the government as the official body representing ex-service men, and of course, some £7 million of war time canteen profits.[32]

Byng's proposals did not bring a halt to the activity of the ex-service men. On the contrary, in the charged atmosphere of mid-1919 the NUX grew rapidly. This growth was augmented by the contradictions with which the NFDDSS was beset, as it sought to maintain its policy of helping ex-service men while remaining aloof from, and antagonistic toward, working-class struggle. The shallowness of this approach led the NFDDSS into a disastrous campaign against Bolshevism, to which it attributed a heady array of crimes including "unemployment amongst ex-service men, the reduction of exports and the high cost of living." NFDDSS officials were worried about the growing influence of revolutionary socialism on ex-service men, and to convince them of its heinous nature it distributed and promoted a film entitled "Bolshevism: a message of its evils". At a time of great working class sympathy for the beleaguered Soviet state, this was too much for many within the NFDDSS, especially the socialist activists who had remained members in the belief that the organization could be won from within to socialism. From the time of the anti-Bolshevik campaign, defections of individuals and branches from the NFDDSS to the NUX began to occur on a large scale. Between May and November 1919 the NUX expanded from a single branch of 50 members into a national organization of over a hundred branches and a membership of nearly 100,000.[33]

Meanwhile the government found itself in the invidious position of having to formulate social policy in the context of an increasingly polarized society in which the labor movement was daily more assertive. Between the extension of the out-of-work donation scheme in May 1919, and its proposed expiry in November 1919, many unions passed resolutions demanding that either the dole be made permanent or that the government provide work for the unemployed. Although the trade revival meant that unemployment had dropped, this served only to strengthen the hand of the unions, while through rapidly escalating prices it worsened the position of unemployed ex-service men. Discontent was sufficiently disturbing for the *Manchester Guardian* of 14 August 1919 to view the proposed reduction of the Rhine Army with consternation, because it would mean an addition to the already crowded ranks of the unemployed ex-service men.[34]

On September 1919 the Minister of Labour, Sir Robert Horne, circulated a memorandum to the cabinet in which he argued that because of the precedent of the donation scheme "we must start from the assumption that to allow the donation scheme to expire and to put nothing in its place is impossible." Intelligence reports backed up Horne's assessment of the government's predicament. On 13 November 1919 Basil Thompson, head of the Directorate of Intelligence, struck a rare note of panic in his report to the cabinet. "My Liverpool correspondent even goes so far as to say that there will be serious trouble if doles are withdrawn during the winter . . . . The discontent among ex-soldiers is not diminishing. There is a possibility of disturbances in the London district when the unemployment donation is stopped."[35]

At the same time as the cabinet was being given such cheerless news, the Labour Party scored a triumph in the first municipal elections held since the war. A total of 573 Labour and socialist members were returned, compared to the previous 48. Labour now controlled twelve boroughs, the base upon which Poplarism—an alliance of local labor politics with the politics of the unemployed—was to be built. This result was a further disturbing portent for Lloyd George's government. The out-of-work donation scheme had been due to end on 24 November 1919. The government fearfully and prudently resolved to again extend the scheme for ex-service men until 31 March 1920. In the end the donation scheme for ex-service men was to be extended a further three times, and was not to be terminated until 31 March 1921, after which the ex-service men were able to receive the dole under the aegis of the unemployment insurance scheme. What had begun as an emergency measure to prevent disaffection among soldiers in the period between demobilization and employment had by 1921 supplanted the poor law as the major method of providing relief. Among many others, William Beveridge saw the donation scheme as a turning point. "It damaged the whole principle of insurance", he wrote in 1930. "From the donation scheme dates the term 'dole' indiscriminately applied later to insurance benefit; also from it dates the conception of largesse in which all were entitled to share." In the face of the discontent of the unemployed during a highly volatile period the paradigm of welfare had been fundamentally altered.[36]

But it was only the unemployed ex-service men, with their military training and strong sense of alienation, who frightened the government and moved it to action.

Of the unemployed civilians the government was neither frightened nor concerned. Horne had recommended in his memorandum of 5 September 1919 that a large extension of contributory insurance be made. The government acted on this by hastily preparing a bill that extended unemployment insurance to all workers earning less than £250 a year, excluding domestic servants and agricultural workers. The bill went before the House of Commons in February 1920 and finally came into effect in November 1920. With only 135,185 civilians claiming the out-of-work donation in November 1919, the government felt confident in ending the donation scheme for unemployed civilians and leaving them to the mercies of the workhouse and destitution until such time in the distant future—a year as it eventually transpired—that they could be relieved through the unemployment insurance scheme. The ending of the dole for unemployed civilians met with only a limited amount of protest, which included the resurrection of pre-war unemployed tactics in Coventry by Tom Mann, who led a demonstration of unemployed into the cathedral during the mayor's annual service. But if the government had correctly gauged the situation in discarding the civilians, it had not in its hope of placating the ex-service men. For while the protest of the civilians soon fizzled out, the continuation of the dole for ex-service men did not buy their acquiescence.[37]

Unemployment was becoming the dominant issue for the ex-service men's organizations. Socialists began to interest themselves in the militant activity of the unemployed ex-service men. When twenty-eight unemployed ex-service men who had marched from Manchester arrived in London in late September 1919, a welcoming meeting in Trafalgar Square was addressed by David Ramsay, a leading shop steward, and Arthur MacManus, an SLP leader. The Manchester marchers met twice with the Minister of Labour, Sir Robert Horne. On the second occasion, on 29 September 1919, Horne entertained the men at a luncheon and succeeded in obtaining a large motorbus for their return journey. Horne seems to have been more aware of the implications of the march than the marchers themselves were. A few days prior to their meeting he had appealed to a conference of employers and trade union representatives, asking that industry employ ex-service men. "Men who were idle", Horne told the conference, "were always thinking of their troubles and were a source of unrest to the community." Behind Horne's appeal and his later hospitality lay a concern not with the plight of unemployed ex-service men, but with the grave problem of social and political order.[38]

Unemployment was leading militant ex-service men into agitating among the unemployed in general and not just among ex-service men. We find the first examples of this near the end of 1919 when some branches of the NUX, such as North Kensington, began to hold meetings outside labor exchanges. The North Kensington NUX, said a spokesman, was "fighting for the cause of all unemployed, whether ex-soldiers or civilians", while a local rival, the North Kensington NFDDSS, was at the same time pressing its national executive to organize not just ex-service men but all the unemployed. At the end of its life, Mander was to claim that the NUX had "introduced a new Labour force to politics." Insofar as the NUX anticipates the NUWM, Mander was correct. As the NUWM was often to prove a force in local politics, so too did the NUX prove an important source of electoral strength in the 1919 municipal elections. Similarly to the NUWM, the NUX—albeit on a minor scale—actively assisted striking workers. The NUX foreshadowed a major area of the NUWM's work in its development of legal case work—the fighting of the individual cases upon problems encountered with unemployment donation, pensions, housing, and training. Most importantly, the NUX, along with the IUX, pioneered some forms of street politics that were later to be associated with the NUWM. During the autumn of 1919 unemployed ex-service men began to fight evictions (later a favorite NUWM tactic) in a manner sufficiently widespread that by November 1919 the Minister of Health, Christopher Addison, felt driven to warn the cabinet of the mounting "social unrest" caused by evictions, and "the possibilities of serious disorder consequent on such evictions." He recommended a softening of existing legislation in favor of the tenant to try to defuse the situation.[39]

The first major organized protest of unemployed ex-service men since the summer of 1919 came on 1 March 1920. A large procession of unemployed ex-service men tried to march on Downing Street, but were dispersed at Westminster Bridge by a violent police baton charge. This was merely the continuation of the government's policy of physical repression, but this time it excited something of a backlash among the ex-service men. On 18 April 1920 a large demonstration of ex-service men, variously estimated at between 10,000 and 50,000 people, took place at Hyde Park, and, as well as the more usual resolutions concerning unemployment, pensions, and gratuities, passed a resolution calling for an enquiry into the action of the police on 1 March. A more aggressive response with longer term implications came in the growing support within the NUX and the IUX for a policy of physical force. In the wake of the Downing Street march, one NUX leader, Frank Gilden, wrote to the *Woolwich Pioneer* that ex-service men "would be justified in taking such means to protect themselves as they thought necessary." The idea of physical force came to mean more than protection and became associated with the idea of forming a red army in Britain in which the ex-service men would act as a nucleus. The importance of physical force had been minimalized by the wartime shop stewards, who believed that revolution could be achieved, and physical force thus made superfluous, through effective industrial organization. The re-emergence of physical force as a revolutionary tactic shows how because of ex-service men's experience of unemployment revolutionary thinking was rapidly and dramatically altering during 1919-1920.[40]

After the Downing Street march the idea of forming a red army, first called for in November 1919 by Jack Leckie, secretary of the Clyde Defence Committee and later an unemployed leader, began to catch on. At the NUX's first national conference in April 1920, a Glasgow delegate urged that the union "should adopt the same methods as the Sinn Feiners in Ireland to show the Government that it meant business". Though this was not adopted as official policy, many ex-service men clearly were sympathetic to the notion of physical struggle. Some branches of the NUX began considering the formation of Red Army sections. The Paddington NUX agreed that its members "should be placed at the disposal of Labour for the purpose of forming a local Soldiers Council or section of the Red Army." Eden Paul, a socialist propagandist, addressing a meeting of unemployed ex-service men in Trafalgar Square on 25 July 1920, described "the new Communist Party as the spearhead of the revolution and the International Union [of ex-service men] as the nucleus of the Red Army which would safeguard the revolution." IUX leaders began to see the formation of a Red Army as their primary aim. "We will form a Red Army in England and fight the capitalists", John Steele, a London IUX leader, secretary of the Hyde Park CPGB, and later to be an NUWCM activist, told a meeting in Hyde Park in August 1920, adding, "Before very long we will have the 'Red' Flag flying over the constitution." For this "insulting language" Steele was imprisoned.[41]

Groups of unemployed ex-service men began to regard themselves as Red Army units. In the summer of 1920 600 unemployed ex-service men in Leicester took to forming up regularly in the market place and then marching under the orders of ex-noncommissioned officers to the offices of the Distress Committee and the Labour Exchange. They were regarded as "a section of the Red Army", and by the end of September 1920 were reported to be "in a very ugly mood and almost out of hand." The idea of unemployed ex-service men forming the basis of a British Red Army reverberates through the politics of the unemployed in the 1920s and 1930s, and was especially potent during the marches. "We are only the nucleus of the red army", Tom Dingley, a former NUX member and NUWCM leader, was to tell the 1922 hunger marchers. John Supple had been unemployed for two years when he set out on the 1927 Welsh miners' hunger march on London. He died on the way, leaving a widow and seven children. In his last letter to his wife he wrote: "Dont worry about me. Think of me as a soldier in the Workers' Army. Remember that I have marched for you and others in want." Many unemployed marchers similarly saw their role as being that of soldiers in the class war, and this as being in stark contrast to their role as soldiers in World War I. "I can assure you", wrote Len Jackson to Lewis Jones after the 1936 hunger march, "that I am far Prouder of the fifteen (15) [*sic*] days I spent in the March to London on behalf of Trade Unionism and the Unemployed than I am of the four and a half years I spent in the War as a Soldier fighting for my Country but now I realise and have for a long time it was for the Capitalist Class and not for the people." Far from being idle rhetoric this was deeply held conviction. That many active in the politics of the unemployed saw themselves as soldiers of the working class is undeniable, and this conviction found concrete and courageous expression during the Spanish Civil War. Out of the 2,000 British who volunteered to fight against Fascism in Spain in the International Brigade, over 500 were members of the NUWM.[42]

During 1920 syndicalist ideas of direct action began to be taken up by some ex-service men's groups, most notably by the British IUX. A man named G. Gilmore, who seems to have been influenced by Sylvia Pankhurst and her ultra-left Workers' Socialist Federation (WSF), formed a branch of the IUX in Bristol during December 1919. Unlike other ex-service men's organizations, including the rest of the IUX, the Bristol IUX had civilians for one-half of its executive and ex-service men for the other half, arguing that this was "a very advanced policy" because it made for an organization that combined "the function of a Trade Union with that of an ex-service Men's movement." Such a policy, claimed the Bristol IUX, "means power and that is the primary essential required at the moment."[43]

Such sentiments proved popular. By early June 1920 the Bristol IUX had 1,500 members, had opened up a second branch that had 200 members, and sold 150 *Workers* every week. The methods of the Bristol IUX were those of direct action. When an ex-service man was arrested, a bomb was thrown in protest at the prison gates. The windows of the Bristol labor exchange were smashed; and an empty house was seized and a war widow and her two children installed in it. When an ex-service man and his family were evicted, the IUX sent a party to deal directly with the landlord. "Damage done to the property of other oppressive landlords had taught the authorities what to expect, and 70 policemen were on guard to protect the landlord." In "an impulse of fury" IUX members smashed up trams upon which women were working as conductors, a job that, prior to World War I, had been an exclusively male province. In July 1920 the Bristol IUX decided to stage a march to London with the object of raising people's political awareness, and of getting in touch with "like elements" in the capital. There was a slightly lunatic panache about most things the Bristol IUX did, and their march was to be no exception. They tramped the 120 miles to London headed by a barrel organ. There was little organization, and the twenty-five marchers slept in the fields at night. They marched into Trafalgar Square on 25 July 1920, still with the barrel organ leading and, one presumes, playing, to be welcomed by a thousand-strong demonstration organized by the Communist Party (British Section of the Third International) (CP(BSTI)). A few days later a deputation of the marchers met with the Minister of Labour, Dr. T. J. Macnamara, and some officials to whom they presented their demands, the chief of which were for the absorption of all unemployed persons in industry and the removal of Winston Churchill from the cabinet on account of his militaristic propensities.[44]

The IUX had been trying to organize in London since late 1919, but only after the arrival of the Bristol marchers did its efforts meet with success. It began to make an impression not in the East End where it had previously concentrated its efforts, but in west London, which, as we have seen, already had some record as a place of radical activity by unemployed ex-service men, and where the IUX was able to gather support upon the issue of unemployment. On 27 July 1920 the IUX held the first of many meetings of unemployed ex-service men outside the Shepherds Bush labor exchange, and soon the Shepherds Bush ex-service men took to marching to other labor exchanges, or visiting the mayor of Hammersmith, who on 10 August 1920 was solemnly warned that if the government failed to give every ex-service man unemployment benefit by the end of the week, "we shall agitate upon every field of social activity with a view to bringing about a social revolution." It comes as no surprise to discover that R. James, who along with Wilfred Lyle organized the IUX in London, had been expelled from his post as full time organizer for the NFDDSS for advocating direct action. By mid-September 1920 the IUX had established a small but active presence in west London with branches at Shepherds Bush, North Kensington, Acton, West Chiswick, and at Waltham Green in the north of the city. Branches later opened up in the northwest of the city at Willesden and Harlesden.[45]

The IUX also began to organize unemployed ex-service men over the issue of unemployment in Dundee during August 1920. Only in Glasgow did the IUX fail to mobilize ex-service men over unemployment, and in consequence the Glasgow IUX was inactive and ineffectual. The IUX leaders, themselves Glaswegian, came to despair of the organization in their own city. "When are the Glasgow boys going to adopt Direct Action?" asked Cox in August 1920: "Glasgow is supposed to be the home of revolution, but in my opinion it is only the home of resolution." It is significant that unemployed ex-service men only became prominent in Glasgow's politics from late October 1920 after John Maclean began to organize them over unemployment.[46]

A second attempt to unite the IUX and the NUX in late 1919 came to nothing, the similarities between the two bodies still far less than the sectarian differences that divided them. These remained sufficiently clearcut in April 1920 for the IUX to declare that the difference between the NUX and itself was "the old question of Reform or Revolution". The NUX was at that time still close enough to the Labour Party for its delegation to the socialist International Congress of Ex-service Men, along with the German delegation, to lead the vote successfully against proposals to establish relations with the newly established Communist International. In the swirling waters of socialist politics in 1920 this position soon altered. The NUX shifted to the far left of the Labour Party by allying itself first with the BSP, and then from its formation in August 1920, with the Communist Party of Great Britain. (CPGB).[47]

By the middle of 1920 the NUX had altered from a body that, although aligned with the Labour Party, was specifically concerned with ex-service men's grievances, to a body that had begun to take on some characteristics of a radical mass working-class movement. This was reflected not just in the continuing growth of the NUX, which by July 1920 had over 250 branches and 300,000 members, but also in its waxing pre-occupations that were far more catholic by mid-1920 than they had been a year before. A mass meeting of the NUX at Trafalgar Square on 4 July 1920 called not for the setting right of the particular problems experienced by ex-service men, but instead made a series of demands that reflected broader working-class aspirations. These included the alleviation of unemployment, housing of a high standard, nationalization of land, withdrawal of all armies of occupation, amnesty for all political and military prisoners, immediate cuts in the cost of food and clothing, the electoral enfranchising of women on the same basis as men, and the complete disarmament of all belligerent forces.[48]

More revealing and certainly more dramatic was the NUX's attempt in the summer of 1920 to organize a national rent strike with the aim of forcing the government to bring the cost of living down. The issue at hand was not a particular grumble of ex-service men but the high prices that afflicted all the working class.

The method of a rent strike was one which the NUX recognized would be fought not by ex-service men, but largely by working-class women. The NUX was both hopeful of their support, and saw them as part of the same movement and struggle to which ex-service men belonged. In the event the NUX failed to garner enough support to go ahead with the rent strike. But that it felt sufficiently confident even to contemplate a rent strike of two million families (the number it believed necessary to win) is evidence of a body that saw its role as mobilizing extra-parliamentary, extra-industrial working class forces in the fight against capitalism, that saw the rent strike as being, in its own words, "one form of attack on capitalism in which everyone can join". It could equally be seen as evidence of foolhardiness; but the NUX was in no way a foolhardy body. Through careful organization and calculated agitation it had built itself up in a little over twelve months into being the second most important ex-service men's organization in Britain. If the NUX was deluded in its hopes of a national rent strike, it probably had the good grounds of knowledge of considerable support upon which to be deluded. The very conception of a national rent strike as a method of waging class struggle remains to this day a breathtaking (and untried) proposition, and one that illustrates just how much more than an ex-service men's organization the NUX had become by the summer of 1920.[49]

Above all other things the NUX was radicalised by unemployment. Something that tells us a good deal about how the specific issue of unemployment could lead to a radical working-class position is a draft unemployment bill published by the Camberwell NUX in September 1920 in the one and only edition of its newspaper, *The Fighter*. In essence the bill called for an irreducible minimum wage for "all mental and manual workers"; equal wages for equal work for both sexes; abolition of piece work; minimum wage payments to all widows, maimed, blind, and aged people; maintenance of all hospitals by the state; the creation in every district of Workers' Committees composed of workers, widows, and maimed, blind and aged people, to assess monthly the wages of workers, and whose permission was necessary for the dischargement or engagement of any worker; nationalization and cultivation of all land; and two pounds per week for every unemployed person. Called an unemployment bill, this was in conception a radical working-class manifesto. When a deputation of ex-service men took this bill to the Minister of Labour, Macnamara, he expressed surprise: "he thought he was going to meet the usual deputation, who were only going to discuss the Ex-service Men Unemployment instead of dealing generally with it as they did." In the unemployment bill of the Camberwell NUX there are both continuities with the past of the politics of the unemployed and with the past of the ex-service men's organizations. In its attempt to resolve grave social problems through legislation it harked back to the Right to Work Bill of 1907. In its prescription of Workers' Committees are echoes of the support given to the shop stewards by the IUX. The bill also drew upon the experience of World War I when national aims had demanded the temporary elimination of unemployment, and had called for physical, mental, and emotional sacrifice from every member of the working class. "Everybody in the community", declared *The Fighter*, "has the right to live, to be fed, housed and clothed, unemployed or employed, because every person is needed at one time or another. Unemployment can be alleviated immediately".[50]

More than anything else it is this sense of a brutally fractured and dishonored social contract, when coupled to the belief, also born of World War I and bolstered by the example of Soviet Russia, that unemployment was not inevitable, that provided the dynamic for the politics of the unemployed in inter-war Britain, and that is summed up in the placard seen at the "Battle of Downing Street", a peaceful demonstration of the unemployed on 18 October 1920 that turned into a riot following an attack by the police. "Oh that bread should be so dear", read the placard, "and flesh and blood so cheap." The unemployment bill of the Camberwell NUX shows us how far the aspirations of ex-service men moved between 1918, when they had been concerned only with their own plight, and 1920. The bill embraced all the problems that engulfed the working class, and not just those that afflicted ex-service men. It is a harbinger of the remarkable events of the next two years, when the unemployed would coalesce into one distinct national body that saw itself as the cutting edge of the class struggle.[51]

Preceding the outburst of unemployed protest in late 1920 the NUX stood at the summit of its achievement. As we have seen, it was a body second in size only to the NFDDSS, but whereas the membership of the NFDDSS was declining, that of the NUX was growing. The NUX's approach to working class struggle would seem to have complemented the forthcoming unemployed protest. Yet at the moment of its greatest possibility the NUX collapsed as a national organization because of an internal financial scandal about which almost nothing is known. Although an internal committee of investigation was later to clear Ernest Mander and the NUX executive of any allegations of financial impropriety, fatal damage had been done. A national referendum of members in early October 1920 decided on a process of reconstruction of the NUX as a federation of autonomous local bodies, but this was never effected and the NUX ceased to exist as a cohesive national body. Some branches, such as in Coventry, dissolved themselves into unemployed committees, others went over to the CPGB, while in London they were to be at the forefront of the unemployed struggles in late 1920, before being swallowed up by the ubiquitous unemployed workers' committees, to whom they imparted something of their militancy and political commitment.[52]

The demise of the NUX was greeted with glee by the IUX, who saw the time as ripe for their advance. In London, particularly in the west of the city, the IUX was at its most active during October 1920. But after November 1920 nothing more is heard of it in London; and in December the IUX was, like the NUX, beset by an obscure financial crisis that spelled its doom. Early that month the IUX executive announced that it was reorganizing itself with the aim of becoming self supporting. "Too long", said the IUX executive, "have we depended on others to assist us", though precisely who the others were was never made clear. Most likely it was the SS&WCM, who had been the main prop and inspiration of the IUX through its short life. We know that the SS&WCM, inspired by the example of the Coventry

Unemployed Workers' Committee, and concerned about the independence of the Glasgow unemployed movement, was swinging around to a belief in the need for a national organization of the unemployed, the development of which rendered the existence of the IUX superfluous, and therefore an unnecessary splitting of SS&WCM's energy and effort. It seems probable that the SS&WCM decided to end its support for the ailing IUX, and instead to devote its energies to assisting the many unemployed shop stewards (such as Tom Dingley in Coventry and Wal Hannington in London) who were beginning to organize the unemployed on a different basis, though one derived from that of the ex-service men's organizations. By the end of December 1920 IUX membership had fallen below its 1919 levels to 6,000 members, and its finances were in a bad way, the organization owing £27. After December 1920 the IUX is not heard of again.[53]

There were general reasons why the socialist ex-service men's organizations disappeared that were inherent in their development from ex-service men's organizations to radical working class bodies. The IUX and the NUX had come to the fore in 1920 as a result of the peculiar and unfortunate position that a sizeable and growing group of ex-service men found themselves in: unemployed, unwanted, and finding life daily more difficult because of inflation. While a body such as the British Legion has been able to survive well over half a century by refusing to identify the cause of ex-service men with any grouping or body other than itself, the socialist ex-service men's organizations doomed themselves when they identified their cause with that of the working class. Mander had argued in May 1919 that the general interests of ex-service men were identical to that of the working class. The special interest of ex-service men upon which the IUX and the NUX had built themselves had been unemployment, and when this too became general to all the working class there was no longer a basis for the IUX and the NUX. From the moment the Camberwell NUX submerged its own problems in those of the working class so completely that it failed to mention the words "ex-service men" in their unemployment bill, the extinction of the NUX and the IUX became inevitable. When, in the autumn of 1920, the post-war boom came to an end and the depression started, the fine distinction between unemployed ex-service men and unemployed civilians blurred in the suffering experienced by all. Unemployment soared from 0.8 percent of the insured workforce in April 1920 to 11 percent nine months later (see Table 5.1). The unemployed ex-service men were no longer a distinct category, and only the tattered remnants of khaki uniforms marked them out from the many others who now came to join them on the gray dole lines.

The Meaning of the Politics of the Unemployed Ex-Service Men

It is not wrong or incorrect to say that ex-service men were radicalized by unemployment, but such a phrase fails to do justice to the full enormity of what had happened to these men in both war and peace, and avoids a good deal of the more difficult questions about their political activity. Brutalized by war—and how little these words convey of what this truly meant—they were forced to survive in a post-war world indifferent to them and their fate. The socialist ex-service men's organizations were an expression of the complex emotional experience of ex-service men, a tormented mix of alienation and isolation, of distorted bodies and shattered psyches, of broken dreams and nightmares that knew no end.

If some unemployed ex-service men, even a sizeable proportion of ex-service men, were involved in the radical activities of the NFDDSS, the NUX and the IUX, a far greater proportion were not. If I have stressed the alliances that the NUX, for example, built up with the police union, it is as well to remember that 90 percent of the men enrolled by the Liverpool Watch Committee to break the second police strike were unemployed ex-service men. The Black and Tans, infamous for their reactionary brutality in Ireland in the early 1920s, were recruited from the ranks of unemployed ex-service men. Ex-service men's anger at unemployment was often channeled not into socialist activity, but racist and sexist violence. Ex-service men played a leading role in a race riot in Cardiff in June 1919 that left fifteen people injured and two dead. There is anecdotal evidence that domestic violence was much worse in the wake of the war, one of the more remarkable pieces of which is the comment made by Sir Nevil Macready, the chief commissioner of police, how "Before the war a man was content to clip his wife under the ear and then go to the public house but now he thinks nothing of bashing her on the head." We find a revealing convergence of racism and sexism in the case in mid-1919 of unemployed ex-service men in London's dock area, who beat up some black workers who had been seen in the company of women who worked as prostitutes, whose services the ex-service men could not afford.[54]

Yet it would be wrong to propose a simple and clear line of cleavage between, on the one hand, reactionary unemployed ex-service men who scabbed on strikers, helped with murderous intent to try to crush the Irish revolution, and beat up women and blacks; and, on the other, revolutionary unemployed ex-service men who formed the radical ranks of the NFDDSS, the NUX and the IUX. Such a division would not allow us to recognize the immense day to day difficulties under which unemployed ex-service men lived, and which might lead them to take part in an unemployed demonstration one week as a protest, and the following week join the Black and Tans as an escape. Such a division, in short, does no justice to the pressures that unemployment places upon people, or to the extremes, sometimes assertive, sometimes degrading, often both, to which people are driven trying to cope with such pressures. Nor does it make allowance for the powerful and often contradictory processes of personal fragmentation experienced by so many soldiers returned from the war.

This becomes clearer if we examine the experience of just one ex-service man as he recalled it many years later:

> Ended up in the trenches in France. Wounded three times. I was back an' forward in an' out of hospital. I got a bullet in me thigh an' shrapnel in the back of the leg. . . . But after all that trouble, when we got discharged they gave us six months money at twenty-nine shillings a week. . . . I was unemployed, no jobs to do an' no money coming in. Bitter? I should say

I was. But what could you do? All you could do was look after number one; you felt you had a right to things you didn't want to have to pay for it all, so a lot of young blokes just got it whatever way they could. You was feeling revolutionary. I know I did nearly go off the deep end. Only those who went through it knows. That was when we nearly had a revolution in Bristol, smashed the tram cars up. But I don't bother with it, don't bother with politics. I joined no party, not many did. All politicians is poison, in my eyes.[55]

Within this description we find many of the contradictions of the post war revolt: an apolitical self-centeredness that is at the same time revolutionary; "feeling revolutionary" juxtaposed with "nearly going off the deep end"; the dynamic for external revolutionary activity being not the attempted resolution of external social crisis but the attempted resolution of internal individual breakdown and disintegration. At the heart of the revolutionary act, the smashing of the tram cars, is the paradoxical motive that is no motive, the soldier's imperative "to look after number one" in a man no longer a soldier. The politics of the unemployed ex-service men were not the revolutionary antithesis to the reactionary activity of other ex-service men. Rather they were the organized expression of such contradictions.

Running like a thread through the activity of unemployed ex-service men was the need to assert a masculinity proven in war but threatened by unemployment. In November 1919, William Earl walked into the Lyons Corner Tea House in Piccadilly, and proceeded to smash the tables with an axe. He was subsequently asked in court if he had known what he was doing. "Oh yes, I know what I am doing", replied Earl, "I cannot get work. I came here to show my manhood and smash the tables. I did not intend to hurt anyone, only to make them jump about." Later during the trial Earl began to shout: "Leave me alone. Give me a job. You want to, but you shan't down me. I want you to kill me. I want to die. Let me alone, and give me work." Earl wanted people to be shocked into recognizing that an unemployed worker was as much a man as an employed worker was. In many ways the politics of the unemployed ex-service men were the torment of William Earl writ large.[56]

It is far too easy to view the unemployed of the inter-war and the unemployed ex-service men of 1919-1920 as revolutionary. Rather than attacking a system that denied large sections of the working class employment, unemployed ex-service men within the radical ex-service men's organizations often chose to instead attack vulnerable elements of the working class that had the good fortune to be in employment. So it was that within the radical context of such bodies as the NFDDSS, the NUX, and the IUX, the politics of the unemployed ex-service men could at times be profoundly reactionary. We find a direct link between the experience of unemployment and the reproduction of racist and sexist attitudes in the demands made by the unemployed ex-service men of Liverpool, who were led by the NFDDSS. A deputation from a demonstration of 5,000 unemployed ex-service men on 23 April 1919 met with the deputy lord mayor and complained that women and "coloured men" were occupying jobs that were rightfully the ex-service men's. Two months later the Liverpool ex-service men were demanding that if the "coloured men" who were employed in warehouses could not be deported, they ought to be segregated to make sure, as an NFDDSS official put it, "they would not be able to mix with whites".[57]

The group who came under most attack from unemployed ex-service men were working-class women. As unemployment among ex-service men grew, so did the crescendo rise for the removal of women from jobs that, as one ex-service men's paper put it, "morally belong to men". At the NFDDSS mass meeting on unemployment held at Hyde Park in May 1919, the chief steward, B. Baldwin, told the ex-service men that the government had failed in its duty to them. "Thousands of 'flappers' were employed in Government offices," he told the meeting, "but discharged and demobilised soldiers could not get work". His words fell upon a receptive audience: any woman driver passing the demonstration was met with cries of "Pull her off". By midsummer 1919 resolutions by ex-service men's organizations calling for the termination of women's employment wherever possible were becoming commonplace. Such antipathy toward women was, by 1920, often taking on a threatening, and on occasions, violent aspect. We have already seen how the Bristol IUX smashed up tram cars upon which women worked as conductors. In a similarly threatening fashion large numbers of unemployed ex-service men in Reading in August 1920 took to marching through the streets to leading factories and business houses demanding the sacking of women and girls so that work might be found for ex-service men. Earlier that same month a procession of several hundred ex-service men in Liverpool sounded an ominous threat when they told the Liverpool Brewers' Association that if 2,000 barmaids engaged by them were not replaced by ex-service men, steps would be taken to remove the barmaids.[58]

Under intense economic and social pressure unemployed ex-service men did not always attack capitalism and its bourgeois supporters. Rather than viewing their problem as being part of the general oppression of their class, they often engaged in attacks upon vulnerable sections of their own class, succumbing to the myths of racism and sexism as partial explanations of their plight, and as criteria for which parts of the working class were attacked, and which were not. Such attitudes did not necessarily exist in isolation and opposition to revolutionary sentiments but in tandem with them. They led to the violent misogynism and the distorted assertions of manhood that made the protest of the unemployed ex-service men take upon forms that were essentially masculine and hence exclusive. While to some extent the NUX and the IUX had by mid-1920 begun to transcend such masculine forms, most notably in the NUX's attempt to organize a nationwide protest of women with the rent strike, they were never to disappear, and remained a strong strand in the later history of the unemployed. In this, and in so many other ways the politics of the unemployed ex-service men illuminates the dusky recesses of the origins of the NUWM. In concerns, theory, practice, militant tone and membership, the radical ex-service men's organizations were the harbinger of the NUWM; equally, and because of this, they also anticipated the darker side of the NUWM and its failings.

None of this should lead us into dismissing the politics of the unemployed ex-service men as reactionary, but rather to an awareness of the complexity of its contradictory aspects. In October 1920 the shop steward David Ramsay wrote despairingly of the politics of the unemployed: "Bluster and pleading, heroics and weakness, patriotism and contempt of country, respect for law and suggestions of revolt-all these follow one another in the course of a single speech delivered by a hungry man suffering from conditions inseparable from capitalism." Yet it was precisely from this tension between the reactionary and the revolutionary that the politics of the unemployed ex-service men gained its volatile, unstable, and threatening nature in a society over which the ruling class was trying to establish new forms of control and discipline. It was the unemployed ex-service men who first declared that no stable social compact could be forged while mass unemployment remained. "We realise that it is in the interests of the capitalist class to keep a certain amount of surplus labour, in order to break strikes and keep down wages", the IUX was to resolve at its congress in February 1920, adding, echoing the Camberwell NUX: "We do not desire that ex-service men should be pitted against the worker. All men and women should have the right to live, and as long as the question of unemployment is unsolved, there can be no peace." While it was to be the NUWM who would honor this vow, we do well to remember that it was the unemployed ex-service men who first made it.[59]

5

One Big Union? The National Unemployed Workers' Committee Movement, 1920–1929

I am a Communist, yes, and proud of it. I am a Communist, not because I like being one. Conditions have made me a rebel. Conditions are rotten. Out of rotten conditions you get dissatisfied persons. . . . I have been thrown up.

—*George Garrett, Liverpool unemployed leader, to 1922 hunger marchers, Trafalgar Square, 19 Nov. 1922*

We call you to the Colours to fight against these things, and it is not merely a fight for 36 shillings a week, for the national demands. In my estimation it is a fight for the workshops and the factories, for the land, for those things that go to make life worth living. That is the fight, the greatest fight. No matter how many doles you get, so long as Capitalism remains in existence, so long as a small class owns and controls everything, you will always be slaves. Rally to the red banner of international freedom. Gird on the armour and victory will be yours.

—*Gordon Currie, Dumfries unemployed leader, to 1922 hunger marchers, Trafalgar Square, 19 Nov. 1922.*[1]

In the autumn of 1920 the post-war boom came to an end and an economic slump unparalleled in British history began. By 1921 over one million were unemployed, and there was never to be less than this number unemployed until World War II. While the 1920s are not normally associated with heavy unemployment, it can be seen from Table 5.1 that unemployment remained at a high level throughout the 1920s, steadying at a constant hopelessness of about one in ten always being out of work.

The old staple industries—coal, shipbuilding, iron and steel, engineering, and textiles—were to be the worst hit and never to recover their previously dominant position in the British economy. While the slump was national in effect the concentration of the staple industries in certain regions, and the almost total reliance

Table 5.1. *Unemployment, 1920-1929*
Percentage of insured workers registered as unemployed, Jan. 1920-Dec. 1929.

	1920	1921	1922	1923	1924	1925	1926	1927	1928	1929
Jan	2.0	11.0	17.7	13.3	11.9	11.2	11.1	12.1	10.7	12.2
Feb	1.2	12.9	17.1	12.4	10.6	11.3	10.5	10.9	10.4	12.1
Mar	0.9	15.0	16.0	11.7	9.8	11.1	9.8	9.9	9.5	10.1
Apr	0.8	19.9	15.9	11.5	9.7	10.9	9.2	9.4	9.5	9.8
May	0.9	23.0	14.6	11.2	9.4	10.9	14.5	8.8	9.8	9.7
Jun	1.0	21.9	13.7	11.3	9.3	10.9	14.7	8.9	10.7	9.6
Jul	1.2	17.4	13.1	11.6	9.8	11.2	14.6	9.3	11.6	9.7
Aug	1.3	15.1	12.8	11.8	10.5	12.1	14.2	9.4	11.6	9.9
Sept	1.9	13.9	12.7	11.7	10.6	12.0	13.9	9.4	11.4	9.9
Oct	4.1	14.3	12.6	11.7	10.9	11.4	13.6	9.5	11.8	10.3
Nov	3.3	16.9	13.0	11.5	10.8	11.0	13.5	10.0	12.2	10.9
Dec	5.6	17.7	12.8	10.6	10.7	10.5	11.9	9.8	11.2	11.0

Sources: Henry Clay, *The Post-War Unemployment Problem* (1929), p. 34; B. B. Gilbert, *British Social Policy, 1914-1939* (1979), pp. 314-316.

Table 5.2. *Regional Unemployment, 1912-1936*
Percentage rates of unemployment by region, 1912-1936.

	1912-1913	1922	1929	1932	1936
London	8.7	13	4.7	13.1	6.5
South-East	4.7	12	3.8	13.1	5.6
South-West	4.6	15	6.8	16.4	7.8
Midlands	2.8	18	9.5	21.6	9.4
North-East	2.5	18	12.6	30.6	16.6
North-West	2.7	16	12.7	26.3	16.2
Scotland	1.8	21	18.8	38.1	28.5
Wales	3.1	12	18.8	38.1	28.5
Britain	3.9	15.2	9.7	22.9	12.6

Notes : Percentages are for July of each year, with the exception of 1922, which is for August. The figures for 1912-1913 are averaged out.
Sources: D. H. Aldcroft, *The Inter War Economy: Britain 1919-1939* (1970) p. 80; J. J. Astor et al,*The Third Winter of Unemployment* (1923), p. 16.

of these regions upon those staple industries, meant that some areas were to be devastated by unemployment in a manner not experienced in other parts of Britain. For example, in Glasgow in June 1922, where 19.7 percent of the workforce was registered as unemployed, over 50 percent of the unemployed (44,805 out of 85,244 unemployed) were from the shipbuilding and engineering industries. In the same month out of 392,000 unemployed nationally in the engineering industry, 102,000 came from the northeast, where they accounted for nearly half of the area's total unemployment. These tendencies grew more pronounced as the years passed. Of the 44.5 percent insured unemployed in the eastern area of south Wales in 1934, over 20 percent had been unemployed for over four years and they tended to be concentrated in areas officially termed derelict: Blaina with 71.4 percent unemployment, Brynmawr with 72.5 percent, and Merthyr Tydfil with 67.6 percent.[2]

As Table 5.2 shows the geographical pattern of unemployment was reversed in the inter-war period. Whereas before 1914 unemployment had tended to be short term, at its worst during cyclical troughs in London, the Midlands, and the south, from 1920 onwards the new phenomenon of long-term, heavy, structural unemployment persisting through all stages of the trade cycle emerged in the traditional industrial areas, particularly in industrial Scotland, the north, and south Wales. In the south, the Midlands, and London, the new industries—automobiles, electrical goods, and chemicals—emerged as major new sources of employment, and were responsible for these areas' relative prosperity. It was not to be the disparate assortment that was the metropolitan working class, but the traditional industrial proletariat, with its high degree of community solidarity, homogeneity of outlook, and a history of class-conscious activity, that was to be the group who bore the brunt of unemployment in this period, and who accordingly was to shape the politics of the unemployed in this era. Leavening this mass was a small but highly committed and gifted group of Marxist activists whose strongholds were these very same working-class communities of the old industrial regions. Befittingly it was the denuded pit village, the quiet mill town, and the smokeless heavy industrial city, that were to provide both the physical and social basis of the politics of the unemployed during the inter-war period.

In both the old industries as they reorganized under the rubric of "rationalization", and in the new expanding industries, the emphasis was upon the new mass modes of production reliant upon large numbers of semi- and unskilled workers, but with as little need for the skilled craftsman—the labor aristocrat—as was possible. "The wider skill associated with the older forms of craftsmen is therefore not only required but becomes a positive disadvantage if it finds its way in the form of false values into the cost of the finished product", Sir James Lithglow, owner of one of the largest shipbuilding companies in Britain, told the Institute of Welding in his presidential address in February 1939. "Opportunity should be taken to fix the type of operator and the scale of pay appropiate to the particular job, without reference to the peculiarities of the job which is displaced." If the politics of the unemployed in the interwar played in the theater of mass joblessness, we should not forget that the backdrop to the action was rationalization and all that this implied. "We are the Red Front", sang the Workers' Theatre in 1932, the black heart of the depression,

The Workers' Red Front
We show you how you're robbed and bled . . .
Speed up and wage cuts
And unemployment
Have brought starvation to our door.
With stage and film show
They're always striving
To hide from you the real class war.[3]

In coal mining, for example, virtually no coal was cut by machine prior to 1914, but by 1927, 58.5 million tons were being cut mechanically and by 1939, 142 million tons. What this meant to those who worked in the mines is well conveyed in the miner Harold Heslop's 1935 novel *Last Cage Down*, in which a coal hewer rues how he has been "reduced from the proud eminence of the skilled craftsman of the pick to a mere shoveller of coal. Any chap from London could do the same! . . . The mine had been Fordized. They were turning out coal like they were turning out cars, and almost as cheaply. Wages were falling, and production was increasing." Many craftsmen found themselves and their skills as obsolete as Edwardian horse drawn hackney carriages, and as little in demand. They were the victims not simply of capitalism, but of a particular historical moment of capitalism, as it emerged sated and enervated from the war, set to embark upon its new stage of monopoly capitalism, with increasingly concentrated ownership of the means of production, the final triumph of unskilled forms of mass production (in which workers had no control) over the last vestiges of handicraft forms of production (in which workers had some control), and the explosive growth of an impoverished proletariat. The politics of the unemployed in the inter-war period was, as much as anything else, a protest by such men against the fundamental changes taking place in the forms of capitalist production: "you will understand", wrote Arthur Horner, an unemployed coal miner and NUWM leader during the 1930s, "how bitterly we felt about the skill of our people being ignored and wasted."[4]

It is then less than surprising that the official labor movement came to occupy a generally antipathetic position toward the politics of the unemployed. For while the unemployed were in a sense in revolt against this new era of capitalism, the official labor movement, in the form of two conservative Labour governments and such decisive acts by the TUC as the Mond/Turner talks, was seeking to accommodate itself to this new era, to become, as Walter Citrine, general secretary of the TUC put it in 1927, "an integral part of the economic machinery of society". Electorally the Labour Party's primary objective was to win and hold the support of the Liberal working-class vote, and thus it stayed in the center through the 1920s, and was unwilling to adopt any radical program that might seriously combat unemployment. But the failure of the Labour Party to grapple fundamentally with the problem of unemployment cannot be attributed only to its quest for electoral legitimacy. Its slogan remained the late nineteenth-century one of work or maintenance, but by this it meant something much narrower than did the NUWM. Labour's policy was essentially dictated not by the ILP socialists, nor even by its much vilified leaders such as MacDonald or Snowden, but by the big conservative trade unions. Their failure to provide leadership upon the issue of unemployment was dictated at first by their belief that unemployment was simply part of post-war dislocation that would in time rectify itself, and later, when this was shown to be wrong, by their belief that unemployment could not be solved. They wanted the existing unemployment insurance system maintained not so much to help the unemployed as to maintain wage levels and preserve union power. Their primary concern remained for those in work, not for those out of it. Work or maintenance was for them a defensive tool to help preserve their status, whereas for the NUWM it was an offensive weapon, to be used in the opening battles of the class war. While the unions were therefore happy enough to watch the 1929-31 Labour government do little to attack unemployment, they were not prepared to support it when it succumbed to the demand of finance and industry and proposed the 10 percent cut in unemployment benefit. Although the Labour Party did support the notion of some work schemes and other ways of dealing with unemployment, it never had a policy for large-scale work creation. The Labour Party continued to make considerable mileage out of the issue of unemployment, but it was never actually committed to a full employment policy, and was never interested in the radical solutions to the problem proposed by its own left.[5]

As the politics of the unemployed had been aligned with the SDF prior to the war, so they now became aligned with the CPGB. But its politics were never reducible to or identical with those of the CPGB. With the creation of its own national organization, the NUWCM, the politics of the unemployed came to be the expression of other revolutionary and radical currents within the working class, which the CPGB, with its Bolshevik structure and ideology, was both unable and unwilling to give tongue to. While the CPGB was by and large to provide the leadership of the inter-war unemployed movement, the politics of the unemployed in this period continued often to be spontaneous, rarely disciplined, and almost impossible to subjugate to the whims of democratic centralism. In many ways it represented the continuation of older forms of radical working-class politics reliant upon mass consent and involvement, and this meant that it was often anathema to the CPGB. This was particularly the case in the early 1920s, when the NUWCM was to be an anarcho-syndicalist body standing in almost heretical contrast to the CPGB. Later, in the 1930s, the NUWM (as the NUWCM styled itself from 1929) was to follow its own star rather than toe the party line, to the extent that after 1935 it was to be such an embarrassment to the party that they attempted to liquidate it. The conflict between the politics of the unemployed and the official labor movement during the inter-war period cannot be reduced to the entirely different although related issue of the growing institutionalization of the differences between social democratic and communist politics then occurring on a worldwide scale. Given their fundamentally different approaches and responses to the changing forms of capitalism, conflict between the politics of the unemployed and the official labor movement was inevitable and was to lead to the formation, for the first time in history, of a national unemployed movement.

The labor aristocrats, who had been so conspicuously absent from the politics of the unemployed prior to the war, now were to emerge as the leaders of this national movement. Jack Williams, casual dock laborer and sometime house painter, and the appropriately titled "Docker" Waites, were to be replaced by the likes of Wal Hannington, a center lathe operator, and Harry MacShane, an engineer. These were people used to strong union organization; in consequence the inter-war unemployed movement, unlike its predecessors, was conceived of and run as something like a union, with some of trade unions' strengths and weaknesses, with radical trade unionist dreams of one big union, and with a reactionary disinterest in the participation of women. The labor movement's rejection of the NUWM as anti-labor particularly rankled with the NUWM's labor aristocratic leadership who in some ways had very traditional trade union values: toward the end of his life Hannington wrote with pride of how the NUWM had stood up and fought "for real trade union principles". Unlike the old SDF and ILP agitators who had been agitators first and foremost, the typical post-war unemployed agitator tended to be a trade unionist first, and an unemployed agitator only second. From the time the London District Council of Unemployed Organisations called for funds in 1921 "to build an unemployed movement such as this country has never seen before", its aim to work with "organised labour" to "abolish the curse of unemployment once and for all", the unfulfilled hope of the inter-war unemployed movement was to work within the labor movement to fight unemployment.[6]

The new social basis of the politics of the unemployed gave it certain organizational strengths, but it also contained weaknesses. The unemployed were not only socially isolated; they were also in the inter-war period to be geographically segregrated, and their plight was never to be the passionate concern of the ruling class that it had been in Victorian and Edwardian London, when the unemployed had routinely paraded under the very noses of their rulers. Nor was it to be of overriding interest to those who worked in the prosperous areas. The condition of those in the working class who remained in steady employment on the whole improved in this era. Despite regional fluctuations, and cuts in some industries in the early 1920s and 1930s, nominal wages remained steady, while retail prices fell 15 percent between 1923 and 1937. The political tone of the era for those with work was set not by the labor movement, but by the Conservative Party, who had replaced the Liberals as the predominant party of British capital, and who dominated the inter-war era electorally. Their identification, particularly under Baldwin, with a mythical traditional Englishness, hid the extent to which they had moved from a traditional laissez-faire position, and were to oversee the growing and increasingly close relationship between state and industry. Even if the hostility of the labor movement toward the unemployed movement had not existed, this prosperity, when allied to the conservatism of the era and combined with the geographical isolation of the majority out of work from the majority in work, mitigated against the alliance of unemployed and employed against unemployment that the unemployed militants dreamt of. Compounding all these difficulties was the attitude of many of the artisans of the old industries themselves, who did not consider unemployment to be for them a normal state, in the way that many of the London casual poor prior to the war had done. Many artisans had at best a lukewarm commitment to an organization whose basic premise was that their plight was permanent and structural; to join the NUWCM or later the NUWM could seem an admission of failure to find work, and therefore an abandonment of status. "It is not easy", wrote Aneurin Bevan (who was himself an NUWCM activist in the early 1920s prior to his distinguished parliamentary career) of the NUWM in 1936, "to give organisational expression to circumstances from which men are trying desperately to escape."[7]

The Origins and Formation of a National Unemployed Movement

"It must be remembered in the event of rioting," the Director of Intelligence warned the cabinet on 2 September 1920, "for the first time in history the rioters will be better trained than the police". Who were the rioters likely to be? Primarily they would be ex-service men who had known some employment immediately after the war and were now unemployed. By mid-October 1920 there were 187,000 such unemployed ex-service men, the greater part of whom were between twenty-five and thirty years of age and who were mostly unskilled laborers. Their experience mirrored the changes then taking place in the processes of production. The war had seen the acceleration of mass production techniques, the widespread introduction of the scientific management of labor, and a general replacement of skilled labor with more sophisticated machinery tended by semi- or unskilled operatives, processes that led to the deskilling of sections of the workforce. Many unemployed ex-service men had not always been unskilled laborers, but had experienced such deskilling. Government enquiries into the status of unemployed ex-service men in London and Bristol "showed a similar marked tendency to change from skilled to unskilled work".[8]

But the rioters were not all to be unemployed ex-service men, as Basil Thomson, Director of Intelligence, knew only too well. He informed the cabinet on 23 September 1920 that in addition to the growing unrest among unemployed ex-service men, "revolutionary feeling" was rapidly "growing in all parts of the country among the younger workmen." Some of these younger workmen had been politicized through their active involvement with the Shop Stewards' and Workers' Committee Movement (SS&WCM). The history of the SS&WCM has been traced elsewhere, and we need only to observe that above all else the shop stewards believed in the supremacy of industrial action as the key to the revolution. Power lay in control of production, and they believed that this could be secured through effective workplace organization. Within Glasgow, the heart of the shop stewards' movement, the efficacy and importance of non-industrial struggle in the working-class fight had been demonstrated by the successful women's rent strike of 1915, but although the shop stewards' movement was associated with this, it was slow to pick up on the lesson that the rent strike provided. While the shop stewards were concerned about such issues as unemployment they felt they could even fight for such non-industrial issues industrially—a line of thinking that reached one end point in the famous and now almost mythical 40 hours strike in Glasgow in January 1919, which, as the manifesto of the joint strike committee made clear, had been initiated over the issue of unemployment.[9]

Under the influence of the Russian example the shop stewards' ideas about revolutionary struggle began to broaden beyond a sole concern with industrial organization. In November 1919, inspired by the idea of soviets, the Scottish Workers' Committee called for the development of "social organisation" in the form of "social committees" to complement strike organization. The aim of the social committees, however, was narrow and remained subordinate to the industrial struggle, existing only to ensure the control of food and fuel during a revolutionary crisis. By early 1920 the SS&WCM was finished as an industrial force with nearly all of its national administrative council out of work due to victimization sackings, but it did not immediately ossify in its thought, and began to develop ideas about enlarging the scope of the class struggle. At its national conference on 10-11 January 1920 the SS&WCM agreed to allow ex-service men's organizations to affiliate with workers' committees, indicating for the first time a willingness to look beyond the factory gate. This line of thought was taken a great deal further when SS&WCM delegates to the Rank and File Convention met again at the International Socialist Club on 12 March 1920. The delegates agreed that the workers' committees who organized the workers "Industrially where they work" needed to be "supplemented by the organisation of revolutionists *Socially where they live*"in anticipation of, and as preparation, for revolution. The aim of these social organizations was to be much more than ensuring the control of food and fuel supplies, as they were now also expected to "propagate the Soviet idea" and most importantly, "to provide a field not only for the activities of revolutionary *industrial* workers, but also of revolutionists who for one reason or another cannot directly share in the industrial struggle." This applied both to women and to the unemployed. This new unit of social organization was to be called the "social soviet", and the ever-faithful IUX proudly announced that it had "taken the lead in forming Social Soviets in London." The increasing concern of the shop stewards with organizing the non-industrial sections of the working class, and the politics of the unemployed ex-service men were to come together in a dramatic fashion at Coventry in September 1920. There a new politics of the unemployed, which differed radically in tactics, organization, and aspirations from the politics of the unemployed prior to 1914, was to be forged.[10]

Coventry was from the outset badly affected by the slump. Between July 1920 and July 1921 unemployment in the city ballooned out from 1,535 to 12,534. In late September 1920 the Conventry NUX came together with the remnants of the shop stewards' movement in the city to organize the unemployed. At a mass meeting of the unemployed the Coventry Unemployed Workers' Committee (CUWC) was formed. Also known as the Coventry Soviet, it ran on what it termed "Soviet principles", electing a committee of ten of whom three were ex-service men. This committee was bound to immediate recall and to act only as directed by mass meetings. The CUWC was distinguished from pre-war unemployed bodies not only in being run by the unemployed themselves, but in its shop steward-influenced ideology and tactics. Over the autumn the CUWC became a formidable presence on the Coventry streets. It staged large unemployed demonstrations almost daily, outside and sometimes inside factories and workshops "to make those at work realise . . . that a solution could be found only in the workers themselves producing for use and not for profit."[11]

The leader of the CUWC was Harry Emery, engineer, shop steward, leader of the Manx national strike of 1918, and former SLP member now associated with the ultra left of the British revolutionary movement, the CP(BSTI), which he represented as a delegate to the CPGB unity convention at Leeds in late January 1921. For Emery, the former shop steward, unemployment offered a crucible in which craft sectionalism, the bugbear of the shop stewards' movement, could be melted down and forged anew into a true working class solidarity. It emphasized, he wrote, "the essential need for the workers to organise and unite as a class, and not sectionally as skilled, semi-skilled and unskilled . . . by organising on Industrial Union lines". To help the worker become fully class conscious, the CUWC encouraged the unemployed to seek out relief as a method of breaking down the hegemonic hold that bourgeois notions of respectability had upon the worker. This task was undertaken, wrote Emery, "knowing full well that once you have got the worker, especially the skilled worker, to break through his bourgeois pride you have gone a long way in freeing him from bourgeois concepts altogether, and also have allowed him to see his class position and unite with the unskilled as workers."[12]

The CUWC was a far more radical body than the London organization of the unemployed that was to arise over the next few months. Unlike their London counterparts the CUWC refused to organize relief for the unemployed or to accept any funds for any purpose other than propaganda. In part this reflected the underlying tension between the ultra-left and the CPGB, the latter being to the fore in organizing the London unemployed. Fred Tyler, in a contemporary review of Emery's pamphlet "The Coming Revolution in Britain", argued that there were two schools of revolutionary thought, that of "the BSP Communists, who want a quick route to government (revolution), [which] would probably lead to the indefinite subjection of the workers to the authority of Communist politicians", while the school "represented by Comrade Emery, [believe in] the temporary necessity of the machinery of the state to aid in the defeat of the counter revolution." Emery was in any case contemptuous of the activity of the London unemployed, and wrote in early 1921, "I venture to assert that our tactics are more revolutionary, more dangerous to Capitalism than those of committees who go about bragging that they are armed and urging their fellow workers to seize a library."[13]

The significance of the near daily mobilization of thousands on the streets of Coventry over the issue of unemployment was not lost upon British revolutionaries. It was evident that there was a great divide between the pre-war politics of the unemployed and the activities of the CUWC. "The old features of pre-war unemployed demonstrations are entirely absent from these manifestations", observed the CPGB's newspaper *The Communist* of the events in Coventry. "Here is no cringing body of half starved men, begging for bread, or, on the other hand, a crowd of potential rioters out for loot. It is an ordered demonstration by intelligent organised workers that they will not starve at the behest of capitalism." It was not to be the youthful CPGB, still more intent on consolidating its embryonic organization than anything else, but the shop stewards who took the initiative in organizing the unemployed. *Solidarity*, the journal of the SS&WCM, called on revolutionaries to "Set up a Committee from amongst the unemployed, and follow the lead of the Coventry workers". David Ramsay, a shop stewards' leader, now called upon the shop stewards to organize the unemployed. He wrote of how the shop stewards in the past had "confined all organisational work to the inside of the factories. It has only catered for the men and women who are in work, and no serious attempt has been made to maintain contact and influence with those who are temporarily on the scrap heap. This has got to be rectified at once." Ramsay's strategy still rested ultimately upon taking industrial action over the issue of unemployment, with the unemployed playing a supporting role. Those in work, with the help of those out of work, were to condemn and combat overtime, piecework, and bonus systems as products of unemployment. If laid off, wrote Ramsay, workers should "refuse to leave the works, open their gates to the unemployed, and be prepared to defend their position against 'law and order.' " Ex-service men were to be prepared to use their military experience "on behalf of their class interests". One month later, on 29 November 1920, the Central London Council of Shop Stewards issued a manifesto in which it announced its intention to create a London-wide unemployed movement "to work in conjunction with the shop stewards in the workshops for the purpose of preparing to take control of industry for the benefit of the working class."[14] But events had overtaken the shop stewards not only in Coventry but in Glasgow and London.

John MacLean, who had been an unemployed leader in 1908 and who became a revolutionary famed throughout Europe during the war, had begun to organize the Glasgow unemployed in conjunction with the IUX in early October 1920. As well as being a Marxist MacLean was a Scottish nationalist, and he argued for the revolutionary establishment of a Scottish Workers' Republic independent of England. Accordingly (and also because of his suspicions of the reformist tendencies of the CPGB) MacLean was at the same time attempting to build a Scottish Communist Party independent of the CPGB, using the SLP as its organizational framework, and the Glasgow unemployed as its shock troops. MacLean's prestige and considerable following meant that his plans represented a threat to the attempt then being made by the CPGB, formed only a few months earlier in August 1920, to establish a hegemonic hold over all revolutionary activity in Britain. The battle was fought over the body of the Glasgow unemployed. Attempts to split the Glasgow unemployed away from MacLean were led by two prominent CPGB members, J. R. Campbell and Willy Gallacher. The Clyde Workers' Committee, now a rump under the leadership of Campbell, fastened on to men discharged from the Albion Motor Works and Parkhead Forge, who, inspired by the CUWC, had met at Glasgow Green and talked of seizing factories. Campbell unsuccessfully tried to use these men as a basis for opposition to MacLean's movement. Some of MacLean's meetings were disrupted by Gallacher and others; and an attempt by Campbell to capture an unemployed meeting at the city hall on 27 December 1920 ended in Campbell being voted down, and, according to MacLean, he "would have been struck down as well but for my intervention".[15]

Because the capture of the Glasgow revolutionary movement was so important to the CPGB, it was prepared to use any methods to defeat MacLean, and Gallacher began to spread rumors that MacLean was of unsound mind.[16] It seems not coincidental that J. R. Campbell, chairman of the SS&WCM, called in *The Worker* of 18 December 1920 for the organization of the unemployed on "a national scale"; for whatever advantages a British organization presented to the unemployed, it cut right across MacLean's hope of using the unemployed as the basis for a separate Scottish revolution. We can only speculate on what influence this had on the decision, less than two weeks later on 1 January 1921, by the CPGB-dominated London District Council of Unemployed Organisations to begin to organize a national unemployed movement, a decision that would ultimately lead to the establishment of the NUWCM.

"The Gallacher gang thrice tried to seize control [of the unemployed] out of my hands and failed absolutely", MacLean later wrote. MacLean, and his lieutenants Sandy Ross and Harry McShane, retained the loyalty of the Glasgow unemployed because they were able to secure concessions for them. It was, until the end of April 1921, illegal in Scotland to give outdoor relief, and MacLean's agitation thus revolved around obtaining the necessities of food and shelter. By the end of October 1920 MacLean had obtained the use of the city hall twice weekly for meetings that over 3,000 unemployed regularly attended. By January 1921 MacLean believed his support in Glasgow to be "stronger than ever before", and the following month his organization became known as the Glasgow Unemployed Workers' Committee (UWC), who had the motto "Food, Clothing, and Shelter." By late February 1921 the Glasgow UWC was holding regular work gate meetings, as well as continuing with large unemployed processions through the city that were "controlled and disciplined by ex-service men"; one procession, on the occasion of the Prince of Wales' visit to Glasgow, being a mile long. On 19 February 1921 a provisional Scottish Unemployed Committee was formed at a conference of delegates from Glasgow unemployed district committees and from the Dundee unemployed, with Sandy Ross as chairman and John MacLean as secretary. But when, on 17 May 1921, Ross and MacLean were each imprisoned for three months on charges of sedition, the independent Scottish unemployed movement came to an end. It had to a large extent depended on MacLean's charisma and indefatigable energy, and in spite of his efforts to build an effective independent Scottish unemployed movement, there was little solid organization that could survive his absence. Into the vacuum created by his imprisonment stepped the well-funded CPGB with its impeccable Bolshevik credentials. A disheartened Harry McShane felt that in spite of the manifold drawbacks of the CPGB, it did offer the only firm basis upon which revolutionary activity could be organized. He went over to the CPGB and the Glasgow unemployed followed, in some cases, such as in Clydesbank in July 1921, CPGB branches actually being formed out of unemployed commitees. The Scottish unemployed movement was to prove a vital force in the inter-war history of the politics of the unemployed, and it operated in a semi-independent fashion to the NUWCM, and later the NUWM. But the revolutionaries among the unemployed now worked for a Soviet Britain, and not a Workers' Republic of Scotland.[17]

Partly inspired by the CUWC, an unemployed movement developed in London in the final months of 1920 that spawned the London District Council of Unemployed Organisations. While nowhere near as radical as its Coventry or Glasgow counterparts, it was the London District Council of Unemployed Organisations that was to create and dominate the NUWCM.

Between 1 September and 1 November 1920, the slow growth of unemployment turned into a rapid increase. The total number of unemployed in Britain rose to nearly a million and a half, and the number in London doubled in these two months. At first, the only bodies organizing the unemployed were the ex-service men's organizations, and for a short time their activities prospered. The NUX and the IUX began to organize marches to and from their meetings, some of the men carrying arms. On 15 September 1921 some 200 IUX members were evicted by police from inside the Harlesden labor exchange where they were trying to hold a meeting; five days later the West London IUX marched a "monster demonstration" of unemployed from Wormwood Scrubs to Hyde Park. The Willesden IUX was by October 1920 holding daily meetings of the unemployed; and early in November 1920, 300 Camberwell unemployed ex-service men marched behind an NUX banner to the Gordon Road workhouse demanding to be admitted. By mid-November 1920 London branches of the NUX were experiencing "great activity" and growing rapidly.[18]

But the lack of effective central coordination consequent upon the collapse of the NUX as a national body, the blurring of ex-service men and civilian unemployment, and the need to make alliances with local labor and socialist activists led to NUX branches being absorbed into the rising unemployed committees. We find a harbinger of this process in early October 1920 when a home was seized at East Ham for two ex-service men and their families, and the local NUX branch in conjunction with the local trades council and the Essex Protection League issued a manifesto announcing their intention to occupy all empty houses in the district that landlords refused to rent to ex-service men. Similarly, at the Siemens works at Woolwich on 7 December 1920, the NUX and the Electrical Trades Union staged a demonstration against overtime. Such alliances had by the end of 1920 evolved into the ubiquitous unemployed workers' committees (UWCs). Thus we find that the Camberwell unemployed who were initially organized under the aegis of the NUPPO and the NUX are soon being organized by the Camberwell UWC; that it is the members of the Islington NUX who form the militant element of the Islington Unemployed Relief Committee; and that Strachan, a young NUX leader, was by late December 1920 chairman of the West Ham UWC.[19]

The formation of the UWCs was given a fillip by the "Battle of Downing Street", a peaceful demonstration on 18 October 1920 turned into a riot following an attack by the police. A conference of London Labour mayors held on 22 September 1920 decided to put the unemployed's case to Lloyd George personally, backing themselves up with a peaceful demonstration of the unemployed. The same day that the mayors, accompanied by representatives of the London Trades Council, the NFDDSS and the NUX, met with the prime minister, the price of a quartern loaf of bread rose from 1 shilling to 1 shilling and 4 pence. Twenty thousand workless, women, old men, and young men with war decorations, marched on a raw cold afternoon behind the banners of the NFDDSS, the NUPPO, and red flags to Whitehall.[20]

The police baton-charged the crowd in an attempt to clear Downing Street, and a battle developed between the police and the unemployed, many of whom were unable to retreat because of the density of the crowd, and who were faced with the unenviable choice of either fighting or being clubbed down. An attempt by some unemployed to rush Downing Street was preceded by a barrage of half-bricks, stones, flints and pieces of iron. The police baton-charged the unemployed from the front, while mounted police wheeled into Whitehall, broke into a canter, and charged them from behind. "Their new long staves", reported *The Times*, "rose and fell with such energy that some were seen to break." Twenty people were reported to have been treated at hospitals for various abdominal and head injuries, though the number of civilian casualties was almost certainly far higher than this figure, for twenty-nine policemen were injured by stone-throwing alone.[21]

The mayors left their meeting with Lloyd George empty handed, but the treatment of the unemployed at Whitehall by the police received great publicity. It seems to have shocked the unemployed and made them far more receptive to suggestions of a more aggressive, organized approach to their activities. Within a fortnight, delegates from twelve unemployed committees met at the Bookbinders Hall in John St., Clerkenwell, and formed the London District Council of Unemployed Organisations (LDC). Wal Hannington, a young unemployed engineer who was to become the national leader of the unemployed for the next two decades, later claimed the credit for the formation of the LDC for himself and the other unemployed shop stewards.[22]

Hannington is a key figure in our story: a street politician of genius and integrity who was imprisoned for extended periods six times; an autodidact who wrote several books, two of which, *Unemployed Struggles* (1936) and *The Problem of the Distressed Areas* (1937), are classics of their genres; a foundation member of the

Communist Party who remained to his death in 1966 a devoted Communist, yet like so many other members of the NUWM (such as Lewis Jones, leader of the Welsh unemployed, the only man at a Moscow meeting who refused to stand when Stalin entered the room) not one to blindly and obediently toe the Party line; a committed trade unionist who believed in many of the conservative values of unionism but who at the same time was something of a political adventurer, proud of having shouldered a rifle in Hamburg during the failed insurrection there in 1924. When considering titles for his autobiography Hannington considered a play upon the title of a well known 1950s film, by calling it "A Rebel with a Cause."[23]

Hannington, born in 1895, grew up in north London in a Camden Town basement, one of several children of a bricklayer. In consequence of his father's trade, in which long periods without work were routine, Hannington grew up with an acute awareness of what unemployment meant to working-class people. From his childhood he was a rebel, at one time leading a revolt of his branch of the Boys' Brigade against the new vicar who wished to transfer the branch's allegiance to Baden Powell's new and burgeoning boy scout movement. In the photographs of him as a young man, resplendent in a sharp suit with haircut to match, Hannington looks a little like a teddy boy gone astray. But in his adolescence bored youths listened to street corner orators rather than Bill Haley for entertainment and inspiration, and from them Hannington gained his initial interest in socialism. In 1915 as a young apprentice engineer, he joined the Kentish Town branch of the BSP, thereby joining both a party (the BSP having been the SDF) and a branch with a tradition of involvement with the unemployed, the latter having been sporadically active in the politics of the unemployed since the 1890s. Through his work he became involved with an equally profound influence on his life, the shop stewards' movement. By early 1920, only in his early twenties, Hannington was a member of the London District Committee of the Amalgamated Engineering Union (AEU), and chairman of the Slough Transport Depot's works committee. "I must have been a very precocious young man", he observed of himself as a more reflective old man. By mid 1920, unemployed as the result of a victimization sacking and having been blacklisted, Hannington found himself driven to live on poor law relief.[24]

He soon found himself at the center of the burgeoning unemployed movement and played an important role in the formation of the LDC, but the image he presents in his works of the omniscient shop stewards taking it upon themselves to offer correctly class-conscious direction and leadership to an apolitical rabble of unemployed is false, and tells us much more about the survival of the SDF's paternalistic attitudes toward the unemployed in its successors the BSP and the CPGB, than it does about the state of the unemployed movement in 1920. As we have seen, the unemployed through the ex-service men's bodies, and their interaction with all hues of socialist thought and organization, had developed their own organizations that were both political and active. The politics of the unemployed by the end of 1920 was the product of varied and often conflicting forces; yet it had developed a powerful momentum and was characterized by a rich diversity of practice and thought in Coventry, in Glasgow, and in London. To it the shop stewards brought their undoubted skills of organization and their own committed political standpoint. But the shop stewards did not create the unemployed movement, as Hannington implies: rather they indicated to the unemployed movement new directions in which it might venture.[25]

Hannington claimed that at his instigation the St. Pancras Unemployed Ex-service Men's Organisation, of which he was a member, led the push for the formation of the LDC. It seems though that this accolade rightly belongs to the Islington Unemployed Relief Committee, in which, as we have seen, the NUX was the militant element. The LDC had a five man executive: Hannington was the organizer; Percy Haye and Jack Holt, both shop stewards, were secretary and chairman; while the other two positions were filled by a man called Phillips, and Dennis Jennett, the shoemaker who, as an SSAU member, had been arrested for his involvement in the May 1919 Parliament Square riot. Jennett was now a leading figure among the Islington unemployed, and by January 1921 was to be chairman of the Islington UWC. The LDC had its headquarters not, as might be expected if one were to believe Hannington's account, in St. Pancras, but at the Islington library in Essex Road, which had been seized by the Islington Unemployed Relief Committee for its headquarters when it had formed early in October. The police retook the library on 29 December 1920 and seized the LDC's correspondence. In spite of a bloody street battle in early January 1921, the LDC was unable to take the Islington town hall as recompense, and afterward shifted its headquarters to the International Socialist Club.[26]

The spate of squatting that formed much of the unemployed activity during November and December 1920 was not instigated by the LDC as Hannington later claimed, but by Islington activists. The occupation of empty houses in which to accommodate the homeless unemployed began, as we have seen, when the East Ham NUX occupied a house in early October; and the occupation of public buildings to house unemployed committees began with the occupation of the Islington library, some weeks before the formation of the LDC. By early December the unemployed were in possession not only of numerous empty houses but also the public baths at Walthamstow and Camberwell, the public libraries at Camberwell, Finsbury, Fulham, Islington and Walthamstow, the territorials drill hall at Hackney, a barracks at High Wycombe, and the town halls in Edmonton, Poplar, and Tottenham. In London, the cabinet was told on 9 December 1920, that "something akin to mob law has begun." The credit for this was due not to the LDC, but, in the words of the Directorate of Intelligence, to "a certain group of Islington extremists [who] were going from district to district inciting ex-service men and unemployed to seize halls and houses."[27] "To the Islington Unemployed Relief Committee", said *The Communist* of 9 December 1920, "is to be given the credit for starting the direct action campaign of the unemployed. . . . In Edmonton, Tottenham, Walthamstow, Hackney, Southwark, Camberwell, Peckham and St Pancras similar movements are now organised."

Local Labour activists sympathized and often supported the unemployed in their activities. Following the violent ejection of the unemployed by the police from a house they had seized in Richmond Road, William Anning, house decorator and a Hackney Labour leader, alderman and chairman of the housing committee of the Hackney borough council, told a meeting of 400 unemployed: "It is useless to attempt to seize any house unless you are armed. I want you to come back tomorrow morning fully armed. Bring the biggest sticks you can find. Some of the police are marked men, and we want to get our own back. They are served out with revolvers. We know the police are the friends of the capitalist class." For these words Anning was later bound over to keep the peace for twelve months with a surety of £100.[28]

What seems to have been taking place in London late in 1920 was a large outburst of sporadic, often emulative, but rarely coordinated activity by the unemployed, led at a local level by Communists, Labour Party activists, and NUX and IUX militants. Having said this, it should be borne in mind that in 1920 it was possible, even likely, for a Communist, a Labour Party activist, and an NUX militant to be one and the same person. In many ways the activity of the London unemployed in 1920 remained a protest of unemployed ex-service men, and the intelligence reports received by the cabinet up until the end of 1920 stressed the role of the ex-service men's organizations and almost totally ignored the role of the LDC in organizing the unemployed. Nowhere is this more evident than in the military manner in which nearly all of the seizures and subsequent occupations of public buildings were carried out: the 300 unemployed who occupied the Finsbury public library on 25 November 1920, some bearing arms and ammunition, all entered "in military formation"; while the unemployed ex-service men from Camberwell who seized the Peckham public library on 1 December 1920 quickly established a cookhouse with ex-army cooks in charge and appointed corporals and orderly sergeants, and, said the *Daily Herald* of 2 December 1920, "conducted themselves quietly and orderly, in accordance with full military discipline." No women took part in the seizures, and bound up with the masculine nature of this form of protest was an essential respect for order. Even *The Times* of 3 December 1920 was led to comment upon the "orderly fashion" in which the unemployed men withdrew from the Tottenham town hall after being offered alternative premises, and spoke sympathetically of the unemployed men who had seized the Edmonton town hall: "their orderly conduct suggested that very many of them had not forgotten their military training".[29]

Here were the reassuring signs of respect in revolt; and here we have an insight into the heart of the London unemployed movement in late 1920, for in spite of appearances it was never a radical or threatening movement. Above all else it was up until at least March 1921 a movement of collective self-help, seeing its major role as that of dispensing relief. The Shoreditch unemployed committee distributed coal and foodstuffs; the Southwark unemployed committee provided a free breakfast; and even radical unemployed groups, such as Hannington's St. Pancras unemployed organization, doled out bread, while the Camberwell unemployed distributed food, and the Islington Unemployed Relief Committee was weekly distributing parcels of food, each worth 13 shillings, to over 250 families.[30]

Yet the activity of the London unemployed, this strange self-help that took both aggressive and compliant forms, did bring forth immediate success. The 1920 Unemployment Insurance Act, which as we have seen was a product of fear of the unemployed in 1919, took effect on 8 November 1920. Ironically, although it was intended to extend insurance to most sections of the working class, by the time it came into effect many were already out of work and on the streets, and therefore unable to pay the necessary contributions to qualify for benefit. These unemployed had no recourse but to the poor law, and in areas where agitation was strong the unemployed were able to force boards of guardians to concede high scales of relief, often funded from inadequate rates. This led many boards to complain and protest to the central government, which responded by blessing areas where the unemployed were particularly active—such as Tottenham and Edmonton—with relief work on arterial road construction, and by rushing an emergency bill through Parliament in December 1920 which waived the contribution rule, and allowed eight weeks' benefit to all who could prove that they had been in insurable employment for four weeks during 1920.[31]

The government also tried to break and divide the unemployed movement by officially encouraging them to resort to their former innocuous practice of collecting in the West End, and by pursuing a deliberate and systematic policy of arresting extremist speakers. In spite of these measures Macnamara, the Minister of Labour, was less than sanguine in private. Lord Riddell recorded in his diary a conversation he had with Macnamara on Christmas Day, 1920. "Macnamara very gloomy about unemployment. He says the next three months will put the Government to a serious test. He doubts whether the Cabinet appreciate the strength of the feelings of the ex-soldiers, and that they will be the ones who will cause the most trouble. He added, 'They have most justification.' "[32]

Many of the local Labour authorities were sympathetic to the organization of the unemployed. George Lansbury gave the NUWCM great prominence in the *Daily Herald*, and when Hannington was on poor relief actually gave him money. In 1920 Lansbury was mayor of Poplar, and in that year he raised the cry of "Unemployed, Go to the Guardians!" in an article of the same name in the *Daily Herald* of 18 December 1920. Although this old SDF slogan was later claimed by the NUWM as their battle cry, it was Lansbury who suggested its usage, and his article reads like a manifesto for the unemployed movement of the 1920s. He called for a national organization of the unemployed, which would focus its strategy upon pressuring local government for adequate relief. "What Parliament and the Government won't do Poor Law Guardians must do, if organised *Labour and the unemployed will but stand together and compel them to carry out the law*", wrote Lansbury. His article received great attention and was subsequently reprinted as a leaflet and distributed free of charge. But its influence as a call to arms was, for the time being, disappointing, and it was not to be until the following winter that the unemployed were to "go to the guardians" in great numbers, and the phenomenon of "Poplarism" was to be established as both a fierce political weapon and a household word. In the meantime the workless placed their faith not in their own activity, but in the activity of their working brethren, and attempted to persuade the national labor movement to take decisive industrial action to force the government to do something for the unemployed.[33]

But where the local labor movement was active and supportive the national labor movement was inactive and sometimes hostile. This was less surprising than it may seem, given the lessening heterodoxy of the national labor movement, its parallel and growing obsession with gaining parliamentary power, which, when coupled to its old commitment to a parliamentary path to change represented important new forces of stability and conservatism in British society that were recognised as such. "Labour itself, moreover, is more self conscious and coherent," said *The Times* of 22 December 1920 in a leading article on unemployment, "a circumstance of advantage to the state". The unemployed's hopes were to be cruelly dashed against the rocks of a Labour leadership concerned primarily with parliamentary success; "public doles, Poplarism, strikes for increased wages . . . not only are not Socialism, but may mislead the spirit and policy of the Socialist movement", Ramsay MacDonald was to write in 1924. But the dangers of being so misled were not apparent to many in the labor movement in 1921, and the LDC met with considerable support in its call for a twenty-four hour general strike to demand the restoration of trade between Britain and Russia. An LDC deputation met with the joint secretaries of the Council of Action on 21 December 1920; with Labour MPs on 22 December 1920; and then with the full Council of Action on 23 December 1920. The Council of Action refused to include unemployment in its agitation, but agreed to propose an emergency resolution demanding full maintenance at the special Labour Party conference being held to discuss the Irish question on 29 December 1920. The conference, which was addressed by LDC representatives, passed the resolution and appointed a subcommittee to investigate the question of the unemployed. This committee in turn convened a national Labour conference to take place on 27 January 1921. A strong feeling in favor of direct action on the issue of unemployment manifested itself at this conference, and there was a great protest when it was announced that the LDC deputation would not be received. Despite attempts by the leadership to limit the agitation to parliament, a resolution asking all unions to test the feeling of their membership upon the question of using direct action against the government was passed. Concern at the rapidly escalating levels of unemployment was growing among the trade union rank and file, and by 23 February 1921, when the conference resumed, support for direct action over the issue of of unemployment was running high. Many unions, even such conservative bodies as the Union of Boot and Shoe Operatives, returned with a clear mandate for a general strike that the Labour leadership was to deny.[34]

An LDC deputation was refused permission to address the conference, Arthur Henderson saying "that the delegates represented the unemployed as much as anyone". Herbert Morrison argued that a general strike would demonstrate the movement's weaknesses rather than its strength, and in clear reference to the unemployed movement said that the labor movement should not play to the gallery and the mob. Parliament, said Jimmy Thomas in a direct refutation of the notion of a general strike, was the only body that could deal with unemployment. But it was by the tactical refusal of the platform to discuss any resolution other than the official resolution, rather than such arguments, that the possibility of direct action was quashed. The official resolution was an endorsement of parliamentarianism that evaded any mention of a general strike, instead content to call upon every trade union "to promote a Labour candidate for every constituency." After two hours of stormy and futile debate, the official resolution was put to the vote and inevitably carried, and the conference, and with it the LDC's hope of pushing the national labor movement into direct action, came to a premature end. The conference had been of critical importance to the national labor movement in endorsing its policy of parliamentarianism and defusing the support for direct action. It strengthened the position of the conservative Labour leaders, and was a premonition of the events of Black Friday, less than two months later, when the leaders of the Triple Alliance would fail to take sympathetic strike action in support of the miners.[35]

"We now have to rely upon our own strength and solidarity," wrote Wal Hannington following the failure of the Labour conference to take action, "and for this purpose we are convening a National Conference." The LDC, as we have seen, first made its desire to organize the unemployed on a national basis clear at the start of 1921, but only after its strategy of forcing the labor movement to take action on behalf of the unemployed had failed did it turn to national organization as a serious option.[36]

The LDC aims were nowhere near as radical as those of the CUWC: it stood for work or maintenance at trade union rates, the reestablishment of trade with Russia, and recognition of the Soviet government. In part this was a recognition of the largely apolitical nature of the London unemployed movement, which even in March 1921 remained at heart a cooperative relief movement. The LDC was still sufficiently respectable for the Ministry of Labour in mid-January 1921 to worry that it was "in danger of being used for political ends". When the LDC launched its attempt to form a national unemployed movement in March 1921 it was then, far from being a revolutionary body, a body with a largely apolitical membership and only moderately radical aims. Nor was it even in full control of the London unemployed movement, for while controlling most of the unemployed committees in the inner city boroughs, the LDC was having trouble winning over the unemployed committees on the outskirts of the capital. Even the twenty-two committees affiliated with the LDC by mid January 1921, while subject to the majority vote of the LDC on general issues, retained full local autonomy, and interventions by the LDC were not always welcomed. When the LDC imposed a 5 percent levy on UWCs to fund itself, the executive of the Battersea UWC resigned in protest.[37]

Nevertheless the LDC was becoming a power: by March 1921 it had its own regular paper, *Out of Work*, edited and published by Mrs. Lily Thring, a Russian Jew who had her government pension stopped because of her involvement in the women's suffrage movement. A former WSF member, member of the International Workers of the World and the CPGB, she was one of the leaders of the house-seizing campaign, had been instrumental in the formation of many of the unemployed committees, and seems to have believed in the efficacy of physical force: three bottles of petrol found on Reuben Gilmour, "a coloured man" and secretary of the Poplar Unemployed Committee, on the occasion of the unsuccessful attempt to take the Islington town hall, had been prepared in her rooms (decorated with portraits of Lenin and Trotsky), and she was later arrested for possession of two German machine guns. She was to be the outstanding woman leader of the unemployed in the 1920s, had the honour to be described by the Directorate of Intelligence as "a woman of loose habits", and by the autumn of 1921 was an unemployed leader of sufficient prominence to warrant her own bodyguard, described by the Special Branch as "irresponsible boys who are ready to render her absolute obedience."[38]

The unemployed were by the spring of 1921 organizing not only in London, Glasgow and Coventry, but in Liverpool, Merthyr, Edinburgh, Leicester, Gorton, Openshaw (Manchester) and Sheffield. On 12 April 1921 a national conference of unemployed organizations took place at the International Socialist Club. Over 100 delegates from London and the English provinces attended, though none came from Scotland, where MacLean still led the unemployed. Although the idea of establishing a National Administrative Council (NAC) to coordinate the work of the scattered organizations had to be abandoned for want of funds, a national framework was established, and from this time the unemployed began to organize nationally, although it was to be a further six months before they could lay claim to being a truly national movement. Shortly after the conference funds were found to establish the NAC, which was in existence by May 1921.[39]

From the beginning the inter-war unemployed movement saw itself as only part of a larger working-class struggle, but exactly what part of that struggle depended upon the extent of unemployed activity in relation to the prevailing fortunes of the labor movement. Thus, in the periods when the working class was in profound retreat and the unemployed movement was meeting with some success, such as late 1921 to early 1923, and late 1931 to 1935, the unemployed movement often began to view itself as the vanguard of the working class movement, while in alternate periods when the labor movement was, if not winning (a rare occurrence in the inter-war years) then neither losing, and the unemployed were quiescient, the unemployed movement saw itself as butressing the work of other working-class projects. The rebuff that the unemployed had experienced from the Labour conference may have served as the catalyst for a separate national organization of the unemployed, but it did not lead them into an antagonistic attitude toward the organized working class (the same cannot be said of its attitude to the official leadership), and the radical leadership of the LDC attempted to build an identity of interests between unemployed and employed workers. This was done through the pages of *Out of Work*; through declarations of intent such as the LDC's resolution in April 1921 "that in no circumstances" would unemployed LDC members allow themselves "to be used as instruments for blacklegging" against the locked out miners; and through such actions as applying for affiliation (which was refused) with the London Trades Council. There were also attempts to whip up industrial activity by the unemployed: on 11 March 1921 the Willesden unemployed, led by Hannington, marched into the Central Aircraft Factory at Kilburn, shut down the motors, addressed the workers on the need not to accept low wages or work overtime because they led to unemployment, and extracted a pledge from the management that overtime would not be worked. This tactic was repeated a fortnight later in a raid on the J.A.P. works at Tottenham. But its well-founded attempts to demonstrate that the unemployed were not the enemy of the employed workers but rather that they were brothers in arms sounded hollow in the face of the reality of mass unemployment. Even if if no LDC member scabbed, or accepted less than trade union rates, the heart of the matter was that there were many, many more unemployed outside of the LDC driven by the desperation of their position to scab, to take lower wages, to accept worse conditions, who did threaten the position of the employed worker. Even at its mightiest, the NUWCM could not deny this fundamental truth of mass unemployment: that it did set worker against worker, employed against unemployed. But the NUWCM could, and did, challenge that this should always be so.[40]

The continuing organization of the unemployed perturbed the government. In a memorandum circulated to the cabinet in February 1921 Macnamara wrote, "The premium which the State has paid for its security so far as unemployed ex-service men are concerned has, during the winter, been 20s. per week unemployment donation." But with the continuing growth of unemployment and the latest extension of the out-of-work donation scheme to end shortly, a new scheme was urgently needed. Macnamara recommended that ex-service men be brought within the unemployment insurance scheme. Rather than antagonize the ex-service men by reducing their dole from 20 shillings to the 15 shillings paid to an unemployed insured worker, Macnamara proposed raising the standard benefit from 15 shillings to 20 shillings. "I do not say that 20s. may not suffice to keep the country steady", Macnamara wrote. "I hope-though I am not sure that it may. But I warn my colleagues that to pay less would be a decision that may be fraught with disaster." Macnamara also proposed to continue the system introduced in December 1920 of paying benefit that was not covered by contributions. This became known as uncovenanted benefit, and a bill was rushed through in late February 1921 embodying Macnamara's proposals. Whereas claimants had previously only been allowed fifteen weeks benefit in one insurance year, claimants now were allowed to draw twenty-two weeks of uncovenanted benefit in the thirty-five weeks between 3 March, when the bill became law, and 2 November 1921. In this way the dole was melted into the benefit until all that was left was the irreducible element—dole—recognized by the working class as its right in hard times.[41]

But the government countered the activity of the unemployed not only by altering the fundamental conception of the unemployment benefit; for it also systematically set about arresting and imprisoning unemployed activists and Communists. "The absence of disorder and even of violent speeches during the past week is testimony to the value of a centralised policy in the prosecution for incitement to sedition" the cabinet was told in mid-March 1921. Harry Emery was imprisoned for two months on a charge of sedition in March 1921, and following a resurgence of unrest in the army and navy in May 1921, the government moved in on the CPGB, raiding its headquarters and arresting and imprisoning its national organizer and its secretary. Within a week unemployed activists such as J. H. Binney in Rotherham, Jack Leckie in Birmingham, John MacLean and Sandy Ross in Glasgow, and Tom Dingley were arrested. The Party went partially underground. The LDC was caught off balance and temporarily lost momentum, and nationally the unemployed movement was quiet through the summer.[42]

But none of this could avert the crisis the government now faced: the abandonment of the actuarial principles upon which the unemployment insurance scheme had been based, when combined with the continued high level of unemployment, left the insurance fund teetering on the edge of insolvency. The government, having temporarily broken the unemployed agitation, tried to protect the fund by reducing men's unemployment benefit from 20 shillings to 15 shillings, and women's from 16 shillings to 12 shillings. These cuts were effective from 1 July 1921, and on 11 July the LDC staged a large unemployed demonstration in London. A deputation of Holt, Hannington and Straker went from the meeting to Whitehall where they had an interview with Macnamara. They were stunned when told that the government had made provision for paying 15 shillings to 1,250,000 unemployed for the next twelve months. "We the unemployed have got to remain content with *at least* another 12 months existence on 15s. per week" wrote Holt in *Out of Work*. "REMAIN CONTENT! HELL! IS IT POSSIBLE?"[43]

The Revolt of 1921

The short answer was that it wasn't possible. During the quiet summer of 1921 the NAC had built up a national framework of organization, holding area conferences, establishing new committees, strengthening the allegiance of old committees. By September 1921, 100 committees were affiliated with the NAC of which thirty were in London. The NAC was to oversee a massive outburst of political activity by the unemployed in the autumn of 1921, paralleled in its magnitude and ferocity only by the events of late 1932. Here it is possible to comment only on some of the general features of what took place in those few short, remarkable months.[44]

Compounding the cuts in benefit, the benefit, as we have seen, was paid only for a limited amount of time. This meant that there were many among the unemployed whose benefit had run out, and who had nothing save the poor law to survive upon. The major gaps in payment of benefit thus corresponded with the peaks in the numbers seeking and receiving outdoor relief. By mid-September 1921, 380,000 unemployed had run out of benefit, and by 3 November 1921, when the new period of benefit started, there were expected to be half a million unemployed off benefit. But the struggle of these people revolved not around trying to force the government to raise benefit and eliminate the gap, but around forcing local authorities to pay adequate outdoor relief without conditions. It was about going to the guardians, and from August onwards countless demonstrations and deputations throughout the country trod the same path.[45]

In the final week of August 1921 demands by the unemployed led to the rates of relief being raised in Bethnal Green, Camberwell, Islington, Bermondsey, Holborn, and Clerkenwell. With these victories under their belts, unemployed leaders began stressing to their audiences "that the unemployed must be prepared to act not only in their own districts, but anywhere else where the right to work or full maintenance is not conceded." In early September the LDC widened the campaign to include non-Labour councils such as Lambeth and Hammersmith, which did possess sufficiently large Labour minorities to act in concert with the unemployed. As the government began imprisoning Poplar councillors in the first week of September 1921, and with the number of those who had run out of benefit now growing rapidly, the NAC launched a massive countrywide campaign for work or full maintenance, and demands were made by the unemployed on guardians, according to one Special Branch report, in practically every English county. To some extent the organized unemployed existed in a symbiotic relationship with sympathetic Labour-controlled local authorities who, while willing to make concessions to the unemployed through a liberal interpretation of poor law statutes, found the mass activity of the unemployed of critical importance in justifying making these concessions, and in legitimizing their own power. Some ruling Labour groups used the street politics of the unemployed to its fullest, and the phenomenon of Poplarism would have been stillborn were it not for the unemployed agitation mounted by the NAC from September 1921 on.[46]

The immediately apparent feature of this agitation was its aggression and violence. While not all of the extraordinary number of demonstrations ended in rioting and street fighting between police and the unemployed, many did. The object of damage by the unemployed seemed normally to be either commercial property such as shops and banks, or public buildings; though on occasion it could be public figures of authority, such as the lord provost of Dundee and his family, whom while in a taxi cab were stoned by a crowd of some thousands of the Dundee unemployed. In Liverpool a deputation from a demonstration of 10,000 unemployed included a radical young Baptist minister, the Reverend J. Vint Laughland. They met with the mayor who as he greeted them smiled in a patronizing way. Laughland grabbed the mayor's chain, and threatened to pull "that damn dog-chain off".[47]

In the Special Branch reports and newspaper accounts the unemployed are portrayed as the instigators of violence, but this does not seem generally to have been the case. A normal pattern of events would be for a peaceful demonstration to be baton-charged and dispersed by the police leading to sporadic street fighting between police and unemployed that often degenerated into rioting. In Sunderland, for example, twelve unemployed men were treated for scalp wounds and several others injured when an unemployed demonstration, waiting upon the return of its leader from an interview with the board of guardians, was baton-charged by the police. If we look at the case of the 150 Liverpool unemployed who attempted to hold a meeting in the Walker Art Gallery on 12 September 1921, we can gain some idea of how violent the police could be. The police locked the unemployed in the gallery, sealed all exits, and without any provocation drew their batons and proceeded to beat all who were trapped inside. George Garrett, an eyewitness, later wrote:

Men yelled aloud as they were batoned down. Others dashed around panic stricken. A few desperate ones dropped from an open window into the side street and got away. Those attempting to follow were struck from behind. The police closed all windows and doors. There were no further escapes. Batons split skull after skull. Men fell where they were hit. The floor streamed with blood. Those lying in it were trampled by others who were soon flattened out alongside them. Gallery workmen were battered too. The police had gone wild. The old police striker [Tissyman], appealing to their decency, had his arm broken and his head smashed. The young parson [Laughland], protesting was knocked bleeding to the floor and as he lay unconscious he was batoned again.[48]

The unemployed's response to such violence was summed up in an article in *Out of Work*: "We are not going to sit indoors and starve, we are coming outside; if it is to be a fight, well, we are not the provokers. . . . We can march orderly, but, by Christ! we will not stand everything." While there was some pressure to organize on a para-military basis to fight the police, this was rejected by both the unemployed and their leaders. A conference of the Red International of Labour Unions (RILU) in October 1921, attended by Wal Hannington among others, rejected out of hand a proposed amendment that the delegates "return to their branches, with instructions to move that an armed force be created in the unemployed organisations to retaliate to the actions of the police." "We are not maintaining the peaceful attitude for inherent love of the police," explained a speaker called Bishop to a large London unemployed demonstration on 18 October 1921, "but because we realise that it is not worthwhile for one or two individuals to lay out one or two coppers . . . the present time is not opportune for such tactics . . . but the day is coming."[49]

The utterly defensive nature of the organized unemployed at this time is well illustrated by the Liverpool unemployed, who concluded from the beating they got in the Walker Art Gallery that they had to become a disciplined body. Under the leadership of Jack Braddock, a member of the International Workers of the World and the CPGB, they registered 8,000 of Liverpool's 40,000 unemployed within a week, grouped them under district headings, split each district into neighbourhood units of twelve and put each unit under the control of an ex-non-commissioned officer who was termed the street captain, and who was responsible for the discipline and conduct of the unit. Each district elected its own leader. "In back streets, shuttered cellars, and on waste lots the units were secretly put through their paces," wrote George Garrett. At the end of a march the unemployed would form up into an "Army", "Section Commanders" would be appointed who would then drill the army. The purpose of this martial discipline was not to encourage violence but to prevent it through intimidation of the police, the unemployed being ordered not to antagonize the police but to be ready to disarm them if they tried to draw their batons. The Liverpool unemployed were never again in the 1920s to be attacked ruthlessly by the police. The politics of the unemployed could be highly aggressive, but the unemployed organizations recognized the fundamental weakness of their own position, and rather than being seduced by insurrectionary fantasies they always tried to prevent such aggression escalating into direct confrontation with the authorities.[50]

A second feature of the unemployed agitation of 1921 was that in contrast to 1920 women were again becoming involved. Within the working class women particularly suffered from unemployment. After World War I women were pushed back into either the traditional female trades of laundry and domestic industry with their traditional bad wages and worse conditions, or unemployment. Even if such work paid less than unemployment benefit, women had to accept it or be cut off benefit. By 1921 the proportion of women in employment was less than in 1910. Led by Lily Thring the LDC had from early 1921 broadened the basis of its support by beginning to organize women. Over 400 women were enrolled for the demonstration to the ill fated Labour conference on 23 February 1921, a women's unemployed committee was established in Edmonton, 500 women from Hoxton formed one of the processions to the LDC demonstration at Hyde Park on 11 July 1921, and Lily Thring led a deputation of women to Downing Street on 2 November 1921 and interviewed the prime minister's secretary. The effect of unemployment in forcing women to work as prostitutes was for the first time raised as an issue by male unemployed activists. Representatives of the unemployed told the Cardiff board of guardians how "there were women prepared to go out on the streets as Mary Magdalenes"; while after the Reverend B. H. Pemberton, a Brighton guardian, opposed the request of an unemployed deputation to raise the scales of relief, one of the unemployed threatened to kill him "with my own hands". "We are fighting for the lives of our womenfolk", he continued: "The parsons of this country are driving the women out to prostitution."[51]

Women began to feature again in demonstrations, but their role within the demonstrations was often ambiguous, one object of their involvement being to render the work of police in breaking up demonstrations more difficult. A procession of unemployed to the West Derby guardians in September 1921 was headed by forty to fifty women carrying babies. The unspoken accusation was not simply that men are unemployed, but that in consequence of their unemployment they were now unable to provide for their wives and children, and had thus failed as men. The West Derby unemployed were presenting unemployment to the guardians as a total dislocation of accepted family structures, and of their own status as men within that structure, through the medium of the opposite of the ideal wife, the starving woman, who—and not the men—led the demonstration.[52]

Women's involvement was limited generally by the awesome amount of domestic work that working-class women were expected to undertake whether in work or out of it (unlike unemployed men), and particularly by the antagonism of men toward women within the unemployed movement. "I think it will need a great amount of 'persuasion' to make the men see that it is essential that women become class conscious and fully understand the position," wrote Lily Webb, active in the Manchester unemployed movement, "so it is up to us to do the persuading." Lily Thring argued that the unemployed movement would never be successful unless women were fully involved. "If the unemployed organisations are going to be effective then they will have to cease confining their activities to the stronger sex," she wrote, "as there has been a tendency to do up until now, and we will have to set to work pretty quickly if the unemployed organisations are not going to be wiped out by the forces of law and order. The participation of activities [*sic*] by women would make a very great difference to the National Unemployed Movement. Women are the majority of the population and should therefore be in a majority in the working class struggle." Or, as she more succinctly put it to a meeting of Woolwich workers: "it was impossible for men to progress unless the women kept pace". Lily Thring constantly tried to increase the involvement of women, and at one stage was attempting to organize the unemployed women of London as a separate body. Because of the unemployed agitation of 1921-22 some women, such as Bessie Braddock in Liverpool and Ellen Wilkinson in Manchester, were able to gain valuable political experience that would lead them into prominent lifetime involvements with the labor movement. But by May 1922 Lily Thring was admitting defeat; the organization of women had failed, she told the NAC, "owing to the lack of support from the men."[53]

While women remained marginal to the unemployed movement in 1921, their involvement shows both how the nature of the politics of the unemployed had altered rapidly since the height of the masculine politics of the unemployed ex-service men in 1920, and yet how the unemployed movement continued to be conceived of, and organized as a masculine body, and the limitations this imposed. When unemployed men had seized the chapel in Walworth in late 1920, they had decided not to permit women inside on the basis that "the arrangements would not permit admission of the female sex." Their comment could stand as one epitaph for the politics of the unemployed in the inter-war period.[54]

A third feature of the politics of the unemployed in late 1921 was the highly assertive, almost belligerent way in which they forced guardians to concede their demands. The Bexley unemployed, for instance, imprisoned members of the Bexley Urban District Council in the council chambers throughout the night of 7-8 December 1921 until they agreed to accede to the demands of the unemployed. During the night the unemployed redecorated the clerk's office, running red tape all over the electric lamps and covering the walls with revolutionary posters. When tactics such as these did fail,as sometimes they did, the unemployed would enter the workhouse as an organized body, with the view to completely disrupting the administration of the workhouse until their demands were met. Let us look at one workhouse invasion in detail: that of Battersea in July 1921 after all outdoor relief there had been stopped. Like so much of the politics of the unemployed there was a tremendous sense of street theatre about the occasion. One thousand people, men enveloped by women and children to prevent the police baton charging, marched behind a drum and bagpipes to the workhouse. The streets were lined with onlookers, some of whom openly wept at the prospect of the marchers having to enter the workhouse.[55]

Once inside they established a parallel system of authority, refusing to recognise the authority of the workhouse officials but acting according to the decisions of their own committee. When called upon by the workhouse master to say grace they sang the "Red Flag", they also held meetings continuously, flew the red flag from the roof, and opened a Red Flag Free Shaving Saloon. Such tactics depended on a high degree of solidarity both inside and outside the workhouse. The unemployed who had not entered the workhouse held meetings, marched nightly to the workhouse walls and sang the "Red Flag" (those inside joining in), and kept in communication by signaling with flags to a flag signaler on the workhouse roof. To quell the revolt a large body of police was brought in to enforce workhouse discipline; the food and conditions made steadily worse and the unemployed subjected to various indignities. In the following days many unemployed left, and by Sunday only 400 remained of the 700 who had first entered. Hanlon, one of the leaders, burst into tears while addressing a meeting. The babies became sick from the bad feeding, but the hard core of 400 remained. That they did so attests not only to considerable individual courage, but also to a strongly held and shared belief in the essential rightness of what they were doing. This cohesion was only possible because of the growing politicization of the unemployed movement during 1921, and because of the ability of that movement to offer a longer-term and more political vision to the unemployed, than just a few hours of marching in the hope of scaring immediate relief out of the guardians. A week after the unemployed first entered the workhouse, the guardians announced concessions in the giving of outdoor relief, and the unemployed walked out of the workhouse victorious.

This politicization was also reflected in the phenomenon of factory raiding. In the last two months of 1921 over a dozen factories in London were raided, as bands of unemployed entered large works that worked overtime or piece work, shut them down, and then held a mass meeting of the workers to persuade them to refuse to do overtime. Any factory that could be persuaded, as some were, to stop overtime would then have to employ more workers. Practically this was a form of direct action that brought tangible (however minimal) results to the unemployed; ideologically it demonstrated the unity of interest of employed and unemployed workers.[56]

During October 1921 the NAC was sufficiently bolstered in confidence by the upsurge of unemployed activity to call for a second national conference. The NAC's hand had been strengthened in a number of ways. It had successfully formalized relations between itself and the unemployed committees, and had established a middle level of district committees. By requiring unemployed committees to remit part of their members' contributions to the NAC, it now had an ongoing if precarious financial base. The NAC had set a national scale of relief demands that had been adopted by unemployed committees throughout the country, and it had staged a successful week of national agitation in mid-October 1921. Following John MacLean's second imprisonment for the year in September

1921, the NAC had entered into preliminary negotiations with the Glasgow unemployed. An indicator of support for the NAC can be had in the circulation of *Out of Work*, now the unemployed's national organ, which by early October 1921 had reached 51,000, leading Percy Haye to predict that its sales would soon equal those of the *Daily Herald*.[57]

"The Only Solution For Unemployment is the Abolition of Capitalism" read the large red banner that formed a striking backdrop to the second national conference of the unemployed, held at Manchester on 21-23 November 1921. The conference established the basis upon which the unemployed would be organized for the next two decades, all unemployed being eligible to join the movement upon payment of a weekly membership fee of one penny. Special Branch agents viewed the proceedings with trepidation and a certain element of prescience: they described the conference as "revolutionary in character", and were of the opinion that "the unemployed organisation will prove a more insidious body than the Communist Party." Already the new geography of the politics of the unemployed was evident: of the 219 affiliated committees there were 66 committees in the northeast, 60 in Wales, and 48 in London, with the remainder scattered around the country. There were 150 delegates, some of whom, wrote Hannington, "had rather conservative views, but before the end of the conference the militants had won the support of all delegates." More precisely, the CPGB militants of the LDC succeeded in taking control of the NUWCM from its inception. A new NAC was elected, which was identical to the old LDC executive, with Jack Holt elected chairman, A. Squair treasurer, and Lily Thring women's organizer. The conference ratified the original objects of the LDC, and took for itself the name National Unemployed Workers' Committee Movement (NUWCM) showing yet again the influence of the shop stewards, whose old organization, the SS&WCM, had been known since January 1921 as the National Workers' Committee Movement (NWCM).[58]

The rise of the Labour Party both before and after World War I was inextricably bound up with the politics of the unemployed, a process as apparent at the local as at the national level. Yet in spite of this, or perhaps, because of this, the response of the national labor movement to the growth of the unemployed movement was necessarily duplicitous. On the one hand, to a modern mass party committed to parliamentary representation, the politics of the unemployed represented an older and seemingly archaic form of working-class political activity neither easily controlled, nor even, in its denial of the constitutional forms of decision making, sharing the same aspirations as the labor movement. On the other hand, the unemployed had mobilized mass support for their cause that could be used to great electoral benefit by the labor movement. It is a measure of the ability of the Labour Party to make itself the bearer of so many hopes and aspirations of the working class that it was able to divert much of the seething river of unemployed discontent into the exceedingly narrow gutter of electoral support. Thus the leader of the Labour Party at the time, J. R. Clynes, (in an echo of 1904-1905) attempted to channel the activity of the unemployed into a mass campaign for a recall of Parliament to discuss unemployment. "In that way", said Clynes, making no bones about what he thought the politics of the unemployed was useful for, "the hands of the Parliamentary Party would be strengthened."[59]

Not only was the Labour Party electorally inclined to do little about unemployment and structurally bound by the unions against doing much, it was also intellectually unable to offer any real solutions. It shared in a prevailing consensus that the most important role of government was to preserve the principles of sound finance, albeit in a more humane way than their opponents, and followed the orthodoxy of its predecessors in seeking a revival of international trade as the only solution to the continuing problem of unemployment. The leaders of the party believed with Philip Snowden that "the great part of the money which has been spent in relief works . . . has been from the economic point of view almost wholly wasted."[60]

The politics of the unemployed dissolved the oily rhetoric of the likes of MacDonald and exposed the Labour Party as having little idea what to do for the unemployed. Much as it contributed to the rise of the Labour Party, the politics of the unemployed also generated forces that threatened the Labour Party's legitimacy, and the legitimacy of the leadership of the labor movement. "It is impossible to say how far their attitude is inspired by the fear that their followers may revolt", reported the Directorate of Intelligence to the cabinet in January 1921 upon the trade unions' revitalized interest in the unemployed. Implicit in much of the politics of the unemployed was a challenge to the position of the Labour Party as representatives of the working class, a challenge that during late 1921 was given physical expression, Arthur Henderson being persistently heckled by the unemployed at various meetings in Sheffield, Jimmy Thomas being similarly howled down and forced to leave one meeting, and Ramsay MacDonald being "severely heckled" by unemployed followers of John MacLean in Glasgow. At a meeting of the Woolwich Labour Party on 12 September 1921, convened to discuss unemployment, a party from the local unemployed committee mounted from the local platform amidst cheering. Their organizer, McCarthy, started to berate the Labour councillors and guardians on the platform, accusing them of jobbery. The chairman and some of the Labour politicians left the platform "amidst great booing", and the unemployed took over the meeting. A little over a fortnight later at a meeting of the LCC, Harry Gosling, leader of the LCC Labour group, stated that "the Labour leaders were on the brink of losing their control over the unemployed". On that same day a large unemployed demonstration gave substance to Gosling's words. It had assembled on the Embankment and, the LDC having been forbidden by the police to lead it to Trafalgar Square, some Poplar councillors not in prison had taken charge and led the demonstration to Hyde Park. Once there the unemployed were berated by Hannington for having followed the councillors "like sheep". He asked the crowd if they would support him and march back to the square, even if it meant being arrested, "and practically the whole of the audience put up their hands." Hannington, whose power derived solely from the support the unemployed were willing to give him at demonstrations, had been willing to gamble his authority upon asking the demonstration to choose between the lead given by the Poplar councillors, whose popularity in the East End was then at its height, and the lead he offered, and he had won.[61]

The state's reaction to the explosion of activity by the unemployed was a mixture of qualified concessions, repression, and guile. The latter was to the fore in the actions of the chief constable of Wolverhampton, who on 13 October 1921, decreed by the NAC as a day of national demonstration, arranged a football match for the unemployed, which attracted 7,000 people and, reported the Special Branch, "proved a great success and prevented a demonstration". Most chief constables lacked the ingenuity of their Wolverhampton colleague and contented themselves with attempting to deny the unemployed the use of the streets by, as we have seen, beating them up and arresting their leaders who could then face a further beating once inside the police station. The judiciary blatantly acquiesced in this, and many unemployed activists were imprisoned with hard labor on charges of either (ironically) disturbing the peace or sedition. But the days when the politics of the unemployed could be crushed by a measure of repressive policing had passed. Macnamara warned his cabinet colleagues on 17 September 1921 that whatever the financial problems, the problem of the unemployed "has to be faced if grave civil disorder is to be avoided." On 18 October 1921, two days after the NAC's week of national agitation had ended, the government announced that from 10 November 1921 dependent's allowances would be paid to those receiving unemployment benefit. These benefits were 5 shillings per week for a wife or husband, and 1 shilling per week for each child, to a maximum of four children.[62]

In making this provision the government was giving de facto recognition to the argument that 15 shillings a week was totally inadequate, and that benefit had to be sufficient to survive upon. By the end of 1921 unemployment insurance was totally different from the original concept of 1911. The scheme was no longer actuarially sound, and far from being centered upon the need for fostering the virtues of self-help and thrift among the working class, it was now based upon the grudging recognition that the state had to provide adequate maintenance to the unemployed or face considerable political unrest. From Addison's scheme to provide an out-of-work donation separate from insurance in 1918, this radical sequence of change had been formed by the state's response to the threat, both real and imagined, from the unemployed. The political activity of the unemployed had proved of crucial importance at every stage of this total reformulation of the state's attitude to, and relation with the unemployed, and thus had been of critical import in shaping how the unemployed were now viewed, and of what unemployment now meant to the unemployed.

The state also sought to control the unemployed through what was regarded by contemporaries as a very large program of total relief works. By late December 1921, 792 relief schemes had received grants of a total capital value of £7,900,000 from the Ministry of Health. This does not include any of the money granted for road construction relief schemes funded by the Ministry of Transport.[63] Nobody was in any doubt as to why this program had been initiated, and altruism on the part of the state did not figure largely in the analysis of either the right or left. "It is both the interest and the duty of the nation to provide work for the whole number who are willing to work", said *The Times* of 19 September 1921, "... so as to keep them from starving and the loss of their homes, and at the same time to prevent an increase in the numbers of the frankly revolutionary band."

Although the state had been forced to initiate relief works on a previously unknown scale, the unemployed did not have it all their own way. The Ministry of Health grants were conditional upon local authorities paying unskilled men 75 percent of the ordinary wage rate, thereby maintaining the poor law principle of less eligibility. The ramifications of this upon the wage levels of local labor markets was obvious and some Labour councils even refused to apply for relief scheme grants because of this stipulation, while there was a spate of NUWCM-led relief workers' strikes. While forced to take action, the state had shaped its response in an ambiguous form, which at best represented a highly qualified victory for the unemployed. Because the unemployed were for the state a political and not a social problem, it was prepared to accede to employment demands only to the extent necessary to keep political order, not to the extent of seriously attempting to ameliorate the condition of the unemployed. "The situation in many parts of the country continues to be dangerous, and is likely to be for months yet", wrote Sir Alfred Mond, Minister of Health, in a memorandum to the cabinet on 21 December 1921, in which he argued that to discontinue funding for relief schemes "would play into the hands of the extremists" and would be to "dangerously relax the all important efforts made by Local Authorities to keep in peaceful channels the disaffection aroused by unemployment, a result which may be disastrous to the well being of the country". Mond was convinced "that anyone who thinks that the danger is past and that there does not still exist a large amount of highly dangerous material, quick to explode under provocation, is deceived. I feel quite sure that none of my colleagues will dissent from this statement." Mond felt that the unemployed needed concrete proof that the government was seriously trying to help them. "One of the principal reasons why there is a better state of mind among the unemployed is the definite evidence, up and down the country, that the Government have seriously tried to do what they can to deal with unemployment." Not to do so, thought Mond, "would be to put the most effective weapon that could possibly be forged into the hands of those who are only too anxiously watching for an opportunity to disturb the social peace."[64]

In January 1922 the government was finally forced to make concessions to the phenomenon of Poplarism, and laid down a uniform scale of relief for London, which became known after the Minister of Health as the Mond scale. This represented important advances for the unemployed in the recognition of the principle of outdoor relief for the unemployed, and in the standardizing of relief funding from a central body, the Metropolitan Common Poor Fund. But again it was a highly qualified victory. The Mond scale, while higher than that paid by some boards of guardians, was lower than that which had been secured by the unemployed in other boroughs. The second problem was that outdoor relief under the Mond scale had to be 10 shillings less than a laborer's standard rates of wages (defined by the government as that given to Grade A workers under the agreement of the London District Industrial Council for Non Trading Services (Manual Labour)), thus ensuring less eligibility, and third, Mond laid down regulations that grafted the household means test on to outdoor relief.[65]

Most importantly, the Mond scale succeeded in destroying the alliance that had been built up between the unemployed and sympathetic Labour-run local authorities, who now found their hands tied behind their backs by Mond's regulations. Ironically, this can be nowhere better seen than in the case of the Poplar board of guardians, who were asked on 25 January 1922 by a deputation of the local NUWCM branch, backed by a thousand unemployed, to raise the relief scales to the level of those laid down by the NUWCM. To the considerable surprise of both the unemployed and the guardians, Charlie Sumner, the chairman (who had himself marched with the unemployed in 1905) told the unemployed that their scale was too modest, and he successfully moved that the rate for every man and wife be 40 shillings (as opposed to the NUWCM's 36 shillings) and for every child 6 shillings. But the intricacies of the regulations governing financing introduced alongside the Mond scale were such that the Poplar board was unable to fund their new scales, and within a week they were forced back to their previous scale of relief. The unemployed felt betrayed and 900 of them, accompanied by three bands, invaded a meeting of the Poplar board on 6 February 1922, and refused to let the guardians leave until 4.30 A.M. the following day. "You appear to be hopeless and are merely the bulwark between us and the capitalist class to keep us in subjection" Melvina Walker castigated the captive guardians. This was not only an unfair judgment, but also a grossly inaccurate assessment. Boards of guardians since 1834 *had* been such a bulwark, and when some people, such as the Poplar guardians, had begun to refashion this bulwark into a working-class weapon, the government had set about stripping them of their powers, leaving them not so much hopeless as powerless.[66]

On the day the previous year that the government had begun arresting the Poplar councillors, *The Times* in a leading article on "Communism in Practice" had already realized some of the possibilities that existed for the ruling class in acceding to the demands of Poplarism. "The case for equalising the Poor Law rates is a strong one, though a uniform rate would of necessity involve the establishment of a central control over expenditure", said *The Times*, leading up to its point: "But a central control would not accord with the purpose of the Communists." Here were the first stirrings of an idea that was to gain increasing support over the next two decades: the denial of what small power the working class could exercise over welfare through the imposition of a central control over unemployment relief. As the old bulwarks crumbled, the state set about building new earthworks to contain the surging waters of the politics of the unemployed.[67]

One Big Union: Syndicalism and the Unemployed

The seeds of the downfall of the unemployed movement of the early 1920s lay in its very success. The wave of activity in the autumn of 1921 had its effect and sufficiently substantial (though barbed) concessions had been won that though distress was still ameliorated in only a minimal fashion, discontent largely evaporated. As Jack Braddock, leader of the Liverpool NUWCM, put it about his city, "the Liverpool Unemployed Workers' Committee Movement had satisfied the basic needs of the men, and they were no longer interested in it." At the same time the economy picked up slightly, and unemployment dropped from 17.7 percent in January 1922 to 12.8 percent in December 1922 (see Table 5.1), a figure around which unemployment levels were to more or less stay for the rest of the decade.[68]

But 1922 was not just a year of decline for the politics of the unemployed: it saw the NUWCM develop a much firmer hold over the unemployed movement, and it was also the year in which the movement passed through the most radical phase of its existence. The NUWCM leadership certainly wanted to radicalize the unemployed movement. "Not only must the unemployed have a fighting organisation", wrote Wal Hannington on January 1922, "but they must also have knowledge and a clear understanding of their class position . . . in order to combat the organised attacks of the employing class". But this radicalization came not only from above. While unemployment declined nationally, it was to continue to bite deep into the traditional heavy industries. In consequence union militants continued to join the dole lines and become active in the NUWCM, contributing to the drift leftwards. At the same time many of the conservative unemployed committees, founded and run more on soup kitchen than direct action lines, had seen the policy and methods of the militant committees yielding immediate and substantial results. Being able to offer no credible alternative to the militants' line, they fell by the wayside for lack of support. By September 1921 collecting boxes had disappeared from unemployed demonstrations, and many unemployed committees consciously shed their relief functions; the Tottenham unemployed committee, for example, declaring that charity was no substitute for work, announced in January 1922 that it would no longer accept provisions provided by local tradesmen, including 400 loaves of bread a week.[69]

By the end of 1922 all unemployed joining a committee affiliated to the NUWCM had to swear an oath of loyalty with the NUWCM that concluded: "Further, realising that only by abolition of this hideous capitalist system can the horror of unemployment be removed from out midst, I here and now take upon myself a binding oath, to never cease from active strife against this system until capitalism is abolished and our country and all its resources truly belong to the people." From an ill-defined collection of committees with varying and conflicting interpretations as to the nature of unemployment and of their role with regard to the unemployed, the LDC militants had created a national movement where the unemployed now swore loyalty to the leadership of the NUWCM, and an oath to participate actively in the abolition of capitalism.[70]

This did not mean that the unemployed movement became tightly controlled and rigidly orthodox. To the contrary it remained heterodox, embracing many committees pursuing highly different approaches to organization and policy, but sharing a belief in militancy and a general far left sympathy. Far from being a Bolshevized movement—an impression Hannington subtly imparts in his works—the NUWCM was criticized by the CPGB for its "loose organisation", and as late as 1924 the CPGB was still calling for the NUWCM to be Bolshevised. If anything the NUWCM inclined not to the Bolshevik model, but to that of its revolutionary rival, anarcho-syndicalism, particularly as it was propounded by the International Workers of the World (IWW).[71]

It had been the IWW, known as the Wobblies, who had first popularized the idea of the "One Big Union" (invariably the term was capitalised both by its proponents and opponents). Established in America in 1905, by Daniel De Leon, Eugene Debs, and William "Big Bill" Haywood, the IWW was based on the writings of De Leon, which emphasized the role of industrial action, as opposed to purer forms of politics, as fundamental in the creation of a socialist society. Supporters of the IWW argued for one big union embracing all workers as the best method of enabling effective revolutionary action. The keenest supporters of De Leon in Britain were the members of the Socialist Labour Party (SLP) who had been highly influential in the shop stewards' movement, particularly in Glasgow, during the war. While many SLP members went over to the CPGB upon its formation, some did not, and were active in the early unemployed movement. The NUWCM seems to have had many links with the IWW. The NAC ordered 600 IWW songbooks in January 1922, and the English organizer of the IWW wrote to his American supplier hinting that the NAC might also take a quantity of other IWW publications. Leading members of the NUWCM were directly involved with the IWW. Lily Thring, A. Squair, Jack Braddock (who signed his reports of the activities of the Liverpool NUWCM "Wobbly"), Jack Leckie ("Leckie is a physical force Anarchist and ardent antiparliamentarian, who breathes dynamite, and talks red armies. Has been in America, and knows all about the IWW. Some guy, believe me!" reported *The Socialist* in October 1920), and Gunnar Soderberg, for a time the NUWCM's London organizer, were all up until at least 1922 members of the IWW as well as of the CPGB. The anarcho-syndicalist tendencies of the NUWCM were to become pronounced during the engineers' lockout of 1922.[72]

The NUWCM recognized that the unemployed were a convenient tool to use to break strikes and to lower wages. Because their analysis stressed the need for a unified struggle of the whole working class, the NUWCM believed the unemployed should be organized not only upon the limited issue of their own welfare, but so that they were actively opposing the roles, such as blacklegging, that the unemployed were normally ascribed in a capitalist society. In the program that the NUWCM adopted at its 1921 conference was a clause pledging unemployed committees to assist striking workers in every way, and to seek representation on strike and lockout committees. But it was not until the NUWCM began to lose momentum early in 1922 that it began actively to organize its members to participate in industrial struggles. The NAC recognized that it was "coming to a standstill, if not on the verge of a retreat" and that it was necessary "to devise fresh ways and means of attacking the citadels of capitalism". The NUWCM was involved in some small local strikes in Bethnal Green, Ipswich, and Reading in February 1922, but it was with the national lock out of engineers in March 1922 that the NUWCM found itself with an opportunity to alter and extend its organization on a national basis.[73]

We have seen how the unemployed raided factories working overtime in early 1921 to demonstrate the need for working-class unity. These raids had a secondary aim of forcing the Amalgamated Engineering Union (AEU) leftwards over the issue of overtime, which had been a festering sore for the engineers since 1918. On 16 January 1922, 1,000 unemployed led by an NAC deputation marched to the AEU's Peckham headquarters, where Hannington harangued an AEU official saying that if the AEU was unwilling to act on the issue of overtime, the unemployed were "ready and willing" to raid factories to prevent it. If the trade unions lacked "sufficient decency and moral courage to put up a fight against overtime", said *Out of Work* in January 1922, ". . . then the National Unemployed Workers' Committee Movement will have to do it".[74]

When the engineers were locked out in March 1922 the NAC called upon its committees to "stand by the engineers". The unemployed were going to play "an important part" in this fight, wrote Hannington. "Don't be afraid of the unemployed pinching your jobs. They are better organised today than you are." At first the unemployed's rôle was to prevent blacklegging and to assist in mass picketing, but the NUWCM leadership constantly pushed for a more active and militant role for the unemployed. Hannington told a meeting of unemployed in Coventry on 12 March 1922, "not only to picket and demonstrate outside the Factory Gates, but if there are blacklegs inside go inside and fetch them out". By late March 1922 to "stand by engineers" meant the formation of "Joint Councils of Action", of which the unemployed committees were to be the nucleus. Believing that the collapse of the trade unions was an imminent possibility, the NUWCM now called for the establishment of alternative organizations "not based as on present lines, mainly concerned with sickness benefits, etc, but vigorously class conscious and prepared for ACTION." The alliance between the unemployed and the engineers, discouraged by the AEU executive who ruled that no unemployed man other than those locked out could sit on lockout committees, was by no means universal and was often—as in Liverpool—shunned by the engineers. But in some areas—Sheffield, Barrow, and parts of London—it did meet with success. Most remarkably, the unemployed ended up running the lockout in Coventry.[75]

We have already seen how the strongly syndicalist influenced Coventry UWC met with some success in 1920. In 1922 the leaders of the Coventry UWC—Tom Dingley, Jack Leckie, and Len Jackson—were able to fight for relief in a way that the AEU knew not, and were able to mobilize thousands of unemployed for picketing in a way the AEU could not. By May 1922 the Special Branch was reporting that "a grave situation" had arisen at Coventry, where the Coventry UWC was now able to rally up to 10,000 at demonstrations and was boasting that the whole district would soon be scab-free. It is clear from Special Branch reports that there was great concern about the embryonic attempt being made by the unemployed to find common cause with striking workers, to the extent that the Special Branch vested it with a revolutionary significance. The government responded by arresting and imprisoning many of the unemployed leaders, including Wal Hannington, Tom Dingley, Lily Thring, and Harry McShane.[76]

The support rendered by the unemployed to the engineers was sufficiently encouraging for the NAC on 28 April 1922 to call upon all unemployed committees "to form Unemployed and Employed Workers' Councils where ever possible." The councils, said the NAC, were the only way of "wresting power from the hands of officialdom and placing it in the hands of the rank and file". This was a flashback to the sovietism that had been popular among the syndicalist shop stewards between 1918 and 1920, and the NUWCM made no secret of its hope "that the great achievements of the Workers' Councils of Russia will be equalled by our own." Gunnar Soderburg took the whole thing one step further in a front page article in *Out of Work*, by declaring that "the unemployed movement is the germ or beginning of the ONE BIG UNION." Such ideas were only deepened, rather than destroyed by the defeat of the engineers: "the Union Bureaucracy, which is driving the working class movement into a state of despair, can be broken by the National Unemployed Workers' Committee Movement", claimed *Out of Work* in August 1922; "a movement like ours . . . can bring about the resuscitation of the whole working class movement." In advocating that it, and not the CPGB, should organize the employed worker, the NUWCM was laying down an unspoken challenge to the authority of the CPGB. In suggesting that mass workers' councils rather than a Leninist vanguard would spearhead the revolution it was propounding a theory of revolutionary struggle clearly at odds with that of the CPGB, who only recognized workers' councils in a token way. Whether or not this was apparent to the NUWCM it is not easy to say, but certainly it was to the CPGB leadership. The CPGB had repudiated the idea of the one big union, and by 1922 the people advocating the one big union, such as John MacLean, who had set up a "One Big Union Publicity Committee", and Sylvia Pankhurst, who was attempting to organize the Fourth International (of Opposition Communist Parties, not Trotsky's Fourth International, founded much later) in Britain upon the basis of support for the one big union, were the CPGB's revolutionary rivals.[77]

The NUWCM was condemned in the Communist Party press for having allowed "talk of the One Big Union to become prevalent in the organisation, until quite a number of the unemployed dreamt of their organisation gradually enrolling unemployed members, until they superseded the present Trade Unions by One Big organisation of employed and unemployed." At its fifth congress in October 1922, the CPGB strongly condemned the idea of joint unemployed and employed workers' committees. The story of the NUWCM's syndicalist outburst does not quite end with this condemnation, but with the tantalizing questions that are raised by a Special Branch report made a few weeks prior to the congress. "Communist officials are trying to induce Hannington, Haye and Holt to convert their organisation into a National Employed and Unemployed Workers' Committee Movement, as a basis for a 'One Big Industrial Union': it is stated that funds would be available for the project." The Special Branch report does not name the officials, so who were they? It seems extremely unlikely that they were representing the CPGB leadership, which would seem to leave two alternatives. Either they were members of rival Communist sects, or CPGB officials trying to organize an opposition within the party to the process of Bolshevization. Either way it would indicate that there was hope of using the NUWCM as a revolutionary alternative to a Bolshevized CPGB; either way it probably tells us much more about how the NUWCM had become the repositry of outmoded revolutionary theories and aspirations than it does about any significant opposition to the bolshevised CPGB in the 1920s. These theories were, as we will shortly see, nearly to destroy the NUWCM in 1923.[78]

This leads us to the fundamental question of what exactly was the relation between the NUWCM and the Communist Party. It may seem that this is a relatively unimportant question, one that is peripheral to our main enquiry. It may seem that an unusual and unnecessary weight is placed upon this relationship in both this and the next chapter. But to arrive at any understanding of the NUWCM it is first necessary to understand the precise nature of the relationship between the CPGB and the NUWCM. When the 1922 hunger marchers arrived in London there was great public interest in them and their cause. To discredit them the newly elected government of Andrew Bonar Law arranged "for publicity to be given to the Communist character and record of the leaders of the unemployed marchers." This devious attempt to smear and dismiss the entire march as a Moscow plot resulted in every newspaper (excepting the *Daily Herald*) publishing on 22 November 1922 a list supplied by the Special Branch of the leading marchers, accompanied by a description of their police record and every scurrilous detail that could be found against them, in every case laying great stress on these men's association with the CPGB. And ever since, in a way, the inter-war unemployed movement has been reduced to being explained as some sort of creation of Moscow, existing only as an extension of the CPGB and its aspirations. Any study of the inter-war unemployed movement, to have any value, must therefore enter the labyrinthine world of far-left politics in the inter-war period and seek to disentangle the reality of the NUWCM and later the NUWM from the rhetoric, ideology, and practice of Communist politics. Some of these themes are pursued further in Chapter Six; here we will limit our investigation to the NUWCM in the early 1920s.[79]

It seems clear that while the NUWCM received occasional handouts from the CPGB, it was not funded on any regular basis by them. While most of the leadership were CPGB members, we cannot assume that they had anywhere near the same sense of commitment to the party line that was to characterize the CPGB in later years. It is difficult to ascertain how much loyalty the leaders of the early unemployed movement felt toward the CPGB. The concept of "the Party" and the rigid discipline and unswerving loyalty it required, as it was to become understood in the 1930s and 1940s, was not immediately and automatically accepted. While, by the 1940s, virtually every member referred to the CPGB as "the Party", as if there was only one true Party, only one Party that mattered, one way, one truth, many of the members of the early CPGB probably still regarded it in much the same way as they had regarded the old socialist societies—vehicles for discussion and propaganda, but not the determining political fact of their lives. For them the important political activity in their lives was whatever movement they were currently involved in—the shop stewards' movement until 1920, the unemployed movement from 1921 onwards—and their Party loyalties were a consequence of this activity, and not the inverse. The Executive Bureau of the RILU criticised the British Bureau of the RILU in 1924 for not actively combatting the "tendencies of the non-Party revolutionary workers to keep their organisations independent of Communist influence", and particularly for being "insufficiently positive . . . in the leadership of the unemployed movement." In the following year the CPGB's Central Commission in its confidential report to the Party congress concluded that there "had been little or no effective contact between the Party as a whole and the Unemployed Movement; and that the question, politically and organisationally, has still to receive adequate attention." Perhaps most tellingly of all, the NUWCM at its third conference in 1923 passed a resolution calling for the organization of the unemployed to fight for the overthrow of capitalism, 59 votes to 24; but rejected a resolution calling upon the NUWCM to form a united front with the CPGB, 55 votes to 52. Immediately after, another resolution instructing the NAC to affiliate with the RILU was carried 85 votes to 13, indicating the NUWCM's desire to be associated with industrial revolutionary politics, but not to be a tool of the CPGB. It demonstrated that while the NAC was sympathetic to the CPGB and peopled by its activists, NUWCM branches, and hence the movement as a whole, was never subordinate to the CPGB. Witness the coded admission of failure by the CPGB's Central Committee in 1924: "a better understanding had been arrived at with all our members actively working within the Unemployed Movement, particularly at the centre," but it felt compelled to add ". . . the way now seems clear to extend that to all districts."[80]

By the summer of 1922 the NUWCM found itself in "grave financial difficulties" and in danger of having to close down its headquarters. In a final attempt to revive its flagging fortunes, the NUWCM organized a national hunger march on London. This had its inspiration in a hunger march made by members of the Birmingham NUWCM to London in August 1922, which had made a large enough impact for the *Daily Herald* to suggest that a national march be organized with the aim of meeting the prime minister. The NAC, deciding that the *Herald*'s suggestion was "a very good idea", set about organizing a national march.[81]

By mid October 1922 the first contingents of unemployed began marching from the far northern towns. At first it seemed that the hunger march would bring about a revival of the fortunes of the NUWCM, with demonstrations beginning to recur, sometimes with an ominous taint. At a demonstration of 1,500 unemployed outside the Stepney workhouse on 24 October 1922 a Mills bomb was thrown at the police as they moved in weilding their truncheons. People momentarily scattered, but the Mills bomb was empty and failed to explode. It lay on the ground without substance and without threat, a symbol for the march that was to follow.[82]

As the marchers advanced on London a general election took place, leading to the return of the Conservatives under Bonar Law. Due to adverse publicity orchestrated by the government London was in a state of some nervousness as to the marchers' possible intentions. On the morning of the day chosen by the NUWCM to seek an audience with Bonar Law (who had made it clear that he would not see them) the NUWCM leaders made an inspection of Whitehall to discover that the government had made elaborate preparations to prevent the unemployed marching on Downing Street. All traffic had been stopped, government office windows were boarded up, barricades were everywhere, and the streets empty save for large forces of police. Some papers had reported that machine gun nests had heen set up in certain buildings, and although the NUWCM leaders were unable to sight them they were not prepared to dismiss the story as "another capitalist lie". The state had readied itself for battle; the unemployed had not. The NUWCM, unwilling to risk the consequences of marching on Whitehall, decided that a deputation would proceed to Whitehall while the demonstration, which ultimately numbered 70,000, would march through the West End to Hyde Park. Hannington attempted to justify the decision not to march on Whitehall to the Hyde Park meeting. "If there had been a fight today we possibly would have been defeated as an army, and the opposing force would have laid down the conditions on which we could work in the future. But there has been no fight and there is no defeat."[83]

But he was wrong, for their bluff had been called and they had lost: and now the NUWCM, in an attempt to make good their failure, was to turn this defeat into a rout. The marchers had originally intended to stay in London less than a fortnight before returning home, but incensed by Bonar Law's refusal to see them, they announced their intention of staying in London until he did. To back themselves up, the NUWCM rashly called for reinforcements of unemployed to march on London. The government responded by instructing poor law authorities, to which marchers had to resort for shelter and food, to discourage the marchers as much as possible, and this was enforced by reducing outdoor relief and paying it in kind to the marchers, and by offering the absolute minimum in the way of food.[84]

By December 1922 the march was falling apart. Many marchers considered further action futile, and keen to return home, some tried to march back, while others pressured boards of guardians to send them home by train. The NAC found they had dug themselves into a deep and dark hole. While many wanted an end to the march, others, including the Scots, were against going back immediately, and threatened to leave the NUWCM if the march was ended, an action that would have destroyed any claim made by the NUWCM to speak for the unemployed of the nation. Compounding these problems were the further 1,000 marchers who were heading toward the capital, who, if the march were to be ended, would have to be contacted and return home without having reached London, a sequence of events that would have greatly, and possibly even fatally, damaged the NUWCM's credibility. The NUWCM had little choice but to try and give a semblance of order to what was becoming a debacle by establishing a relay system whereby marchers arriving in London replaced marchers already there, who then returned home.[85]

The solidarity of the marchers was collapsing. Sixty marchers at the Wandsworth workhouse came out in a body to protest against the bad food. They telephoned

Hannington and threatened a "forcible demonstration" at Queens Square if they were not provided with food. Hannington was forced to give them money, collected and intended for other purposes, to buy food. "A great tactless [*sic*] blunder arose", wrote a chief marshall of the march in a letter home. "Personally I don't think Law will climb down". By late December 1922 there were only 500 of the original 2,000 marchers remaining in London. To try to restore morale, as well as to recruit more marchers, two groups of marchers undertook further marches around southern England in the manner of the pre-war propaganda marches, one contingent being led by Dingley, the other by Hannington. They set out on 24 January 1923, and met back together at a demonstration in Hyde Park on 13 February 1923, neither contingent very much larger. The number of marchers in London was now at its lowest level, and having failed in its objective, the NUWCM was forced to admit defeat. On 20 February 1923, about five months after the march had commenced with such fervor and hope, the marchers returned home and the march drew to an ignominious conclusion.[86]

Beyond failing upon its own terms the march had greatly weakened the unemployed movement by removing the NUWCM activists from the work of local organization during the critical period of early winter, and this, it was later claimed, "had a disastrous effect upon the already scattered organisation". Certainly the winter of 1922-23 was the first since the war not to experience serious unrest on the streets. The achievements of the march had been its most obvious features and were none the less significant for that: 2,000 men had marched to London from all over the nation. The effect of the march upon the men who took part is difficult to ascertain, but for some, like Tommy James, who marched with the Rotherham contingent of forty men and a pony and cart, it was a decisive experience that was to lead to a lifelong commitment to Communism, and would ultimately take him to the battlefields of Spain as an international brigadier. The great irony of the 1922 hunger march, as with all the hunger marches, was that while it concentrated on immediate specifics that it could not win, it did have a potent afterlife in the activity both of those who marched, and of those who were affected by the march, and it is in this largely intangible area that the true success and the great significance of the marches lies.[87]

The Collapse and Rebuilding of the NUWCM, 1923-1929

"The unemployed strategists have reached the end of their tether;"wrote the Communist R. Page Arnot in 1923; "driven by the lowness of the state dole they were able for a time to exploit the resources of local government. 'Go to the Guardians' was good tactics, but it has yielded the inevitable result that the Guardians are either bankrupt or have been replaced by hard faced men whose business it is to guard the rates." But what was the NUWCM to do? Not only was its organization verging on bankruptcy, its support among the unemployed slipping, and its structure thrown into disarray by the march, but unemployment was falling slowly, but significantly, from 17.7 percent in January 1922, to 13.3 percent in January 1923, to 10.6 percent by the end of 1923 (see Table 5.1). By April 1923 the number of committees affiliated with the NUWCM had slumped in London and the Home Counties from 104 to 65; in the Midlands from 47 to 12; in Lancashire from 66 to 21; and in Wales only a quarter of the 58 committees were functioning. "Those who are engaged in organising the unemployed are constantly crying for new forms of activity to be suggested", wrote G. D. H. Cole in this year of decline for the NUWCM: "But such new forms are not easily devised."[88]

All that was left was what Arnot described as "a sham thing", the illusory hope of affiliation with the TUC. One consequence of the 1922 hunger march had been a meeting of the NUWCM officials and the TUC General Council on 20 December 1922, which led to a day of national joint demonstrations on 7 January 1923, known as Unemployed Sunday. While not a resounding success, it raised hopes of further joint activity. The NUWCM began to press for affiliation with the TUC, and at the 1923 Trades Union Congress at Plymouth it was agreed that the TUC General Council and the NUWCM should establish a joint advisory committee on unemployment. Some joint activity was undertaken as a result of the work of the committee, but it was neither particularly popular nor successful. The General Council grew increasingly hostile to the NUWCM, rejecting both the joint committee's proposal whereby trade unions would recognize an NUWCM card as a clearance for a person joining a trade union upon finding employment, and the NAC's call for a jointly organized great national hunger march; not holding any further meetings of the committee after July 1925 despite calls by the NUWCM, and, following the general strike, from August 1926 refusing outright to convene any further meetings. In 1927 the General Council disbanded the committee, a decision endorsed by the TUC the following year.[89]

On May Day 1923 Wal Hannington illegally left Britain and made his way to Russia to attend an RILU conference. In his absence the NUWCM came perilously close to total disintegration. "We have known for some time that the unemployed movement has not been working successfully and that to a great extent its leadership was passing out of the hands of the party", Ernest Cant, London organizer of the CPGB, admitted on 6 June 1923. The opposition to the Party element was led by Gunnar Soderburg, Liverpool seaman, IWW member, and organizer of the London unemployed. Personal and political differences were to lead Soderburg in July 1923 to form a breakaway organization, the Unemployed Workers' Organisation (UWO), as a rival to the NUWCM.[90]

Soderburg entered into an alliance with Sylvia Pankhurst, who had been expelled from the CPGB for her continued support of ultra-left politics, including anti-parliamentarianism, and in particular because of her support and publicization of the Workers' Opposition, the left wing of the Russian Bolsheviks, who unsuccessfully opposed Lenin's New Economic Policy in the early 1920s. The UWO approached Pankhurst early in July 1923 asking for space in her paper, the *Workers' Dreadnought,* for their manifesto that mounted a scarifying attack upon the NUWCM, claiming it was dominated by professional politicians and had failed to secure a better lot for the unemployed. The NUWCM slogan "Work or maintenance at trade union rates" was dismissed as conservative, and the UWO counterposed their slogan "Abolition of the wage system". The UWO's ultra-leftism was apparent in its dismissal of the CPGB as "reformist", while its strong syndicalism was evident in its use of the word "politician" as a term of utter contempt, and its advocacy of direct action as a means of building a genuine working class revolutionary movement. Sylvia Pankhurst found the manifesto "similar to our views", and published it.[91]

Disaffection within the NUWCM was sufficiently strong that the UWO was able in the summer of 1923 to make substantial inroads into the heart of the NUWCM. The London unemployed committees—Poplar, Bow and Bromley, Camberwell, Edmonton, South Lambeth, Tottenham, Enfield, Ponders End, and Milwall—all left the NUWCM and went over to the UWO. The UWO, as an anti-parliamentary body, was not concerned—as the NUWCM was—with building any alliances with the labor, and instead chose to highlight what they saw as the futility of socialists ever attempting to work from within the state machine. In Poplar a financial crisis, precipitated by the run on outdoor relief caused by the dock laborers' strike, was to combine with a substantial drop in wages and prices to force the Poplar board of guardians (now led by George Lansbury's son Edgar, a Communist) to reduce its scales of outdoor relief. On 26 September 1923 the Poplar guardians were held captive in their meeting room by a demonstration of 200 unemployed organized by the UWO. The police were contacted, and upon their arrival the guardians, after some argument, authorized their entry. The police smashed windows to get inside, and then batoned the unemployed with such viciousness that twenty had to be treated in hospital. The UWO saw the event as a vindication of their policy of anti-parliamentarianism: "we can claim victory for our defeat by being able to prove the fallacy and futility of the local governing bodies in their endeavour to abolish poverty and distress."[92]

Upon returning from Russia in mid-September 1923 Hannington found the NUWCM in debt and the NAC racked with acrimony. He set about salvaging what he could from the wreckage, and went straight into the fight agreeing to a debate with Soderburg, which, according to the *Workers' Dreadnought*, Hannington lost. Worse came in Glasgow in an unemployed meeting where Hannington attacked the UWO for its treatment of the Poplar board of guardians. John MacLean, who only had a few weeks left to live, had published a pamphlet criticizing the use of police at Poplar. When MacLean entered, the meeting turned on Hannington who, for the first and last time in his life, was howled down by the unemployed. The meeting then broke up in disorder. The UWO's philosophy was sufficiently popular for the revolt against the NUWCM to spread briefly to centers outside of London, and by January 1924 the UWO was claiming a membership of 3,000.[93]

But the times were unpropitious for any organization of the unemployed, far less one without any backing, and engaged in a constant battle with the entrenched NUWCM. The year 1924 saw an economic upswing, and unemployment fell to 9.3 percent in June 1924, the lowest recorded monthly figure between 1921 and 1939 (see Tables 5.1 and 6.1). The first Labour government was formed in January 1924, and although it failed to live up to the hopes it had generated about how unemployment would be cured when the Labour Party came to power, it did abolish the gap; increase the period of uncovenanted (now renamed extended) benefit to a maximum of forty-one weeks; and increase benefits for men from 15 shillings to 18 shillings a week, for women from 12 shillings to 15 shillings, and for a child dependent from 1 shilling to 2 shillings. These changes represented small but material improvements for the unemployed, which, combined with the faith many vested in the first Labour government, did much to calm the temper of the unemployed and reduce agitation further. The UWO crumbled and then disappeared. Ultimately the UWO was important not for its achievements, which were negligible and transitory, but for what it signified about the changing nature of the politics of the unemployed. In this sense the UWO was more than an isolated outburst of ultra-left sectarianism; more, even, than a final expression of the radical revolutionary politics of the preceding decade, that could no longer be fitted into the mold that being forced upon revolutionary politics by the CPGB. It was at heart a misdirected cry of anguish at the collapse of a form of unemployed politics, the symbiotic relationship between local Labour representatives and unemployed activity, that had, for over a quarter of a century, been the bedrock of the politics of the unemployed and a fecund area for the growth of a radical, grassroots working-class politics.[94]

Meanwhile the NUWCM languished, and from what can be gathered from the report of its fourth conference, held at Sheffield on 6-8 December 1924, had been lucky to survive at all. The NUWCM had just one pound in hand and the NAC officials had been able to get Sheffield only by using money collected at meetings the previous week. Even Wal Hannington, a man who would always find the indelible imprint of working-class advance stamped upon the face of the worst defeat, could do no better than to urge the delegates "not to lose heart because of the apathy of the unemployed." At the 1924 conference it was evident that the NUWCM as it had been was coming to an end. The leaders of its heroic years had gone or were going. Percy Haye resigned as secretary, embittered and wearied by the events of 1923. Harry McShane was to disappear to the Yukon for some years, while Tom Dingley was no longer active, having suffered a breakdown following the 1922 lockout. Jack Braddock had left the CPGB and no longer worked with the unemployed. Harry Emery, after being caught stealing guns for the IRA, had fled to Russia. Hannington had been transferred by the CPGB from his work with the now moribund NUWCM to the Minority Movement (MM), established by the CPGB in August 1924 in the hope of creating a national rank and file movement in industry under Party control. From the MM's inauguration Hannington was on its national executive, and he later became national organizer of the Metal Workers' Minority Movement (MWMM). As he worked full time with the MM, his role as NUWCM organizer became largely token, leading to some disgruntled—and hastily refuted—rumblings at the NUWCM's fifth national conference in 1926.[95]

Between 1924 and 1929 the NUWCM limped along, slowly building a new unemployed movement, different in structure, ideology, and social basis than the old NUWCM. From 1925 onwards the relative inactivity of the NUWCM allowed Party activists to associate themselves much more closely with the NUWCM not just at the level of national leadership, but at the local branch level. While it was largely only Communist activists who, under instructions, had any interest in keeping the NUWCM alive, it is important to remember that the CPGB was, through the 1920s, primarily concerned with the struggles inside the factory and the workshop, and not those outside of it. The CPGB was the first British Marxist party to attempt to organize its members on a trade union basis, and it was upon industrial organization that the Party concentrated its efforts through the decade in attempting to create a revolutionary ferment in Britain. Within this model a comatose NUWCM, whose officials had to beg to pay their fares to their own conference, did not loom large. Only in this context can Communist work within the NUWCM, and at the same time the NUWCM's continued independence, be understood. "The eyes of all Communists should be turned to the factory, to the factory gate", said the CPGB Organising Committee in 1925. In the paradigm of the industrial proletariat resolutely marching toward class victory, eyes were averted when the unemployed straggled into view.[96]

While unemployment between 1926 and 1930—relative to the rest of the inter-war—was low, it became concentrated in certain black spots in Scotland, north England, and south Wales. Here Communist activists rebuilt the NUWCM, keeping otherwise defunct branches ticking over, resuscitating dead branches, and occasionally building new ones. It is significant that the only unemployed activity of any import between 1923 and 1929 was the south Welsh miners' hunger march of 1927. Very occasionally, near total unemployment, such as was to become commonplace in the south Welsh mining valleys, acted as a solvent on the restraints upon radical activity in devastated communities, and the Communists were for a short time able to create counter communities based on a radical proletarian culture. No "Little Moscow" was ever founded in areas of low or even medium unemployment. A feature of the structural decline of the old industries was the simultaneous decrease in the size of the working population and an increase in the number unemployed. In coal mining, for example, the national workforce shrank by nearly half a million between 1920 and 1934, yet the level of unemployment in the industry, which was 3 percent in 1923, was 29.7 percent 11 years later. Those that left went to the south or the Midlands where there was at least hope of getting work. But not all found it easy to uproot themselves; bound by tradition, family ties, sentimental attachment, mortgages, and friendship, they were what has been described as "the trapped generation". With no prospect of work, little political and no industrial power, they resorted to the politics of the street—demonstrations, eviction fights, and the like to protect what little dignity and few possessions remained. In such areas the NUWCM became only another hat which the politics of the community wore when dealing specifically with issues of unemployment: thus the Mardy lodge of the South Wales Miners' Federation (SWMF) allowed the local branch of the NUWCM to be merged into it. In areas of high unemployment outside the "Little Moscows" the distinction between the local NUWCM and the local CPGB also often became blurred, even in the eyes of the activists themselves. *The Red Challenger*, news sheet of the Merthyr CPGB in the late 1920s, focused generally on unemployment; and the word "we", which was often used, denoted not Communists, but unemployed. The conflation and confusion of both is apparent in the declaration that "we must build up the NUWCM. The unemployed must be organised for the coming struggle. Therefore join the Communist Party without delay."[97]

Yet the overall impression is that of Communists working within a movement, rather than controlling it. Certainly in London this seems to have been the case. In August 1925 the London DC of the CPGB asked branches for "the names and addresses of all nuclei leaders in Trade Union branches and NUWCM committees", implying that the NUWCM was no more CPGB run than the trade unions, hence the need for organization of party activists within both. In March 1926 the Young Communist League (YCL) was calling for improved cooperation with the NUWCM, while the London district committee of the CPGB issued a string of calls ordering all unemployed Party members to take an active part in the work of the NUWCM. These seem to have been so unpopular that one call late in 1927 concluded by requesting branches to forward particulars of anybody failing to comply with the call "in order that the necessary disciplinary action may be taken." While the NUWCM cannot then be dismissed as a Communist front organization, it is clear that Communists were critical in ensuring the survival of the NUWCM.[98]

To concentrate only on the political alignments of the unemployed movement is to obscure its more fundamental achievement. The various left-wing organizations of the unemployed in the 1920s may have differed in ideology, but they all shared an overriding preoccupation with winning some immediate relief for the unemployed. The cry remained "work or maintenance", but it was maintenance that was sought and often won from local bodies. John MacLean thus may have hoped for the establishment of a Scottish Workers' Republic by the unemployed, but the agitation he led focused upon obtaining food with which to survive. As he put it at his trial, "so far as we were concerned, it was a case of food first, work came second." While MacLean and his followers advocated, in the words of Sandy Ross, "the forcible possession of the necessaries of life", MacLean later stating that they had always told the unemployed who felt they "could not hold out it was their business to go out and take food rather than die of starvation", their tactics revolved around pressuring the Glasgow council for food. While the NUWCM required members to swear an oath that ended with a call to fight to abolish capitalism, its interests lay not just in the broader political struggle, but equally in addressing the immediate problems of the unemployed, the first part of the oath declaring that the aim of the NUWCM was to ensure "that no man, woman or child suffers hunger or want this winter." The NUWCM was always as committed to the immediate problems of relieving distress as it was to the revolutionary struggle, a point Hannington was many years later to stress strongly in a letter to the historian L. J.

MacFarlane. And their achievements in this regard were not inconsiderable. The real value of unemployment benefit increased greatly. Though attended by numerous exclusive qualifications, benefit, between November 1920 and August 1931, rose 92 percent for a single man, and 240 percent for a man with a wife and two children. Not only had the benefit so risen, but it was by 1930 paid almost continuously, and rather than its amount being determined by actuarial principles, it was determined by social considerations: rather than representing a return upon an amount paid in that bore no relation to how much an unemployed person needed to get by, it now represented the bare minimum deemed necessary to survive.[99]

Reaction

Reaction to the outburst of unemployed activity in the 1920s was to have a considerable impact upon the later history of the politics of the unemployed. The hysterical edge of bourgeois reaction took numerous forms: one was a revival of interest in the pseudo-science of eugenics and the endorsement of the idea of the compulsory sterilization of the unfit; Mrs. B. I. Drysdale at the Fifth Neo-Malthusian conference in July 1922, referring to the "growing discontent and unrest . . . found among the unemployed workers", concluded, "Civilisation in its own defence, and for its own continued existence, must limit the amount of poor quality citizens." Another form was the numerous spying organizations set up by frightened capitalists, one of which in Liverpool, financed partly by Cunard, claimed in a secret report in 1925 to have destroyed "the Unemployed Movement".[100]

More substantial was the reaction of the state in subtle reworkings of the welfare system. Through the gradual tightening up on the application of the "not genuinely seeking work" clause almost three million claims for unemployment benefit were to be disallowed between 1921 and 1930. The clause required applicants for unemployment benefit to prove that they were genuinely seeking employment and were unable to obtain it. Originally only applied to those on uncovenanted benefit, it was extended to those on covenanted benefit (those who were fully entitled to benefit under the actuarial principles of 1911) by the 1924 Labour government. The clause in operation was bureaucracy at its cruelest and most degrading. Applicants were forced to tramp from worksite to worksite knowing only too well that there was no work to be had, but that the charade had to be acted out in order to obtain benefit. Margaret McCarthy, Bradford spinner and NUWCM activist, was to recall that "the genuinely seeking work clause, above all else, set our pride on edge. To genuinely seek work in Lancashire in the years of the depression was a farce." It is a cliche, but in this case true, that the clause seared itself into the minds of people. One Welsh unemployed activist visited two unemployed friends at a mental hospital where they had been for six months. He recalled that "they were standing by a wall, nothing in their hands, but acting as if there was. And I asked 'Well, what are you doing?' And he said, 'I'm trying to write out a list of where I was looking for work last week.' " Perhaps the worst of the test was that unlike a cut in the rate in unemployment benefit, it did not affect all the unemployed equally. The test had originally been intended to get married women off benefit, and it was not to be until 1929, when the test began to affect large numbers of unemployed men, that there was any significant protest about it. To the extent that the unemployed failed to take action over this issue, they remained prisoners of their own conservatism, of the false beliefs that most women did not really want waged work, and that men struck off under the test were similarly uninterested, and thus were malingerers.[101]

Terrible as the test was, it was nowhere near as important to the history or the politics of the unemployed as the changes then occurring in the relations between central and local government. Neville Chamberlain, Minister of Health from 1924 to 1929, was determined to end the practice of boards of guardians acceding to working-class pressure and paying high scales of relief, a practice that went under the catch all title of "Poplarism". There was pressure within the Conservative Party, originating from the far-right British Empire Union (BEU) to have those on relief disenfranchised. The lunacy of a system that allowed those on relief to vote upon how it was spent "reached its climax", according to the BEU, "when the National Organised Unemployed who were running candidates at Guardians elections demanded a National Scale." Prior to the general strike Chamberlain drafted a bill that gave the Minister of Health the power to take over a board "unable to discharge its functions", in reality any board paying relief regarded as extravagant. But not until after the general strike did Chamberlain feel emboldened enough to have his bill enacted as the Guardians Default Act. As a warning to other local bodies, he used it to supersede the West Ham board of guardians in 1926, and the Bedwellty and Chester-le-street (Durham) boards in 1927. All these bodies had Labour majorities and were considered generous in their scales of outdoor relief. But Chamberlain was not content to rely only on intimidation. In late 1928 he introduced the Local Government Bill into Parliament, and it was enacted the following year. This measure abolished boards of guardians and transferred their powers to country councils and county boroughs, who were now to administer the poor law through Public Assistance Committees (PACs). Funding for relief was no longer to be drawn from local rates, but henceforth from block grants from the Exchequer. Instead of the system of triennial election for the boards of guardians, the PAC was to be appointed by the county or borough council, who now only had to face the annual election of one-third of its members, which meant that previously dynamic swings in electoral fortune, such as in 1918, would be muted. Additionally, ultimate responsibility for PAC decisions rested with the council. In this way the relationship between local government and the central state was also fundamentally altered, and the aim of the BEU to disenfranchise the unemployed subtly realized.[102]

Far from weakening the edifice of the poor law, the act shored it up by removing it from the corrosive influence of the politics of the unemployed. Even where a county or borough council could be successfully pressured by the unemployed, its scope of activity was severely circumscribed as it had to answer to its new paymaster, the central government. What had been established was what *The Times* had advocated on 1 September 1921 in reaction to Poplarism: "a central control over expenditure" that "would not accord with the purpose of the Communists". It is grimly ironic that of all the legacies of the politics of the unemployed this was to be the most enduring.

6

Are We Red? The National Unemployed Workers Movement, 1929–1939

When trade has become as brisk as anyone can naturally expect trade now to become for this country, we shall still have a residuum. We shall still have a population which were they not human beings, one would describe—merely for the sake of making quite clear what their position was—as "scrap".

—Ramsay MacDonald, Prime Minister, 23 November 1932.

Some people work and some do not
It depends on how much cash they've got.
So if you're hungry now I guess
Well, next week you may be getting less.

—Stephen "Johnny" Hicks, Stepney boxer poet and NUWM member.[1]

The history of the politics of the unemployed in the inter-war period can be divided, with some precision, by the sixth national conference of the NUWCM between 14 and 16 September 1929. There the politics of the unemployed took on a fundamentally different appearance from the loose coalition of often anarchistic unemployed committees formed in the heady atmosphere of the early 1920s. Gone were the revolutionary overtones of the early days when members swore an oath against "this hideous capitalist system", "to never cease from active strife against this system until capitalism is abolished and our country and all its resources truly belong to the people". In place of this, the NUWCM in 1929 adopted a new constitution, object eight of which rather meekly vowed "that our movement shall keep before itself the ultimate goal of working class power for the overthrow of capitalism and the establishment of the Workers' Socialist Republic." The times were not revolutionary, and nor were the unemployed activists. Gone were many of the larger than life figures of the early 1920s, existing in the dark shadow of post-war European revolutionary politics, with furtive now largely lost connections to all sorts of insurrectionary groups. There is no John MacLean with a dream of a Scottish Workers' Republic, no Lily Thring with her machine guns and body guard, no Harry

Emery prepared to raid a Birmingham arms factory for the IRA, and upon being caught, to flee on bail to Ireland, and from there to Russia.[2]

At the sixth conference of the NUWCM a new conception of unemployed politics, very different from that of the early 1920s, was being promulgated; and it was a conception, first and foremost, of the unemployed fighting within the system, and not outside of it and seeking to overthrow it. In many ways the program adopted by the NUWCM in 1929 was exceedingly moderate. Embodied in the new constitution and the resolutions were calls for the repeal of the Guardians Default Act and of the various other poor law reforms, reestablishment of the boards of guardians, abolition of test and task work, all of these demands being summed up in object four of the new constitution: "To fight for the removal of the many administrative grievances that exist in the Unemployed Insurance Scheme and the Poor Law." The essence of the conference was distilled in a resolution moved by Sid Elias upon poor law reform, which called for direct representation of NUWCM members on Public Assistance Committees (PACs), thereby seeking to be incorporated into the existing welfare structure.[3]

The structure of the NUWCM was subtly but definitely altered with power now residing at the top with a Headquarters Advisory Committee (HAC) "composed of capable comrades residing in the London area, selected by the NAC", who were vested with the all-important job of "effectively controlling and supervising" the work of the National Headquarters in between meetings of the National Advisory Council (NAC), effectively giving the reins of the organization to Communist Party activists in London. The NAC was to be composed of the executive elected by conference and one delegate from each District Council (DC). Each DC, in turn, was composed of delegates from local branches over whom it enjoyed certain powers. Any decisions it made were binding upon all its branches and all branches were obligated to participate in any joint work prescribed by the DC. All of this left the branches with very little constitutional power. It is possible to see elements of the Bolshevik principles of democratic centralism being built into the structure of the NUWCM, but in practice the NAC and the HAC lacked the organization and the powers to enforce this structure. The NUWCM headquarters were, to some extent against their will, to remain in thrall to the pulse of the branches, being compelled to follow the leads of rank and file activists, rather than the inverse. When in 1935 the NAC passed a resolution calling upon the unemployed to take "all possible action" against Fascist Italy following Mussolini's invasion of Abyssinia, copies of the resolution were sent to branches with a circular making it clear that this was only the opinion of the NAC and not of the whole movement, explaining: "The NUWM exists for the express purpose of leading the fight against unemployment. . . .The NAC recognise that on other questions of political importance there are many shades of opinion within the NUWM. . . . we recognise that on such an issue there may be strong differences of opinion within our Movement and because of this greatest toleration must be shown to comrades who honestly differ with us on this question."[4]

The tension between overt political aims and the immediate needs of the unemployed had been apparent since the earliest days of SDF involvement. Part of the success of CPGB activists during the inter-war period was their ability to subsume their political desires within unemployed work. "The members of the Comunist Party have cut out all theory stuff", reported Tom McKay, one of the 1922 hunger march leaders, to the NUWCM headquarters in the same year, "and are doing some good rock bottom work." However differently this new structure was to operate in practice, its adoption demonstrated the great difference between the unemployed movement of the early 1920s and the movement that was about to enter the 1930s. This profound change is best illustrated by the decision of the NAC meeting a month after the 1929 conference to shorten the name of the movement to that of the National Unemployed Workers' Movement (NUWM). The word "committee" and with it all the old syndicalist dreams of establishing a new order based on workers' committees, was dispensed with and the UWCs became, more prosaically and less independently, branches of the NUWM, a body that had forsaken its dreams of a revolution for a program that sought some amelioration of the plight of the unemployed through militant activity. At the same meeting it was reported that in Chatham an unemployed man had been imprisoned for six months for stealing a loaf of bread. Four days after the NAC meeting Wall Street crashed; self-defenestration, in John Hepworth's memorable phrase, became fashionable; and while a man from Chatham spent half a year of his life in jail pondering the criminal consequences of hunger, capitalism entered the greatest crisis of its history.[5]

Regrettably, this chapter does not seek to chronicle the remarkable and myriad activities of the unemployed in these years of crisis, for which a work at least the size of the book would be required to do any justice. Pressure of space limits this chapter to the humbler aim of exploring exactly what the NUWM was, and what it meant to working-class people. To do this it attempts to answer the following questions, which seem central to any understanding of the NUWM. First, what was the relation of the CPGB to the NUWM? Second, what was the meaning and effect of the unemployed protest in the 1930s? And third, what part did women play in the NUWM?

The CPGB and the NUWM

Within and without Communist historical writing the NUWM is referred to as a subsidiary Communist Party organization, an approach that blurs the real shape and import of the NUWM. This is a significant issue if only because too many of both the NUWM's friends and enemies, both at the time and since, have denied the importance of the NUWM and all that it represents by claiming that it was a Communist organization. The close and false association in the minds of authorities between communism and unemployed protest both in Britain and elsewhere was given wonderful comic expression by Charlie Chaplin in his classic movie *Modern*

Times (1936), in which the tramp loses his job, gets caught up in an unemployed demonstration, and is promptly arrested and imprisoned as a Communist agitator. It may seem that even if the NUWM was a Communist front, this is largely an irrelevancy, that it does not necessarily imply anything about the NUWM's worth or otherwise. But as Communist parties were distinguished by a certain type of ideology and structure—particularly the notions of democratic centralism and iron discipline—it does imply that the NUWM was characterised by the same praxis as the CPGB. It suggests that the NUWM was a puppet of the CPGB, passive players in a piece of agit-prop theater directed from Russia, unemployed protesters being "the misguided dupes of Moscow", as the *Daily Mail* of 25 January 1934 characterized the hunger marchers of that year. Within such a paradigm the NUWM seems a lifeless body characterised by Marxist hyperbole and practical failure, for the wooden questions historians ask of such a wooden body are as obvious as they are irrelevant to the reality of the NUWM: if the NUWM was a Communist organization, why did it fail to make a revolution among the unemployed at such a time of discontent? In this way the fundamental significance of the politics of the unemployed is ignored. As George Lansbury put it at the height of the 1932 unemployed revolt, "There is no sense in blaming the Bolshevists as disturbers of the peace. The foul conditions of life imposed on three and a half millions of our citizens are alone responsible for the unrest."[6]

If we are to arrive at any understanding of the NUWM it is necessary to elaborate and examine the distinctions between the politics of the unemployed and those of the Communist Party. We have seen how the NUWCM grew out of the peculiar circumstances of the early 1920s as a genuine working-class movement. In it individual Communists played a very important role, but it never was a Communist organization, and this continued to be the case through the 1930s. The CPGB "always felt that the Unemployed Workers Movement should be controlled by the Party", Len Youle was to recall many years later. Youle had left the CPGB but remained general secretary of the Yorkshire NUWM, the result being that the CPGB "tried to remove me from the position. . .but I had too strong a hold on the unemployed in Yorkshire for them to succeed. . . .the Unemployed Movement was not controlled by the Communist Party, and if people would consult Maud Brown and myself they would find that is true." Ironically, when the CPGB's leader Harry Pollitt addressed the seventh congress of the Comintern, the most significant achievement he could claim for the CPGB was the successful fight against the cutting back of unemployment relief, which was in reality largely the work of the NUWM.[7]

From the founding of the Communist International (Comintern) in 1919 the policy followed by communist parties throughout the world had been that of the united front, of working with and within social democratic organizations, which, wrote Lenin, were to be supported "in the same way as a rope supports a hanged man." In 1928 this all changed with the adoption by the sixth congress of the Comintern of the policy of the Third Period, which was to be popularized under the slogan "Class against Class". This recognized three periods of history since World

War I: a revolutionary period from 1917 to 1921; a period of capitalist stabilisation from 1921 to 1927; and the third period from 1928 onwards in which the contradictions of capitalism would become increasingly pronounced, leading to a revolutionary crisis. In this crisis social democrats would act in the interests of the bourgeoisie to partially resolve such contradictions, and hence were the enemies of the working class. Over the next two years the new line grew more extreme. It was argued that reformist working class leaders—both political and industrial—had gone over into the bosom of capitalism; that their institutions, the trade unions and social democratic parties, were hopelessly bourgeois and hence of no use to the working class who, as the crisis deepened, were rapidly moving leftwards. In this stunning refutation of reality, social democracy was damned as "social fascism", and the role of the Communist Party defined as leading the masses to victory, independent of any other working class organization.[8]

The effect of this new policy upon the NUWM was contradictory, reflecting the curious and confused status of an organization peopled with Communist activists yet existing outside of the CPGB. The Comintern strategists recognized that organizing the unorganized sections of the working class such as women, the unemployed, and youths was one way in which Communists might begin to assume leadership of the working class. Within the CPGB this at first meant renewed support for the NUWM, and then later meant the attempted liquidation of the NUWM. At its tenth and eleventh congresses, both held in 1929, the CPGB passed resolutions stressing the importance of supporting the NUWCM. The Party transferred Hannington from his job as full-time organizer of the Metal Workers' Minority Movement (MWMM) back to the NUWCM in 1928, and in January 1929 the Party's central committee announced that Hannington had been "Released from all other Party obligations" in order to work full time organizing the unemployed.[9]

To bring the unemployed movement firmly under party control the Comintern began to advocate the abolition of the NUWM and the creation of a mass movement of unemployed and employed led by the Minority Movement (MM). It says much about the distance between the CPGB—which following the purge of its leadership in late 1929 was fully subservient to the Comintern line—and the NUWM, that the NUWM not only resisted this attempt to destroy it, but prospered in spite of the hostility of the CPGB. At first the CPGB, as it had done with every other aspect of the Third Period policy, was content to pay lip service to these new ideas. Harry Pollitt, former MM head and now a member of the Party secretariat, meekly observed in late 1929 that the MM had "to give the issue of organising the unemployed more serious attention". The NUWCM at its 1929 conference passed an ingenious resolution that called for the exchange of executive members between the NUWM and the MM to ensure a closer relationship between the two bodies. As the activities of the NUWM and the MM were so bound up together that it is not always possible to tell precisely which body is responsible for what, the resolution was in reality a formula that preserved the independence of the NUWM by recognizing the work that many MM activists did for the NUWM, and vice versa.[10]

For a short time the ruse worked, but by early 1931 doubts were being raised within the Party about the role of the NUWM, and criticism of the NUWM's tendencies toward "legalism" was made in a meeting of the CPGB Political Bureau. During the 1920s the administrative maze through which the unemployed had to find their way to unemployment benefit had grown steadily more complex. The NUWM took to offering the unemployed legal and administrative advice and representing them in front of statutory bodies. By 1929 this aspect of its work was important enough to warrant the establishment of a National Legal Department, which distributed information and advice to NUWM branches and took up test cases. The rubric "legalism" was employed by the CPGB to deride all these activities as reformist rather than revolutionary. The NUWM saw its legal work differently, as both an important service and as an inducement to join their movement. Although a few branches concentrated almost exclusively upon legal work, some even becoming corrupt in the process, most regarded it as only one aspect of their work. But it was over the ostensible issue of legalism that the CPGB, under great pressure from the Comintern, attempted to destroy the NUWM. In their opposition to trade unionism proponents of Third Period policy would stress the role that trade unions played in mitigating the worst effects of capitalism by successfully working within the system, winning concessions without attacking the root cause of oppression. This line of reasoning began also to be used as far-left critique of the NUWM, who, it was argued, had become part of the very system they were supposed to oppose. "Just as the trade unions had a stake in the continuation of capitalism", it was argued at the general council of the RILU in Moscow, "so, precisely in the same way, but unconsciously of course, the NUWM was coming to have a stake in the continuation of unemployment, which was the sole reason for its existence".[11]

In February 1930 the theses of the sixth session of the RILU central council were published and these internal arguments were for the first time publicly hinted at. The RILU compounded the problems of the NUWM by calling for an International Unemployed Day of Struggle on 6 March 1930, which while meeting with success in some countries was a failure in Britain. The NUWM claimed at the end of 1929 to have increased its membership by 100 percent from 10,000 to 20,000, and while the true figures may have only been half these totals, it is undeniable that the NUWM had rebuilt itself during 1929 back into a cohesive organization. Yet it remained small, and anything but national in scope. An examination of the branches represented at the 1929 NUWM conference reveals that support at that time had retreated to a few enclaves in north England (thirty-three branches), and some outposts in south Wales (seven branches), with a further two Scottish branches, Edinburgh and Kilmarnock, and two London branches, Battersea and Chatham, making up the total of forty-four branches represented. International Unemployment Day cruelly spotlighted the weakness of the NUWM. Demonstrations of any size only took place at Bradford and London, the latter remarkable only for having formed the subject matter of the first ever socialist newsreel to be made in Britain. This failure to mobilize mass support signaled the beginning of a general attack

Table 6.1. *Unemployment, 1929-1939*
Percentage of insured workers registered as unemployed, Jan. 1929-July 1939

	1929	1930	1931	1932	1933	1934	1935	1936	1937	1938	1939
Jan	12.2	12.4	21.1	22.1	23.0	18.6	17.6	16.2	12.4	13.2	14.4
Feb	12.1	12.9	21.3	21.9	22.7	18.1	17.5	15.3	12.0	13.1	13.4
Mar	10.1	13.7	21.0	20.8	21.9	17.2	16.4	14.2	11.6	12.7	12.2
Apr	9.8	14.2	20.4	21.3	21.3	16.6	15.6	13.6	10.5	12.7	11.6
May	9.7	15.0	20.3	22.0	20.4	16.2	15.5	12.8	10.7	12.8	10.5
Jun	9.6	15.4	21.2	22.2	19.4	16.4	15.4	12.8	10.0	13.2	9.5
Jul	9.7	16.7	21.9	22.8	19.5	16.7	15.2	12.4	10.1	12.9	8.9
Aug	9.9	17.0	21.9	23.0	19.1	16.5	14.9	12.0	9.9	12.6	
Sept	9.9	17.5	22.4	22.8	18.4	16.0	14.9	12.1	9.7	12.8	
Oct	10.3	18.5	21.7	21.9	18.1	16.3	14.5	12.0	10.1	12.7	
Nov	10.9	18.9	21.2	22.2	17.9	16.3	14.5	12.0	10.9	13.0	
Dec	11.0	19.9	20.7	21.6	17.5	16.0	14.1	12.0	12.1	12.9	

Source: B. B. Gilbert, *British Social Policy, 1914-1939* (1979). pp. 314-16

upon the NUWM. Hannington was the butt of much criticism at a meeting of the CPGB Political Bureau on 21 March 1930. R. Page Arnot reproached the NUWM for its tendency "to become a kind of trade union." Like many in the RILU Arnot objected to making members pay their due of a penny a week, believing that this prevented people from joining.[12]

The survival of the NUWM was now at stake. It was forced into the invidious position of having to stage a mass action to prove itself at a time when it had no mass support. Its third national hunger march, staged in April 1930, was doomed to be the only one of the NUWM's six national hunger marches that was an outright failure. It was both the smallest, only 350 marchers taking part, and the least successful in garnering popular support. Labor and union activists who had supported previous marches were less than willing to do so for a march that, in true Third Period fashion, styled itself "Against the Labour Government". The hostility of the official labor movement was fiercer than ever, the Scottish marchers being preceded southwards by Mary Sutherland, Scottish Women's Organiser of the Labour Party, who advised local labor activists to do nothing to assist the approaching marchers. While unemployment was growing rapidly (see Table 6.1), the unemployed had as yet no major grievance with the Labour Party, who had not begun to attack the unemployed, and whose Unemployment Act of 1929 effectively ended the "not genuinely seeking work" clause. While this had been foisted on an unwilling government by the pressure of the radical ILP MPs, it was misinterpreted by many as evidence of the government's good will, a perception not weakened by the act's marginal raising of unemployed benefit. The NUWM's march thus took place at a most unpropitious time, and served to compound rather than solve the NUWM's dilemma.[13]

The attacks upon the NUWM grew in number and ferocity. It was publicly chastised in the *RILU Magazine* for its failure on International Unemployment Day. The CPGB newspaper, the *Daily Worker*, carried this criticism a good deal further, concluding that the NUWM "must be made an integral part of the Minority Movement." Hannington retained his nerve, and published a carefully worded reply in the *Daily Worker* seemingly in line with CPGB pronouncements up until the final sentence, in which he managed to turn all the arguments for the liquidation of the NUWM upon their head by appending the slogan "Build the NUWM." Only in this way, a naive reader would assume, could the mass activity of the unemployed, the unity of unemployed and employed, and the ending of legalism be achieved, and not as the CPGB would have it, through liquidation of the NUWM into the MM. The attacks grew more strident, honed upon the grindstone of the NUWM's intransigence. Calls were made for the "complete over-hauling" of the NUWM, which "at present acts as a separate organization." Worse came at the fifth congress of the RILU at Moscow in August 1930 when Salomon Lozovsky, RILU's head, damned the NUWM in his report as having "stagnated in its development". Lozovsky went on to emphasize that the NUWM must be reorganized under the MM's "direct leadership".[14]

Then a remarkable thing happened. The NUWM ignored the instructions from Moscow, and continued to lead the unemployed precisely as it had done before. Over the next year the NUWM would periodically issue carefully worded statements acknowledging the leading position of the MM without actually conceding in any way its own independence. From the time the dole queues had begun to lengthen in late 1929 the NUWM had experienced unspectacular but steady growth, with the exception of the period of the 1930 hunger march, when membership actually declined. Demonstrations and deputations began to recur, though on a much smaller scale than that of the early 1920s. The NUWM became involved in eviction fights and rent strikes, and was to the fore in forming Tenants' Defence Leagues in Chelsea, Tottenham, and Lochgelly. The NUWM was also active in, and ultimately the driving force behind, the Workers' Charter campaign, a failed attempt by the greatly weakened CPGB, its membership at an all-time low of 2,555, to break out of its position of isolation by creating a new mass movement. What little effect the campaign had, derived from the growing ability of the NUWM to convert grievances about unemployment into political activity. The campaign signaled both the end of the MM, and the beginning of an open fight by the NUWM against those counseling its extinction.[15]

Meanwhile the attacks upon the NUWM continued unabated in the Comintern press. Comintern thinking at this time was greatly influenced by Germany, which had the largest communist party outside of Russia, and where it had long been expected the next revolution would come. The success of the Nazis in mobilizing ever-increasing numbers of the unemployed as stormtroopers gave a sense of urgency to the need to organize sections of the working class outside the traditional ranks of the class-conscious factory proletariat. From 1929 onwards the German Communist Party (KPD) vested the unemployed with revolutionary significance and sought to organize them in mass committees centered on labor exchanges. This, coupled to the explosive growth of unemployment throughout the world, strengthened the important role accorded the unemployed by Comintern strategists. In April 1931 the RILU instructed its sections to revive the unemployed movement in all countries, and in August 1931, in conjunction with the Comintern, it held an unemployed conference in Prague of communist parties, red trade unions, and unemployed organizations. The Prague conference called for the British unemployed movement to be radically reorganized, along the lines of the KPD's unemployed organizations, into non-fee-paying, broad united front committees based at every labor exchange.[16]

Wal Hannington, emboldened by the growth of the NUWM, asserted its independence at the Prague conference. At first he told the conference, the NUWM had been an "auxiliary organization of the Party" whereas "now it acts as an independent organization". He went on to criticize those who had pushed for the liquidation of the NUWM because it had "not become a stronger mass movement". For a leading communist, Hannington could be unusually blunt in his opposition to aspects of the Party line when he felt they impinged upon the independence of the NUWM. At the eighth session of the RILU central council in December 1931 he declared, "quite frankly, I don't believe that the unemployed in Britain prefer to have an organization which they don't pay for." The NUWM interpreted the Prague resolutions as the establishment of broad unemployed committees that would be led by the NUWM, thereby strengthening the importance of the NUWM, rather than rendering it superfluous, as was the intent of the conference. With the decision of the National government in late 1931 to cut the dole by 10 percent and introduce means testing upon transitional benefits (renamed transitional payment to emphasize that they were paid in way of privilege rather than right), the NUWM found itself at the head of a mass movement of protest by the unemployed. After late 1931 little more was heard about dissolving the NUWM. "Instead of the Prague resolutions having been carried out", commented a writer in the *Communist Review* in 1933, "they have been allowed to remain largely a dead letter."[17]

There were other factors beyond Comintern hostility that served to distance the NUWM from the CPGB. First, the CPGB was never a party of the unemployed in the way that, for example, the KPD was with 80 percent of its membership unemployed by 1931. At the height of the depression just over half of the CPGB was still in employment and the party was never comfortable with that part of its membership that was unemployed: "no Communist", wrote Idris Cox in August 1932, "can remain satisfied with the. . .unsatisfactory social composition of the membership." Cox argued for "a mass Party, *firmly rooted in the factories and trade unions*", echoing the CPGB's major aim in the early 1930s. Although the Party directly gained from the work of the NUWM, its membership exploding from 3,000 to over 6,000 members during the outburst of unemployed activity in late 1931, only about half of the party's unemployed members—less than a thousand people—

were active in the NUWM. After 1931 the Party was content to leave the organization of the unemployed to the NUWM, rather than instruct its activists to directly organize the unemployed. "In other words", wrote a Communist in 1933, "the work is contracted out to that body [the NUWM]." This lack of interest at a national level was compounded by the unwillingness of many Communists to join the NUWM, which they believed ought to have been liquidated in line with the Prague resolutions. In part because of this mix of indifference and hostility, and in part because of the explosive growth of the NUWM in 1931 and 1932, which overwhelmed Communist organization in many areas, there was an almost complete absence of Party fractions within NUWM branches. The lack of direct grass roots input by the CPGB led to the situation where CPGB organizers would "criticise" NUWM branches for "mistakes", the Barnsbury CPGB, for example, opposing the Barnsbury NUWM's idea of organizing an outing for workers' children as "reformist". Pat Devine, an NAC member, noted that in "consequence a feeling of antagonism has arisen all over the country between comrades in the NUWM and the party organisers."[18]

Great has been the criticism of the policy of "Class against Class". The antagonism of the KPD toward the Social Democratic Party has been blamed for the success of Nazism, a theory popular with Ernest Bevin and many since, but one that ascribes to the KPD an historical importance it never had. It is undeniable that the sectarianism generated by "Class against Class" did much to cripple the international revolutionary movement, and that in Britain the Communist party dwindled and was at its most ineffective in the years of the Third Period. And, as we have just seen, it was at this time that attempts were made by the CPGB to destroy the NUWM. Yet it is too easy to view "Class against Class" as a disastrous policy imposed by Moscow. It was a policy that found great resonance within the CPGB. "It accorded completely with our mood of frustration and despair," recalled a woman who had been an unemployed CPGB member in the 1920s, "with our lack of confidence in the recognised Labour leadership, our desire for something short, sharp and spectacular to end the hopeless stalemate of our existence." The myth of the disastrous Third Period policy is especially important to some Communist Party historians who use it as a method of exorcising the demon of Stalin, who is blamed for every fault, drawback, and failure of communist parties throughout Europe. Against the dark night of the Third Period is contrasted the roseate dawn in 1935 of the Poplar Front, when boilermaker and burgher joined hands and resolutely marched together against the forces of Fascism.[19]

Yet as far as the NUWM was concerned "Class against Class" was not an unmitigated disaster. In the increasingly polarized world of inter-war working-class politics the trade union movement came to be dominated by a fiercely anti-communist leadership, who, from 1931 on, were also effectively to control the Labour Party. The official labor movement's post-1926 *jihad* against all things deemed Communist masked more fundamental concerns to create a cohesive, centralized, and monolithic mass movement that no longer had room for dissidents of any sort, a brutal intolerance to other points of view viciously epitomized in

Ernest Bevin's action in having George Lansbury's microphone switched off while Lansbury was speaking to the 1935 Labour Party Conference. The losses inherent in such a process were most immediately apparent to the unemployed. They were forsaken by most trade unions and seemingly forgotten by the Labour Party. The secretary of the Labour Party Local Government Department wrote to one prospective Labour candidate in 1937, warning her to avoid getting involved in any arguments regarding Labour's record on unemployment. "You will note that insurance benefit since October 31, 1935 is at every point as high or higher than in 1930-31, under the Labour Government."[20]

For the NUWM this had three contradictory consequences. One was that it meant any joint activity with the official labor movement was out of the question. The TUC refusals to support any of its six national hunger marches were always couched in the same terms: the NUWM was a Communist body whose aims were antithetical to those of the labor movement. When the Labour Party issued the first of its infamous Black Circulars proscribing Communist organizations in 1930, the NUWM was listed. "The truth", said T. Scollan, a delegate to the 1939 Labour Party conference, "is that the unemployed movement in this country was for a long time simply used in the war between the Communist Party and the Labour Party." At the same time the NUWM, even at the height of the Third Period, never relinquished its dream of working within and through the organized working-class movement, in particular the TUC, upon whose annual congresses the NUWM would often stage hunger marches, only, as in the case of the 1932 TUC, to be met with police batons outside, and contempt and ridicule inside. Another was that because of the failure of the labor movement in the 1930s either to help or to lead the unemployed, because of the rightward drift of the official party, and in consequence, because of such lunacies as the Jarrow hunger marchers (pointedly the only one of all the inter-war marches not organized by the NUWM, but a local Labour initiative) being sometimes helped in some towns by Tory activists but denied help by the labor movement, many disillusioned Labour activists came to passively and actively support the work of the NUWM. This meant that while the distance between official labor and the NUWM opened up into an uncrossable abyss, the relations between grass-roots socialists of all persuasions were strengthened through unemployed activity, the ILP, for example, overcoming its reservations in 1933 to pledge its full support to the NUWM. The members of the NUWM were the navvies who built the bridges over which the CPGB would later trot to the Popular Front, where, somewhat ironically, it would come to regard the NUWM as an embarrassing reminder of its sectarian dark ages. A third, and perhaps the most important, consequence was that "Class against Class" allowed the NUWM to assert proudly, and make a virtue of, the isolation into which it had been driven by the official labor movement. This was marvelously symbolized by the gesture of having the resolution ending the NUWM's attempts to work with the TUC being put at the NUWM's 1929 conference by Phil Hicken, brother of the charismatic Derbyshire miners' leader, Henry Hicken. The NUWM might have been a prodigal member of the family of labor, but it was still a member.[21]

"Class against Class" lent the NUWM activists a sense of historical destiny. "To organise the unemployed meant to come to grips with capitalism", muses the unemployed miner, James Cameron, a character in the miner Harold Heslop's Third Period novel *Last Cage Down* (1935). "He knew that they [the unemployed] ought to be taking a conscious part in the historical processes of the transformation of society". But the Third Period did not, as it has since been represented, postulate a mechanistic view of this transformation of society. The activity of the working class was now all-important in wresting power from the bourgeoisie. Of course, the working class had the advantage, or so it was believed, of having history upon its side in the struggle, for the bourgeoisie was doomed and the victory of the proletariat assured. As NUWM activist Margaret McCarthy later wrote: "One belonged to the mighty fundamental forces of creation. And, to crown all, one marched with history, not struggling in a petty, selfish, greedy and soul demeaning way to stem the onward surging tide, but swelling forward with it, one with the movement across the centuries, forward into an unimaginably magnificent future of human brotherhood. History and we were one."[22]

The unemployed in their day-to-day lives saw little reason for hope under the existing system. They experienced not progress but worsening poverty and increasing repression. The NUWM was able to act as a catalyst for a significant, if short-lived movement of protest in 1931-32 because its belief in class war, and its belief in the historical certainty and importance of the unemployed's struggle, for once coincided with the popular mood. In such a situation their words rose above rhetoric and became a call to arms that resonated in the hearts and minds of the unemployed. But the seeds of failure of this protest were inevitably sown in the conditions of its genesis: the NUWM operated in a vacuum, making it, for a short time, a virtuous and even popular place to inhabit. But there existed no escape from the vacuum, no route to the broader working-class movements and alliances that could have lent the unemployed protest the broader social and political import it so desperately needed. And so the movement of protest, which grew so splendidly in forced isolation, withered and died for want of support and protection.

It might have been expected that the Popular Front would have enabled the NUWM to escape such a quandary. But for the NUWM, whose class-loaded politics became an embarrassment to the CPGB, it spelt doom. In line with the Popular Front strategy of working with social democratic organizations and the progressive elements of the middle class against fascism, the CPGB wanted to dissolve the NUWM into a new united unemployed organization composed of TUC unemployed associations, National Council of Social Service unemployed clubs, and NUWM branches, which would exist under the control of the TUC; but its efforts came to nothing in the face of TUC hostility. Although the CPGB later claimed its efforts had "been hampered by sectarianism inside the NUWM", the NUWM did try to get the TUC General Council to propose an All-in Conference of Unemployed organizations, and Hannington wrote personally to Walter Citrine asking for an informal talk to discuss the possibility of forming a new TUC unemployed organization.[23]

Popular Front politics brought few rewards to the NUWM. Its willingness to make concessions to the official labor movement, which were normally reciprocated only with vitriol, greatly weakened the movement. In south Wales the NUWM, under pressure from the South Wales Miners' Federation (SWMF), agreed in 1937 to cease recruiting unemployed miners in that region. As far as south Wales was concerned, wrote the SWMF's general secretary, "the NUWM is dissolved". By 1938 there were only nine NUWM branches remaining in what had once been a NUWM bastion. The Popular Front was about anti-fascism, and the unemployed had utility only insofar as they constituted an anti-fascist force. Some Communists were little inclined to assist the 1936 national hunger march, seeing it as a wasteful diversion of energy from the campaign for support for the beleaguered Spanish Republic. Unemployment had dropped to 9.7 percent by September 1937 (see Table 6.1), and this coupled to the adverse effect of Popular Front politics robbed the NUWM of much of its strength. Yet, as in the late 1920s, it was the indefatigable energy and the sense of responsibility of Communists that kept the NUWM going. George Stalker, Communist and NUWM district organizer in Dundee, wrote in 1939 to NUWM headquarters:

> I am doing this in a hell of a rush Comrades. I wish I had more time to give you the accurate information which you must have for your valuable work, but honest to Christ between COR [Court of References], UAB [Unemployment Assistance Board], PAC [Public Assistance Committees], Domestic problems, Insurance Policy, Party secretariat, Branch Committee, Party Branch meetings and education, one has to be a bloody automaton. She says I've ceased to be a husband and become a machine. But someone has got to do it Comrade.[24]

A downswing in trade saw unemployment levels rise from late 1937 (see Table 6.1) but brought no corresponding rise in the fortunes of the NUWM. The NAC was forced to make "serious economies" in April 1938, and the only mass activity in that year was some regional hunger marches in Scotland. In London the winter of 1938-1939 saw a series of publicity stunts masterminded by Scottish International Brigadier Donald Renton. Groups of unemployed would lie down across Oxford Street to bring peak-hour traffic to a halt; the Ritz was invaded and the unemployed had tea there; an attempt was made to deliver a black coffin marked "Unemployed. He asked in vain for appeasement" to 10 Downing Street; and groups of unemployed took to chaining themselves to railings outside public buildings. These events succeeded in attracting much publicity, and had, in such escapades as entering the Ritz, a certain poignancy. But the tactics were those of a well-organized pressure group, not a mass movement, and were symptomatic of the weakness of the NUWM in the late 1930s. The NUWM was now not so much in decline as supine. Its remaining branches settled down to a modest but heavy workload of representation at UABs, PACs, and CORs. Many took on the nature of free general legal aid bodies, dispensing advice on divorces, separations, housing, old age pensions, and sackings. They had become, as George Lasker of the Dowkins NUWM put it, "a place where the workers could have their complaints against the Authorities taken up."[25]

The rearmament program reduced unemployment significantly through 1939, from 14.4 percent in January, to 8.9 percent six months later, the lowest level since December 1920 (see Tables 5.1 and 6.1). NUWM branches shrank in size and in overall numbers. The NAC only survived on what it could get from trade union branches, Left Book Club groups, and sympathizers. With the advent of the war the NUWM recognised that mass unemployment, which had been its basis for two decades, would no longer exist. Accordingly the NAC decided to suspend the NUWM for the duration of hostilities, with the intention of rebuilding the movement after the war, when it expected mass unemployment to return. To maintain its headquarters, the NAC set up a guarantor scheme whereby sympathetic trade union branches agreed to maintain the NUWM headquarters over the war through a monthly donation. Wal Hannington returned to his trade, and in 1942 became national organizer for the AEU.[26]

The NUWM did not come to a complete halt with the beginning of the war. Eric Edney, an International Brigadier, ran NUWM headquarters single-handedly between 1940 and 1942. The NUWM helped people with problems arising from pensions and allowances, war injuries and damage, and military hardship cases. NUWM branches still had occasional minor success, such as that of the Liskeard branch gaining an improvement in the condition of laundry workers in 1941, and the Cumberland NUWM district council succeeding in the same year in enforcing payment of agricultural workers at county rates. Occasionally new branches were formed, and membership cards were issued up until 1943, when in the March of that year it was decided to close the NUWM down for good. A memorandum issued in the name of the National Headquarters Committee (NHC) concluded that if mass unemployment were to recur after the war, it would be "a matter of concern for the entire working class community to accept responsibility for devising the form of organization and action necessary to combat it". This was the NUWM's death knell. As late as March 1942 an NUWM circular to branches declared how after the war the NUWM "will have no small say in the solution of post-war difficulties". It is impossible to know whether this about face by the NHC was simply because the NUWM was £87 in debt, or if it was related to international Communist politics, and the decision of less than three months later to dissolve the Comintern. By 1944 Hannington was privately writing that he hoped if mass unemployment recurred after the war that "the responsibility will be taken up officially by the Trade Union Movement, and that the unemployed will not be left to form its own defensive organization. That will be the line I will work for." The affairs of the NUWM came to a formal end in 1946, when the £25 that remained after its assets had been sold and its debts paid was invested in the People's Printing Press, publisher of the *Daily Worker*. But the legacy of the NUWM was far greater than the few pounds it bequeathed to the CPGB's newspaper. While the CPGB was a key element in the politics of the unemployed in this era, the politics of the unemployed were a much broader phenomenon during the inter-war period than the CPGB, and the NUWM was to enjoy a mass legitimacy that the CPGB was never to rival. The NUWM embraced, and was embraced by, a far larger world than that of British Communism, and it is to that we now turn our attention.[27]

The Meaning of Unemployed Protest

When the NUWM is examined upon its own terms we discover a paradox: a body that while presenting a public persona of a truly correct Communist organization—with all the rigidities and clumsy translations of reality this required—was in practice a dynamic movement, capable of responding in infinitely subtle ways to the requirements of the unemployed, and innovative in forging a radical politics that went far beyond the limited strictures of Stalinist ideology in its constituency, programs, and analysis of the state. The NUWM was a juncture between a wide radical working-class activism, which possessed a long and honorable tradition, with the far narrower world of a disciplined radical political sect, the CPGB.

In this light a typical story is that of the women of Cambuslang, Scotland. From 1933 through to 1939 these women, using the NUWM, waged an on-and-off campaign to secure housing improvements. While the ultimate outcome of this campaign is unknown it is clear from the fragmentary evidence that the NUWM was a sufficiently accessible form of organization for these women to make use of, and that rather than imposing rigid organization and ideology upon the women, the NUWM was pliant enough to serve as a vehicle for the women's protracted campaign of protest for a period of six years. Rather than viewing the NUWM as organizing the unemployed, it is better to see it as a vehicle that the unemployed could shanghai at times of acute tension to use for their own economic and social struggles. This was not a one-sided process, for the NUWM cast such struggles into an explicitly political form, and in the case of Cambuslang, the housing agitation resulted in the election of two Communist councillors in 1935. The campaign included eviction fights, petitioning, and lobbying in force, such as in 1936 when fifty women and the local NUWM secretary, at the women's instigation, paid a visit to the Lanarkshire County Council headquarters in Glasgow. The convenor of the council's housing committee refused to meet with the women, and so the women waited outside the council meeting room for him. At midday all the councillors came out for dinner, except for the frightened housing convenor and the chief sanitary inspector. Officials asked the by now indignant women to move on, which they refused to do, and so the police were called in. Arguing that the police had no right to eject ratepayers the women succeeded in having the police sent back. Finally the chief sanitary officer and the housing convenor had to be smuggled out through the coal cellars, away from the wrath of the women of Cambuslang.[28]

The figures upon which Table 6.2 are based would have to be considered approximate rather than accurate. Wal Hannington admitted many years later that while many would pay up to join the NUWM, generally only executive members of local branches would regularly pay their weekly membership fee of a penny. Any estimate of the NUWM's influence would be myopic if it concentrated only on

Table 6.2. *NUWM Membership, 1928-1932*
Publicly claimed totals of NUWM membership, Dec. 1928-Oct. 1932

1928	December.	10,000
1929	-	5,000
	December	20,000
1931	August	20,000*
	December	37,000
1932	October	50,000

*A further 20,000 unpaid members were claimed at this time.
Sources: *Inprecorr*, 30 Oct. 1931, p. 1008; *RILU Magazine*, 1 Feb. 1932, p. 64; *Communist Review*, Oct. 1932, p. 484.

membership statistics. A not overly sympathetic witness, the Pilgrim Trust, in its study *Men Without Work*, found that "the majority of those [unemployed] who spoke about it [the NUWM] evidently valued it." No table of membership statistics can explain the tens of thousands of unemployed the NUWM could on occasion mobilize in industrial centres throughout Britain.[29]

A familiar theme in the writing of Lenin, and, indeed, many other revolutionaries is the belief that sheer economic misery would propel the people to revolution. Of his own country Lenin could typically write: "starvation and unemployment are with elemental and inevitable force undermining the foundations of the autocracy." Yet nothing could be further from the truth, and Lenin in some of his other writings, and most certainly in his actions, keenly denied such a narrowly determinist view. There was nothing intrinsic in the actual misery of unemployment that guaranteed that the NUWM would generate the mass support that it sometimes did.[30]

Sometimes suffering would smoulder into futile acts of individual retribution. Joe Rawlings, later to be an NUWM activist and leader of the 1932 Birkenhead riot, and his family were once evicted, and while he and his wife went searching for some accommodation for the evening their seven-year-old daughter, while playing in the street, was run over by an automobile, and in consequence lost a leg. Embittered by the accident, Rawlings went to a leading Conservative's home under the cover of darkness and smashed all the house's windows. In 1932 Owen McKeown, a bricklayer, had his transitional payment stopped under the means test, and was left with an 8 shillings a week pension to live on. He went and smashed two windows of the Lloyds Bank in Oxford. For this he was arrested, and, when in court asked if he admitted to the offenses, replied: "If I broke the glass on behalf of the working class it is not a crime. If it is a crime I shall have to plead guilty . . . . I did it as a protest against the operation of the Means Test by the PACs . . . . The Means Test is one of the most cowardly attacks ever made on the working class. Some people are only allowed 2/- a week. What do they expect these people to do?" McKeown was sentenced to one month's imprisonment with hard labor. Both McKeown's and Rawlings' actions had radical overtones that represent a political response to unemployment. Yet such actions, undertaken individually, were as much an expression of rage at their own impotence, as they were an outburst against their miserable plight. The question arises as to why and how the NUWM was on occasion able to channel such feelings of impotence into more effective forms of protest.[31]

To answer this question it is enlightening to look at what the unemployed actually got angry about and protested against. The unemployed did not protest against their unemployment as such, although an outrage against a system that allowed unemployment was always very much the backdrop to the politics of the unemployed in this era. There is no utopian hope for the right to work, as there had been in the 1900s, and no revolutionary promise of a new world as there had been in the 1880s and in 1919-1921. Instead there is simply a grim desire to see the dole administered with a measure of humanity. It is absurd to attempt to quantify the amounts of suffering wrought by various pieces of legislation in this period, but it is nonetheless true that the unemployed suffered greatly from legislative and administrative measures other than the means test. Yet it was the means test that became the motif that towered over all other, that became the great symbol of the injustice and wrongs of the inter-war era, and not the "not genuinely seeking work" clause, not the anomalies regulations, and not the dole cut. By December 1931 we can see a decisive shift in the object of unemployed protest from an attempt to prevent the 10 percent cut in unemployment benefit, to a much more straightforward fight for the removal of the means test. Other issues—local demands, the Anomalies Acts, the cut in the dole—were to figure in the demands of the unemployed over the next few years, but it is the means test that predominates again and again as the injustice which rankled most, and against which the unemployed were prepared to do battle; its predominance in the politics of the unemployed at this time summed up by Leo McGree's words to a crowd of 18,000 unemployed at Birkenhead just before the famous 1932 riot: "We must fight to the end. On Monday the Means Test must be a thing of the past in Birkenhead." While the revolt of 1932 had complex causes deserving of a separate book, there can be little dispute about the motif around which that revolt took place: the means test.[32]

The means test was not only a personal means test but also a household means test. This meant that a man might be refused the dole and told to look to his two working sisters for support. As the criterion was not family but household it could also mean that a friend who had taken up lodgings in a home might be expected to ask his hosts for support. The means test, wrote Wal Hannington, "was an enquiry which we regarded as a terrible blow against the sanctity of family life". In essence, as was readily admitted up until 1932, but often denied from then on, the means test grafted the ideology and practice of the poor law onto unemployment insurance. "Transitional payments are unmistakeably public assistance" said the Ministry of Labour in late 1932. "They differ in character from the public assistance administered under the Poor Law only in being a charge on the national exchequer and not the local exchequer."[33]

In a national survey undertaken in 1931 it was discovered "that, in the minds of the people, there is a sharp distinction between the other social services, whether contributory or not, which give relief, and the Poor Law." The poor law retained much of its old stigma, and of the 2,354 unemployed who had been struck off benefit and who were the subject of this survey, only 17 percent resorted to poor law relief after losing the dole, as opposed to nearly half—some 46.8 percent—who had resort to relatives for support. "It seems indeed that the reluctance to be associated with the Poor Law affects more than the individual concerned and others than those legally liable for his support. It is felt by the whole circle of which he is a member. Undoubtedly it was this vicarious sense of pride or self-respect which induced many relatives and friends to give support to disallowed persons in their time of need." The odium, stigma, and pain of the poor law now fell on all recipients of transitional payment. Jack Cook, the respectable unemployed miner in the novel *Means Test Man*, reflects, "It was something else besides a means test, it tested one's soul, one's being, and the soul and the being were the poorer every time. It could not but leave them worse, disturbing as it did the calm and quietness of the inner life. However far back into one's self one retreated, still the test followed, measuring, measuring."[34]

Much of the popularity of the 1942 Beveridge Report, the blueprint for the post-World War II welfare state, derived from its proposal to create a system of social security that guaranteed subsistence level incomes that did not include the means test. It was, wrote Beveridge, " a plan of insurance . . . as of right and without means test." Beveridge acknowledged "the strength of popular objection to any kind of means test."[35]

The means test was reviled not simply for what it was and how it affected people, but also for the fact that it affected so many people. During 1932, the worst year for unemployment during the depression, 46 percent of the insured population experienced unemployment at some time during the year. Between 25 January 1932 and 7 January 1933 of the 1,341,480 initial applications for transitional payments, 678,747 were allowed at the same rate as that of unemployment insurance benefit, 420,884 at less than that of the full benefit, and 241,849 refused payment of any kind, on the basis of the means test. Of the 8,185,922 applications for renewals and revisions of transitional payments, 4,758,190 were allowed at the same rate as that of unemployment insurance benefit, 3,114,220 at less than that of the full benefit, and 313,512 refused payment of any kind, on the basis of the means test.[36] A little under a half of all unemployed were, on these figures, getting a good deal less than the dole, and in a significant minority of cases absolutely nothing, because of the means test.

The means test posed new organizational problems for the NUWM. We have seen how alliances between local left representatives and unemployed activists had been of crucial importance in the politics of the unemployed up until the mid-1920s. One uncommented consequence of the operation of the means test was to further weaken this ever-more tenuous connection by driving yet another wedge between local Labour representatives and unemployed activists. For the NUWM the issue was unambiguous: Labour members of PACs should not administer the means test, with the aim of making it impossible for the government to implement the measure. For Labour representatives the issue was more complex. The means test had been introduced by the Labour Party and for some time after the election of the National Government the Labour Party's opposition to it was equivocal. The means test originated not, as is commonly thought, in the financial crisis of 1931, which led to calls for severe cuts in public spending. Rather it stemmed from the desire to reduce wages by reducing the level of the dole. Support for this point of view had been building steadily through the late 1920s and acquired disciples in the 1929-1931 Labour government, in particular Margaret Bondfield. Not until November 1932, after Ulster, after Birkenhead, after the national hunger march against the means test, did the Labour Party finally adopt the abolition of the means test as part of its policy. "The Means Test is so cruel that I dont want to have anything to do with it," a Labour woman member of a PAC told Fenner Brockway in early 1932, "yet I know I've been able to get a few extra shillings for this family and that, and I feel for their sakes I ought to go on". The dilemma for local Labour representatives, who could see both the savagery of the Means Test, and the possibility of a minor subversion of it that would benefit the unemployed, was cruel and compromising. "We are being asked to administer an Act", she continued, "which no-one with a human feelings can administer with a clear conscience." A conference of working-class bodies and trade unions held in Cardiff at the time of the threat of supersession to Glamorgan passed a motion calling for the immediate repeal of the means test. The seconder of the motion, Councillor P. M. Evans, member of the Llanelly Guardians Committee, which was also under the threat of supersession, said he would "prefer that commissioners, rather than Labour men and women, should administer the means test." In the ensuing discussion most speakers "were of the opinion that the unemployed would receive more consideration from the guardians committee and that, however distasteful it might be, it was far better that they should continue to discharge their duties in this manner". There were a few notable exceptions, such as in Oldham, where Labour members of the PAC refused to participate in administering the means test for nearly a year, and in consequence gained six seats in the local council elections of 1 November 1932, and Stoke-on-Trent where local Labour PAC members behaved similarly.[37]

At first this seemed a reasonable position to take, given that many local authorities were able to administer the means test in a relatively humane manner. But having conceded the principle of the means test they found they were trapped in a corner when in March 1932 the government announced its intention to take "recalcitrant authorities seriously in hand." Generally the threat of supersession by government-appointed commissioners was enough to whip rebellious authorities, such as the Glamorgan, Bridgend, and Lincoln PACs, into line, and where threats proved insufficient, supersession—such as occurred with Rotherham and Durham PACs—solved the problem. After that time, the NUWM found local victories, so essential for establishing and maintaining the support of the unemployed, more difficult to come by. But the government did not have it all its own way. Although the alliance between local Labour representatives and the unemployed was further weakened, because of pressure by the unemployed there continued to be as great a variation between different local authorities in administering the means test as there had been with the poor law. After the disturbances of 1932 there was a general relaxation of the administration of the means test, which helped to allay discontent in later years and prevent a recurrence of the events of 1932, and which the government preferred to ignore as long as local authorities did not openly and blatantly challenge the principle of the means test.[38]

The government's failure in the face of unemployed activity to administer unemployment benefit as strictly as it desired strengthened the position of those who argued that such strictness was only possible by removing the control of relief from local authorities and giving it to the central government. This line of thought led to the Unemployment Act of 1934 that created the Unemployment Assistance Board (UAB), which took control of unemployment relief away from local government and gave it to the central government.[39]

Collectively the vast gamut of unemployed activity—the marches, demonstrations, deputations, and eviction fights—were the tangible aspect of widely held notions about the relationship between society and its poorest members. Part of these notions was the belief that the poor had the right to live with some dignity. Underlying this was the idea that the state is not the representative of all the people, but only of some, the ruling class; and that the relationship between the unemployed and the state is thus necessarily always antagonistic, and that change came only through conflict. These ideas could be expressed politically, as, for example, Joe Rawlings put it: "the ruling class never make any concessions to our class out of a sense of civic responsibility. Or for the human welfare of the common people. The unemployed had to agitate, demonstrate, organise hunger marches to London. . .to secure improvements".[40]

The consequence was a politics that focused very largely upon the state. What was created was an apolitical militancy that narrowly saw the state, and not the wider form and nature of society, as the problem. This meant that the unemployed had a remarkably clear conception of the state. The unemployed never believed in the idea of the state as some impassive authority or terrain or body that could be won over to unequivocally better the lot of the unemployed. The state was for them another aspect of capitalist society. Though purportedly the public sector, it was the sector that most intruded into the private spheres of working-class life. "It is no good ignoring the state and hoping that it will play no part", wrote Tom Mann in 1933 after his imprisonment for three months because of his role as NUWM treasurer. "The capitalist state is continually in action against the workers, police baton us, and the law courts send us to prison." This attitude made for a politics that was aggressive but not always radical. A packed public meeting of the NUWM in Bootle in January 1935, was told by a Mr. McKenna:

When members of the Birkenhead Council had asked what would happen if they refused the demands of the unemployed, the reply came in a single word, "Riots!" . . . No authority can compete with us. There are 10,000 unemployed in Bootle and about 6,000 to 8,000 on relief. If we do not get this extra money, what will happen? The same as in Birkenhead and West Ham—Riots! That is what the authorities fear, and we fear the baton. But you should not fear the baton, because that is only to put you out of your misery for a few minutes. You will soon be back in the fray again. Once you've had the first crack you get into the way of it.

In an extreme form such ideas could even make for a politics that was, if anything, anti-political. At the same meeting in Bootle, the principal speaker, Owen Kelly, said: "The Unemployed Workers Movement was not concerned with what form the future state in England would take, whether Soviet, Fascist, Labour or National Government. What they said was that whoever was in power they would fight them for the standard of life which was rightfully theirs." The NUWM often criticized the labor movement for their unnecessarily narrow focus upon parliamentarianism. But the NUWM could be as narrowly obsessed with the state as the Labour Party was with Parliament.[41]

The use of conflict as a vehicle for organization and agitation was central to the success of the NUWM in transforming individual discontent into effective protest. Without conflict, as was the case in the late 1930s, the NUWM atrophied. Conflict in the charged atmosphere of the early 1930s meant violence, and in the words of Rhondda NUWM leader (and later secretary of the NUM) Will Paynter, the unemployed "met violence with violence". But while the British state did keep unemployed activists under regular and sometimes intense surveillance, while it would at moments of stress resort to imprisoning numerous activists, and when faced with large and angry unemployed demonstrations, do nothing to contain the brutal behavior of the police, it never resorted to the same level of violence in dealing with the politics of the unemployed as did some governments in other countries. There is, for example, no equivalent to the decision of President Herbert Hoover in July 1932 to turn the United States of America's army on the Bonus Army, some thousands of unemployed, patriotic, anti-communist World War I veterans who had converged upon and set up shanty towns in Washington in the hope of being paid a bonus by the government for their war service. Led by General Patton, four troops of cavalry, four infantry companies, a machine gun squadron, and six tanks destroyed the shanty towns and routed the veterans after fierce fighting that left two veterans dead and many wounded. Nor is there any parallel to the shooting dead of four hunger marchers and wounding of dozens more by private security guards at the gates of Henry Ford's Rouge plant in 7 March 1932.[42]

But given this qualification there can be little doubt that the early 1930s were the bloodiest era of the politics of the unemployed in Britain, with pitched street battles between police and unemployed running for hours and sometimes days throughout the major industrial centers of Britain. This is not to say that the NUWM encouraged or organized such violence. The NUWM leadership, as committed revolutionaries, were if anything, ideologically predisposed to the use of violence as a form of political action, but only in certain situations. The fight of the unemployed was not such a situation: to organize on the basis of physical force would be to invite a mighty retribution on the same basis. Early in his career as an unemployed activist Wal Hannington had concrete experience of the most extreme form of street politics: urban warfare. Returning from an illegal trip to Russia in 1923 Hannington found himself stuck in Hamburg, unable to find a ship in which sympathetic sailors would stow him away for his return to England. Germany in late 1923 was in social turmoil, the economy in crisis, inflation gone mad, and with three million workers taking part in the general strike of August. On one day alone, 13 August, 110 people died in street battles. When Hannington arrived in Hamburg, he found himself in a major European city on the verge of revolution. There was grave disorder, with daily shooting battles between the police and the KPD paramilitary organization, the Hundertschaft. The Hamburg Communist Party was dominated by the ultra-left, and Hamburg was to be the only city to rise in armed revolt in October 1923 after the planned German revolution ended in disarray and confusion. While in Hamburg Hannington lived in the home of a Hundertschaft member who was under orders not to allow Hannington, as an international Communist delegate, to become involved in any street fighting, and when Hannington asked for the use of some of his weapons he was refused. In spite of this, Hannington seems to have been determined to assist the workers' militia, for he makes oblique references in his books to having been involved in some of these street battles. The violent street politics of Weimar Germany certainly made a great impression upon Hannington, for he devotes several pages in both *Unemployed Struggles* and his autobiography to his experiences in Hamburg. Yet Hannington was never to seek to introduce any of the organization or methods with which he became familiar in Hamburg to the streets of Britain.[43]

The NUWM did not precipitate violence, and there is no known example of the unemployed initiating a riot in the 1930s. This is not to deny that on occasion small acts of provocation and sometimes violence were condoned, if not openly encouraged, but this represents, particularly in the charged atmosphere between late 1932 and early 1933, a point of divide rather than of consensus between the leadership and some rank and file of the NUWM. With the advent to power of the confrontationist National government in 1931 conflict was inevitable, and from the outset the National government recognized that its policy of reducing unemployment benefit and introducing the means test meant violence, as a memorandum by the Home Secretary makes clear: "Demonstrations by the unemployed would certainly be organised in all the large cities and clashes with the police would be frequent. There might even be rioting with loss of life."[44]

This prediction was to be fulfilled in 1932, a year of bloody violence that saw troops firing upon unemployed demonstrators in Belfast, leaving two dead. In Liverpool police used motor cycle combinations, each motorcycle with three or four constables upon it, all of them, excepting the driver, with drawn batons, to charge and break up unemployed demonstrations. In Birkenhead vicious street fighting between police and the unemployed, which lasted several days and led to several areas of the town becoming no-go areas for police, culminated in the police storming and taking tenement buildings one by one, beating up men and sometimes their families. One witness wrote many years later: "on Sunday night there wasn't a murmer [*sic*], most had gone to bed, but about 11 o'clock there was a commotion, the street was full of police cars. They started from the first lobby, the staircase had iron railings, so they ran their batons up and down the railings shouting 'Come out now you parish reared lot of B———' ...The screams was terrible ..." Sometimes the women would fight back, one describing how when the police stormed their building, "I tried to prevent them hitting my husband. Then they commenced to baton me all over the arms and body. As they hit me and my Jim, the children and I were screaming, and the police shouted 'Shut up, you parish-fed bastards!' "[45]

Conflict meant many people suffered physically, as the statements above indicate. It also often meant imprisonment for those involved: five of the ringleaders of the Birkenhead disturbances received sentences ranging between four months and three years. At one stage in 1932 it was estimated that over 400 unemployed were serving sentences in prisons for offenses related to their political work with the unemployed. But conflict also conferred benefits; in Birkenhead it led to the raising of relief paid under the means test to full unemployment rate; the setting in hand of £170,000 of work schemes for the unemployed; and a commitment from the council to pressure the government to end the means test.[46]

As in 1908 the efficacy of conflict threatened the chosen parliamentary path of the Labour Party, which, while having swung (temporarily) leftwards after its disastrous showing in the 1931 election, was opposed to street politics. The Labour Party saw the politics of the unemployed as representing a threat not just to itself, but to the very idea of parliamentary democracy that it had worked so hard at selling to the working class. "The lesson for the unemployed was unfortunately only too plain", said J. R. Oldfield, a Labour London County Council (LCC) member, during an LCC debate on unemployment in October 1932. "Nothing was done for them unless there was disorder and riot." "The respect for political democracy was in danger of being wiped out", George Lansbury, now Labour Party leader, warned the House of Commons on 19 December 1932.

> At Birkenhead after the riots a great concession was made to the men who had demonstrated, and in Belfast the same thing had happened. If they were going to turn over a new leaf in this business, let the Government make an announcement at once, and not allow people to believe that the only way to get any concession was by creating disturbances.... Concessions made after violence gave those who did not believe in political democracy the right to say "Riot, and you will get concessions."

Of course, the politics of the unemployed represented a greater threat ultimately to the Labour Party than it did immediately to the government for the government, through violence and suppression, could contain the unemployed. There was even a sense of betrayal on the part of Labour, that the government by its bloody-mindedness had left its loyal protecters in the lurch. Witness the revealing appeal made in Parliament to the prime minister by the prominent left-wing MP Stafford Cripps at the height of the unemployed disturbances in 1932.

What were they to say to the unemployed of Bristol who pointed to Birkenhead? When they told the unemployed that they could achieve nothing by rioting, they were met at once by the argument of what happened at Birkenhead and Belfast. . . .Was anybody going to convince an unemployed man ~~who was told~~ by a Communist that the way in which he could force relief out of a local authority was by rioting that these concessions had not been given as the result of force?

If only the Prime Minister would give some expression of his intentions, vague though it might be, it would assist those people who were trying to preserve law and order in the country. . . .What he begged the Prime Minister to do , for the sake of ther country, was to give some indication, as to whether the Government intended to make some concession on the Means Test.[47]

Let us take just one case of where conflict benefited the NUWM, that of Bristol in the early 1930s. Bristol had special significance for the NUWM because of the existence there of the Bristol Unemployed Association (BUA), formed in the 1920s by the Bristol Trades Council. With the decision of the TUC General Council in January 1932 to create a rival organization of the unemployed based on the BUA model (see Chapter Seven), the NAC placed great emphasis upon the success of the Bristol NUWM, which had been formed during the period of rapid growth that the NUWM experienced in 1931. By early 1932 the Bristol NUWM enjoyed about the same level of popular support as the BUA, each body averaging an attendance of 200 people at their meetings. This balance was to alter significantly in favor of the NUWM during February 1932 as a result of a number of violent demonstrations.[48]

The spark for these events was the amalgamation of the Bristol *Evening World* and the Bristol *Evening Times*, which led to a curb in the rates paid to the 700 hawkers of these papers. The news vendors retaliated by striking and set up a joint committee with the NUWM. A demonstration of 4,000 organized by the NUWM in support of the striking news vendors on 9 February 1932 was dispersed with considerable violence by the police. The NUWM experienced a sudden and dramatic surge in popular support. Its meetings swelled to over 400 unemployed. Maby, the chief constable, tried to repress any further activity by refusing the NUWM permission to hold a march on 23 February 1932, which had been decreed by the NAC as Unemployed Fighting Day. The NUWM decided to break the ban and issued a leaflet calling upon the unemployed to

SMASH THE EDICT OF CHIEF MABY!
RALLY TO THE STRUGGLE AGAINST POLICE BRUTALITY!
FIGHT FOR THE FREEDOM OF THE STREETS!
FIGHT FOR THE RIGHT TO DEMONSTRATE![49]

The immediate demand had become not the ending of the dole cuts and abolition of the means test, but the right of the unemployed to demonstrate. Unemployed protest was never simply a manifestation of anger against the appalling wretchedness of being jobless. Nor was it always just a demand for work or maintenance, or even, during the 1930s, a protest against the means test, important as all these things were.

It was also about the determination of the most oppressed and isolated sections of the working class to be politically active. "They couldn't deny you, you and the rest of the Broo folk here the right to lay bare your grievances", thinks an unemployed Scot marching in an unemployed demonstration in the Scottish Communist writer Lewis Grassic Gibbon's classic novel *Grey Granite* (1934, published 1946). "Communionists [*sic*] like Big Jim might blether damned stite but they tried to win your rights for you." Between 6,000 and 10,000 people tried to march to the Bristol council house on 23 February 1932. The police attacked them without provocation in Old Market Street. Many in the front rows were felled senseless to the ground where they were then kicked by police. The police attack rapidly lost focus, and not only demonstrators but any bystander in Old Market Street stood in danger of being beaten up. One witness "saw a young woman, standing about three yards from the pavement with a baby in her arms, pushed by a Policeman, which she resented. He then hit her in the face with a baton; the baby fell to the ground with the mother on top; the baby being about 3 months old." Another witness standing outside Wakefield's shop "saw an old man, who appeared to be about 60 years of age, take refuge in the shop doorway and a Policeman deliberately followed him with his baton drawn, giving him a severe blow on the head then left him lying on the ground." The unemployed fought back, their only weapons apart from fists being pieces of coal and bricks, and it was only after two hours of fighting that the police succeeded in dispersing the crowd.[50]

What were the consequences of this street fighting? First, it discredited the police and won for the unemployed the right to demonstrate. When a third demonstration of 15,000 unemployed took place in pouring rain on 8 March 1932, it was not attacked by the police. Second, the BUA and its constitutional tactics were discredited in the eyes of the unemployed. The BUA had refused to join in the February demonstrations, and lost much support in consequence. Even Councillor Winchester, who had been president of the BUA for five years, was forced to admit the claims of the NUWM, and he called upon the BUA and the NUWM to form a united front. Third, it greatly bolstered the NUWM, and Bristol was to remain an NUWM stronghold throughout the 1930s. For a time its meetings became so large that overflow meetings had to be held in an outside lane. The unemployed accorded loyalty to those whose methods proved effective. At a time of austerity and confrontation this was much more likely to be a no-holds-barred organization like the NUWM, rather than the constitutional BUA. The council, which had refused to have anything to do with the NUWM up until the end of February 1932, was compelled to receive a NUWM deputation on 8 March 1932 as representing the unemployed of Bristol. A deputation from the BUA had asked the Bristol Council in mid-December 1931 to abolish the means test, but not until after the NUWM demonstrations of February 1932 did the council temporarily suspend the operation of relief cuts.[51]

The NUWM's politics derived their power from the way the NUWM asserted them on a mass basis out on the streets. This was the case not only in Bristol, but anywhere the NUWM organized. Max Cohen, an unemployed cabinet maker, saw his first unemployed demonstration from atop a tram in Forgeton in the autumn of 1931, a time when an angry tide of protest at the reduction of unemployment benefit and at the introduction of the means test was beginning to rise throughout Britain.

The tram proceeded down the main street and suddenly I beheld a spectacle which electrified me. It seemed as though a mighty flood of people stretched down the street, into the distance, as far as the eye could see. I had never seen such a large crowd. The black flood surged impetuously toward the direction from which the tram was coming. It was a black flood flecked with red-red banners on which were slogans in white letters. Everybody on top of the tram-car was standing up, craning eagerly in the direction of the demonstrators, gazing with wonderment and incredulity.

Suddenly, more astonishing than the pouring stream of people, a vast elemental roar smote the sky, reechoed and vibrated from the tall buildings. "Not - a - penny - off - the - d - o - ole!" "Not - a - man - off - benefit!" "Down - with - the - Means - Test!" I got off the tram-car just before the demonstration reached it. For a moment I hesitated on the pavement as the river of people swept past me, and then I plunged into it.[52]

Why did so many unemployed on certain occasions join an unemployed demonstration? First, it would seem that there was a feeling of excited relief that the individual's problem was shared by many others, who were now collectively registering their dissent with their condition. If unemployment was in so many ways about the alienation of the individual from society, unemployed demonstrations represented a temporary reconciliation with the social world, hence the feeling of almost joyful relief when Max Cohen, for the first time since losing his job, plunged back into "the river of people". The NUWM was able to garner mass support for its demonstrations because before they were anything else—political demonstrations, challenges to authority—they were public assemblies of the unemployed asserting their existence as part of society, and not as individuals isolated from it. "It is difficult to describe the feeling one had marching through this lane of cheering people, swaying and surging behind a wall of policemen", Will Paynter wrote of the arrival of the 1932 hunger marchers in Hyde Park, where they were greeted by a large demonstration. "The intense emotion of their demonstration not only thrilled one's being but had a physical effect so that one's feet seemed scarcely to touch the ground."[53]

An unemployed Bristol man described how he was moved by the public form of unemployed protest to join a demonstration:

A procession of the unemployed had started to wind its way from the Horse fair. The banners read, WORKERS OF THE WORLD UNITE, DOWN WITH THE MEANS TEST, WE WANT WORK NOT DOLE. I felt excited to think that someone had the guts to protest. I stood watching until two men carrying a banner which read JOIN THE UNEMPLOYED WORKERS MOVEMENT shouted, "Get in the ranks if you're out of work". And I became one of the demonstrators.

The sheer emotional power created by the simple mass assertion of the fact of unemployment cannot be over-estimated. One women recalled the hunger marchers entering Carlisle:

They came from all over, but the most pathetic sight was the Scots. They had marched every foot of the way from Glasgow. Ragged, footsore, hungry, heads bent. Our lads had marched in singing Cumberland's own song *John Peel.* Other contingents had marched in singing *The Red Flag.* But the Scots hadn't the strength to sing. We knew they were coming before we saw them because of a rhythmic sound which as they drew nearer became a chant, 'Are we Red? Yes we're Red!' Repeated over and over. I stood on the pavement with my two wee ones in the pram and cried.

As individuals the unemployed were powerless, but as part of a mass demonstration upon the streets they could manifest a power pregnant with both threats and promises, which however transistory was nevertheless obviously real for demonstrators, spectators, and the authorities alike. Because of this emotional responses became personal political lessons: Alaric Jacob remembers the hunger marchers entering London "like a series of living illustrations to Marx's work." And, also because of this, for the unemployed who took part the marches and demonstrations offered the less political but more fundamental chance of hope. However fleeting, it was this that lay at the heart of all unemployed demonstrations. The unemployed Scot in Lewis Grassic Gibbon's *Grey Granite* describes an unemployed demonstration:

Boomr-oom went the drum and you were all singing. . . .it gave a swing to your feet and you all felt kittled up and high by then and looked back by your shoulder and saw behind the the birn of the billies marching like you, you forgot your wife, that you hadn't a meck, the hunger and dirt, you'd alter that. . . .Singing, you'd never sung so before, all your mates about you, marching as one, you forgot all the chave and trauchle of things, the sting of your feet, nothing could stop you.

James Barke in his novel upon the Glasgow NUWM wrote:

Despite all the apathy and despair engendered by years of unemployment, starvation and hopelessness, the music, and the marching of the men and women behind it, had effect. . . .There was the feeling as music entered the impoverished blood, that here at last was an expression of revolt, an over throwing of despair.

It was hope that the demonstrations generated, and it was hope that lent the unemployed the strength and dignity they needed to survive.[54]

This product of the politics of the unemployed, while intangible compared to winning a few pennies more at the PAC, was ultimately one of far more importance. It is for this reason that the Welsh historian Gwyn Alf Williams so eloquently described the massive and successful unemployed protests in 1935, when 300,000 Welsh people marched against the cuts in benefit proposed by the Unemployment

Assistance Board (UAB) Act, accordingly: "What God himself seemed to have abandoned, these ordinary men and women defended, and they saved the sum of a human society in the valleys of south Wales for a bob on the benefit."[55]

Women and Unemployed Protest

Unemployment affected women differently, and in general, more severely than it affected men. Recent research has revealed the key role women's work played in the economy of the working-class family in the inter-war period. Most of this work took place in what has been termed the "informal" economy and not in the recognized industrial sphere. As such, though all working-class women were workers, only a minority were recognized as "employed", and qualified for the receipt of the dole. Even the small number of women who were eligible for unemployment benefit found themselves singled out for attack through the Anomalies Regulations, introduced by the Labour Government in 1931. Under these regulations it became almost impossible for a married woman to receive benefit. Women's experience of unemployment thus found little expression in the official unemployment statistics of the era, yet this scourge was a fact of life for many working class women.[56]

A silent area of women's experience of unemployment, and also an area that seems to have been conveniently ignored in writings upon the informal economy is that of prostitution. Many unemployed women were compelled to work as prostitutes in order to survive. The *Islington Woman Worker*, a Communist Party factory paper, attacked the 1927 Blanesburgh Report's recommendations that unemployed benefit be reduced on the grounds that many girls "rather than go into the work-house, will be driven onto the streets to keep them from starvation." In NUWM activist Harry Davies' unpublished novel about the NUWM in Nottingham, one of the main characters, Edna Turner, is driven to work as a prostitute. Her husband, a fitter, is unemployed and her children are starving. Edna confides to her friend Mary:

> when yer old man's out of work and walks his bleeding legs off looking for a job that's not there, til he comes home like a dog wi his tail between his legs after somebody had been beating him. Its all bleeding wrong Mary. Do they think that I like to see my kids running round clammed with cold and half filled bellies and bleeding rubber daps on their feet? What else can a woman do? They blame yer when yer keep yer legs shut and when yer keep them open. Thats why I took th quick way out Mary. Does any bugger think for a moment that I liked doin it? Its th love for my kids that matters. That made me do things. Yer forced to do things yer don want to and they condem yer all the same time. Its about time Mary that some of us blighters were born wi a silver spoon in our mouths then there'd be no need for open legs to keep our kiddies.[57]

The bitter experience of the women forced to work as prostitutes because of unemployment is but one aspect of the broader exploitation unemployed women were faced with. Women could be cut off unemployment benefit for refusing to take domestic work, though this was both an uninsurable occupation (meaning that domestic workers failed to qualify for unemployment benefit once they were again unemployed) and rightly carried the stigma of being little better than prostitution. The NUWM campaigned vigourosly against such state-decreed exploitation, as it did for better maternal facilities and extra food for mothers and children, and one outstanding feature of the NUWM in the 1930s is the large involvement of women at a grass-roots level. "I believe we women have done good work marching side by side with our men", said Emmie Lawther, 1936 hunger marcher, addressing a mass meeting upon her return to Blaydon after the march. "We marched against starvation, against privation and the vicious inquisition which our women people have to undergo under the Means Test. I believe that women are the people who suffer most under the Means Test."[58]

As the drive to get women off the unemployment registers began in 1930, so too began the agitation of women. In the period 1930-31 many local demands made by the unemployed betray an orientation toward issues of principal importance to women. Demands such as free maternity treatment, free clothes washing facilities, free feeding for school children, extra relief for pregnant women and waiting facilities for women outside labor exchanges were all symptomatic of the renewed involvement of women. Some NUWM branches had large women membership, 214 of the 494 members of the Chesterfield NUWM in 1931 being women; 79 of the 166 members of the East Kirby NUWM; and 247 of the 730 Kircaldy NUWM. But the mass participation of women in the movement was not reflected in the leadership of the NUWM, which tended to be male-dominated, and women often labored under great difficulties in the branches; the Plymouth NUWM, which had over 200 women members, did not allow women on a deputation to the mayor "until they forced themselves on it". There was a machismo about much of what men did in the NUWM that could have hardly helped women working within the movement. The NUWM attracted a certain type of person, often keen on physical pursuits (there was a preponderance of boxers in the organization) and outdoor activity, something of political mavericks as far as the CPGB and the Labour Party went, but at the same time people who developed a deep commitment to working-class struggle through their involvement with the NUWM. "A strong feeling of adventure enlivened our activities during the early 1930s" wrote Will Paynter, himself to be an International Brigadier. "This was as true of Liverpool or Glasgow as it was of the Rhondda. There was excitement and a certain element of danger in our struggles against unemployment." As we noted in Chapter Four, out of the 2,000 British who volunteered to fight against Fascism in Spain in the International Brigade, over 500 were members of the NUWM. The endless official exhortations of the NAC for branches to organize women did little to dent traditional patriarchal attitudes, driving Maud Brown, national women's organizer of the NUWM, to comment that "the comrades fail to understand the importance of work among women."[59]

In some ways women were the typical NUWM supporters in the 1930s. Witness the mix of forlorn revolutionary hopes and overt sexism when George Orwell attended a social evening organized by the Wigan NUWM to raise funds to defend the imprisoned KPD leader Ernst Thaelmann. Instead of finding hearty socialist proletarian men, he discovered

About 200 people, preponderantly women, largely members of the Co-op . . . and I suppose for the most part living directly or indirectly on the dole. Round the back a few aged miners sitting looking on benevolently, a lot of very young girls in front. Some dancing to the concertina (many of the girls confessed that they could not dance, which struck me as rather pathetic) and some excruciating singing. I suppose that represented a fair cross section of the more revolutionary element in Wigan. If so, God help us. Exactly the same sheeplike crowd—gaping girls and shapeless middle aged women dozing over their knitting—that you see everywhere else.[60]

In spite of the impression Orwell imparts of ovine quiescence, women, as they had done in the first decade of the 1900s, gave to the fights of the unemployed a militancy often lacking from all male protests. The methods of the unemployed women were often more intimidating, and far less constitutional than those preferred by their menfolk. Mrs. Williams, secretary of the Gorseinon NUWM in 1930, was officially warned about her regular threatening of the local relieving officer with grievous bodily harm. During 1938-39, the Tyneside NUWM ran a campaign against the local Unemployment Assistance Board. Publicity was given to various unjust decisions handed down by the board, especially to one case where a child died because of underfeeding before birth. The wife of the UAB area officer was forced to leave the district for some time "because of unpleasantness adopted against her by women folk". The campaign proved successful, and the area officer told T. A. Richardson, Tyneside NUWM organizer, that he "would not refuse any more [diet and household help allowances] because of the child's death". In Nottingham in 1934, a deputation of NUWM women invaded the office of Mr. Bentley, the Area Officer of the UAB. Laura Johnson, a member of the delegation, recalled that

We women . . . raided his office. We went in a group . . . he jumped up but his telephone had been fixed properly, so he got the wires round his legs whilst trying to get from behind the counter. I turned round and locked the door, but the police had been sent for. Quite a struggle developed. He got hold of me trying to take the key out of the door. June Ellis jumped on his back and Mrs Ellis was tugging his arm. I think he thought he'd come to a proper old hell hole . . . he wasn't there a month before he asked for a transfer.[61]

Andy Croft, in his 1983 introduction to the novel *Means Test Man*, written by unemployed miner Walter Brierly in 1935, argues, "Unemployment in the 20s and 30s, as now, destroys people. It does not politicise people." In one sense this judgment is correct, for it cannot be shown that unemployment radicalized the working class of the inter-war period, or for that matter, of any other period.. But it also begs the question as to what the words "politics" and "politicize" mean in relation to the unemployed.

In 1935 in Merthyr Vale a thousand women marched upon the local UAB office, smashed its windows and destroyed its records following the announcement of the new cuts in benefits. This incident was fictionalized in an interesting manner in Lewis Jones' novel *We Live* (1939), emphasising not any revolutionary aspect of the protest—as might be expected from a committed Communist writer and NUWM activist such as Jones—but as a specific action taken to achieve a definite and particular result. In Jones' novel, the women smash their way into the UAB office and confront a cowering official.

'But what can I do, what can I do?' he wailed, rubbing his hands helplessly through his hair. 'Don't operate any more cuts and send a wire to the Government telling them of our demands', shouted Mary . . . 'Well what is your answer? We don't want to be here all day'. She glanced around the room. 'Some of these women still have ten miles to march before they get home'. The man looked helplessly at her, then managed to whisper. 'What if I refuse?' The answer came from all the women simultaneously: 'You'll stop in this room till you change your mind.'[62]

While the women of Merthyr could not be said to have been politicized, they had chosen to take decisive action to affect their destiny, and to the extent that they were seeking to create and assert power through collective activity their action was political. At certain crucial moments through the 1920s and 1930s, large numbers of unemployed, under the auspices of the NUWM, took such action. No estimate of the membership of the NUWM can account for the latent support the body enjoyed among the unemployed in certain areas, and which could on occasion, be mobilized, on national, local, or individual issues. At certain key junctures large numbers of the unemployed were prepared to act in a concerted fashion to correct what they felt was a just grievance. While only a few unemployed (though an extremely committed and later to be an influential few in labor politics) developed a political commitment from their involvement, all the unemployed who protested were mobilized with political explanations and solutions being used as rallying cries, and were attempting, similar to the women of Merthyr, to redefine the relationships of power, even if only momentarily, that defined them as politically irrelevant.

Within a few short years of the protests of the women of Merthyr the antagonisms that had characterized the inter-war period had been temporarily resolved in the concessions of the post-World War II state, which themselves represented new battlegrounds for future class conflict. The authorities through the 1920s and 1930s had sought, in both ideology and practice, to destroy any vestige of a system susceptible to working-class pressure, and to erect in its place a social welfare edifice in which the unemployed, and not the authorities, would be the prisoners. The coming of the welfare state, for all its shortcomings and failings did, initially at least, spell a measure of material betterment for the working class. But it did not eradicate unemployment. Alexander Keyssar has written of how what emerged in the post-World War II United States of America was not an "era of steady work and stable incomes but rather . . . an era of managed unemployment",[63] and his judgment applys equally to Britain. What was denied the working class after World War II was the power, often slippery and always tenuous, but nonetheless tangible and real, over determining some aspects of their life when at its bleakest, a power they had been used to exercising for at least sixty years prior to 1945. The state's aim was not to end unemployment but to cauterize the suffering and the consequent political dangers that flowed from such suffering.

7

The Free Hand of The State Machine: The National Council of Social Service and the Unemployed Club Movement, 1932–1939

This is not charity. It is something to keep the unemployed from brooding.
—*The lord mayor of Nottingham, opening an occupational workshop for the unemployed, 5 December 1932*

Needless to say the whole scheme is non-political.
—*Professor Peers, advocate of unemployed clubs, 1 November 1932*[1]

So far we have looked at our subject only within the context of Marxist and socialist politics. There were, of course, other attempts to organize the unemployed, generally in opposition to the socialist-led unemployed bodies, but as this opposition, and not the condition of the unemployed, was their sole dynamic, they were unable to attract support. From the time of the Social Imperialists' Central Unemployed Organisation Committee in 1893, this strand of the politics of the unemployed is a record of failure. The Loyal Liverpool Unemployed Distress Committee was typical of this genre of organization. Formed in 1922 by Liverpool industrialists concerned about the success of the Liverpool NUWCM, it failed to gather any following, was to be successfully infiltrated by the NUWCM, and ended up distributing Communist Party literature. There is one exception to what, if expanded, is a dismal litany: that of the unemployed club movement between 1932 and 1939, the one major non-socialist attempt to organize the unemployed that met with some success. For this reason it forms part of our subject, and makes for an important comparison with the preceding history of the politics of the unemployed. This chapter briefly examines two other failed attempts to organize the unemployed in the 1930s, and then goes on to analyze in detail the National Council of Social Service and the unemployed club movement.[2]

The first attempt in the 1930s to organize the unemployed on a basis different to that of the NUWM was made by the General Council of the TUC in January 1932, in the wake of the unemployed disturbances that had greeted the announcement of the dole cuts and the imposition of the means test. The TUC decided to establish unemployed associations under the control of trades councils. These were to provide educational and recreational facilities, as well as providing machinery for dealing with unemployed appeal cases. Unofficially it was explained that the associations "meant a definite attack by the General Council on Communistic control of the unemployed workers". While a few associations did take a militant line, most would have concurred with the president of the Goldthorpe Unemployed Association when he said that they devoted "their energy to secure a working class majority on the council instead of useless marching and empty gestures with no real effect". But the associations were never a success. Hampered by the indifference and on occasion hostility of some trade unions, the sympathy of many trades councils for the NUWM, and the restrictive attitude of the TUC, the total membership nationally never seems to have risen much above 20,000.[3]

More sinister was the attempt made from 1933 onwards by Oswald Mosley's British Union of Fascists (BUF) to establish a power base among the unemployed. Mosley, who had resigned from the Labour government over its failure to deal with unemployment, believed (and not without good reason) that it was rising unemployment that had brought the Nazis power in Germany, and, he later wrote, it was upon the growing crisis of unemployment that "I rested my whole action". Interestingly, the BUF at first tried to organize the unemployed not after the manner of Hitler's paramilitary force of unemployed, the stormtroopers (SA), but through a body known as the Fascist Union of British Workers (FUBW), which aped the aims, language, and some of the methods of the NUWM. The BUF was attracted by the mass populist character of the NUWM, and, initially, before turning to vilification, the BUF seemed to be almost wooing the NUWM. The BUF newspaper *Blackshirt*, for instance, described how "Hannington electrifies his audience by the smashing clarity of his language." Such flattery was in vain, and only three NUWM members are known to have joined the BUF. At first led by Michael Goulding and a former leader of the Battersea NUWM, J. D. Paton, the FUBW ostensibly aimed "To protect the interests of the workers, whether in employment or unemployed, to fight against wage cuts and all reductions in the standards of life". The BUF stressed its belief "in the principle of the right to work rather than doles", and the FUBW helped the unemployed in a somewhat similar fashion to the NUWM, fighting appeals and gaining publicity protecting tenants in eviction cases. But the FUBW never used the mass militant tactics of the NUWM, preferring to assist the unemployed in more obvious though less effective ways, such as recommending FUBW members to sympathetic employers and offering work selling Fascist papers. In Manchester the BUF distributed coal to "needy people", while in London the FUBW was at one time planning to open an employment bureau. Always the BUF stressed "the practical assistance given by the FUBW to the unemployed." The FUBW seems never to have been capable of the militant violence that characterized the Nazi SA. Rather, and in spite of its language, it remained a conservative body employing conservative methods. It was never the volatile force that the SA and on occasion the NUWM could be, and remained a minuscule and pallid imitation of the NUWM. Its leadership was taken over in April 1933 by Charles Bradford, but after mid-1934 the FUBW was wound up, its work with the unemployed taken over by the Industrial Section of the BUF.[4]

The BUF continued to attempt to organize the unemployed, holding many of its meetings outside labor exchanges, continuing to fight unemployed cases, and emphasising its concern for the unemployed. But it failed to create the power base that it desired among the unemployed, in part because while it condoned and organized street violence, the BUF tried to maintain its respectability by not organizing the forms of mass activity so characteristic of the NUWM and so important to the success of the NUWM. But it also failed because of the existence of the NUWM, which, from 1934 onwards, saw itself as an anti-fascist body. Until we have a study of anti-fascism in the 1930s we will be unable to determine how important the role of the NUWM as an anti-fascist body was, but it is clear that the NUWM was often to the fore of the violent anti-fascist street politics, and the record of NUWM members in the International Brigade shows that many were passionately committed to the anti-fascist cause. Perhaps more important than its direct anti-fascist work was that the NUWM continued through the 1930s to set the agenda for the politics of the unemployed. The BUF, unable ever to seize the initiative for itself, was instead continually reacting to the lead of the NUWM. After the NUWM's 1934 national hunger march, for example, the front page of *Fascist Week* was given over to an article headed "Justice for the Unemployed", which effectively only repeated the demands of the march, with the limp addition of a defense of Mosley's record in this area. Because the NUWM so dominated the politics of the unemployed, an important element of the BUF's push into the East End in the late 1930s was propaganda aimed at discrediting the NUWM, and in this it met with some limited success. "In 1933 and 1934 the general mood of the unemployed in Poplar was Communist," wrote the socialist Leslie Paul, "four years later it had become Fascist." But Mosley's efforts to win the unemployed nationally failed. His strategy of converting the unemployed to Fascism may have taken a very different path if unemployment in Britain had ever reached the huge proportions that it did in Germany in the early 1930s. But given this qualification, there seems to be more than a grain of truth in Hannington's own final assessment. "I have always considered that one of the most important political achievements of the NUWM was our defeat of Mosley's efforts . . . to get control of the unemployed", he wrote in a letter in 1959. "He tried desperately hard but he miserably failed because of the activities and the strength of the NUWM. History would certainly have been different in this country if Mosley could have established his fascist organization amongst the unemployed as Hitler had done."[5]

The State and the National Council of Social Service

The unemployed revolt of 1932 rocked the bourgeoisie but seemed to achieve nothing. The cuts, the anomalies regulations, and the means test all remained.

Although numerous concessions were won locally, no concessions were made nationally. What effect, if any, had the unemployed revolt had? James Barke, in his novel upon the NUWM in Glasgow, *Major Operation* (1936), wrote of the authorities attitude toward the unemployed: "Weak they would bully them: strong they would humour them: dangerous, they would call the military in to mow them down." The largest, most sustained, and the most important attempt to humor the unemployed in the wake of the large scale unemployed protests of 1932 was to be the unemployed club movement.[6]

Following the resumption of Parliament on 22 November 1932 it was expected that Ramsay MacDonald, the prime minister, would deliver a speech announcing some softening of the means test in response to the tumultuous events of the autumn. Days passed, and then weeks, and no statement was forthcoming. Then, on the evening of 19 December 1932, MacDonald made an eagerly awaited broadcast on the BBC entitled "The Nation and the Unemployed". It was an extraordinary talk, managing to discuss the plight of the unemployed without once mentioning the cuts, the anomalies regulations, or the means test. Instead, MacDonald talked of "personal service", and announced that in November the government had approached the National Council of Social Service (NCSS) to "strengthen and widen their organization for the purpose of coordinating the work of all voluntary bodies" who were helping the unemployed. "With the approach of winter", continued MacDonald with a measure of understatement, "it became clear that the time had come for further co-operation and activity in voluntary service for the unemployed". He went on to cite such examples of voluntary service as gym instructors keeping men fit, a group of unemployed men who had turned a waste spot into a paddling pool for children, and the retired merchant marine skipper who was teaching the unemployed how to make mats out of bits of old rope, with which to furnish their homes.[7]

But these were no mere sops for the unemployed. MacDonald, whose gift for obfuscation was legendary, was on this occasion unusually clear as to the purpose of "personal service". "The problem of the better use of enforced leisure is one that has become of supreme importance. . . . We cannot afford to have class divisions and conflicts ruling our social and industrial life. We cannot afford great masses of unemployed people." Here was an attempt to infuse society's relationship with the unemployed with the new spirit of corporatism. This was a concept far removed from prevailing notions of charity, a point MacDonald was keen to emphasize: "Separate all these things, I beg of you, from the idea of giving something in charity to somebody in distress. It belongs to a different class of idea altogether. It is an attempt on a national scale to find new ways of employment, to put a new spirit of co-operation and independence into our people, so that through distress and failure we may find a way to national unity and commonwealth well being." "Personal service", said MacDonald in a telling (and chilling) phrase, "is the free hand of the State machine".[8]

The same evening as MacDonald made his broadcast, it was revealed by the government in the House of Commons that it was giving £10,000 to the NCSS to assist them in their new role as the central body coordinating voluntary work amongst the unemployed. A little over a year later there were to be 2,125 unemployed clubs with a membership estimated in excess of 200,000 existing under the aegis of the NCSS. By 1936 the NCSS was to be receiving from the government a yearly grant of £390,000 for their work among the unemployed. State support of the NCSS did not stop with national funding, but extended to the local and personal level. "It would, indeed, be difficult to pay too high a tribute to the voluntary service, that is being given throughout the country by the Ministry's [of Labour] local officers", effused the NCSS Unemployment Committee in mid 1933. The NCSS, for its part, made sure to reciprocate such favors. For example, the Liverpool Council of Social Service (LCSS) received from the various Liverpool charities lists of people who had received help. The LCSS regularly forwarded the names of these recipients of pints of milk, free meals, and clothing to the Liverpool Public Assistance Committee, who then checked them against their records of people on local government relief. Anyone unfortunate enough to have received both relief and charity would be referred to the relieving officers, who, acting upon the basis of this information, would then cut the amount of relief.[9] The NCSS survives to the present day, and is now known as the National Council of Voluntary organizations (NCVO), a body that in 1986 received 57 percent of its income from statutory sources, a total of £1,513,000 worth of government funding.[10]

The history of the NCSS sheds much light on both the social and political history of the inter-war years, yet it has been largely neglected by historians. All that we have is an official history of the NCSS by Margaret Brasnett, a turgid and uncritical account that totally ignores the major theme of the history of the NCSS: the symbiotic relation between the rise of state welfare services and voluntary welfare services. Only slightly less uncritical is an article upon the unemployed club movement in the 1930s by Ralph Hayburn, which, while based upon work of some detail in Lancashire, ends up accepting the NCSS at its own estimation. Hayburn considers the unemployed clubs to have been "a more worthwhile alternative open to the unemployed" than the street politics of the NUWCM. This was precisely how the NCSS viewed itself. More fundamentally, it was the reason for the clubs' existence in the first place, a point Hayburn chooses to gloss over. As he accepts the general premise of the unemployed clubs, so too is Hayburn content to accept without question the particular form of the clubs' activities, to the extent of aping the language of the NCSS propagandists. The men involved in the unemployed clubs "would otherwise have continued to spend their time in idleness: instead they were able to occupy their time purposefully", writes Hayburn, for whom only activity by the unemployed within the context of the unemployed clubs would seem to be purposeful. The question Hayburn chooses not to ask is this: for what purpose were the clubs instigated and supported? To be able to answer this we need to know something more of the history of the NCSS prior to the fateful evening of 19 December 1932.[11]

World War I witnessed a great extension of the statutory social services, and charities, in their close relationship to these services, simultaneously blossomed. Old charities grew to unprecedented size, and new charities appeared everywhere.

This concerned the government, who saw the pre-war edifice of the poor law, carefully buttressed by private charity, giving way to an "outburst of spasmodic, unregulated energy". In response the Local Government Board called for the establishment of local representative committees to coordinate the distribution of relief. This indirectly led to the setting up of a Joint Committee of Social Service, which included both representatives of the new local committees and the major charities, and representatives of the state. The meetings of this body were chaired by Aubrey Vere Simmons, first secretary of the Local Government Board; and it was to be from the offices of the Local Government Board in March 1919 that a memorandum was sent announcing the formation of a new national body of social service, to be known as the National Council of Social Service.[12]

The founding members of the NCSS were a dozen central and local government bodies, and the same number of voluntary organizations. At its inception the NCSS was an initiative of the state attempting, upon a national basis, to integrate the work of the charities with the actions of the state, and to mediate between the decisions of the state and the activities of the voluntary social worker. In this the NCSS stood in stark contrast to the relations that had previously prevailed between the voluntary agencies and the state, which were at best a demarcation of separate interests, at worst mutual hostility. The new relationship between the state and the voluntary agencies was personified in Aubrey Vere Simmons, who in addition to his work as first secretary of the Local Government Board now became the first chairman of the NCSS. But we must not make too much of the importance of the NCSS in the period up until 1932. If the NCSS was an attempt to place voluntary social work in intimate and subordinate relation to the policy of the state, it was until 1932 an attempt that failed. Throughout the 1920s the NCSS remained small and ineffectual: its total direct expenditure in 1927 was only £4,330, though it did distribute ten times that amount to charities. While it did meet with some limited success setting up rural community councils with Carnegie Trust funding, its urban councils of social service were generally failures, and those that did not collapse claimed only the humblest of achievements. In Sheffield blood donors were organized; in Stafford a car roster for hospitals was set up; and in Belfast a survey was undertaken of blind babies. It is apposite that the NCSS displayed no interest in the unemployed during this period.[13]

Ironically, the NCSS was first propelled into work among the unemployed as a direct consequence of the extra-parliamentary politics of the unemployed. The 1927 hunger march of Welsh miners to London, organized by the NUWM, did much to prick the bourgeois conscience, and as a result the lord mayor of London opened a million-pound fund for the relief of distress in south Wales. The NCSS was given the task of administering the fund, and through subsequent funding from the Carnegie Trust (though this was used only for music and drama classes and not relief), they were able to continue their work among the unemployed in south Wales and Durham during 1929. The onset of the depression and the mammoth increase in unemployment that was experienced through 1930 and 1931 brought, however, no corresponding increase in activity among the unemployed by the NCSS. The violent demonstrations by the unemployed in October and November 1931 against the National government's economy measures only elicited some isolated local initiatives in voluntary schemes.[14]

On 27 January 1932 the NCSS organized a meeting in the Albert Hall where the Prince of Wales made a speech upon unemployment that was broadcast simultaneously to the nation. The prince had become the patron of the NCSS in March 1928 and was an enthusiastic supporter of its work. In his speech the prince called upon the people to refuse to be paralyzed by the size of the problem, "to break it up into little pieces", to see unemployment "as a national opportunity for voluntary social service". This speech later became enshrined in NCSS mythology as heralding an immediate and glorious outburst of altruistic effort throughout the nation. Brasnett, one imagines rheumy-eyed, gives a touching rendition of this particular untruth. "The response to the Prince's appeal was immediate and overwhelming. . . . From all parts of the country came reports of initiative by individuals, voluntary service organizations, councils of social services, and special committees." In reality only a few centers were opened, and quite a number more, opened in the fright of October 1931, were actually closed down in the summer of 1932. We will examine the precise form of the growth of the unemployed club movement later. What is of consequence here is that the myth of a spontaneous movement of voluntary service from below was later to be of great use in legitimizing the unemployed club movement as a creation of apolitical self help by the people, rather than as what it was: an intervention by the state. As the Prince of Wales so beguilingly put it in a follow up speech made at Newcastle in April 1932, "we are not here to consider how industrial or political action can help us in our present difficulties. We are here to consider how we ourselves can help each other."[15]

Following the unemployed revolt of the autumn of 1932, the government was faced with a dilemma. It had to be seen both as doing something positive to help the unemployed, and of doing something to prevent a recurrence of the revolt. Given that the National government's reason for existence was to enforce the economy measures, it was firmly set against any increase of public expenditure upon the unemployed. But at the same time the government was compelled to act. It is then less than surprising that in late October 1932, at the time of the arrival of the hunger marchers in London, the National government's Unemployment Committee turned for help to the NCSS. Here was a body that could be relied upon to organize the unemployed in a manner wholly sympathetic to the aspirations of the government, but which at the same time would be seen as independent of that government. Added to this exhilarating mixture of private intimacy and public distance was the virtue that the NCSS came very, very cheap.[16]

The NCSS, for its part, saw in unemployment the power base it had for so long lacked, and in it the chance finally to fulfill the lofty ambitions of its genesis in 1919. On 8 November 1932, seven days after the hunger marchers had attempted to take their petition to Parliament, and three days after they had finally left London, a memorandum written by Eva Hubback and Alan Collinridge was circulated within the NCSS. The memorandum stressed the urgency of immediately setting up a central body within the NCSS to organize the unemployed. This body would have to command the confidence of all interested organizations, including those of labor, though it advised against having labor representatives upon the central body. Hubback and Collinridge concluded that "there are certain steps which it is of the highest importance to take at once if more of the present winter is not to be lost". What very quickly followed was a coordinated campaign by the NCSS, the government, and associated forces that included newspapers, the BBC, and the Prince of Wales. On 21 November 1932, the NCSS formed a special Unemployment Committee, and the following day the Ministry of Labour officially asked the NCSS to act as a national central body, coordinating voluntary efforts to help the unemployed, and to forward an estimate of the amount of money that they would require to undertake this task. The NCSS, on 16 December 1932, decided that it needed £8,000: £4,000 to expand its own internal administration, and £4,000 for the appointment of six "outside Advisory Officers". Sir Henry Betterton, the Minister of Labour, gave them £7,500 the following day, which was increased two days later to £10,000, and followed, in early 1933, by a second grant of £15,000 for funding local schemes.[17]

To further finance its new field of activity, the NCSS decided to raise an extra £15,000 with a private appeal. We can, to some extent, gauge the support that this new project enjoyed among financial and industrial capital from the fact that this appeal easily overran its target, having reached the figure of £21,000 by April 1933. The major contributors were the large banks (£9,135), Unilever, Shell, I.C.I., Imperial Tobacco Company, Woolworths and J. A. Player, (£5,850) and Sir William Morris (£4,000). Morris, well-known as a philanthropist, had agreed to donate £4,000 annually for six years, a total of £24,000.[18]

On the evening of 19 December 1932, while Ramsay MacDonald broadcast to the nation, Betterton told the House of Commons that he "had decided against setting up an ad-hoc body, which might be said to be the creature or agent of the government", and had instead decided to utilize the NCSS as a central body to coordinate voluntary effort among the unemployed. A great virtue of the NCSS was that although it was just such a creature of the government, it would be difficult for people to establish that this was so. Meanwhile, in a well-orchestrated manner, the Prince of Wales, who was eager to do all he could for the NCSS in its new role, toured unemployed centers in the north of England in his capacity as NCSS patron. He used these visits to publicize a series of talks by S. P. B. Mais upon the unemployed centres, which were broadcast on the BBC early in 1933.[19]

The political impulse that set the NCSS in motion in November 1932 determined the form that the NCSS activity among the unemployed was to take. As a consequence of the frightening behavior of the unemployed in late 1931 and the autumn of 1932, bourgeois society now had a number of urgent and related needs regarding the unemployed, which the NCSS strove to fulfill. The previous months had seen a dangerous radicalization of the unemployed that presented both short-term problems, such as the controlling of a malcontent reserve army of labor; and longer-term problems, like the dangers of politicized unemployed workers reentering the workforce at a later date with a brooding antagonism against capitalism derived from their experience of unemployment. The NCSS understood what was expected of it. "It is well to remember", ran an NCSS pamphlet of 1933, "that the main purpose of these schemes is to keep men fit, mentally, physically and morally, against the day when they find work again". "The tragedy of the position", wrote John Buchan in his foreword to an NCSS booklet published in 1932, "lies less in the meagre livelihood to which hundreds of thousands are condemned than in the fact that they are losing their technical skill through idleness, and having their minds dulled and soured. They are deeply malcontent with the situation and are only too eager to find a way out."[20]

Correspondingly the job of the NCSS lay not in ameliorating the meager livelihood of the unemployed, but in the prevention of the "souring" of their minds. S. P. B. Mais, in his final broadcast upon the unemployed clubs, quoted passages from a letter written to him by an unemployed Lancashire man, in whose town there was no unemployed club. "We have no club, or reading room," he wrote; "no learning how to mend shoes, make this, make that, or the other; we just loaf about. . . . I am not a politician, nor a Communist, but sometimes I feel that if this goes on I shall become revolutionary. I am an ex-serviceman—if that makes any difference—I served in France." Mais used the letter as an allegorical tale upon the unemployed club movement. Here was an essentially temperate man, desirous of little save some activity, as provided by the clubs, with which to fill his empty days. Without the club, without this activity, there was the danger of revolution, a threat reinforced by the military experience of the man—"if that makes any difference"—which of course it did. But trouble could be averted, the revolutionary in the breast of the provincial man thwarted, by starting up a club. "I hope that convinces you", said Mais, commenting upon the letter and concluding his series of talks, "that there is still work for you to do." The activities of the NCSS were not to be an attempt to alleviate the social problems of the unemployed, but a campaign to defuse discontent with their lot. The job of the NCSS was to politically emasculate the unemployed.[21]

If certain of the goals they desired, the NCSS was at first unsure how to achieve them. Personal social service along the lines of the COS was neither acceptable to the working class nor particularly effective as the political weapon the NCSS sought. The COS, even in the 1930s, continued to operate like a Victorian charity. Applicants in London's East End still faced severe questioning to discover whether or not they were deserving, and every entry in the social worker's record book still had to conclude, "applicant expressed gratitude". This sort of personal service was more likely to antagonize than pacify those unemployed who had already suffered the indignities of the means test. In 1929 Sir Wyndham Deedes, in his capacity as NCSS assistant secretary, toured Britain looking at the work of the NCSS, and in the course of his travels became highly critical of the older notions of personal service as practiced by bodies such as the COS. In 1927 the Workers' Educational Association had established a club for the unemployed at Lincoln, where articles could be made by the unemployed for others. As unemployment grew in the early 1930s a number of similar clubs were established, as well as some "settlements" for the unemployed. It was to these, and its own experience with educational projects in Wales and Durham, that the NCSS now turned for a new model of personal service.[22]

Upon its formation the NCSS Unemployed Committee defined its immediate purpose as being to stimulate and support the growth of indoor occupation centers, physical training facilities, outdoor work on allotments, and educational activities. Although the NCSS was for the rest of the decade to support all these activities, the major, and most successful, aspect of their work among the unemployed was to be the unemployed clubs. These took many forms and were known by many names-service centers, unemployed centers, occupational centers, recreational centers and unemployed clubs. For the sake of clarity I have referred to them generally as unemployed clubs, and it is upon these that the rest of this chapter focuses.[23]

Unemployed Clubs and Street Politics

At the most basic level the NCSS saw the unemployed clubs as an alternative to the politics of the street, where the activity of the unemployed was determined by the unemployed themselves. The first aim of the clubs was to get the unemployed off the streets, their own environment, into a club, where their activity could be observed, structured, and disciplined in an environment over which the unemployed could at best exert minimal influence. This was seen by sympathetic observers as the clubs' main function. William Teeling, an aspiring Tory politician and Fascist sympathizer, in December 1932 and January 1933 donned the rags of a tramp and thus spuriously disguised, traveled England visiting unemployed clubs. Subsequently he wrote a book of his experiences in which he gave a highly favorable account of the clubs. Teeling was greatly concerned by unemployment, and he believed that because of it "the discipline of our youth is very bad." His patrician soul was stirred, however, by his discovery "that England really wants the Government to take action and give a lead and do something to save the generation we younger politicians will one day have to rule, from becoming a generation of undisciplined and irresponsible voters." For Teeling the clubs were a way of disciplining unemployed street brawlers and turning them into passive, responsible voters.[24]

The unemployed clubs were generally divided into two types: the recreational center, which provided shelter and some facilities for unorganized indoor amusements such as cards, dominoes, draughts, darts, and newspaper reading; and the occupational center where there was a constant round of organized activity, bootmaking, carpentry classes, educational sessions, craft lessons, and physical exercise sessions (known by that idiomatic British phrase, "physical jerks"). S. P. B. Mais, in one of his BBC talks upon the unemployed clubs, made a revealing criticism of the Oxford unemployed club. The club, said Mais, was "*Purely recreational*, and scarcely raises the men from apathy more than the street corner. They seemed soured, suspicious and listless. Where games and rest are the predominating characteristics a club becomes no more than a street with a roof on." We may ask whom the unemployed were suspicious of and sour toward, and the answer we get is that it was the middle-class interloper Mais. Such class antagonism was an acknowledged feature of the street, which is why Mais saw the club as merely the street with a roof above it. The danger was that such antagonism would find expression in activity typical of the street, which in the Britain of 1932-33 was as often as not directed against the bourgeoisie. The idea of the unemployed club was to dispel disaffection, not provide it with a focus. The aim of the unemployed clubs was, in the words of the South East Lancashire and North East Cheshire Advisory Council, "to organise enforced leisure, to provide an alternative to the street corner."[25]

So important was this aim that it came to determine the unemployed clubs' very structure. Because the clubs were meant to provide a different environment than that of the street, the recreational centers came to be viewed as failures, for they reproduced the street and its social relations, with the working class and not the bourgeoisie in control. For this reason the NCSS concentrated on transforming recreational centers into occupational centers, and establishing new clubs upon occupational lines. From the outset the NCSS Unemployment Committee saw its principal task as " the development of useful and constructive occupation for those who are suffering from enforced idleness", while it regarded recreational centers "where there is no programme of constructive activities" as having "no permanent value". "It may even be found wise," thought the committee, "to require as a condition of membership that a man should join one of the group activities of the club." A policy that favoured the development of occupational centers was not easy to implement, given that a recreational center was far cheaper to establish and easier to run than an occupational center. In spite of this the NCSS persisted and met with success. Out of 760 unemployed clubs extant in February 1933, 314 were occupational centers, and 446 were recreational centers. By November 1934, out of 2,162 clubs, the number of occupational centers had quadrupled to a total of 1,405, while the number of recreational centers, 757, was not even a doubling of the February 1933 total.[26]

Unemployment was thought to "demoralize" the unemployed, "demoralize" being a curious term which covered a number of prejudices against the unemployed, and which primarily meant that unemployment often led to bitter thoughts against a society that no longer seemed to care. But society, as evident in the occupational clubs, could present the fiction that it did care, and, what is of importance, give little time for the unemployed man, between physical jerks, play reading, boot repairing, toy making, and his allotment, to formulate any plans for retribution against a larger, heartless world that had cast him out.

The Unemployed Clubs as an Ideological Weapon

The unemployed clubs represented far more than an attempt to organize the unemployed along reactionary lines; and our analysis would be flawed if it stopped at this point. The unemployed clubs also represented an ideological battle fought against those who saw in unemployment capitalist society's rejection and alienation of the very people who were supposed to constitute the productive core of that society. As the Northern Ireland Council of Social Service put it, voluntary service was essential for "destroying in them [the unemployed] the sense of having been scrapped by a society to which never the less they still belonged." The unemployed clubs represented an attempt to claim back the unemployed, and to deny the political construction put on unemployment by the likes of the NUWM: that a society that no longer had a place for masses of men and women was a society that could no longer justify its own existence. It was because of this that the work of the NCSS represented such a force for stability in the troubled years of the depression. Voluntary social service among the unemployed was, wrote L. F. Ellis, secretary of the NCSS, much more than "helping unemployed people through a bad time"; it was "a means to help forward a more general adjustment to new conditions". By "new conditions" Ellis meant "a period of reconstruction which must inevitably cause prolonged dislocation". Voluntary social service was then also about teaching the unemployed to accept rather than challenge their lot. It was upon these particular grounds that the government, through the Ministry of Health, asked local authorities to render every assistance to NCSS work among the unemployed. In a circular sent out to local authorities on March 1933, it was stressed that "individual victims of involuntary idleness may in the consciousness of deteriorating abilities and the apparent remoteness of the prospect of regaining work, suffer from anxieties which all good citizens must be anxious to mitigate to the best of their capacity." Good citizens, so concerned, were to help the NCSS.[27]

But there were difficulties. In the classic 1938 study *Men Without Work* a discussion about an NUWM member who feels great resentment toward society concludes that "such feelings as these are almost always, in some degree, present. One of the greatest problems that the voluntary agencies working among them are set to do is to break down these feelings without breaking down a man's self respect, and it is one they find very hard to solve." Precisely because it was an ideological battle within which bourgeois society had to be shown as caring, it was of the utmost importance that the movement was seen to remain voluntary, its dynamic altruism. The moment it was revealed as working hand in glove with the government by introducing an element of compulsion, its dynamic would stand revealed as political, and the movement would lose all credibility. Given the close ties between the government and the NCSS the fiction of altruism was not easily maintained. The shadow of the government hung long and black over the unemployed clubs, and provoked much opposition and antipathy in consequence. L. F. Ellis wrote in 1934 of those who saw the unemployed clubs as the "forerunners of a compulsory scheme, regarded the Council as the stalking horse of the Government. The widespread prejudice which existed seriously handicapped the growth of voluntary activities". The NUWM in particular saw the unemployed clubs as part of a plan whereby the unemployed would ultimately be made to work in centers without wages, fears that were to be to some extent realized in the Unemployment Act of

1934, which in one clause gave the government the power of making attendance at government training centers compulsory upon pain of loss of benefit.[28]

What is interesting about this clause is that it actually brought the NCSS and the government into disagreement. The success of the unemployed clubs depended on the voluntary support given them by the unemployed, and the 1934 act threatened this support in two ways. First, it reinforced the perception of the NCSS as "the stalking horse" of the government; and second, it fractured the illusion that the unemployed clubs were there simply to help the unemployed. The NCSS was worried about this problem as early as May 1933 when A. D. Lindsay, master of Balliol College, Oxford, and chairman of the NCSS Unemployment Committee, wrote to Ramsay MacDonald asking for reassurance upon this matter. NCSS work, wrote Lindsay, "is concerned only with one aspect of the problem—what people call the psychological effects of unemployment. It is in that limited sphere that we regard it as essential to preserve the voluntary character of all that is done." MacDonald replied that the government had "no intention of doing anything to impair the voluntary basis", but plans for the bill of the following year were already being prepared. This left the government in the position of sanctioning the principle of voluntary attendance, but attacking its practice with the 1934 Unemployment Act. The NCSS felt sufficiently strongly about the offending clause to lobby unsuccessfully for its removal. Ellis, the NCSS secretary, wrote to Betterton, the Minister of Labour, on 22 November 1933 asking for the clause to be removed. If it was to be implemented, wrote Ellis, there was a "danger that compulsion may destroy the moral values of effort and lead to resentment". The final twist to this tale came after the enactment of the legislation, for although the government now had the power to make attendance at training camps compulsory, it never openly used it.[29]

But the ideological battle was not fought solely by rocking the unemployed's head upon the bourgeois bosom, cooing softly in its ear that all was well. The NCSS sought to curb the discontent of the unemployed by redefining, to an extent, what unemployment was, and therefore what to be unemployed meant. Rather than being unemployed meaning being without a job, it came to mean (in the world of voluntary service) being possessed, rather enviably, of a surfeit of time for leisure. Using this idea of leisure the NCSS sought to break down the sense of isolation and resentment felt by the unemployed, which the NCSS defined as being antisocial.

To achieve this they had first to destroy the unemployed's sense of identity as being unemployed. "The Council's aim", wrote L. F. Ellis in late 1934, "has always been to break down the division between employed and unemployed."[30] By this Ellis meant something quite different from the unity of employed and unemployed worker against the bourgeoisie preached by the NUWM. Ellis meant the forgetting of the particular experience of oppression and suffering experienced as an unemployed member of the working class, and the merging of the unemployed's consciousness into that of the bourgeoisie. For Ellis the division of unemployed and employed was not a schism within the working class, but the larger divide between working class and middle class. The breakdown of such a division was to be achieved by defining the unemployed as different only in their fortune of having plenty of leisure time, and the unemployed are referred to not as the unemployed, but as "the leisured members of the community" or "those with more leisure than their fellow beings" or just, simply, "the leisured." Archbishop Temple of York referred to the unemployed as "the uneducated leisured classes", a definition of some power, managing both to rob the unemployed of their identity as part of the working class, while firmly establishing them in a new position of inferiority to the bourgeoisie, who were, after all, the educated leisured class. Of course the voluntary service movement did not just define the problem of the unemployed as an excess of leisure. They also had the answer.[31]

"The correct use of leisure is of such importance in our modern world", gushed the 1934 annual report of the Brighton Centre for the Unemployed, immediately switching to a tone of contrite humility: "It is in an attempt to solve, in part, this problem that the Brighton Centre for the Unemployed goes on with its work, quietly and unobtrusively, striving to fill the vacant hours of those unfortunate members of our community." As we have seen, the South East Lancashire and North East Cheshire Advisory Council saw part of its role as being "to organise enforced leisure", while Ramsay MacDonald regarded the problem of "enforced leisure" as one that had "become of supreme importance". In this context unemployed clubs became, rather frighteningly, "laboratories in which experiments can be made of the best way in which to employ the hours of leisure that the mechanisation of a scientific age involves." In this way, the fundamental problem of unemployment, created by a specific social system, was transformed into the trivial conundrum of what the unemployed were to do with the unlimited leisure bequeathed by a brave new scientific world.[32]

If leisure, and not unemployment, was the primary difficulty, it became possible to talk about the unemployed without talking about unemployment. It even became possible to see personal service for the unemployed as a denial of the fact of unemployment. The East Shropshire Association of Mutual Services Clubs, set up at the instigation of the NCSS in 1935, had as its object one of the glibber pieces of sophistry deployed by the voluntary service movement: "To extend the facilities for the profitable employment of leisure time (having special regard to the leisure caused by unemployment) in existing clubs." The logic of this was such that an unemployed person in east Shropshire could find him or herself in the historically unique situation of being in "profitable employment" without having a job.[33]

The last word on the idea of leisure and its possible uses should go to William Teeling, who, in addition to looking at schemes for the unemployed in Britain, had also examined similar projects in Fascist Italy, a country of which he was a keen advocate. Teeling concluded that "There is much being done in Italy and England to-day that if not exactly the same is at least very similar in regard to dealing with the leisure hours of those that work or once worked." Teeling's conclusion stands as an indictment of those that bandied about the seemingly innocent concept of leisure, without questioning either its origins or its uses.[34]

Structure and Nature of the Clubs

Thus far we have analyzed what may be termed the ideology of the unemployed club movement. This has led to two broad conclusions: (i) that the unemployed club movement, far from being an exercise in altruism, was an exercise in encapsulating and preserving a certain relationship of power between bourgeoisie and working class, and (ii) that the aim of this was to curtail the political activity of the unemployed.

But does this analysis stand up? It could be fairly objected that it is based not upon the reality of the clubs but upon the bourgeois ideal of the unemployed clubs. One way in which the analysis can be checked is to examine the concrete reality of the clubs themselves, and to see if this either reinforces or contradicts what we have so far found out. If we are to do this, there are four important questions which need to be answered: first, who founded the clubs? second, who ran the clubs? third, who attended the clubs? and fourth, what were the clubs like and what did they do?

The NCSS orthodoxy in regard to the first two questions was well put by Richard Clements, an NCSS advisory officer, in a speech he made in 1935. "The movement", he emphasized, "was a typical British product; it was not planned from above but grew out of the needs and feelings of the people. A wave of enthusiasm swept the country." Let us look at the contention that "a wave of enthusiasm swept the country" in the wake of the Prince of Wales' speech in January 1932. If this were the case we would expect to find that the vast majority of clubs were formed by the winter of 1932-33.[35]

We find from Table 7.1 that the vast majority of clubs were formed not in 1932, but in 1933. Although we can see that the "wave of enthusiasm" took place in 1933 and not 1932, we lack statistical evidence for the number of clubs in 1932, so we still cannot say for certain that the Prince of Wales' appeal did not spark off a movement of some magnitude. There is other evidence though, which, while not conclusive, does point to there being little interest in the unemployed clubs until the winter of 1932-33, with the vast majority being formed after November 1932.[36]

If we use the unemployed clubs visited by Prince George in Birmingham on 27 November 1933 as a sample, we discover that only one club had been established prior to November 1932, and of the remaining six, four had been founded during November and December 1932. Of the twenty-one unemployed clubs in the Midlands Prince George visited in a more extensive tour the following year, we find that only two had been formed prior to November 1932, one in 1931 and one in 1928. Of the remaining nineteen clubs, five were formed in the period November to December 1932, eight in the period January to April 1933, and two in 1934. In the case of London there is a remarkable example of virtually no response to the prince's appeal, followed by rapid growth in the winter of 1932-33. In July 1932 the NCSS reported "that although there were a few social and recreational centres available for the unemployed in London, very little had been done to start occupation centres".

Table 7.1. *Unemployed Clubs, 1933-1938*

Date		Occupational	Recreational	Total
*				
1 Feb.	1933	314	446	760
1 March	1933	593	619	1,212
1 April	1933	729	636	1,465
1 May	1933	837	732	1,569
1 June	1933	934	723	1,657
1 July	1933	1,059	826	1,885
1 Oct.	1933	1,148	863	2,011
1 Jan.	1934	1,243	882	2,125
1 Feb	1934	1,305	910	2,215
1 Oct.	1934	1,388	756	2,144
1 Nov.	1934	1,405	757	2,162
	1936			1,542
	1937			1,600
30 Sept.	1938			1,450

Sources: NCSS, Schemes to Aid the Unemployed Progress Report, April 1933; NCSS Unemployment Committee Progress Report, June 1933; 13 Jan. 1937; 30 Sept. 1938; NCSS Unemployment Committee, Secretary's Report, 10 Oct. 1933; 1 March 1934; 22 Nov. 1934; NCVOA-NCSS Box 5.

* No accurate figures available prior to 1 Feb. 1933; after 1935 the NCSS no longer distinguished between occupational and recreational clubs.

In January 1933 the London Council for Voluntary Occupation was formed. Before disbursing any money it undertook a survey and discovered that there were now nearly 200 unemployed clubs in existence in London. Some voluntary service organizations and activities did result as a local response to unemployed protest late in the autumn of 1932. It is no surprise, for example, to find in Bristol—one of the storm centers of NUWM activity in 1932—the Bristol Unemployed Welfare Association being formed in October 1932, at a special conference chaired by the mayor and attended by representatives of religious, social, educational, and other bodies. Another obvious, if totally inadequate, response to the revolt of 1932 was the commencement of gymnastics classes for the unemployed in Liverpool on 5 October 1932, a few weeks after the violence of the Birkenhead and Liverpool unemployed riots. But as Eva Hubback and Alan Collinridge, in their memorandum of 8 November 1932, emphasized, the NCSS had "to take the initiative in the overwhelming number of localities in which nothing adequate is being done." The NCSS Unemployment Committee was formed not in response to a groundswell of voluntary social work among the unemployed, but in order to bring such a movement into existence.[37]

Once the NCSS Unemployment Committee was established, and a concerted campaign begun by them and the government to encourage voluntary social service, unemployed clubs mushroomed all over the country. Often, as in Stockport in December 1932, the mayor would convene a town meeting at which an organizing body comprising representatives of local charities and local government would be set up. Funds for such bodies were obtained from both the NCSS and a mix of local capitalists. The unemployed clubs in Liverpool, for example, were sponsored by, among others, the Liverpool Steamship Owners Association (who had in the 1920s funded the attempts at sabotaging the NUWCM made by J. McQuirk Hughes), the Liverpool Retail Grocers' Association, and the Liverpool Institute of Chartered Accountants. At first the NCSS grant aided unemployed clubs directly, but later it developed and funded a structure of supporting regional bodies, which in turn initiated, supervised, and funded local clubs. The unemployed clubs were then founded and funded from above by a body subservient to the state, a process in which they were supported by local bourgeoisie. "It became fashionable to 'do something for the unemployed,' " wrote Ellen Wilkinson in 1939. "Out of this feeling came the social service movement, as we know it, with its clubs for the unemployed". Shortly before Christmas of 1932, Wal Hannington, serving a sentence of three months in Pentonville prison in consequence of the 1932 hunger march, was visited by a church minister who told Hannington that the march had "stirred the conscience of the other class to the need for providing some kind of social life for the unemployed".[38]

The NCSS claimed that the unemployed clubs "were a spontaneous creation of the unemployed men, were financed entirely by them, and remained entirely under their control". We have seen that far from this being so, the clubs were a planned creation of the bourgeoisie. But is it possible that the unemployed may have controlled the clubs? Generally there were two committees involved in the management of an unemployed club. The first was a general committee, composed of representatives of the local authority, voluntary organizations, and the churches. This was very much a middle-class committee composed of local dignitaries and social workers, and it would be responsible for the formation, structuring, and funding of the unemployed club. In all these functions it would expect to enjoy the support, advice, and funding of the regional voluntary service organizations established by the NCSS. Upon establishment of the club there would be formed a club committee, composed of representatives of the unemployed and of the general committee, which would then be responsible for the day-to-day running of the club. Theoretically, this second committee would then be its own master, the general committee restricting itself to a paternal role of fundraising and guidance. Sometimes the unemployed would have delegates on the general committee, and in other cases, though this was rare, there would be just the one committee composed of the club's promoters alongside some of the unemployed.[39]

Whatever the particular form of the clubs' management, the general reality was of middle-class control over the working-class membership. While members of the unemployed club were entitled to vote at the election of some of the representatives for the club committee, they had no say whatsoever in the selection of the general committee which decided policy and controlled funds. In reality the general committee was a self-selecting middle-class oligarchy, and it was they, and not the unemployed working-class club members, who were the real power base of the unemployed club. In private the NCSS recognized that "the central organization has remained in the hands of comparatively well to do citizens". "It is only in rare cases that the representatives of the workers are to be found in counsels of either the national or local Voluntary organizations", wrote Sir Wyndham Deedes in 1937. "The Governing bodies of Voluntary organizations are composed for the most part of middle class people and intellectuals, and their financial resources are drawn from what in some quarters are known as the 'capitalist' classes."[40]

While members of the unemployed clubs paid one or two pence as a weekly membership fee, one of the most common complaints of the unemployed members was that they were "not allowed to know how the main funds of the club were being spent". Many of the middle-class members of the general committee who did control the funds, after their initial enthusiasm for voluntary work died following the club's formation, never visited the unemployed club they ran. Inevitably they were often ignorant of the problems of the club and of the unemployed in general. Some voluntary service organizations were quite blunt in their determination not to allow the unemployed any control of club finances. Here was the cutting edge of middle-class power, where NCSS talk of democracy was slashed into meaningless strips. The NCSS inspired Nottingham County Unemployed Workers' Committee (somewhat misnamed as not one unemployed worker was on the committee) decided that while "the unemployed men should be given every opportunity to participate in their development by being represented on all committees", no unemployed would be allowed to sit on the finance committees of their clubs.[41]

Notwithstanding such middle-class control, we should not assume either that the clubs always ran the way the middle class wanted them to, or that the unemployed who patronized them were content passively to mold themselves into the grateful cobblers and physical jerks enthusiasts of NCSS propaganda. "There were unfortunate examples", writes Henry Mess, "of groups of men being granted the use of buildings and turning them into gambling dens and rough houses, the right to use the buildings only being saved by the trustees stepping in and exercising a firm control." Use of the unemployed clubs by the unemployed was therefore totally conditional upon their forms of behavior being acceptable to the bourgeoisie. Firm control normally took the form of installing a full time salaried supervisor of the unemployed club. These supervisors were responsible not to the unemployed members of the clubs, but rather to either a town committee or a regional council. William Teeling, in his gauche but revealing way, gives an interesting picture of one supervisor, Miss Jowitt (sister of Sir William Jowitt) who ran a settlement for the unemployed at Seaham Harbour. Teeling had told her of a friend who ran a small racing stable "for excitement". "She looked at me, this tall, handsome woman. 'Do you mean to tell me they still look for excitement there? Is there not a million times more thrill where under your very eyes you often see men rescued from being almost animals and turned into real men, real assets to their country.' " A chastened Teeling conceded, "There certainly is a thrill in such work." Jowitt's harangue captures the patronising essence of many a patrician NCSS activist, and gives us an insight into just how class-based was the nature of much voluntary work amongst the unemployed.[42]

But it would be wrong, (though tempting), to write off all who worked under the aegis of the NCSS as being similarly minded. Many people who took up such work did so for the best of reasons. Yet their well-meaning efforts took place within an organization whose guiding principles were political rather than humanitarian. No matter what their individual motives, all voluntary workers operated in structures designed to reproduce rather than minimize the unequal power relations that prevailed between bourgeoisie and working class in society at large. Even within the very notion of voluntary service these power relations were encapsulated, and it is therefore not surprising to find A. D. Lindsay writing: "In practice our difficulty, I think, is not the difficulty of voluntary service, but the difficulty of who directs voluntary service. If we can get somebody to organise the unemployed from below for this purpose then we should do the trick." The trick was to shroud the true nature of the power relations within voluntary service, a trick that the NCSS tried to pull off in two ways. First, it sought the support of the TUC, and in this it was unsuccessful. The TUC was suspicious of both the unemployed clubs, which it regarded as potential (and sometimes actual) sources of products made by unpaid labor, and the NCSS, whose intentions it doubted. The TUC refused to have anything to do with the activities of the NCSS, and although trades councils remained free to cooperate, this does not seem to have occurred on a very widespread basis. In spite of this rebuff the NCSS attempted to maintain friendly relations with TUC unemployed associations, though this good will was never allowed to extend to the NUWM, a point upon which the NCSS was emphatic. The NCSS never gave up wooing the TUC, hoping this might give them some credibility among the working class. "We should try to retain cordial relations with the TUC", wrote Leonard King, secretary of the South Yorkshire Unemployment Advisory Council, in a letter to L. F. Ellis in 1936, "otherwise we give grounds for suspicion that we are an Employer's body. This particularly applies to a Council such as ours financed very substantially by Coal owners."[43]

The second way in which the NCSS attempted to hide its real face was (as Lindsay had suggested), by molding some selected unemployed members into the sort of leaders it required. Unemployed members deemed suitable were shipped off for instructional courses in leadership at one of the five residential centers run by or through the NCSS. Here they would be trained for three to six weeks in leadership, club management, and running club activities. The clubs did not operate in a vacuum. After returning to their club the unemployed leaders would be subjected to the continuing external influence of the NCSS. For advice and help they were greatly dependent upon an infrastructure of support provided by the NCSS, and this acted as a very important influence upon the nature of the clubs. There were talks broadcast by the BBC, at one stage every Monday, Tuesday, and

Friday, about what made for a good club and what made for a bad club. There was an unending stream of instructional memos, pamphlets, and leaflets; and even in the most innocuous of these the middle-class bias of the NCSS would sometimes be betrayed. For example, in 1933 the NCSS issued a list of objects that could be made in the clubs, which contained suggestions that ranged from the practical—chairs, stools, tables, window boxes, to the pointless—spoons and hinges; to the ironically futile—paperknife, pipe rack, wireless cabinet, and meat chopper; and which in their hollow imitation of middle-class life made a mockery of the unemployed's poverty.[44]

There would also be regular visits from NCSS advisory officers. The NCSS placed great emphasis upon the role of the advisory officers, and as early as April 1933 the NCSS had nine such officers working full time. Later, as the NCSS fostered area and county committees to give a regional backbone to its organization of the unemployed, it made grants to these bodies to enable them to form "a nucleus advisory staff of travelling instructors". In addition to the numerous advisory officers it thus indirectly supported, the NCSS was by 1939 funding forty-two full-time advisory officers of its own. The advisory officers were expected to travel about the country initiating new clubs, as well as giving personal advice on management, organization, development, and conduct of activities in clubs. They were very much the grass roots ideologues as well as the organizers of the voluntary service movement, being required to have "a clear understanding of the special aims and purposes of the work which Occupation clubs and kindred institutions are endeavouring to carry out." Their ideas were fashioned by their training, and subsequent heterodoxy was avoided by attendance at the ubiquitous NCSS conference that "offered the best means of building up a body of common thought and principle throughout the movement".[45]

Ellen Wilkinson, in her harrowing account of the destruction of the shipbuilding town of Jarrow, *The Town that Was Murdered*, drew a graphic picture of an advisory officer putting "the common thought and principle" of the NCSS into action.

> An organiser to justify his job, decides that certain towns must have centres. Perhaps a few sympathisers are collected, premises are taken, and then the unemployed are invited to become members. Often a young University graduate arrives and commences to "organise" men old enough to be his father. These men have a hatred of being organised in that way-whether for education or recreation. Men who have been independent and efficient workmen-and often taking a responsible part in the activities of their union cannot be regarded as social casualties in need of guidance. Many of them have the ability to organise their own activities. . . . Already, as a result of the way in which the social service movement has been organised, a kind of stigma is being attached to social service activities.[46]

To answer our second question: the unemployed did not run the unemployed clubs. They were run and controlled by the middle class, who reproduced their dominance over the unemployed in the structure and activities of the clubs. But as the aim of the unemployed club movement was to stifle unemployed political activity, it would have been curious if this had been otherwise.

The answer to our third question—who attended the clubs?—is less obvious than it first seems. While it was unemployed members of the working class who patronized the clubs, it was only particular sections of the unemployed. For a start club members were largely men, the club movement a man's movement. It proved extraordinarily unsuccessful in attracting women. Of an estimated membership in 1936 of 200,000 only 16,000 were women. The NCSS did little, if anything, to attract women into the unemployed clubs. The clubs' activities were male-focused, with endless woodwork classes, but few needlework classes. A report made for the NCSS in early 1933 found in Liverpool, for example, that while there were thirty clubs for men, there was only one for unemployed women. In Glasgow there were only three clubs for unemployed women, and in Shoreditch it was reported that there was "a strong feeling that all money and effort should be concentrated on the men". About the only specific activity for women undertaken by the NCSS was running "homecraft" classes for women in the Special Areas in 1935-36, and this was done at the specific behest of the commissioner for Special Areas. Even if the NCSS had manifested a vague interest in working among women (which it didn't), it was tied to the government's indifference to unemployed women, the Ministry of Labour maintaining that unemployed men's wives were not unemployed and therefore should not benefit from Ministry grants.[47]

Among unemployed men the clubs experienced great difficulty with the old, who were seen as being without hope, and the young, who were, the NCSS told the Beveridge Committee in 1942, "a disturbing influence on the clubs". According to the NCSS, "The voluntary basis of membership and organization required a sense of responsibility within the Club, for which the unstable employment records of the younger people were the worst possible preparation." The NCSS then made an unusually candid admission. "As far as the younger men were concerned, particularly those under 20 years of age, the clubs frankly failed". From this we can surmise that the clubs tended to be the province of unemployed working-class men, who would more often than not be middle-aged. The clubs' appeal was limited even within this group, and by 1937 it was admitted in some NCSS quarters that it was "doubtful if the clubs will ever cater for more than ten or fifteen per cent of the Unemployed".[48]

Finally, we need to know what the clubs were actually like. The official image was of enthusiastic unemployed cheerfully toiling away in humble but homely surroundings. The reality was different. The NCSS Unemployment Committee recognized in mid-1933 that most unemployed clubs were "very poor in quality", and the picture was not to improve with the passing of the years. John Newson, in a talk broadcast to unemployed clubs in 1935, chastised members for the poor condition of their clubs in a characteristic NCSS manner: "Too often the club is housed in accommodation that would never appeal to a man in paid work and to which members dont feel they'd like to ask their wives. Now that is not good enough!" In 1937 the South East Lancashire and the North East Cheshire Advisory Council described clubs as being housed in "generally deplorable premises". The most vivid description given of the unemployed clubs is that written by a man who probably saw more of them than anybody else, the Prince of Wales. His description is all the more striking given that he was both a sympathetic witness, and one who saw the clubs at their very best: Rhymney Social Centre, for example, being hastily ordered to have thirty pounds worth of emergency reconditioning and reconstruction before the prince (now King Edward VIII) visited in late 1936.[49]

Yet in spite of such artifice, the underlying reality was too strong to be denied. "Despite sincere attempts to make the clubs cheerful, " wrote the duke of Windsor some years later,

> they were for the most part dreary places-unused public halls, makeshift wooden structures often ill-lit and shabbily furnished with hard, almost forbidding, benches and tables. The walls were bare except for coloured lithographs of my parents and other national figures. The prevailing despair and resentment were often too heavy even for [NCSS chairman] "Bill" Adams' salty buoyancy to lift. More than once I found myself walking the length of one of the big rooms past row after row of crowded but silent benches, hearing nothing save the creak of floor boards under my weight. This reproachful, almost sullen, silence was a new experience for me; I was accustomed to cheers.[50]

In this remarkable description the unemployed clubs, far from being a compliment to the bourgeois soul, have become an uncomfortable accusation. This is not so surprising when we consider that the unemployed clubs existed not to benefit the unemployed but to control them. What emerges from the vast number of photographs and descriptions of the clubs' activities is the pointlessness of the endless repetition of activity that created no future: a numbing circle of horse vaulting, arm waving exercises, boot patching, rope mat making, and continuing, repetitive tedium, ad nauseam.

Admittedly the NCSS recognized the limited range of activities as a problem. Predictably its only solution was to introduce more of them. These new activities and the way they were implemented again reveal the political role of the clubs in disciplining and controlling the unemployed. "No one wants to go on indefinitely making boots or bookshelves", admitted the Prince of Wales in a BBC broadcast in January 1934, "and we realise that all these kinds of activities are only a stop gap." With its emphasis on the need for constant useful activity, the NCSS began to encourage educational and cultural activity in the clubs. But this took a particular form: Teeling observed that classes in the unemployed clubs "steer clear of politics and history". At a time when revolutionary politics were not without their appeal for the unemployed, some clubs subtly sought to impart a belief in the worth of parliamentary politics. At the Spennymoor settlement for the unemployed a model parliament along the lines of Westminster was run with full participation by the unemployed: "The result is that they study the subjects of the day and they learn the difficulties of parliamentary government and the procedure at Westminster. For every bill they introduce, the Warden insists some people shall be detailed off to give the Conservative side."[51]

The NCSS used the club movement to seek to determine not just working class behavior, but also working-class culture. The 1930s was a period that saw a most remarkable flowering of self-consciously working-class writing, much of which was concerned with the experience of unemployment. To this movement the clubs contributed nothing, and did nothing to encourage people to be part of it, but instead strived to impress upon the unemployed the great virtue of bourgeois literature. Courses run by the NCSS in play production, play reading, and play writing were, according to a confidential NCSS report of 1938, "More for the purpose of developing taste and judgement in the choice of plays than to help and encourage play wrights."[52]

Physical training was another activity that the NCSS tried vainly to promote in the clubs. Physical training supposedly served the purpose of keeping workers in a good state of fitness, ready for reabsorption into industry at a later date. It was derided by the opponents of the NCSS as preparation for military training, but there seems to be no truth in this allegation. The NCSS was, however, sensitive to these criticisms and told instructors that "methods should be as free as possible from what might be described as 'militaristic' efforts". The major aim of physical training was more ideological than militaristic, and it was viewed as a vehicle for implanting ideas about nationalism: NCSS physical training instructors were told that the major aim of physical training was "To point out the traditional and ever increasing importance of games in the development of the British Citizen and their special importance in relation to the occupation of leisure time."[53]

Physical training was one of the much-touted activities of the unemployed clubs, one of the received images of the 1930s being of unemployed men doing gymnastics or physical jerks displays. Ironically it was the area in which the NCSS met with greatest failure, in spite of the investment of considerable amounts of money and energy. By the end of 1933 facilities for physical training were being provided in 591 unemployed centers and the NCSS trained numerous instructors. But there was little response from the unemployed. An NCSS report in 1935 concluded that "there was no great demand for physical training classes in any area". The inanity of physical jerks was found to have little attraction: "it is useless to start classes in physical training . . . unless some objective is put before them, and, although it sounds very well to talk about inspiring their interest in fitness and giving them a realisation of the value of a healthy body, it is not always easy to create enthusiasm for ideas." "With regard to this new drive to keep the unemployed fit', wrote J. J. Worley, a member of the co-operative movement, ". . . on a starvation diet men had no strength for physical jerks. Physical jerks are no substitute for prime joints". The numbers involved in physical training were small: in February 1939, 4,638 people were reported to have regularly attended NCSS aided keep fit classes, and this figure was an improvement on the tally for 1938. Even this minuscule figure was inflated, for in several areas the keep fit classes were filled with a preponderance of employed people.[54]

Effect of Clubs

In the end we are left with more questions than answers. This chapter has looked at how the NCSS conceived and structured its work in relation to the unemployed, but not at how the unemployed conceived and structured their response to the clubs. It is clear that while many unemployed resented the clubs, for many others they fulfilled a social need for which neither the labor movement nor the NUWM had previously catered, and led the NUWM to make considerable changes in its organization at a grass roots level. "In combating the Social Service schemes we must do more than explain their dangers to the standards of life of the unemployed", Wal Hannington told an NUWM NAC meeting in February 1933. "Our Movement must develop a social life in the work of the NUWM through the organising of educational and study classes, sports teams, libraries, games and Bands, always taking care to guard against any danger of this question becoming predominant in the life of the NUWM." Some clubs did fulfill a permanent need, as evidenced by the Jarrow club, which had a subscribing membership that rarely dipped below the 200 mark.[55]

There are questions that are impossible to answer: if we have established that one aim of the clubs was to control the unemployed, how successful were the clubs in controlling and depoliticizing the unemployed?

In 1937 Y. G. Evans, the unemployed secretary of the Tonyrefail and District Unemployed Social Service Committee (in fact this was a club, if not in name) wrote to Oliver Harris, general secretary of the SWMF, in protest at the conditions of the unemployed: "Our sufferings are already too great and will become unbearable in the near future", wrote Evans, concluding, "We will heartily support any movement that can be made to improve conditions. If nothing can be done trouble is bound to come sooner or later". This was not the sort of talk that the NCSS had been paid by the government to sponsor, and it shows how even in the belly of the beast the unemployed were not so malleable and pliant as to be crushed flat and without fight by years of NCSS initiatives intended to engender the opposite reaction.[56]

One tangible NCSS achievement, and certainly one of its most enduring lies in the image that they gave to many people of the 1930s: not of the unemployed fighting in Whitehall, but cheering the Prince of Wales in devastated industrial towns; not of the unemployed marching for their rights, but vaulting a box for no reason; not of a fearful bourgeoisie mixing concession and force in reacting to the unemployed, but of a benevolent and altruistic bourgeoisie leading the unemployed; not of the unemployed making demands, but receiving charity. In essence, it is the difference between a picture of a passive poor and an active proletariat; of the working class making its own history, or being molded by greater, uncontrollable forces.

By 1947 the NCSS view was sufficiently well entrenched for Henry Mess to write: "There is no reason to think that if the clubs had not existed there would have been more active political opposition. It is more likely that more men would have sunk back into deep lethargy as indeed many of them had done before the clubs were started."[57]

This is a total inversion of history. The clubs were brought into existence and structured in a particular manner as a direct consequence of the activity of the unemployed, with the specific aim of sinking this activity into the lethargy induced by the tedium of physical jerks, cobbling, and craft work. To assert the opposite, that the clubs were brought into existence to combat the lethargy of the unemployed is to be untruthful, and to promulgate a politically and class based myth. Depending on whether this myth is accepted or rejected goes a long way in determining how the 1930s in Britain are viewed.

Conclusion

I stood in the ruins of Dowlais,
And sighed for the lovers destroyed
And the landscape of Gwalia stained for all time
By the bloody hands of progress.
I saw the ghosts of the slaves of The Successful Century
Marching on the ridges of the sunset
And wandering along desolate furnaces,
And they had not forgotten their humiliation,
For their mouths were full of curses.
And I cried aloud,
O what shall I do for my fathers
And the land of my fathers?
But they cursed and cursed and would not answer
For they could not forget their humiliation.

—*Idris Davies,* Gwalia Deserta *(Dent 1938)*

What determined the activity of the unemployed? What, on occasion, propelled the unemployed into challenging the very assumptions that in large part shaped the experience of being unemployed? Man has an infinite capacity for suffering, and suffering alone is never a sufficient spur to action, so no catalogue of the inhumanity of unemployment can explain the activity of the unemployed.

We can try to answer this question by first asking when did this activity of the unemployed take place? The answer to this is straightforward enough: at moments of capitalist crisis. What were such crises of capitalism characterized by? First and most obviously, by an excessively large number of unemployed. Much analysis tends to concentrate upon the weaknesses of capitalism at such moments of crisis, of the capacity for disintegration and failure at such times, and the swelling of the reserve army of labor is often cited as proof of such collapse.

Yet what is equally apparent at such moments of weakness is the capacity of capitalism for radical change, which paradoxically is its great and so far enduring strength. Depressions, together with wars, the most common form of capitalist crisis, are moments in history when capitalism is able to administer surgery to itself under the anesthetic of economic crisis. To take one example, many economists and historians find a contradiction in the inter-war British economy: on the one hand development and improvement, an era in which the foundations of modern-day British monopoly capitalism were laid; on the other suffering and exploitation on a mass and unimaginable scale. Some historians have sought to cut the Gordian knot by minimizing the human cost of the depression, illustrating their despicable intent with graphs and statistics of rising national earnings, rising national *average* infant mortality rates, and the like, which tell us nothing beyond a certain bias, and surreptitiously hide a great deal. The contradiction is in reality no contradiction at all: the record of economic development in the inter-war period was necessarily dependent upon the human agony it created and gorged upon. What we discover during depressions is that trends toward new methods of production and distribution become greatly accelerated, existing patterns of capitalist ownership undergo rapid and decisive changes, and much of this is only possible because of the weakness of the working class due to the existence of a vast reserve army of labor. In all periods of crisis we see a great impetus given to the concentration and centralization of capital—in the 1880s the establishment of cartels and corporations, in the 1920s and 1930s the wholesale push toward monopoly capitalism.

Most importantly for our study was the impetus given to technological change in the labor process. So far we have dealt with unemployment and the unemployed as isolated objects, but this is an analytical fiction, and an irritating one at that. In reality the world of working and not working were two sides of the same coin. In a depression the world of working underwent drastic and rapid changes. In old industries, because the workforce, threatened by unemployment, was unable to offer strong opposition, technological change led to both the deskilling of labor and the displacement of labor. Those who remained working did so upon deskilled work with correspondingly reduced wages, subjected to a new and ever-more ferocious work discipline. Those forced to leave formed the fodder for exploitation by new industries, and had the unenviable choice of taking work at lower wages and worsened conditions, or remaining unemployed. Unemployed protest never just represented the protest of those who had lost their jobs, but instead the cumulative outrage of those subjected to a process of deskilling, increased work discipline, reduced wages, and, finally, unemployment.

To maintain such an obscene state of affairs capitalism needed to promulgate myths about itself to make sure that those who were oppressed and destroyed by its activities felt their oppression and destruction to be both historically inevitable and morally appropriate. At certain moments in history, as we have seen, the unemployed came to feel that their continued acquiescence was no longer morally appropriate, came to believe, if only briefly, that what was immoral was not their inability to find work, but a system that created and condoned unemployment. And during those occassional moments some unemployed saw that there was nothing at all historically inevitable about their unemployment, saw that it was a product of a system that was subject to change or even destruction, and reacted accordingly, pouring their outrage and sadness, their despair and hope into the political activity of the organized unemployed. The politics of the unemployed shaped not just the unemployed's immediate destiny, but the very conception of what to be unemployed meant. While the nineteenth-century idea of "unemployed" equating with personal failure was imposed upon the unemployed, the newer notion of "unemployed" as equating with economic and social injustice was, to a great extent, one decisive outcome of the struggle of the unemployed between 1884 and 1939.

This change in the ideological construction of "unemployed" was neither inevitable, nor a form of gentle progress, but a hard-fought hegemonic battle. That is why for many capitalists unemployment was not primarily an industrial or social problem, but an extremely important battleground of competing political values. In 1922, and again in 1925, Sir Alfred Mond, one of the leading capitalists of the day, proposed a scheme whereby the dole would be paid direct to industries as a wage supplement, with the purpose of increasing employment so as to demonstrate that unemployment could be eliminated under capitalism. Mond, addressing a special committee of the Federation of British Industry set up to examine his proposals in 1925, argued that

> those of us who are in politics realise it more and more, that today it [unemployment] is a challenge to our whole industrial order. Today the Socialist Party accuses us of being entirely incapable of dealing with industry, the management of business or the organization of society, and one of their chief arguments is that we cannot deal with the Unemployment question, and if we say all we can do is to go on as we are doing now, they will say with some truth, "Well you are incapable of finding any solution. We think we have a solution. Let us try ours." . . . The danger of this is very great . . . Your Communists can always bring so many hard cases that it silences you against cases which you know ought not be there at all.

As Keir Hardie observed of public opinion of the unemployed in 1905, "This intangible force does not come into being spontaneously. It is a manufactured article, and represents that amount of agitation and education which any given cause has been able to exert upon the community. The demonstrations in support of the Unemployed Bill created the necessary 'public opinion' to ensure the Bill becoming an Act."[1]

Capitalism produced unemployment, but it did not disgorge the unemployed as it disgorged Model T Fords. The unemployed were only defined and, in this sense, specifically created, through their relation with the capitalist state. Marx could thus perceive and comment upon the reserve army of labor that capitalism had brought into existence, but he did not comment upon the unemployed, because the reserve army of labor had not then entered into a discourse with the immature capitalist state. The capitalist state did not pass from immaturity to maturity for no reason, or for the reason of the unemployed alone; it was propelled there by the changing nature of capitalist production, with which it existed in symbiotic relation. Capitalist production, passing into ever more complex and sophisticated forms, found that an industrial reserve army of labor was not enough. Where this army had been anarchic it had to be controlled; where it had been undisciplined it had to be disciplined; where it had been formless it had to have shape. From the 1880s onwards work practices such as half time, part time, and the entire casual labor market no longer adequately fulfilled the requirements of capitalism in providing labor. As the industrial workforce became more disciplined, so too had the industrial reserve army of labor; as the industrial workforce became more homogenized, so too had the industrial reserve army of labor.

Capitalism produced unemployment, but it was the capitalist state that determined how the unemployed daily related to the employed, how the unemployed daily related to each other, and how they daily related to the world at large. This in turn determined how the unemployed were perceived both by others and by themselves. These perceptions, when accepted and unchallenged, formed the mortar that held the bricks of oppression together. The capitalist state, through the implied or actual use of force (e.g., the workhouse, the means test) produced a conception of unemployed relations that became an accepted consensus. Force and consent are not equals: people may consent in the face of force, but they attempt to mold it on their terms. Such was the experience of the unemployed.

This is not to say that each new consensus did not represent some advance, some progress for the working class, for often it did. An unemployed worker in Britain is materially better off in the 1990s than her or his counterpart a century ago. But if something is gained, something is lost: in the case of the unemployed material betterment—which is not to be derided—has been won at the expense of the possibility of exerting some power. Each major reformulation of the unemployed as a social product (1834, 1886, 1911, 1921, 1931, 1942) has been a reformulation of the relationship of power between the bourgeoisie and the unemployed. People accuse the unemployed of apathy, but in truth they are the victims of the past victories of the unemployed, which led the state to devise new forms of administering welfare over which the unemployed would no longer be able to exert any influence. More than ever the unemployed are defined in terms of their close relationship with the state. Yet in every instance, just when the bourgeoisie feels it has successfully negotiated terms entirely favorable to itself and placed the unemployed within a gilded cage from which there is no escape—lo and behold!—the unemployed discover that no Bastille is impregnable and turn the new construction of the unemployed to their own favor.

It would be reassuring to end this book upon a note of euphoric victory, to present the coming of the post World War II Welfare State as, in part, a triumphant consequence of the politics of the unemployed between 1884 and 1939. But in the 1990s it is not possible to proffer a Marxist qualification of a Whig myth, and say that some of the few benefits of the remnant Welfare State are partly attributable to the past activity of the unemployed. Mass unemployment is again accepted as a fact of life, and the baying of those calling for the return of task work to discipline the unemployed grows louder with each passing day.

And perhaps this was bound to be so because of the very nature of the politics of the uemployed, from the moment in 1870 when the Land and Labour League demanded for the unemployed not the end of wage labour, but simply the incorporation of the unemployed within it. The cry of the Unemployed Workers' Organisation in the 1920s, "Abolition of the wage system", was, as they pointed out, far more radical than that of "Work or full maintenance", the slogan of the NUWCM, from whom they had broken away. But it was also utopian, and throughout the period we have looked at, totally unrealizable. The contradictory problem that beset all the politics of the unemployed, from 1884 to 1939, was that the unemployed were part of the system of wage labor, indeed, not only were they part of that system, they were integral to it, for without the existence of a reserve army of labor, ther could be no army of waged laborers. And, as well as underpinning of the system of wage labor, the unemployed were defined in terms of it, as being without waged labor: any politics of the unemployed began in seeking to try and redress this balance, to transform the unemployed into employed. But how could they? How could you protest against a system into which you were trying to escape? How could you challenge the world of working that created the workless, when what so desperately, urgently needed was work? George Bernard Shaw was right when, after the Trafalgar Square riot of 1886, he wrote of the unemployed, "The sullen fury of the man who has been tramping through the mud all day in bitter weather, vainly seeking a master is not—unfortunately—'revolution in the making'. The unemployed are as great a nuisance to the Socialists as to themselves. Angry as they are, they do not want a revolution: they want a job." And to get a job, they had to publicly establish that they were not one of the old classes of the indigent poor, but members of that modern grouping known as the unemployed. For this reason the battles of the unemployed were as much about having themselves recognised and treated as unemployed, rather than as vagrants or paupers, as they were about getting work or maintenance. This is why the breaking down of poor law provisions that demanded that all entering workhouses be treated as paupers was such an important element of the politics of the unemployed during the 1920s and 1930s, particularly during the hunger marches. As the poor law inspectors admitted after the 1922 hunger march, "the marchers have had a fairly triumphant progress . . . and have successfully upheld their claim that they are not vagrants and should not be treated as such. . . . The guardians and the police must share the responsibilty for the failure to make the marchers amenable to the law." And so ultimately the law changed to accomodate the unemployed as unemployed, when the poor law was abolished and replaced by the welfare state. That was a victory, but a highly ambiguous one.[2]

It is not wrong to commemorate this or the other minuscule victories of the unemployed that stand out so vividly in large part only because of the utter bleakness of the background against which they were enacted. But instead of only remembering the small successes, perhaps we should also walk alongside the ghosts of Dowlais and not forget their humiliation, and ask ourselves why it is that such humiliation continues to this day. And then we might realize that the politics of the unemployed reveals the great historic failure of the labor and socialist movements: to create an economy in which there is a meaningful place for all. The hope of the unemployed needs to become the hope of us all.

Notes

Archives and Collections

The following abbreviations have been used throughout the notes:

BRO	Bristol Records Office
CPA	Communist Party Archives
HP/CPA	Wal Hannington Papers, Communist Party Archives
HP/MML	Wal Hannington Papers, Marx Memorial Library
JJ/BL	John Johnson Collection, Bodleian Library
MML	Marx Memorial Library
MRC	Modern Records Centre
NCVOA	National Council of Voluntary Organisations Archive
PP/JJ/BL	Pollard Papers, John Johnson Collection, Bodleian Library
PRO Cab	Public Records Office, Cabinet Papers
RCA	Ruskin College Archives
SWCA	South Wales Coalfield Archives

Note: *Unless otherwise stated all references were published in London.*

Introduction

1. Ernie Benson, *To Struggle is to Live, Vol. II* (Newcastle 1980), pp. 55-56.

2. D. N. Ashton, *Unemployment Under Capitalism: The Sociology of British & American Labour Markets* (Brighton 1986), p. 15.

3. Ralph Hayburn, "The Police and the Hunger Marchers", *International Review of Social History* (1972); "The National Unemployed Workers' Movement, 1921-1936", *International Review of Social History* (1983); John Stevenson, "The Politics

of Violence", G. Peele and C. Cook (eds.), *Crisis and Controversy* (1976) subsequently republished in various guises; Peter Kingsford, *The Hunger Marchers in Britain 1920-1940* (1982).

4. It is interesting to note that in the late 1930s Hannington began writing a semi-autobiographical novel about working-class life in London, which he was never to finish. The draft first chapter bears strong similarity to the first chapter of Hannington's autobiography *Never On Our Knees*; interview with Eric Edney, 15 March 1986; Wal Hannington, "Three Brothers" unpub. short story, nd, HP/CPA -C2D.

Chapter 1

1. B. Tierney, *Medieval Poor Law* (Berkeley 1959), p. 12.

2. R. H. Tawney, *Religion and the Rise of Capitalism* (1926) (Harmondsworth 1961), p. 260; E. M. Leonard, *The Early History of English Poor Relief* (Cambridge 1906), p. 18.

3. K. Thomas, *Religion and the Decline of Magic* (1971), pp. 564, 601; C. Hill, "The Poor and the People," *Collected Essays Vol. III* (Brighton 1986), p. 260.

4. R. H. Hilton, "Agrarian Class Structure and Economic Development in Pre-Industrial Europe," *Past and Present* (1978), 80, p. 14; Leonard, *Poor Relief*, p. 3.

5. Thomas More, *Utopia* (1516) (Harmondsworth 1986), p. 46.

6. Ranging from G. R. Elton, *England Under the Tudors* (1971), p. 188; to C. Hill, *The Century of Revolution 1603-1741* (1967), p. 27.

7. J. F. Pound, *Poverty and Vagrancy in Tudor England* (1971), p. 29; C. Hill, *Reformation to Industrial Revolution* (Harmondsworth 1986), pp. 262, 84; A. L. Beier, *Masterless Men: The vagrancy problem in England 1560-1640* (1985), p. 23.

8. Beier, *Masterless Men,* p. 66; C. Hill, *The World Turned Upside Down* (Harmondsworth 1984), p. 50; Elton, *Under the Tudors,* p. 260; in spite of this pertinent point, Elton elsewhere makes glib use of the concept of the "unemployed".

9. More, *Utopia*, p. 47; Hill, *Reformation*, pp. 170-71.

10. Beier, *Masterless Men*, pp. 158-60, 164-69.

11. Elton, *Under the Tudors,* p. 456; quoted John Walter, "A 'Rising of the People'?, The Oxfordshire Rising of 1596", *Past and Present* (1985), 107, p. 91; R. H. Tawney and E. Power (eds.), *Tudor Economic Documents, Vol. 2* (1953), pp. 347, 355.

12. Karl Marx, *Capital, Vol. I* (1867) (Harmondsworth 1976), p. 899.

13. Quoted Marx, *Capital*, p. 764; quoted D. C. Coleman, "Labour in the English Economy in the Seventeenth Century," *Economic History Review* (1955-56), p. 281.

14. Hill, *Century of Revolution*, p. 25; Hill, *Reformation*, p. 259; Arthur Young, *Eastern Tour, Vol. IV* (1771), p. 361.

15. Hill, *Upside Down*, pp. 332, 342; quoted Sidney Pollard, "Factory Discipline in the Industrial Revolution," *Economic History Review* (1963-64), p. 258; see also Neil McKendrick, "Josiah Wedgewood and Factory Discipline", *Historical Journal*

(1961), iv, p. 38; John Knott, *Popular Opposition to the 1834 Poor Law* (Sydney 1986), p. 24.

16. Pollard, "Factory Discipline", p. 254; some historians see the workhouse as the ancestor of the prison, the factory, and the charitable institution, see Dario Melossi and Massimo Pavarini, *The Prison and the Factory* (1981), ch. 1; also Marx, *Capital*, pp. 338-39; Joseph Mather "The File Hewer's Lamentation," (1792) Roger Lonsdale (ed.), *The New Oxford Book of Eighteenth Century Verse* (Oxford 1984), p. 789.

17. Knott, *Opposition*, pp. 31, 32-33; M. E. Rose, *The English Poor Law, 1780-1834* (Newton Abbot 1971), p. 18.

18. Coleman, "Labour in the . . . Seventeenth Century," p. 287; E. P. Thompson, "Time, Work-Discipline and Industrial Capitalism", *Past and Present* (1967), 38, p. 72; the only history to date of the tramping system is R. A. Leeson, *Travelling Brothers* (1979).

19. Coleman, "Labour in the . . . Seventeenth Century," p. 294; Raymond Williams, *Keywords* (1987), pp. 325-327, gives the fullest discussion available of the history of the words "unemployed" and "unemployment"; see also *OED* (1926); E. P. Thompson, *The Making of the English Working Class* (rev. ed. Harmondsworth 1968), p. 853n; for an example of a contemporary discussion of the problem of the unemployed see Robert Owen, *Report to the County of Lanark* (1821).

20. Leonard, *Poor Relief*, p. vii; Knott, *Opposition*, p. 51; Andrew Scull, *Museums of Madness. The Social Organisation of Insanity in Nineteenth Century England* (1979), p. 86.

21. Quoted G. R. Boyer, "The Old Poor Law and the Agricultural Labour Market in Southern England: An Empirical Analysis," *Journal of Economic History* (1986), p. 115; Thomas Malthus, "A Summary View of Population" (1830), *An Essay on the Principle of Population* (Harmondsworth 1986), pp. 268-69.

22. D. Fraser (ed.), "Introduction", *The New Poor Law in the Nineteenth Century* (1976), p. 1; quoted Ian Anstruther, *The Scandal of the Andover Workhouse* (1973), p. 16.

23. Quoted Scull, *Madness*, p. 71; quoted Alasdair Clayre (ed.), *Nature and Industrialisation* (Oxford 1985), pp. 148-49; quoted P. Hollis (ed.), *Class and Conflict in Nineteenth Century England, 1815-1850* (1973), p. 122.

24. Knott, *Opposition*, pp. 13-34. The Oldham select vestry, for example, was dominated by working class radicals during the 1820s, John Foster, *Class Struggle and the Industrial Revolution* (1974), pp. 62-63; N. C. Edsall, *The anti-Poor Law Movement 1834-1844* (Manchester 1971), p. 8.

25. Knott, *Opposition*, p. 30-34; this concept was developed by E. P. Thompson, "The Moral Economy of the English Crowd in the Eighteenth Century," *Past and Present* (1971); quoted Clayre, *Industrialisation*, pp. 151-52.

26. Knott, *Opposition*, p. 269; quoted M. E. Rose, "The anti-Poor Law Movement," Fraser (ed.), *New Poor Law*, p. 84; Knott, *Opposition*, pp. 270-71, 129-42; see also Frederick Engels, *The Condition of the Working Class in England* (1845) (1984), p. 316.

27. Engels, *Condition,* p. 120.

28. A Renfrewshire Heritor, *The Unemployed and the Proposed New Poor Law* (Glasgow 1843), p. 28; Rose, *Poor Law,* p. 145; the success of the new poor law can be seen by comparing the percentage of unemployed in certain trade unions, 1851-1889, B. R. Mitchell and P. Deane, *Abstract of British Historical Statistics* (Cambridge 1971), p. 64, with unemployed able bodied men on outdoor relief, 1839-1846, 1849-1861, 1872, 1884-1889, Karel Williams, *From Pauperism to Poverty* (1981), pp. 181-182.

29. T. P. O'Neill, "The Organisation and Administration of Relief, 1845-1852," R. D. Edwards and T. D. Williams (eds.), *The Great Famine* (Dublin 1956), p. 209; M. E. Rose, "Rochdale Man and Stalybridge Riot. The Relief and Control of the Unemployed During the Lancashire Cotton Famine," A. P. Donajorodzki (ed.), *Social Control in Nineteenth Century Britain* (1977); Gareth Stedman Jones, *Outcast London* (Oxford 1971), pp. 45-46; *The Times,* 12 April 1870.

30. In spite of what Royden Harrison suggests, *Before the Socialists* (1965), pp. 221, 245.

31. *The Times,* 16 April 1870; also 18 April 1870.

Chapter 2

1. *Commonweal,* 27 Nov. 1887; also *Pall Mall Gazette,* 15 Oct. 1887.

2. *Standard,* 5 April 1867, quoted Marx, *Capital,* p. 285.

3. Raphael Samuel, "Workshop of the World: Steam Power and Hand Technology in mid Victorian Britain", *History Workshop Journal* (1977), p. 44; quoted H. J. Habakuk, *American and British Technology in the Nineteenth Century* (Cambridge 1962), p. 201; B. F. Duckham, "Introduction" (1969), R. L. Galloway, *A History of Coal Mining in Great Britain* (1882) (Newton Abbot 1969), p. 4; R. W. Breach and R. M. Hartwell (eds.), *British Economy and Society 1870-1970* (Oxford 1972), p. 112.

4. *Daily Chronicle,* 26 June 1893.

5. H. M. Hyndman, *Further Reminiscences* (1912), pp. 252-53; M. S. Wilkins, "The Non-Socialist Origins of England's First Important Socialist organization", *International Review of Social History* (1959), pp. 203-07; quoted E. P. Thompson, *William Morris. Romantic to Revolutionary* (New York 1976), p. 341.

6. P. de Rousiers, *The Labour Question in Britain* (1896), pp. 280, 357.

7. See P. Thompson, *Socialists, Liberals and Labour. The Struggle For London 1885-1914* (1967), ch. 1; Jones, *Outcast London*, ch. 8, p. 343.

8. The photograph of Williams can be found in H. W. Lee and E. Archbold, *Social Democracy in Britain* (1935), p. 56; this account is derived from *Justice,* 21 July 1894; 22 March 1890; 13 Jan. 1906; 10 Feb. 1894; and a more fanciful account given in Lee and Archbold, pp. 44, 86-87; see also H. M. Hyndman, *The Record of an Adventurous Life* (1911), p. 376.

9. B. B. Gilbert, *The Evolution of National Insurance in Great Britain* (1966), pp. 28-32; *Justice,* 30 Aug. 1884.

10. *Justice,* 27 Sept. 1884; 25 Oct. 1884; 7 March 1885; Harry Quelch, "Twenty One Years of Socialist Agitation", *Social Democrat,* Jan. 1903, p. 11.

11. *Justice,* 20 Feb. 1886; H. A. Clegg, A. Fox, and A. F. Thompson, *A History of British Trade Unions Since 1889, Vol. I* (Oxford 1964), p. 467; S. and B. Webb, *The History of British Trade Unionism 1666-1920,* p. 388.

12. E. J. Hobsbawm, "Debating the Labour Aristocracy", *Worlds of Labour* (1984), p. 221; on gender see C. Cockburn, *Brothers: Male Dominance and Technical Change* (1984); *Pall Mall Gazette,* 4 Feb. 1886.

13. Mitchell and Deane, *British Historical Statistics,* pp. 64-65; on the radicalising effect this had upon the labour aristocracy, Webbs, *Unionism,* pp. 378-79; also Tom Mann, *Memoirs* (1923), p. 25; *Pall Mall Gazette,* 10 Feb. 1886; Lee and Archbold, *Democracy,* pp. 105-9.

14. *Justice,* 19 Dec. 1885; there had been some minor unemployed activity prior to this call, *Justice,* 24 Oct. 1885; 28 Nov. 1885; *Justice,* 9 Jan. 1886; 23 Jan. 1886.

15. T. A. Jackson, *The history and working class associations and traditions of Clerkenwell Green* (1934); Lee and Archbold, *Democracy,* p. 126; F. W. Galton, quoted P. Thompson, *Socialists,* p. 115; *Justice,* 23 Jan. 1886; 30. Jan. 1886; 15 May 1886; 7 Aug. 1886; 4 Sept. 1886; 11 Sept. 1886.

16. *Justice,* 23 Dec. 1893; 6 Feb. 1886.

17. Lee and Archbold, *Democracy,* p. 109; *Pall Mall Gazette,* 4 Feb. 1886; also 11 Feb. 1886; *Justice,* 6 Feb. 1886.

18. *Justice,* 19 Dec. 1885; 6 Feb. 1886.

19. On the Fair Trade League and its activities organizing blackleg labour, J. Saville, "Unions and Free Labour: Background to the Taff Vale Decision", A. Briggs and J. Saville (eds.), *Essays in Labour History, Vol. I.* (1960), pp. 331-36; on its connection with the unemployed, Hyndman, *Life,* p. 400; K. D. Brown, *John Burns* (1977), p. 20. *The Times,* 9 Feb. 1886, declared the riot more alarming than the Chartist demonstrations of 1848; the Queen was outraged,Queen Victoria to Gladstone, 11 Feb. 1886, C. Hibbert (ed.), *Queen Victoria In Her Letters and Journals* (Harmondsworth 1984), p. 297; the rioters, she told a daughter, were not the deserving unemployed but socialists and criminals, *ibid*; see also *Justice,* 13 Feb. 1886; *Pall Mall Gazette,* 9-11 Feb. 1886; Brown, *Burns,* p. 21; Jones, *Outcast London,* pp. 292-94; Mann, *Memoirs,* p. 60.

20. Lee and Archbold, *Democracy,* p. 115; quoted C. Tsuzuki, *H. M. Hyndman and British Socialism* (Oxford 1961), p. 75; F. Engels. "Preface to the English Edition" (5 Nov. 1886), Marx, *Capital,* p. 113.

21. Frederick Engels to Laura Lafargue, 9 Feb. 1886, *Frederick Engels, Paul and Laura Lafargue Correspondence, Vol. I.* (Moscow 1959), p. 334; *Pall Mall Gazette,* 9 Feb. 1886.

22. *Justice,* 6 Feb. 1886; *Pall Mall Gazette,* 4 Feb. 1886; 11 Feb. 1886; quoted Tsuzuki, *Hyndman,* p. 74.

23. *Morning Post,* 9 Feb. 1886; *Pall Mall Gazette,* 11 Feb. 1886; 24 July 1886; *The Times,* 17 Feb. 1886; "There are men experienced in observing and dealing with distress", wrote Beveridge over thirty years later about the distribution of this fund in the prevailing post riot climate of fear, "who say that East and South London have scarcely yet recovered from the demoralisation of that orgy of relief", *Unemployment. A Problem of Industry* (1909), p. 158; José Harris, *Unemployment and Politics* (Oxford 1972), p. 111, follows Beveridge on this point, but there was little evidence of orgiastic almsgiving at the time; see *Justice,* 6 March 1886.

24. *Pall Mall Gazette,* 10 Feb. 1886; quoted Harris, *Unemployment,* p. 76; quoted S. and B. Webb (eds.), *The Public Organisation of the Labour Market* (1909), p. 116; Mann, *Memoirs,* p. 25.

25. Harris, *Unemployment,* pp. 76-78; C. D. H. Howard (ed.), Joseph Chamberlain, *A Political Memoir 1880-92* (1953), pp. 109-10; *The Radical Programme* (1885), p. 17; Jones, *Outcast London,* p. 312; Webbs, *Market,* p. 118.

26. Thompson, *Morris,* p. 407; *Pall Mall Gazette,* 13 Feb. 1886; *Justice,* 13 March 1886, 20 March 1886.

27. Lee and Archbold, *Democracy,* p. 125; *Justice,* 8 Jan. 1887; Thompson, *Socialists,* p. 17; *Justice,* 29 Jan. 1887; also 6 Aug. 1887.

28. Basil Thomson, *The Story of Scotland Yard* (1935), p. 176.

29. *Justice,* 13 Nov. 1886; Mann, *Memoirs,* p. 64; Lee and Archbold, *Democracy,* p. 126; Tom Mann, "Introduction", Hannington, *Struggles,* pp. vii-viii.

30. Quelch, "Agitation", p. 15; Frederick Engels to Laura Lafargue, 24 Nov. 1886, *Correspondence,* p. 396; Lee and Archbold, *Democracy,* pp. 125-126; *Justice,* 12 Feb. 1887

31. Lee and Archbold, *Democracy,* p. 119; *Justice,* 10 Sept. 1887.

32. *Justice,* 10 Sept. 1887; *Commonweal,* May 1885; 29 Oct. 1887; on the League and the Norwich unemployed, *Commonweal,* 22 Jan. 1887; 29 Jan. 1882.

33. A number of eyewitness accounts of such attacks are given in *Pall Mall Gazette,* 20 Oct. 1887; in general *Pall Mall Gazette,* Oct.-Nov. 1887. On Bloody Sunday *Pall Mall Gazette,* 14 Nov. 1887; *The Times,* 14 Nov. 1887; *Commonweal,* Nov. 1887; detailed accounts are given in Thompson, *Morris,* pp. 490-491; Brown, *Burns,* pp. 25-27; more sympathetic to the police is R. C. K. Ensor, *England 1870-1914* (Oxford 1936), pp. 180-81.

34. Jones, *Outcast London,* pp. 172-73; *Justice,* 24 Dec. 1887.

35. *Justice,* 12 Jan. 1889; 3 Oct. 1888; 10 Nov. 1888; 3 Dec. 1888; 22 Dec. 1888; 5 Jan. 1889; 26 Jan. 1889; 2 Feb. 1889; 9 Feb. 1889.

36. Clegg et al., *Unions*, p. 55; Webbs, *Unionism*, p. 384.

37. Tom Mann, *Required Now: One Big Union of Boilermakers, Foundry Men, Engineers and Steelworkers* (pamp. 1920), n.p.; Harry Pollitt, "Tom Mann's obituary notice", draft, n.d., Tom Mann papers, Communist Party Archives; quoted Clegg et al., *Unions*, p. 90; *Justice*, 7 Sept. 1889.

38. *Justice*, 22 Dec. 1888; Will Thorne, *My Life's Battles* (1925), p. 80; Clegg et al., *Unions*, pp. 68, 93; *Justice*, 24 Jan. 1891; Harris, *Unemployment*, p. 86; *Justice*, 7 Sept. 1889; Tsuzuki, *Hyndman*, p. 90.

39. H. Llewellyn Smith and V. Nash, *The Story of the Dockers' Strike* (1889), p. 165; quoted Harris, *Unemployment*, p. 83.

40. *Justice*, 4 Oct. 1890; 11 Oct. 1890; 18 Oct. 1890; 1 Nov. 1890; 29 Nov. 1890; 20 Dec. 1890; 13 Jan. 1891; 24 Jan. 1891; 15 Feb. 1891.

41. *Justice*, 9 April 1892; 16 April 1892; 30 April 1892; 29 Oct. 1892; 24 Sept. 1892; 5 Nov. 1892.

42. *Justice*, 3 Nov. 1888; 26 Nov. 1892; 3 Nov. 1892; 17 Dec. 1892; 10 Dec. 1892; 20 Jan. 1894; 14 Jan. 1893; 18 Feb. 1893.

43. *Justice*, 14 Oct. 1893; 21 Oct. 1893; 23 Dec. 1893.

44. *Justice*, 10 Dec. 1892; 7 Oct. 1893.

45. *Justice*, 23 Dec. 1893; 6 Jan. 1894.

46. *Justice*, 17 Feb. 1894; 3 March 1893; 7 April 1894.

47. *Justice*, 5 Jan. 1895; 19 Jan. 1895; 9 Dec. 1893.

48. *Justice*, 19 Oct. 1895; 16 March 1895; 10 Aug. 1901; 19 Oct. 1895.

49. *Justice*, 19 Jan. 1895; 23 Feb. 1895; P. A. Ryan, "Poplarism, 1894-1930", Pat Thane (ed.), *The Origins of British Social Policy* (1978), p. 61; *Justice*, 2 Feb. 1895; 9 Feb. 1895; Paul Watmough, "The Politics of Unemployment in London, 1892-1895" (Univ. of Warwick MA thesis 1975), p. 50; *Labour Leader*, 19 Jan. 1895; *Justice*, 2 Feb. 1895; 16 Feb. 1895; 9 March 1895.

50. *Justice*, 17 Dec. 1892; Thompson, *Socialists*, p. 120; Harris, *Unemployment*, p. 84; *Justice*, 16 Dec. 1893.

51. Watmough, "Politics", p. 36; *Justice*, 23 Dec. 1893.

52. James Hinton, *Labour and Socialism* (Brighton 1983), p. 58; Hardie outlined his plan in an editorial in *Justice*, 11 Feb. 1893; Watmough, "Politics", p. 73; *Labour Leader*, 16 Feb. 1895.

53. *Labour Leader*, 23 Feb. 1895; *Labour Leader*, 16 Feb. 1895; Harris, *Unemployment*, pp. 89-101.

54. *Labour Leader*, 9 Feb. 1895; Smart's idea was not new; John Fielding, an SDF member had suggested something similar in 1887; *Justice*, 10 Dec. 1887; K. D. Brown, *Labour and Unemployment 1900-1914* (Newton Abbot 1971), p. 18.

55. *Labour Leader*, 9 March 1895; Tsuzuki, *Hyndman*, Appendix B; *Justice*, 9 Feb. 1895.

56. Karl Marx, "Economic and Philosophical Manuscripts" (1844), *Early Writings* (Harmondsworth 1977), p. 335.

57. Harris, *Unemployment*, p. 4.

58. Jones, *Outcast London*, p. 281.

59. Webbs, *Unionism*, p. 381; Watmough, "Politics", pp. 10-11; *The Times*, 3 March 1886.

60. *Labour Leader*, 26 Jan. 1895.

61. *TUC Report, 1889*, pp. 47-48; Tom Mann and Ben Tillett, *The "New" Trades Unionism* (1890), n.p.; Alexander Keyssar, *Out of Work. The First Century of Unemployment in Massachusetts* (Cambridge 1986), p. 201; this pathbreaking work shames most British scholarship on the history of unemployment.

62. J. Ramsay MacDonald, "A Rock Ahead", *To-day*, March 1887.

63. *The Times,* 3 Dec. 1902; *Justice,* 6 Dec. 1902.

64. *Justice,* 21 Feb. 1903; 6 Dec. 1902; 10 Jan. 1903; 31 Jan. 1903.

65. *Justice,* 21 Feb. 1903. Examples of more politicized behavior were at Croydon where the unemployed stormed a meeting of the town council, at Walthamstow where 400 unemployed invaded the town hall, and in Hackney, where the unemployed were successful in extracting relief "on a scale almost generous"; *Social Democrat,* Jan. 1903, p. 3; *Justice,* 21 Feb. 1903; 7 March 1903. *Social Democrat,* Feb. 1903, p. 66.

66. *Justice,* Jan.-Feb. 1903; 28 March 1903.

67. *Justice,* 7 Nov. 1903; Brown, *Labour,* pp. 22-30; see *Justice,* 28 Nov. 1903 for the minuscule activity that continued.

68. *Justice,* 21 Feb. 1903; 14 Feb. 1903.

69. Henry Pelling, "British Labour and British Imperialism", *Popular Politics and Society in Late Victorian Britain* (1968); and Richard Price, *An Imperial War and the British Working Class* (1972), ch. iv, seem to think that it wasn't a working class phenonemon, while Gareth Stedman Jones, "Working class culture and working class politics in London 1870-1900", *Languages of Class* (Cambridge 1983), pp. 182-83, 238, seems to think it was, but that we shouldn't blame the working class for it. Sometimes the boot was on the other foot: Tommy Jackson, later a prominent CPGB member, in 1900 joined the SDF in a burst of admiration upon witnessing an SDF meeting put a jingo mob to flight in a street fight; T. A. Jackson, *Solo Trumpet* (1953), pp. 47-48. *Justice,* 30 Sept. 1899; *Labour Leader,* 28 Oct. 1904.

70. *Justice,* 10 Jan. 1903; see also 24 Jan. 1903; 31 Jan. 1903.

Chapter 3

1. *Report of the Annual Labour Party Conference, 1909,* p. 95.

2. F. Engels to L. Lafargue, 24 Nov. 1886, *Correspondence,* pp. 408-9.

3. In 1895 Cecil Rhodes attended a meeting of the unemployed in the East End of London, and there listened to "wild speeches, which", he wrote, "were just a cry for 'bread,' 'bread!' " The meeting confirmed Rhodes in his belief in the necessity of imperialism to create new markets and to find new areas in which to settle "surplus population". "The Empire, as I have always said, is a bread and butter question. If you want to avoid civil war, you must become imperialists." Quoted V. I. Lenin, *Imperialism, The Highest Stage of Capitalism* (1916) (Peking 1975), pp. 93-94.

4. B. Holton, *British Syndicalism, 1900-1914* (1976), p. 32; G. Lansbury, *Looking Backwards and Forwards* (1935), p. 32.

5. R. W. Breach and R. M. Hartwell (eds.), *British Economy and Society, 1870-1970* (Oxford 1972), p. 112; S. Pollard, *The Development of the British Economy 1914-1967* (1970), pp. 2, 24-25; E. J. Hobsbawm, "The Formation of British Working Class Culture", *Worlds of Labour* (1984), p. 184; E. J. Hobsbawm, "The

Making of the Working Class, 1870-1914", *Worlds of Labour*, p. 198; *Labour Leader*, 14 Oct. 1904.

6. B. Semmel, *Imperialism and Social Reform. English Social-Imperial Thought 1895-1914* (1960), p. 234; J. Keir Hardie, *The Unemployed Problem: With Some Solutions For Solving It* (1904), pamp., n.p., Employment Box 9, John Johnson Collection, Bodleian Library (JJ/BL); *Justice*, 15 Oct. 1904.

7. Quoted K. D. Brown, "Conflict in Early British Welfare Policy: The case of the Unemployed Workmen Bill of 1905", *Journal of Modern History* (1971), p. 619.

8. *Labour Leader*, 7 Oct. 1904; *Justice*, 1 Oct. 1904; Brown, *Labour*, p. 37; Brown, *Conflict*, pp. 154-56; quoted J. Harris, *William Beveridge* (Oxford 1977), p. 109; also pp. 110, 112; *Justice*, 15 Oct. 1904; 22 Oct. 1904; 15 April 1905; 3 Dec. 1904; 17 Dec. 1904; 24 Dec. 1904; 19 Nov. 1904.

9. *Justice*, 26 Nov. 1904; 7 Jan. 1905; W. Stewart, *J. Keir Hardie* (1921), p. 216; *Labour Leader*, 4 Aug. 1904; in general see A. J. Kidd, "The Social Democratic Federation and Popular Agitation Amongst the unemployed in Edwardian Manchester", *International Review of Social History* (1984); also *Labour Leader*, 2 Dec. 1904; *Justice*, 26 Nov. 1904.

10. See *Labour Leader*, 28 Oct. 1904; K. O. Morgan, *Keir Hardie: Radical and Socialist* (1984), p. 143; *Labour Leader*, 21 Oct. 1904; 23 Dec. 1904; 30 Dec. 1904.

11. G. L. Bernstein, *Liberalism and Liberal Politics in Edwardian England* (1986) pp. 80-82; Harris, *Unemployment*, pp. 158-59; *Justice*, 11 Feb. 1905; *Labour Leader*, 17 Feb. 1905; Brown, *Labour*, p. 47.

12. Brown, "Conflict", p. 621; Harris, *Unemployment*, pp. 158-59; *Justice*, 6 May 1905; *Labour Leader*, 28 April 1905.

13. *Justice*, 13 May 1905; Clegg et al., *Unions*, pp. 453-54; *Labour Leader*, 2 June 1905.

14. *Labour Leader*, 19 May 1905; quoted Brown, "Conflict", p. 623; *Justice*, 3 Dec. 1904; 4 March 1905.

15. Brown, "Conflict", pp. 623-24; *Labour Leader*, 26 May 1905; *Justice*, 3 June 1905.

16. *Labour Leader*, 9 June 1905.

17. *Labour Leader*, 2 June 1905; *Daily Herald*, 20 Nov. 1922.

18. *Labour Leader*, 19 May 1905; 2 June 1905; Brown, "Conflict", p. 623.

19. R. C. Davison, *The Unemployed* (1929), pp. 64-65; Eddy Jones' Diary, 1936, Eddy Jones papers, South Wales Coalfield Archive (SWCA), University College, Swansea; *Labour Leader*, 9 June 1905.

20. *Justice*, 17 June 1905; J. T. Murphy, *Preparing For Power* (1936) (1972), p. 217; Wal Hanington, "Comments on the [Basil Davidson] novel *An English Tune*", Wal Hannington Papers, Communist Party Archives, E1/c.

21. *Justice*, 10 June 1905; 17 June 1905; *Labour Leader*, 14 July 1905; 21 July 1905; Brown, "Conflict", p. 625; *Labour Leader*, 28 July 1905; 11 Aug. 1905.

22. Quoted Kidd, "Agitation", p. 349; the following account is derived from the *Labour Leader*, 4 Aug. 1905.

23. See K. D. Brown, "The Appointment of the 1905 Poor Law Commission-a Rejoinder', *Bulletin of the Institute of Historical Research* (1971).

24. Quoted *Labour Leader*, 21 July 1905; Clegg et al., *Unions*, p. 386; R. E. Dowse, *Left in the Centre: The Independent Labour Party 1893-1940* (1966), p. 12; Morgan, *Hardie*, p. 148; quoted K. J. Hancock, "The Reduction of Unemployment as a Problem of Public Policy, 1920-29", *Economic History Review* (1962), p. 343.

25. *Labour Leader*, 25 Aug. 1905; 18 Aug. 1905.

26. *Justice*, 2 Sept. 1905; 7 Oct. 1905; 9 Sept. 1905; 21 Oct. 1905.

27. *Justice*, 28 Oct. 1905; *Labour Leader*, 18 Aug. 1905.

28. *Justice*, 25 Nov. 1905.

29. *Justice*, 30 Sept. 1905; 21 Oct. 1905.

30. J. Liddington and J. Norris, *One Hand Tied Behind Us. The Rise of the Women's Suffrage Movement* (1978), pp. 238-39; *Justice*, 15 July 1905; *Labour Leader*, 4 Nov. 1904.

31. *Labour Leader*, 2 Dec. 1904.

32. E. Sylvia Pankhurst, *The Suffragette Movement* (1931) (1977), pp. 128-131, 185; A. Rosen, *Rise Up, Women! The Militant Campaign of the Women's Social and Political Union, 1903-1914* (1974), pp. 29-30; *Justice*, 3 March 1906; *Labour Leader*, 18 Aug. 1905; 4 Nov. 1904; Kidd, "Agitation", p.350.

33. The accepted version, first put about by Sylvia Pankhurst, *Suffragette*, p. 185, and followed by historians since, is that the WSPU only began operations in London after the arrival of Annie Kenney in early 1906. Dora Montefiore, active in the SDF and for a time a leader of the WSPU, refuted this version in her autobiography *From A Victorian to A Modern* (1927), pp. 50-51, writing of how "*the WSPU had been doing good work in London long before Annie Kenney arrived*", p. 51 (orig. emphasis). Given the events of late 1905 Montefiore's version seems far more likely than Pankhurst's. *Labour Leader*, 21 July 1905; Rosen, *Rise*, pp. 60-61; Pankhurst, *Suffragette*, p. 250.

34. *Justice*, 11 Nov. 1905; Pankhurst, *Suffragette*, p. 184.

35. *Justice*, 11 Nov. 1905; *The Times*, 7 Nov. 1905.

36. *Social Democrat*, Nov. 1905, p. 642; for a vivid account of the march see *Labour Leader*, 10 Nov. 1905; poems discussed are St. John Adcock, "The March of the Unemployed", *Labour Leader*, 14 Feb. 1903; T. C. W., "Song of the Unemployed", *Labour Leader* 24 Jan. 1903; Gleaner "The Plight of the Unemployed", *Labour Leader*, 7 Feb. 1903.

37. J. Keir Hardie, *John Bull and his unemployed* (pamp. 1905); Walter Brierly, *Means Test Man* (1935) (Nottingham 1983), pp. 23, 206.

38. W. Hannington, *Never On Our Knees* (1967), p. 86.

39. *Labour Leader*, 10 Nov. 1905; *Justice*, 18 Nov. 1905; 25 Nov. 1905; 9 Dec. 1905; 16 Dec. 1905; 21 Oct. 1905; for example, following the women's march Queen Alexandra on 13 Nov. 1905 gave £2,000 to establish a national unemployed relief fund to which over £150,000 was finally subscribed, *Labour Leader*, 17 Nov. 1905; Beveridge, *Unemployment*, p. 186. Gerald Balfour was dismayed at this display of old-fashioned aristocratic largesse, which would, he wrote, "interfere

with the delicate machinery of administration", K. Young, *Arthur James Balfour* (1963), p. 252; *Labour Leader*, 24 Nov. 1905.

40. *Justice*, 6 Jan. 1906; Williams polled 2,537 votes, *Justice*, 20 Jan. 1906; 10 Feb. 1906; 17 Feb. 1906; 28 April 1906.

41. *Justice*, 31 March 1906.

42. *Justice*, 14 July 1906; 13 Oct. 1906; *Labour Leader*, 21 Sept. 1906; P. C. Gould, *Early Green Politics. Back to Nature, Back to the Land, and Socialism in Britain, 1880-1900* (New York 1988) gives an interesting but inadequate overview of the relation between socialists and the politics of the environment at this time; far better though tantalizingly brief is E. P. Thompson's discussion of what the idea of land meant to the working class, *Making*, pp. 253-56; see also Wal Hannington, *The Problem of the Distressed Areas* (1937), ch. 9, for a history of "back to the land" and its various political uses, culminating in Conservative support for land settlement as a solution for unemployment in the 1930s.

43. On Lewis farms were seized, families moved in, dwellings erected, and government officials warned that Lewis would become a "second Ireland", see *The Times,* 2 Oct. 1920, also 18 Oct 1920; 22 Oct. 1920; an account of these incidents and John MacLean's involvement can be found in *The Vanguard* Sept. 1920; Nov. 1920. *Justice*, 31 Jan. 1908; there was a strong "back to the land" sentiment among the Manchester unemployed, an unemployed meeting in that city in early 1907 declaring its intention to be "to use their utmost powers to get back to natural methods of production on land belonging to the citizens of Manchester, and also to establish a 'land only' register away from police surveillance", *Justice*, 2 March 1907. Keir Hardie, *The Unemployed Problem; Daily Herald*, 5 July 1920; *Report of the Third National Conference of the NUWCM, 1923*, Working Class Movement Library, Manchester.

44. *Justice*, 21 July 1906; 11 Aug. 1906; 18 Aug. 1906; 1 Sept. 1906; 8 Sept. 1906; C. H. Rolph, *London Particulars* (Oxford 1980), p. 51; *Labour Leader*, 27 July 1906; 3 Aug. 1906; 10 Aug. 1906; 17 Aug. 1906.

45. *Labour Leader,* 31 Jan. 1908; also 17 Jan. 1908.

46. *Labour Leader*, 8 March 1907; K.D. Brown, "The Labour Party and the Unemployment Question 1906-1910", *Historical Journal* (1971), p. 601.

47. *The Labour Party and Unemployment*, Labour Party Leaflet No. 35 (1908); the bill was published, along with a commentary, in J. Ramsay MacDonald, *The New Unemployed Bill of the Labour Party* (pamp. 1907); quoted Lord Elton, *The Life of James Ramsay MacDonald* (1939), p. 143; *Labour Leader*, 8 May 1907.

48. *Labour Leader*, 31 Jan. 1908.

49. H. Russell Smart, *The Right to Work* (pamp. 1908), n.p.; Montefiore, *Modern*, p. 59; see also Liddington and Norris ch. 11, *Hand*; Rosen, *Rise*, ch. 5.

50. *Labour Leader*, 17 Jan. 1908; 31 Jan. 1908; *Justice*, 23 Nov. 1907; 25 Jan. 1908; 8 Feb. 1908; *Social Democrat*, May 1907; *Justice*, 2 Feb. 1907; 16 Feb. 1907; 30 March 1907; 16 Nov. 1907; 13 April 1908; Brown, "Question", p. 604;. Harris, *Unemployment*, p. 244.

51. On the SDP's initial support, *Justice*, 2 Nov. 1907; on its later opposition, *Justice*, 25 April 1908; *Justice*, 4 July 1908; 11 July 1908; Morgan, *Hardie*, pp. 172, 176, 218-220, 222, 224.

52. *Justice*, 22 Aug. 1908; 26 Oct. 1908.

53. K. Middlemas, *The Clydesiders* (1965), p. 43; *Labour Leader*, 12 Sept. 1908; H. MacShane, *No Mean Fighter* (1978), p. 24; *Justice*, 19 Sept. 1908; Lee and Archbold, *Democracy*, p. 144.

54. Asked what was the most pressing and important problem facing the Labour party, Arthur Henderson, Labour Party chairman, replied "Undoubtedly the unemployed", *Labour Leader*, 18 Sept. 1908; *Justice*, 3 Oct. 1908; *Labour Leader*, 18 Sept. 1908; Brown, *Labour*, p. 98; on "Docker" Waites' march, *Justice*, 17 Oct. 1908.

55. *Justice*, 17 Oct. 1908; 26 Sept. 1908; 24 Oct. 1908; *Labour Leader*, 9 Oct. 1908; 16 Oct. 1908; quoted Brown, *Labour*, p. 101; Bernstein, *Liberalism*, p. 125; C. Cook, *A Short History of the Liberal Party, 1900-1976* (1976), p. 47; J. Grigg, *Lloyd George: The People's Champion 1902-1911* (1978), p. 171.

56. Brown, "Question", p. 609; Harris, *Unemployment*, p. 275; Bernstein, *Liberalism*, pp. 125-26.

57. *Justice*, 17 Oct. 1908; soon after the LCC put a great deal of work in hand for the unemployed, *Justice*, 24 Oct. 1908; *Labour Leader*, 23 Oct. 1908.

58. P. Wyncoll, *The Nottingham Labour Movement 1880-1939* (1985), p. 145; *Labour Leader*, 30 Oct. 1908; 30 Nov. 1908; *Justice*, 7 Nov. 1908.

59. *Labour Leader*, 20 Nov. 1908.

60. *Labour Leader*, 23 Oct. 1908; 30 Oct. 1908.

61. *Justice*, 24 Oct. 1908.

62. Harris, *Unemployment*, p. 275; *Labour Leader*, 30 Oct. 1908; Brown, "Question", p. 611; *Justice*, 14 Nov. 1908; 23 Oct. 1908; early in November 1908 the London poor law inspector reported that "there appears to be throughout London a general organisation which, for political ends, is exerting pressure on Boards of Guardians to give undue relief"; quoted Harris, *Unemployment*, p. 273n.

63. Keir Hardie to Bruce Glasier, 27 Dec. 1908; cited H. Pelling, *A Short History of the Labour Party* (1972), p. 21; *Justice*, 28 Nov. 1908; 12 Dec. 1908, the "Direct Actionists" were possibly members of the Liverpool Direct Action League, "a particularly important example of anarcho-syndicalist activity at this time", Holton, *Syndicalism*, pp. 46-47; Thompson, *Socialists*, p. 235n; *Labour Leader*, 6 Nov. 1908; 20 Nov. 1908.

64. *Justice*, 28 Nov. 1908; *Labour Leader*, 18 Dec. 1908; 20 Nov. 1908.

65. *Justice*, 19 Dec. 1908; 26 Dec. 1908; 2 Jan. 1909; 9 Jan. 1909; 23 Jan. 1909; 13 Feb. 1909; 18 July 1908; 16 Jan. 1909; 30 Jan. 1909; 6 Feb. 1909; 27 Feb. 1909.

66. *Labour Leader*, 12 Feb. 1909; *Justice*, 20 Feb. 1909; on women's involvement see *Justice*, 6 June 1907; 25 Jan. 1908; 14 Nov. 1908; 28 Nov. 1908; *Labour Leader*, 11 Sept. 1908.

67. *Justice*, 20 Feb. 1909; 27 Feb. 1909; *Labour Leader*, 19 Feb. 1909.

68. Hinton, *Labour and Socialism*, p. 30; *Clarion*, 28 Sept. 1906.

69. *Labour Leader*, 31 May 1912, quoted by Stephen Yeo in his insightful essay "Socialism, the State, and some oppositional Englishness", R. Colls and P. Dodd (eds.), *Englishness. Politics and Culture 1880-1920* (1986), p. 360.

70. Beveridge, *Unemployment*, pp. 263-67; *Justice*, 24 Feb. 1912; quoted Harris, *Unemployment*, p. 365.

71. R. Hay, "Employers and Social Policy in Britain: the Evolution of Welfare Legislation 1905-1914", *International Review of Social History* (1977).

72. Beveridge approvingly quotes Sir Herbert Llewellyn Smith: "the scheme itself will automatically exclude the loafer", *Unemployment*, p. 265; G. D. H. Cole, *A Short History of the British Working Class, 1787-1947* (1948), p. 308; A. Clinton, *Trades councils in Britain, 1900-1940* (Manchester 1977), pp. 46-48.

73. R. Blumenfeld, *The Press In My Time* (1933), p. 49; tariff reform would, said Chamberlain, "secure for the masses . . . constant employment at high wages", *The Times*, 10 July 1906.

74. Beveridge, *Unemployment*, p. 103.

Chapter 4

1. Peter Kingsford, *The Hunger Marchers in Britain, 1920-1939* (1982), p. 69.

2. *Second Congress of the Communist International, Minutes of the Proceedings, Vol. 1* (1977), p. 12; A. Lindeman, *The Red Years: European Socialism vs Bolshevism, 1919-1920* (1976), p. xiii; see also F. L. Carsten, *Revolution in Central Europe, 1918-1919* (1972); for bourgeois reaction see Duff Cooper, *Haig* (1936), p. 403; quoted Andrew Rothstein *The Soldiers' Strikes of 1919* (1985), p. 91.

3. For example, contrast Allen Hutt, *The Post War History of the British Working Class* (1937), pp. 9-40, with H. A. Clegg, *A History of British Trade Unions Since 1889, Vol. II, 1911-1933* (Oxford 1985), pp. 266-302; Clegg would have us believe that the fears of Cabinet were in the main the result of poor briefing, p. 278; anon., *Glasgow 1919* (Glasgow 1974); *Daily Herald*, 4 Aug. 1919; 5 Aug. 1919; quoted P. B. Johnson, *Land Fit For Heroes* (1968), p. 345.

4. PRO Cab 24/67, GT 6047, "Demobilisation and Employment ", C. Addison, 19 Oct. 1918; B. B. Gilbert, *British Social Policy, 1914-1939* (1970), pp. 60-62.

5. Bertolt Brecht, "The Soldier of La Ciotat", in his *Short Stories* (1984), p. 130; anon., "Disabled Through Service" (n.d.), Unemployment, Box 8, JJ/BL; Thomas Bell, *Pioneering Days* (1941), p. 270.

6. On European ex-service men's organizations, Mark Ferro, *The Great War, 1914-1918* (1973), p. 225; J. P. Nettl, *Rosa Luxemburg, Vol. II* (Oxford 1966), p. 775; Robert Soucy, *French Fascism: The First Wave 1924-1933* (1986), p. 216; Conan Fischer, *Stormtroopers: A Social, Economic and Ideological Analysis, 1929-1935* (1983), p. 5; Ferro, *War*, p. 157.

7. *The Ex-Service Man*, 12 July 1919; see also Graham Wootton, *The Politics of Influence: British ex-servicemen, Cabinet decisions and cultural change, 1917-1957* (1963), p. 92. In some areas the NADSS degenerated into little better than a

scab labor organisation, the Leeds NADSS, for example, being strongly opposed to trade unionism and declaring that "its members shall have the right to work, when, how and where they please." PRO Cab 24/87, GT 8082, "Report on Revolutionary Organisations", 2 Sept. 1919; *Daily Herald*, 24 May 1920; *The Times*, 30 July 1917; *The Ex-Service Man*, 5 July 1919; *The Times*, 15 July 1918; 29 July 1918; 2 Sept. 1918.

8. Winston S. Churchill, *The World Crisis: The Aftermath* (1929), p. 65; *The Socialist*, 16 March 1922.

9. R. K. Middlemas, *The Master Builders* (1963), p. 283; Sir B. E. Wyndham Childs, *Episodes and Reflections* (1930), p. 171; Graham Wootton, *The Official History of the British Legion* (1956), pp. 3-4; *The Ex-Service Man*, 12 July 1919; 19 July 1919.

10. *The Ex-Service Man*, 5 July 1919; Alan Howkins, *Poor Labouring Men: Rural Radicalism in Norfolk, 1870-1923* (1985), p. 128.

11. *Daily Herald*, 6 May 1919; *Territorial Service Gazette*, 19 April 1919; 3 May 1919.

12. The only detailed account is Rothstein's unsatisfactory *Soldiers Strikes*; the army was undoubtedly in a rebellious and even threatening mood, see Martin Gilbert, *Winston S. Churchill Vol. IV:l* (1972), p. 462; Churchill, *World Crisis*, p. 61; *The Times*, 29 May 1919; PRO Cab 24/74, GT 6744, "Co-ordination of Demobilisation Scheme", 3 Feb. 1919; W. Arthur Lewis, *Economic Survey 1919-1939* (1965), p. 18; *The Times*, 29 May 1919.

13. C. L. Mowat, *Britain Between the Wars* (1966), p. 27.

14. PRO Cab 24/74, GT 6713, "Report on Revolutionary Organisations", 28 Jan. 1919; McShane, *Fighter*, p. 52; *Daily Herald*, 29 April 1919; 9 May 1919; Lucia Jones, "Sylvia Pankhurst and the Workers' Socialist Federation: The Red Twilight, 1918-1924" (Univ. of Warwick M.A. thesis, 1972), p. 87.

15. Gilbert, *Policy*, p. 62; this clause was introduced into unemployment insurance, with almost identical wording, in clause 3(b) of the Unemployment Insurance Act of March 1921; Alan Deacon, "Concession and Coercion: The politics of Unemployment Insurance in the Twenties", Asa Briggs and John Saville (eds.), *Essays in Labour History 1918-1939* (1977), p. 16.

16. *The Times*, 18 Nov. 1918; *The Times*, 26 May 1919.

17. *Daily Herald*, 27 May 1919; *The Times*, 27 May 1919; PRO Cab 24/77, GT 7091, "Report on Revolutionary Organisations", 28 May 1919; on Jennett, *Daily Herald*, 28 May 1919; PRO Cab 24/128, CP 3309, "Report on Revolutionary Organisations", 15 Sept. 1921; *Out of Work*, No.23 (Jan. 1922).

18. *Territorial Service Gazette*, 28 April 1919; *Daily Herald*, 1 Sept. 1919; *The Times*, 10 June 1919; the conference was later attacked by the left as having been unrepresentative, and although there had been 430 delegates representing over 600 branches present, there does seem to have been some substance to this allegation. Both the decision not to ally with the Labour Party and to admit officers proved very unpopular among the membership. *Daily Herald*, 1 Sept. 1919; *Territorial Service Gazette*, 21 June 1919; 5 July 1919.

19. On the SSAU, PRO Cab 24/82, GT 7566, "Report on Revolutionary Organisations", 26 June 1919; PRO Cab 24/90, GT 8400, "Report on Revolutionary Organisations", 23 Oct. 1919; the SSAU had strong links with the *Daily Herald*; it advised soldiers not to interfere in labor disturbances, made its members pledge to take no action against strikers, and discussed the possibility of a coup d'etat to set up a republic. For a time it was regarded by the authorities as dangerous; PRO Cab 24/76, GT 6976, "Report on Revolutionary Organisations", 10 March 1919; /77, GT 7091, "Report on Revolutionary Organisations", 7 April 1919; /81, GT 7417, "Report on Revolutionary Organisations", 4 June 1919; /93, CP 195, "Special Report on the Daily Herald", 25 Nov. 1919; Basil Thompson, *Queer People* (1922), pp. 296-7; *Daily Herald*, 9 May 1919; on the IUX, *The Worker*, 23 Aug. 1919; 28 June 1919; PRO Cab 24/88, GT 8792, "Report on Revolutionary Organisations", 18 Sept. 1919.

20. *Workers' Dreadnought*, 3 Jan. 1920; *The Worker*, 27 Sept. 1919; a list of IUX officials in 1919 is given in *The Worker*, 9 Aug. 1919; of IUX branch secretaries in *The Worker*, 3 Jan. 1920; and of IUX officials in 1920 in *The Worker* Feb. 1920; *The Worker*, 16 Aug. 1919; 15 Nov. 1919; 4 Dec. 1919.

21. *The Worker*, 15 Nov. 1919; 20 Sept. 1919; 21 Feb. 1920; PRO Cab 24/88, GT 8792, "Report on Revolutionary Organisations", 18 Sept. 1919.

22. PRO Cab 24/87, GT 8036, "Report on Revolutionary Organisations", 21 Aug. 1919; *The Worker*, 21 Feb. 1920.

23. *Daily Herald*, 5 July 1920; 6 May 1920; on Beckett, *The Ex-Service Man*, 30 Jan. 1919; *Fascist Week*, 2 March 1934; 2 March 1934; Beckett was later to follow another virulent anti-semite, William Joyce (later Lord Haw Haw) in splitting from Mosley to form the Nationalist Socialist Party. Subsequently he was secretary of another Fascist sect, the British People's Party; Fenner Brockway, *Inside the Left* (1942), p .206; Robert Skidelsky, *Oswald Mosley* (1975), p. 399. *Daily Herald*, 16 June 1919; Brockway, *Left*, p. 206; Minutes of the Executive Committee of the London Trades Council, 29 Dec. 1919; *The Worker*, 7 Feb. 1920; *The Times*, 29 July 1920; 28 Dec. 1920; *Daily Herald*, 11 June 1919.

24. *The Worker*, 22 July 1919; *Daily Herald*, 7 June 1919.

25. PRO Cab 24/81, GT 7463, "Report on Revolutionary Organisations", 12 June 1919; /84, GT 7742, "Report on Revolutionary Organisations", 17 July 1919; *The Ex-Service Man*, 28 June 1919; /84, GT 7790, "Report on Revolutionary Organisations", 24 July 1919; *Territorial Service Gazette*, 19 July 1919.

26. *Daily Herald*, 22 July 1919; *The Times*, 23 July 1919.

27. The following account is derived from reports of the riot and reports of the subsequent court cases given in the *Daily Herald*, 21-25 July 1919; *The Ex-Service Man*, 16 Aug. 1919; *The Times*, 21-26 July 1919, 28 July 1919, 31 July 1919, 2 Aug. 1919, 11 Aug. 1919.

28. PRO Cab 24/86, GT 7933, "Report on Revolutionary Organisations", 7 Aug. 1919; /84, GT 7790, "Report on Revolutionary Organisations", 24 July 1919.

29. *The Times*, 2 June 1919; PRO Cab 24/86, GT 7933, "Report on Revolutionary Organisations", 7 Aug. 1919; *Daily Herald*, 25 Aug. 1919; J. and B. Braddock, *The Braddocks* (1963), p. 32.

30. Cooper, *Haig*, p. 421; attempts to mollify the unemployed ex-service men included a national scheme for employing disabled ex-service men, inaugurated in August 1919 by royal proclamation, under which employers promised to employ a set percentage of disabled ex-service men, and in return were allowed to advertise themselves as men of benevolence as members of the King's National Roll, *Report of the Ministry of Labour for the Years 1923 and 1924* Cmd. 2481 (1925), p. 94; an attempt by the government to unify the various organizations in late 1918 failed to get off the ground, *The Ex-Service Man*, 1 May 1919; 2 Aug. 1919; 26 July 1919. *The Times*, 26 July 1919; *Territorial Service Gazette*, 9 Aug. 1919.

31. "One unfortunate result of having three or more organisations is that class divisions are being introduced among ex-service men", lamented the *Territorial Service Gazette*, 26 July 1919, suggesting that such class divisions were somehow unknown to ex-service men prior to the formation of these organizations. *Daily Herald*, 14 Jan. 1921; *The Times*, 7 July 1919, also 9 July 1919.

32. PRO Cab 24/89, GT 8290, "The Labour Situation: Report from the Ministry of Labour", 8 Oct. 1919; Wootton, *Legion*, p.13; *Daily Herald*, 25 May 1920; /88, GT 8184, "The Labour Situation: Report from the Ministry of Labour", 17 Sept. 1920.

33. *Daily Herald*, 4 Aug. 1919; *The Times*, 22 Aug. 1919; Cole, *Short History of the British Working Class*, p. 377; PRO Cab 24/89, GT 8228, "Report on Revolutionary Organisations", 25 Sept. 1919; some NFDDSS branches passed resolutions condemning the film, *Daily Herald*, 4 Sept. 1919; PRO Cab 24/93, CP 113, "The Labour Situation: Report from the Ministry of Labour", 12 Nov. 1919.

34. Gilbert, *Policy*, p. 66.

35. PRO Cab 24/88, GT 8123, R. Horne, "Unemployment Insurance", 5 Sept, 1919; /93, CP 125, "Report on Revolutionary Organisations", 13 Nov. 1919.

36. *Workers' Dreadnought*, 8 Nov. 1919; Beveridge, *Unemployment*, pp. 273-74.

37. Wal Hannington, *A Short History of the Unemployed* (1938), p. 21; *Daily Herald*, 22 Nov. 1919; 24 Nov. 1919.

38. PRO Cab 24/89, GT 8250, "Report on Revolutionary Organisations", 2 Oct. 1919; *The Times*, 25 Sept. 1919.

39. *Daily Herald*, 16 Dec. 1919; 1 Oct. 1920; PRO Cab 24/93, CP 184, C. Addison, "Trouble arising from eviction . . ." 24 Nov. 1919.

40. *The Times*, 2 March 1920; PRO Cab 24/104, CP 1129, "Report on Revolutionary Organisations", 22 April 1920; quoted Jones, "Pankhurst", p. 90; for example "Should the Workers Arm?" cited J. T. Murphy, *Preparing For Power* (1934) (1972), p. 124.

41. *The Worker*, 22 Nov. 1919; 7 Aug. 1920; *The Times*, 28 Dec. 1920; PRO Cab 24/104, CP 1129, "Report on Revolutionary Organisations", 22 April 1920; *The Worker*, 2 Oct. 1920; *The Communist*, 12 Aug. 1920; *The Times*, 21 Aug. 1920;

Steele was again imprisoned in November 1920 for sedition and by late 1921 he was reduced to living in a workhouse from where he continued his political work with the NUWCM; PRO Cab 24/118, "A Survey of Revolutionary Movements in Great Britain in the year 1920", Jan. 1921; /129, CP 3436, "Report on Revolutionary Organisations", 20 Oct. 1921; /140, CP 4326, "Report on Revolutionary Organisations", 23 Nov. 1922; *Out of Work*, no. 40.

42. PRO Cab 24/112, CP 1908, "Report on Revolutionary Organisations", 30 Sept. 1920; Kingsford, *Hunger Marchers*, p. 68; quoted Hywel Francis and David Smith, *The Fed: A History of the South Wales Miners in the Twentieth Century* (1981), p. 101; Len Jackson to Lewis Jones, 10 Nov. 1936, Eddie Jones Papers, SWCA; *NUWM National Conference Report 1939*, Wal Hannington Papers, Marx Memorial Library (HP/MML), A III; Noreen Branson, *History of the Communist Party of Great Britain, 1927-1941* (1985), p. 231.

43. *Workers' Dreadnought*, 7 Aug. 1920; *The Worker*, 20 March 1920.

44. *The Worker*, 5 June 1920; 5 July 1920; *Workers' Dreadnought*, 17 July 1920; 31 July 1920; 7 Aug. 1920; *The Worker*, 7 Aug. 1920; the CP(BSTI) was a short lived anti-parliamentarian rival to the CPGB, formed by remnants of the WSF.

45. *The Worker*, 20 Dec. 1920; 6 March 1920; 13 March 1920; 28 Aug. 1920; 11 Sept. 1920; 18 Sept. 1920; 9 Oct. 1920; 16 Oct. 1920.

46. *The Worker*, 28 Aug. 1920; 23 Oct. 1920.

47. *The Worker*, 3 Jan. 1920; 15 May 1920; *Solidarity*, April 1920; *The Call*, 8 July 1920; 15 July 1920; *The Communist*, 19 Aug. 1920.

48. *Daily Herald*, 5 July 1920.

49. *The Communist*, 19 Aug. 1920; see also *The Call*, 8 July 1920; *The Times*, 29 July 1920; 20 Aug. 1920.

50. *The Fighter*, Sept. 1920.

51. *Daily Herald*, 23 Sept. 1920.

52. *Daily Herald*, 12 Oct. 1920; 26 Nov. 1920; *The Communist*, 30 Sept. 1920; F. W. Carr, "Engineering Workers and the Rise of Labour in Coventry, 1914-1939" (Univ. of Warwick Ph.D. thesis, 1978), p. 189.

53. *The Worker*, 16 Oct. 1920; 4 Dec. 1920; PRO Cab 24/117, CP 2352, "Report on Revolutionary Organisations", 23 Dec. 1920.

54. *Daily Herald*, 5 Aug. 1919; A. Hazlet, *The "B" Specials: A History of the Ulster Special Constabulary* (1972), p. 6; *Daily Herald*, 14 June 1919; 24 Jan. 1920; *Workers' Dreadnought*, 7 June 1919.

55. quoted Stephen Humphries, *Hooligans or Rebels? An Oral History of Working Class Childhood and Youth 1889-1939* (Oxford 1981), p. 187.

56. *Daily Herald*, 4 Nov. 1919.

57. PRO Cab 24/78, GT 7172, "The Labour Situation: Report from the Ministry of Labour", 26 April 1919; *Territorial Service Gazette*, 21 June 1919; PRO Cab 24/82, GT 7566, "Report on Revolutionary Organisations", 26 June 1919.

58. *Territorial Service Gazette*, 14 June 1919; *Daily Herald*, 27 May 1919; PRO Cab 24/81, GT 7147, "Report on Revolutionary Organisations", 4 June 1919; Cab

24/84, GT 7746, "The Labour Situation: Report from the Ministry of Labour", 16 July 1919; *The Times*, 1 Sept. 1920; 5 Aug. 1920.

59. *Solidarity*, Oct. 1920; *Workers' Dreadnought*, 21 Feb. 1920.

Chapter 5

1. PRO Cab 24/140, CP 4326, "Report on Revolutionary Organisations", 23 Nov. 1922; *Nottingham Guardian*, 6 Dec. 1932.

2. J. J. Astor et al., *The Third Winter of Unemployment* (1923), p. 327; Wal Hannington, *The Problem of the Distressed Areas* (1937), p. 16; Hywel Francis and David Smith, *The Fed. A History of the South Wales Miners in the Twentieth Century* (1984), p. 244.

3. Ellen Wilkinson, *The Town That Was Murdered* (1939), p. 148; Tom Thomas, "Their Theatre and Ours", *History Workshop Journal*, no. 4, p. 137.

4. M. W. Kirby, *The British Coalmining Industry, 1870-1946* (1977), p. 255; Harold Heslop, *Last Cage Down* (1935) (repub. 1984), p. 229; Arthur Horner, *Incorrigible Rebel* (1960), p. 156.

5. quoted Branson, *CPGB 1927-1941*, p. 12; David Marquand, *Ramsay MacDonald* (1977), pp. 793-95; Sean Glynn, "Real Policy Options", S. Glynn and A. Booth (eds.), *The Road to Full Employment* (1987), pp. 156-57.

6. Wal Hannington to Arthur Pullen, 12 Oct. 1957, Hannington Papers, Communist Party Archives (HP/CPA)-A2c; *The Socialist*, 13 Jan. 1921.

7. London and Cambridge Economic Service, *The British Economy: Key Statistics, 1900-1966* (1968), Table E, p. 8; Aneurin Bevan, "The Unemployed and their Marches, Review of *Unemployed Struggles*", *Labour Monthly*, Dec. 1936, p. 760.

8. PRO Cab 24/111, CP 1830, "Report on Revolutionary Organisations", 2 Sept. 1920; *The Times*, 22 Oct. 1920; the best study of deskilling remains Harry Braverman, *Labour and Monopoly Capital* (1974); PRO Cab 24/114, CP 2036, "Enquiry into the classes of ex-service men in the Bristol area receiving Out of Work Donation", 30 Oct. 1920.

9. PRO Cab 24/111, CP 1885, "Report on Revolutionary Organisations", 23 Sept. 1920; James Hinton, *The First Shop Stewards' Movement* (1973); Joseph Melling, *Rent Strikes: People's Struggles for Housing in West Scotland, 1890-1916* (Edinburgh 1983); the 40 hours strike manifesto is reprinted in *Glasgow 1919. The Story of the Forty Hour Strike* (Glasgow 1974), np.

10. *The Worker*, 22 Nov. 1919; 14 Feb. 1920; *Solidarity*, April 1920.

11. F. W. Carr, "The Formation of the Communist Party in Coventry" (Univ. of Warwick MA thesis, 1969), p. 7; *The Socialist*, 28 Oct. 1920; *Solidarity*, Oct. 1920; *The Times*, 5 Oct. 1920.

12. *Workers' Dreadnought*, 1 Jan. 1921; Carr, "Communist Party", n. 41; PRO Cab 24/118, CP 2475, "Report on Revolutionary Organisations", 20 Jan. 1921; Emery was patronizingly described by *The Times* of 6 Oct. 1920 as "one of those earnest and able young workmen who are irresistably attracted by advanced social

and political movements"; *The Socialist*, 28 Oct. 1920; *Workers' Dreadnought*, 1 Feb. 1921.

13. PRO Cab 24/118, CP 2458, "Ministry of Labour Weekly Report", 15 Jan. 1921; *Workers' Dreadnought*, 8 Jan. 1921; 1 Jan. 1921.

14. *The Communist*, 7 Oct. 1920; *Solidarity*, Oct. 1920; *Daily Herald*, 30 Nov. 1920.

15. John MacLean, "All hail, the Scottish Workers' Republic" (1920), Nan Milton (ed.), *John MacLean. In the Rapids of Revolution. Essays, articles and letters, 1902-1923* (1978), pp. 217-18; on MacLean's nationalism see David Howell's study of MacLean in *A Lost Left. Three Studies in Socialism and Nationalism* (Manchester 1987); the full story of MacLean's attempt to create a separate Scottish Communist Party is given in Walter Kendall, *The Revolutionary Movement in Britain, 1900-1921. The Origins of the British Communism* (1969), ch. 17; *The Vanguard*, Nov. 1920; *The Socialist*, 30 Dec. 1920; 13 Jan. 1920.

16. *The Socialist*, 13 Jan. 1920.

17. John MacLean, "An Open Letter to Lenin", *The Socialist*, 30 Jan. 1921; *The Vanguard*, Nov. 1920; *The Socialist*, 30 Jan. 1921; 13 Jan. 1921; 24 Feb. 1921; 3 March 1921; 17 March 1921; 26 May 1921; McShane, *Fighter*, p. 120; interview with Finlay Hart, 30 July 1986.

18. PRO Cab 24/114, CP 2089, "Report on Revolutionary Organisations", 11 Nov. 1920; /118, CP 2089, "A Survey of Revolutionary Movements in Great Britain in the Year 1920", Jan. 1921; /111, CP 1885, "Report on Revolutionary Organisations", 23 Sept. 1920; *The Worker*, 2 Oct. 1920; 16 Oct. 1920; *Daily Herald*, 11 Nov. 1920; 12 Nov. 1920.

19. *Daily Herald*, 13 Oct. 1920; 8 Dec. 1920; 24 Dec. 1920; 22 Oct. 1920; 11 Nov. 1920; 22 Dec. 1920.

20. *Daily Herald*, 23 Sept. 1920; 19 Oct. 1920.

21. *The Times*, 19 Oct. 1920; *Daily Herald*, 19 Oct. 1920; *The Communist*, 21 Oct. 1920; PRO Cab 24/112, CP 1997, Report on Revolutionary Organisations", 21 Oct. 1920; Kingsford, *Marchers*, pp. 13-15; Hannington, *Struggles*, pp. 16-17.

22. Hannington, *Struggles*, p. 15.

23. Lewis Jones anecdote, Gwyn A. Williams, *When Was Wales* (Harmondsworth 1985), p. 261; "Suggested Titles", HP/CPA-Cla.

24. The Kentish Town SDF formed a St. Pancras Unemployed Committee early in 1895, for example, which succeeded in mobilizing the unemployed to the extent that the local board of guardians acceded to their demand to open up two stone yards to employ the workless, *Justice*, 16 Feb. 1895. Hannington, *Never*, p. 71. The major sources for Hannington's life are his own books, particularly his autobiography *Never On Our Knees*, an entry in *The Labour Who's Who 1927*, and his personal papers held by the CPA.

25. For example, we find the following self-satisfied description of the NUWCM's work in its paper *Out of Work*, no. 48: "We found the unemployed a collection of whining, mumping groups, totally unclass conscious, and material for blacklegging. We (that is, all of us) have given the unemployed direction, discipline and dignity".

26. Hannington, *Struggles*, pp. 17-20; Jones, "Pankhurst", p. 94; Kingsford, *Marchers*, p. 20; *The Communist*, 9 Dec. 1920; *Daily Herald*, 13 Oct. 1920; 30 Dec. 1920; PRO Cab 24/118, CP 2458, "Ministry of Labour Weekly Report", 15 Jan. 1921.

27. Hannington, *Struggles*, pp. 18-19; *Daily Herald*, 13 Oct. 1920; *Daily Herald*, 3 Dec. 1920; the *Herald* admitted its list of occupied buildings was far from complete; the Camberwell unemployed alone had seized twenty-one houses by the beginning of December; *Daily Herald*, 2 Dec. 1920; PRO Cab 24/118, CP 2273, "Report on Revolutionary Organisations", 9 Dec. 1920; /113, CP 2118, "Report on Revolutionary Organisations", 9 Oct. 1920.

28. *The Times*, 4 Dec. 1920.

29. PRO Cab 24/118, CP 2273, "Report on Revolutionary Organisations", 9 Dec. 1920; *The Times*, 26 Nov. 1920.

30. J. W. Holt wrote, "Most of the unemployed committees throughout London are at present concentrating their energies on giving relief to the unemployed", *Out of Work*, 19 March 1921; *Daily Herald*, 24 Dec. 1920; 8 Dec. 1920; 23 Nov. 1920; 18 Nov. 1920.

31. *The Times*, 7 Dec. 1920; Hannington, *History*, p. 28.

32. PRO Cab 24/115, CP 2116, "Report on Revolutionary Organisations", 18 Nov. 1920; *Lord Riddell's Intimate Diary of the Peace Conference and After, 1918-1923* (1933), p. 257; Macnamara had tried to warn the cabinet of his fears three days earlier, see PRO Cab 24/117, CP 2342, "Progress of the Measures to Deal With Unemployment", T. J. Macnamara, 22 Dec. 1920.

33. Wal Hannington, "Notes for autobiography", HP/CPA-C1b.

34. Ramsay MacDonald, *Socialism, Critical and Constructive* (1924), p. iv; a full account of the interviews between the LDC and the Council of Action is given in *The Communist*, 30 Jan. 1920.

35. *The Times*, 24 Feb. 1921; Hutt, *Post War*, pp. 64-65.

36. PRO Cab 24/118, CP 2461, "Report on Revolutionary Organisations," 15 Jan. 1921.

37. PRO Cab 24/118, CP 2461, "Report on Revolutionary Organisations," 15 Jan. 1921; /119, CP 2574, "Report on Revolutionary Organisations", 10 Feb. 1921; /118, CP 2485, "Ministry of Labour Weekly Report", 15 Jan. 1921; *Out of Work*, 19 March 1921.

38. *The Times*, 6 Jan. 1921; 7 Sept. 1922; PRO Cab 24/128, CP 3309, "Report on Revolutionary Organisations", 15 Sept. 1921; /128, CP 3380, "Report on Revolutionary Organisations", 6 Oct. 1921.

39. PRO Cab 24/120, CP 2631, "Report on Revolutionary Organisations", 3 March 1921; Cab 24/120, CP 2765, "Report on Revolutionary Organisations", 24 Feb. 1921; Cab 24/120, CP 2470, "Ministry of Labour Weekly Report", 5 March 1921; Cab 24/121, CP 2765, "Report on Revolutionary Organisations", 23 March 1921; Cab 24/122, CP 2842, "Ministry of Labour Weekly Report", 16 April 1921; *Out of Work*, 21 May 1921.

40. *Out of Work*, 30 April 1921; 2 April 1921; 9 April 1921; Minutes of Executive Meeting of London Trades Council, 31 May 1921; Hannington, *Struggles*, pp. 26-27.

41. PRO Cab 24/119, CP 2562, "Unemployment: The Immediate Future", 10 Feb. 1921; Hannington, *History*, p. 28.

42. PRO Cab 24/120, CP 2740, "Report on Revolutionary Organisations", 17 March 1921; Cab 24/122, CP 2891, "Report on Revolutionary Organisations", 28 April 1921; Cab 24/123, CP 2952, "Report on Revolutionary Organisations", 19 May 1921; Cab 24/125, CP 3010, "Report on Revolutionary Organisations", 2 June 1921; Montefiore, *Victorian*, p. 208. There was an attempt by the LDC to revive activity with a march of 170 "class conscious men" to the Labour Party conference in June 1921, *Labour Party Conference Report 1921*, pp. 182-184, as well as some minor activity in Sheffield and Sussex, Cab 24/125, CP 3055, "Report on Revolutionary Organisations", 16 June 1921; *Out of Work*, no. 14 (c. July 1921); Jane Bellamy et al., *Who was Harry Cowley?* (Brighton 1984) p. 6.

43. PRO Cab 24/126, CP 3138, "Report on Revolutionary Organisations", 21 July 1921; *Out of Work*, no. 12 (c. July 1921).

44. *Out of Work*, no. 14 (c. Aug 1921); PRO Cab 24/128, CP 3309, "Report on Revolutionary Organisations", 15 Sept. 1921.

45. J. J. Astor et al., *The Third Winter of Unemployment* (1923), p. 44; PRO Cab 24/128, CP 3217, "The Unemployment Problem", 17 Sept. 1921.

46. PRO Cab 24/127, CP 3277, "Report on Revolutionary Organisations", 1 Sept. 1921; Cab 24/128, CP 3333, "Report on Revolutionary Organisations", 22 Sept. 1921; *The Times*, 1 Sept. 1921.

47. *The Times*, 8 Sept. 1921; George Garrett, *Unemployed Struggles, Liverpool 1921-1922* (Liverpool n.d.) p. 6; Braddock, *Braddocks*, p. 34.

48. *The Times*, 9 Sept. 1921. On the Walker Art Gallery bloodbath, Garrett, *Unemployed*, p. 13; see also Braddock, *Braddocks*, pp. 35-37; *The Times*, 14 Sept. 1921.

49. *Out of Work*, no.18 (c. Oct. 1921). The RILU, also known as the Profintern, was the Communist international of trade unions, which in Britain attempted to organize rank and file industrial activity. PRO Cab 24/129, CP 3436, "Report on Revolutionary organisations", 20 Oct. 1921.

50. Garrett, *Unemployed*, pp. 20-21; PRO Cab 24/131, CP 3526, "Report on Revolutionary Organisations", 1 Dec. 1921.

51. Gail Brayburn, *Women Workers in the First World War* (1981), pp. 181, 210; PRO Cab 24/126, CP 3138, "Report on Revolutionary Organisations", 21 July 1921; Cab 24/119, CP 2514, "Report on Revolutionary Organisations", 10 Feb. 1921; *Out of Work*, no. 21 (c. Nov. 1921); no. 19 (c. Oct. 1921); *The Times*, 21 Sept. 1921.

52. PRO Cab 24/128, CP 3350, "Report on Revolutionary Organisations", 29 Sept. 1921.

53. Quoted Sheila Rowbotham, *Hidden From History* (1973), p. 135; *Out of Work*, no. 21 (c. Dec. 1921); no. 17 (c. Sept 1921); PRO Cab 24/129, CP 3478, "Report on Revolutionary Organisations", 10 Nov. 1921; Cab 24/136, CP 3983, "Report on Revolutionary Organisations", 16 May 1922.

54. *The Times*, 4 Dec. 1920.

55. PRO Cab 24/131, CP 3561, "Report on Revolutionary Organisations", 15 Dec. 1921; the following account is derived from a detailed article by Lily Thring in *Out of Work*, no. 13 (c. July 1921).

56. *Out of Work*, no. 23 (c. Jan. 1922); Hannington, *Struggles*, pp. 45-48.

57. *Out of Work*, no. 15 (c. Sept. 1921); PRO Cab 24/129, CP 3408, "Report on Revolutionary Organisations", 14 Oct. 1921.

58. PRO Cab 24/131, CP 3492, "Report on Revolutionary Organisations", 1 Dec. 1921; *Out of Work*, no. 20 (c. Nov. 1921); Hannington, *Struggles*, p. 43. "Soon it was a wry joke that the shop steward leaders of 1918 had become the unemployed leaders of the 1920s", James Hinton and Richard Hyman, *Trade Unions and Revolution: the Industrial Politics of the early British Communist Party* (1975), p. 14.

59. While little local work has been done in this area to date, at least one historian, Richard Stone, has shown how in the small Derbyshire town of Glossop, solidly Liberal until 1919, Labour's fortunes were closely tied and partly determined by the activity of the local NUWCM branch, concluding that the major factor in explaining the success of Labour between 1921 and 1924 was NUWCM inspired agitation; Richard Stone, "When town mobilised over unemployment", *Glossop Chronicle and Advertiser*, 1 Jan. 1981; *The Times*, 6 Sept. 1921.

60. Hancock, "The Reduction of Unemployment", p. 343.

61. PRO Cab 24/118, CP 2429, "Report on Revolutionary Organisations", 6 Jan. 1921; Cab 24/128, CP 3380, "Report on Revolutionary Organisations", 6 Oct. 1921; *The Times*, 13 Sept. 1921; Cab 24/128, CP 3380, "Report on Revolutionary Organisations", 6 Oct. 1921.

62. PRO Cab 24/129, CP 3408, "Report on Revolutionary Organisations", 14 Oct. 1921. A detailed account of one such police beating of activists, one a cripple, can be found in *Out of Work*, no. 32. Cab 24/128, CP 3380, "Report on Revolutionary Organisations", 6 Oct. 1921; Cab 24/128, CP 3217, "The Unemployment Problem", T. J. Macnamara, 17 Sept. 1921; Gilbert, *Policy*, p. 85.

63. PRO Cab 24/131, CP 3574, "Works for the Relief of Unemployment", A. Mond, 21 Dec. 1921.

64. *The Communist*, 4 Feb. 1922; *Out of Work*, no. 45; Hannington, *Struggles*, pp. 61-63; "Relief of Unemployment", A. Mond.

65. Noreen Branson, *Poplarism, 1919-1925* (1979), pp. 117-119.

66. Branson, *Poplarism*, pp. 123-28; also PRO Cab 24/133, CP 3725, "Report on Revolutionary Organisations", 9 Feb. 1922.

67. *The Times*, 1 Sept. 1921.

68. Braddock, *Braddocks*, p. 43.

69. *Out of Work*, no. 24 (c. Jan. 1922); no. 17 (c. Sept. 1921); PRO Cab 24/131, CP 3600, "Report on Revolutionary Organisations", 5 Jan. 1922; the relief system also could lead to corruption, such as when cases of syrup donated by Tate and Lyle to the unemployed at the Dockland Settlement did not reach all the unemployed, but only a few who were "prominent in the U. W. M. [*sic*]"; F. Wilson to Wal Hannington, Feb. 1951, HP/CPA-E2a.

70. *Out of Work*, no. 46 (c. Nov. 1922).

71. see E. Stanley, "Unemployed Organisation and the Working Class Movement", *Communist Review*, 1924, p. 372.

72. *The Socialist*, Oct. 1920; Leckie was the secretary of the Clyde Workers Defence Committee in 1919 and later an ardent CPGB member active against John MacLean, Carr, "Communist Party", n. 63. PRO Cab 24/132, CP 3609, "Report on Revolutionary Organisations", 12 Jan. 1922; Cab 24/132, CP 3687, "Report on Revolutionary Organisations", 2 Feb. 1922.

73. *Out of Work*, no. 28 (c. March 1922); no. 32 (c. April 1922); no. 25 (c. Jan. 1922).

74. On the AEU, overtime, and the lockout see Clegg, *Unions*, pp. 337-43. PRO Cab 24/132, CP 3609, "Report on Revolutionary Organisations", 22 Jan. 1922; *Out of Work*, no. 23 (c. Jan. 1922).

75. PRO Cab 24/134, CP 3854, "Report on Revolutionary Organisations", 16 March 1922; *Out of Work*, no. 27 (c.March 1922); no. 29 (c.March 1922); Cab 24/134, CP 3854, "Report on Revolutionary Organisations", 16 March 1922; a full account of the Coventry lockout is given in Carr, "Engineering Workers", pp. 207-218.

76. PRO Cab 24/136, CP 3960, "Report on Revolutionary Organisations", 4 May 1922; Cab 24/136, CP 3917, "Report on Revolutionary Organisations", 31 March 1922; Hannington, *Struggles*, pp. 65-66.

77. PRO Cab 24/136, CP 3983, "Report on Revolutionary Organisations", 16 May 1922; *Out of Work*, no. 32 (c. May 1932); no.40 (c. Aug. 1922); Cab. 24/128, CP 3333, "Report on Revolutionary Organisations", 22 Sept. 1921; Cab 24/138, CP 4132, "Report on Revolutionary Organisations", 27 July 1922.

78. L. J. MacFarlane, *The British Communist Party. Its Origins and Development until 1929* (1966), p. 125; PRO Cab 24/139, CP 4207, "Report on Revolutionary Organisations", 21 Sept. 1922.

79. Cabinet decision quoted *The Guardian*, 5 April 1966; Kingsford, *Marchers*, p. 53.

80. PRO Cab 24/137, CP 3636, "Report on Revolutionary Organisations", 12 April 1922, listed only two NUWCM activists, Leckie and Holt, as being on the CPGB payroll; Cab 24/139, CP 4282, "Report on Revolutionary Organisations," 12 Oct. 1922, mentions, for example, the CPGB giving the NUWCM £25, but there is no suggestion in Special Branch reports that the CPGB was funding the NUWCM in any systematic way. Executive Bureau of RILU, 1924, quoted Roderick Martin, "The National Minority Movement: A study in the organisation of trade union militancy in the interwar period" (Oxford D. Phil thesis, 1964), p. 52; *Report of the Central Commission to the Party Congress, 1925*, Pollard Papers (unsorted), John Johnson Collection, Bodleian Library (PP/JJ/BL); *Report of Third National Conference of NUWCM; Speeches and Documents of the Sixth Conference of the CPGB, 1924* (1970), p. 76.

81. What agitation there was in the summer of 1922 focused upon the "gap" system, introduced by the government to make uncovenanted benefit stretch twice the distance, by having a gap of five weeks in which no benefit would be paid after every five weeks in which benefit had been paid. This extraordinarily unpopular system was modified by the government in July 1922, reducing the gap to one week. In Scotland the unemployed were more active than in other parts of Britain, particularly upon the issue of housing, with thousands gathering to support the NUWCM in its eviction fights in the Gorbals and elsewhere in Glasgow. The Scottish NUWCM called for national action on the rent question, but the NUWCM, who at the height of their influence in September 1921 had rejected the possibility of a national rent strike, were now in no position to do anything so ambitious; *Out of Work*, no. 35 (c. June 1922); no. 37 (c. July 1922); no. 34 (c. June 1922); Hannington, *Struggles*, pp. 70-74; "Revolutionary Organisations", 1 Dec. 1921. *Out of Work*, no. 34 (c. June 1922); no. 39 (c. Aug. 1922); no. 40 (c. Aug. 1922); no. 41 (c. Sept. 1922); PRO Cab 24/138, CP 4171, "Report on Revolutionary Organisations", 24 Aug. 1922; *Daily Herald*, 21 Aug. 1922.

82. PRO Cab 24/139, CP 4292, "Report on Revolutionary Organisations", 26 Oct. 1922.

83. Hannington, *Struggles*, p. 85; quoted Kingsford, *Marchers*, p. 58.

84. Kingsford, *Marchers*, p. 57.

85. PRO Cab 24/140, CP 4337, "Report on Revolutionary Organisations", 30 Nov. 1922; PRO Cab 24/140, CP 4353, "Report on Revolutionary Organisations", 7 Dec. 1922.

86. PRO Cab 24/140, CP 4365, "Report on Revolutionary Organisations", 7 Dec. 1922; Cab 24/140, CP 4375, "Report on Revolutionary Organisations", 21 Dec. 1922; Hannington, *Struggles*, pp. 72-97; Kingsford, *Marchers*, pp. 62-71.

87. E. Stanley, "Unemployed Organisations", p. 370; Brian Lewis and Bill Gledhill, *Tommy James: A Lion of a Man* (Pontefract 1985), p. 10.

88. R. Page Arnot, "The Labour Movement and the Unemployed", *The Labour Monthly*, March 1923, p. 159; *Third National Conference of NUWCM*; G. D. H. Cole, *Out of Work* (1923), pp. 79-80.

89. Arnot, "Labour Movement", p. 158; Hannington, *History*, pp. 36-37; *Third National Conference of NUWCM*; *Report of Fifth National Conference of NUWCM, 1926*, Wal Hannington Papers, Marx Memorial Library (HP/MML), A III; *Report of Sixth National Conference of NUWCM, 1929*, HP/MML-A III.

90. Ernest Cant to all Local Party Committees, 6 June 1923, PP/JJ/BL. Prior to the NUWCM's April 1923 national conference, Cant called a meeting of leading London CPGB members connected with the unemployed, and of the thirty he expected, only four turned up; Ernest Cant to all Local Party Committees, 20 April 1923, PP/JJ/BL. Soderburg seems to have had a dislike of Percy Haye, NUWCM national secretary, and by the time of the 1923 NUWCM conference, this antipathy had developed into Soderburg being "in opposition" to the NAC, and in particular Haye. Soderburg began to raise questions about the expenditure upon the chairman (Holt) and secretary (Haye), and the amount of work they put in; NUWCM NAC Minutes 29 Sept.-2 Oct. 1923. HP/MML-A III. "One of the influences against us has been the London Organiser, Soderburg", wrote Cant in his letter of 6 June 1923: "But, being a strong personality we have not hitherto been able to find sufficient grounds to justify his removal." Sufficient grounds were found in information the LDC claimed to have that Soderburg was a paid agent of Scotland Yard. There is however no evidence in Special Branch reports to corroborate this claim, and Soderburg maintained that he had been framed by the CPGB. It was upon the basis of this allegation that Harry Homer, NAC business manager, moved at an LDC meeting in late 1923 that Soderburg be asked to resign, but before the motion was seconded, Soderburg took the advantage and voluntarily resigned; NAC Minutes, 29 Sept.-2 Oct. 1923. It seems that the resignation call was orchestrated by the CPGB. Certainly the Party never forgave Soderburg. When he was arrested in 1931 and eventually imprisoned in Sing Sing prison for a bombing on the New York docks in connection with a seamen's strike, the American Communist Party refused to help Soderburg in his defense, and publicly repeated the allegation of his connection with Scotland Yard; Gunnar Soderburg to George Garrett, 8 Jan. 1939, quoted M. Toole, *Mrs. Bessie Braddock MP* (1957) pp. 93-94. Soderburg was still in Sing Sing at this time, and claimed he was innocent of the bombing charge.

91. E. H. Carr, *The Russian Revolution, 1917-1929* (1983), p. 31; MacFarlane, *Communist Party*, pp. 67-68. The remnants of the WSF were now known as the Communist Workers' Party, which although an extremely small group still had some influence through the pages of the *Dreadnought*; Jones, "Pankhurst", p. 104. *Workers' Dreadnought*, 7 July 1923; 4 Aug. 1923.

92. *Workers' Dreadnought*, 1 Sept. 1923; 13 Oct. 1923; PRO Cab 24/160, CP 291(24), "Report on Revolutionary Organisations", 5 July 1923; Sylvia Pankhurst's account book 1922-24, International Institute of Social History, Amsterdam, Pankhurst papers, 132(97); Branson, *Poplarism*, p. 192.

93. NAC Minutes 29 Sept.-2 Oct. 1923; *Workers' Dreadnought*, 20 Sept. 1923; Nan Milton, *John MacLean* (1973), p. 200; *Workers' Dreadnought*, 19 Jan. 1924.

94. Hannington, *History*, p. 39.

95. "Headquarters had had a continual struggle for existence," Holt told the conference, ". . . and had it not been for donations from the Executives of various Trade Unions, the Movement would have undoubtedly closed down"; *Report of Fourth National Conference of NUWCM, Dec. 1924*, HP/MML, A III; McShane, *Fighter*, p. 167; Braddock, *Braddocks*, p. 63; Carr, "Communist Party", n. 63; Martin, "National Minority Movement", pp. 57, 385-386; *Report of Fifth National Conference of NUWCM, 1926*.

96. *Towards A Mass Party: Theses of the Organising Bureau of the CPGB, 1925*, PP/JJ/BL.

97. There had been a small revival of unemployed activity in the atmosphere of heightened political tension prior to the general strike of 1926; London District CPGB Circular Letter, 25 Nov. 1925, PP/JJ/BL; *The Times*, 20 April 1926; *Report of Fifth National Conference*. Francis and Smith, *The Fed*, pp. 164, 184-85; on "Little Moscows" generally, see Stuart Macintyre, *Little Moscows: Communism and Working Class Militancy in Interwar Britain* (1980); for comparisons of the size of industries' workforces and their level of unemployment in this period, see Mitchell and Deane, *British Historical Statistics*, pp. 67, 119, 188; Stuart Macintyre, *A Proletarian Science: Marxism in Britain, 1917-1933* (1986), p. 40; *The Red Challenger*, no. 3, 1928, Communist papers, JJ/9.5.78/VQ, John Johnson Collection, Bodleian Library (JJ/BL).

98. London DC circular letter, 20 Aug. 1925, PP/JJ/BL; Resolution on the British League (YCL), March 1926, PP/JJ/BL; London DC circular letter, 1927, PP/JJ/BL.

99. John MacLean, "Speech from the dock", 25 Oct. 1921, Milton (ed.), *Revolution*, pp. 209-10; PRO Cab 24/117, CP 2352, "Report on Revolutionary Organisations", 23 Dec. 1920; Wal Hannington to L. J. MacFarlane, 27 June 1961, HP/CPA-E2d; Alan Deacon, "Systems of Interwar Unemployment Relief", Glynn and Booth, *Full Employment*, p. 34.

100. R. Pierpont (ed.), *Report of the Fifth Neo-Malthusian and Birth Control Conference, 1922* (1922), pp. 37, 39; Wyndham Childs, *Episodes*, p. 216; Ron Bean, "Liverpool Shipping Employers and the Anti-Communist Activities of J. M. Hughes, 1920-1925", *Bulletin of the Society for the Study of Labour History* (1977), no. 34, p. 24.

101. Deacon, "Concession", p. 27; Margaret McCarthy, *Generation in Revolt* (1953), p. 121; Macintyre, *Marxism*, p. 40; Deacon, "Interwar Unemployment Relief", pp. 35-36; in Glasgow in 1925 it was reported that clerks were being paid overtime to spot unemployed women who promenaded regularly, and that these women were then struck off unemployment benefit—no matter how many stamps they had—on the grounds that they were not genuinely seeking work; *Workers' Weekly*, 27 Feb. 1925.

102. *The Empire Record*, April 1927, p. 95; also May 1927, p. 95; March 1928, p. 84; Keith Feiling, *The Life of Neville Chamberlain* (1946), p. 140; Gilbert, *Policy*, p. 221; A. J. P. Taylor, *English History, 1914-1945* (Harmondsworth 1985), p. 325;

A. J. Vinson, "Poor Relief, public assistance and the maintenance of the unemployed in Southampton between the wars", *Southern History* (1980), vol. 2, p. 193.

Chapter 6

1. *Communist Review*, Nov. 1932; Stephen "Johnny" Hicks, *Sparring For Luck: Autobiography of the East End Boxer Poet* (1982), p. 71.

2. *Out of Work*, no. 46 (1922); *Report of the Sixth Annual Conference of the NUWCM, 1929*, HP/MML-AII; McShane, *Fighter*, p. 167; Braddock, *Braddocks*, p. 63; Carr, "Communist Party", n. 63.

3. *Sixth Annual Conference of the NUWCM, 1929.*

4. NUWCM circular, "Explanation Re Vote on War Resolution" (1935) HP/CPA-A2e.

5. PRO Cab 24/139, CP4307, "Report on Revolutionary Organisations", 16 Nov. 1922; NUWM NAC Report, 19-20 Oct. 1929, HP/MML-AIII; John Hepworth, *His book* (Melbourne 1978), p. 151.

6. *The Times*, 11 October 1932.

7. James Jupp, *The Radical Left in Britain* (1982), p. 25; Harry Pollitt, *Unity Against the National Government*, pamp, nd, c. 1935.

8. V. I. Lenin, *"Left-Wing" Communism, An Infantile Disorder* (1920) (Peking 1975), pp. 90-91. The origins of the Third Period policy lay less in acute analysis and more in internal Russian politics; see E.H. Carr, *The Russian Revolution From Lenin to Stalin, 1917-1929* (1979), pp. 137, 165-66.

9. Kate Pohl, "The Role of Women Workers in Modern Economic Fights", *RILU Magazine*, Feb. 1929, p. 206; *The New Line: Documents of the Tenth Congress* (1929), p. 99; *Resolutions of the Eleventh Congress* (1930), pp. 11, 27; Martin, "National Minority Movement", p. 385; after Hannington's departure the MWMM collapsed.

10. Harry Pollitt, "The N.M.M. Conference", *RILU Magazine*, Oct. 1929, p. 336; *NUWM Sixth Annual Conference Report, 1929.*

11. Branson, *CPGB, 1927-1941*, p. 78; *NUWM National Conference Report, 1929.* NUWM branches in the Stoke district, for example, charged commission on cases defended at courts of referees, until Hannington intervened in late 1929; "Plan of Work and Re-organisation for the Stoke District Council of the NUWM", Dec. 1929; Modern Records Centre, Iron and Steel Confederation Papers, 36/U7; *International Press Correspondence* (*Inprecorr*), 6 July 1931, p. 677; Margaret McCarthy, *Generation in Revolt* (1953), p. 172.

12. *RILU Magazine*, Feb. 1930, p. 577. An ironic consequence of the major unemployed demonstrations that took place on 6 March 1930 in the United States of America was the inception of congressional investigations into un-American activities, marking the formal birth of the statutory use of anti-communism as a method of controlling and circumscribing working-class protest; D. Leab, "United We Eat: The creation and organisation of the Unemployed Councils in 1930",

Labor History (USA) (1967), p. 307. *Inprecorr*, 30 Oct. 1931, p. 1008; *NUWM Conference Report 1929;* Bert Hogenkamp, *Deadly Parallels: Film and the Left in Britain, 1929-1939* (1986), p. 44; Branson, *CPGB, 1927-1941*, p. 78.

13. Wal Hannington, *Achievements of the Hunger March Against the Labour Government* (pamp. 1930); Middlemas, *Clydesiders*, pp. 237-38.

14. V. Krause, "International Unemployment Day", *RILU Magazine*, June 1930, p. 62; *Daily Worker*, 19 June 1930; 27 June 1930; L. Zoubock, "Some Fundamental Mistakes of the British Minority Movement", *RILU Magazine*, July 1930, p. 165; *Inprecorr*, 11 Sept. 1930, p. 895, quoted E. H. Carr, *The Twilight of the Comintern, 1930-1935* (1986), p. 209.

15. NUWM NAC Reports 24-25 May 1930, 29-30 Dec. 1930, HP/MML-AI andAII; see also G. Evers, "The Unemployed Movement and the IX Plenum", *RILU Magazine*, 15 Sept. 1931, p. 3; *Daily Worker*, 25 Sept. 1930; A. L. Morton, "Review of The History of the Communist Party", *Our History Journal*, Nov. 1985, p. 4; a song written for the Workers' Charter campaign with the refrain "three pounds a week and the seven hour day" would be sung at meetings by Sid Elias, who saw himself as leader of the campaign, in the expectation that the audience would join in. He was, according to Harry McShane, "a badly disappointed man", McShane, *Fighter*, p. 172; by far the biggest delegation present from a single organization at the Workers' Charter Convention in April 1931, was that of the NUWM, with some 142 delegates; *Road to Victory: Resolutions of the First National Workers Charter Convention* (pamp. 1931).

16. *Inprecorr*, 6 July 1931; 17 Aug. 1931, p. 805; 3 Sept. 1931, p. 873; 10 Sept. 1931, p. 884; Fischer, *Stormtroopers*, p. 48; Eve Rosenhaft, *Beating the Fascists? The German Communists and Political Violence, 1929-1933* (1983), pp. 48-50; Carr, *Comintern*, p. 39.

17. *Inprecorr*, 30 Oct. 1931, p. 1008; *RILU Magazine*, 1 Feb. 1932, p. 64; *Communist Review*, March 1933, p. 145; Russian revolutionary history was invoked on the side of broad-based unemployed committees, it being argued that the St Petersburg Unemployed Council had been central to the failed 1905 revolution; see Sergei Malyshev, *Unemployed Councils in St Petersburg in 1906* (1931); the Russian example proved more influential in the United States of America, see Leab, "United We Eat", p. 302.

18. Ben Fowkes, *Communism in Germany under the Weimar Republic* (1984), p. 176; Idris Cox, "Carrying out the C.C. Resolution", *Communist Review*, Aug. 1932, p. 383; some Welsh Communists claimed that there was an overemphasis within the Party at this time upon mobilizing the unemployed, but while this may well have been true of the devastated south Welsh coal fields, it was not the case nationally; see Horner, *Rebel*, p. 110; Len Jeffries, "Faith in the Working Class", *Communist Review*, Oct. 1932, p. 486; 47 percent of the CPGB were unemployed in July 1931, *Communist Review*, July 1931, p. 292; 49 percent in March 1932, J. Degras (ed.), *The Communist International, Vol. III* (Oxford 1965), p. 187; 49.43 percent were "unemployed and housewives" in June 1932; *Communist Review*, Aug. 1932, p. 385; *Daily Worker*, 20 Jan. 1932; *Communist Review*, July 1931, p. 292; George

Finch, "The Mass Movement of the Unemployed Workers ", *Communist Review*, Nov. 1933, p. 404; "Immediate Tasks before the Party and the Working Class: Resolution of the Central Committee", *Communist Review*, Feb. 1932, p. 64; "May Central Committee Meeting", *Communist Review*, July 1931, p. 275; Pat Devine, "The United Front and the Unemployed", *Communist Review*, Oct. 1932, p. 486.

19. McCarthy, *Revolt*, p. 138; for some Third Period rhetoric as early as 1926 see T. A. Jackson's review of Trotsky's "Where is Britain Going?" in *Workers' Weekly*, 5 March 1926; for a good example of the mythologizing of the Popular Front, see Jim Fyrth (ed.), *Britain, Fascism and the Popular Front* (1985).

20. Ben Pimlott, *Labour and the Left in the 1930s* (Cambridge 1977), pp. 17-18, 55; Jupp, *Radical Left*, p. 13; Secretary, Local Government Department, Labour Party, to Lucy Middleton, 8 April 1937, Middleton papers, MID52/11, Ruskin College.

21. *Labour Party Conference Report 1930*, p. 29; *Labour Party Conference Report 1939*, p. 269; *NUWCM Conference Report, 1929*; Pimlott, *Labour and the Left*, p. 81; *Manchester Guardian*, 17 April 1933; J. E. Williams, *The Derbyshire Miners* (1962), p. 883.

22. Harold Heslop, *Last Cage Down* (1935) (1984), pp. 185-186, 187; McCarthy, *Revolt*, p. 95.

23. Harry Pollitt, *Forward!* (pamp. 1936); *It Can Be Done: Report of the 14th Congress of CPGB, 1937*, pp. 291, also 238; Resolutions of the Tenth National Conference of the NUWM, 1937, HP/CPA-A2g; Wal Hannington to Sir Walter Citrine, 21 Feb. 1938, HP/CPA-Ee.

24. Circular from Oliver Harris, General Secretary of the SWMF, 15 July 1937; also Oliver Harris to David Lewis, 2 July 1937; SWMF papers, F42, SWCA; NUWM Branch List, 1938; HP/CPA-A2g; Pat Devine, "Carry on the Marchers' Struggle", *Discussion*, Dec. 1936, p. 15; George Stalker to Unemployment Research and Advice Bureau (URAB) of the NUWM, 30 June 1939.

25. *Report of the 11th NUWM Conference 1939*, HP/MML-AII; *The Times*, 17 Nov. 1938; 21 Dec. 1938; 23 Dec. 1938; 4 Jan. 1939; 5 Jan. 1939; 7 Jan. 1939; 18 Jan. 1939; 24 Jan. 1939; L. Attach, West Hartlepool NUWM to URAB (NUWM), 10 June 1939, HP/MML-A-VII; Dunfermline NUWM bulletin, May 1939, HP/ MML-AVII-IB; George Lasker to Wal Hannington, 8 March 1939, HP/MML-AVII-IB.

26. NUWM circular, 11 July 1939, HP/MML-A(iv); Memorandum of NUWM NHC Meeting, 2 Sept. 1939, HP/CPA-A2f; Guarantor Plan, 1939, HP/CPA-A2f.

27. NUWM circular, 8 March 1942, HP/CPA-A2h; Eric Edney to Wal Hannington, 13 Sept. 1940, HP/CPA-A2h; J. Shields and P. E. Hall, "Report of the Position of the NUWM Head Office", 22 March 1943, HP/CPA-A2f; Memorandum of NHC meeting, 24 April 1943, HP/CPA-A2f; NUWM circular 8 March 1942; Wal Hannington to W. J. Tucker, 29 Nov. 1944, HP/CPA-E1g; Wal Hannington to Harry McShane, 15 Feb. 1946, HP/CPA-A2f.

28. Henry Miller, "Report on Housing Agitation Organised by the Cambuslang Branch of the NUWM," (1939), HP/MML-AVII, see also *The Pilot and Cambuslang District News*, 25 Nov. 1938; *Scottish Daily Express*, 25 Jan. 1939.

29. *Men Without Work* (Cambridge 1938), p. 162.

30. V. I. Lenin, *Collected Works Vol. 10* (1962), p. 452.

31. Beatrice Burton's Written Reminiscences, 6 March 1976, MSS 14, Ruskin College Archives (RCA); *Oxford Times*, 26 Aug. 1932.

32. Stephen Kelly, *Idle Hands, Clenched Fists. The Depression in a Shipyard Town* (Nottingham 1987), p. 67.

33. Wal Hannington, "Notes for Autobiography", HP/CPA, C1b; that the means test was the same as the poor law was denied by, for example, R. S. Hudson, parliamentary secretary, Ministry of Labour, *The Times*, 24 March 1932; *The Times*, 30 Sept. 1932.

34. R. C. Davison, "General Report on Disallowed Claimants", *First Report of the Royal [Gregory] Commission on Unemployment Insurance, 1931*, Cmd 3872 (1931), p. 112-13; Brierly, *Means Test Man*, p. 263.

35. Sir William Beveridge, *Social Insurance and Allied Services Report*, Cmd 6404 (1942), pp. 7, 11.

36. *Ministry of Labour Report 1932*, Cmd 4281 (1933), p. 65.

37. *The Times*, 12 Nov. 1932; 25 July 1932; 18 Nov. 1932; 29 Nov. 1932; Fenner Brockway, *Hungry England* (1932), pp. 26, 28.

38. *The Times*, 24 March 1932; 2 April 1932; 16 Sept. 1932; *Ministry of Labour Report 1932*, Cmd 4281 (1933), p. 66.

39. Deacon, "Interwar Unemployment Relief", pp. 38-39.

40. Joe Rawlings, "Unemployed Struggles" (typescript, n.d.), MSS 14, RCA.

41. Tom Mann, *Tom Mann and the ILP*, pamp. (nd. c. 1933); *Bootle Times*, 18 Jan. 1935.

42. There can be no doubt that the state did pursue a policy of persecution of NUWM activists. Following the uproar that accompanied the arrest and imprisonment of the 77-year-old Tom Mann, treasurer of the NUWM, in December 1932, Sir John Gilmour, Home Secretary, told Parliament that the government had "adopted this course of action to make certain that it is brought home to those who organise these street demonstrations that such penalties will follow if they refuse to give an undertaking that there will be no disorders", *The Times*, 20 Dec. 1932; such sentiments were echoed around the nation by the judiciary: remanding six men who had been involved with an unemployed demonstration outside Stratford town hall in October 1932, the magistrate, Mr. St. John Morrow, commented that "Members of the local authority must not be intimidated; and he hoped the police would keep far from the district those who would seek to coerce or intimidate the local authority", *The Times*, 6 Oct. 1932; Irving Bernstein, *The Lean Years: A History of the American Worker, 1920-1933* (Boston 1960), pp. 437-455; A. Baskin, "The Ford Hunger March-1932", *Labor History* (USA), 1972, pp. 331-60.

43. Will Paynter, *My Generation* (1972), p. 88; Fowkes, *Communism in Germany*, pp. 100, 107; Hannington, *Struggles*, pp. 109-16; *Never On Our Knees*, pp. 168-70.

44. PRO Cab 24/223/243 (31), "The Present Situation: Memorandum by the Home Secretary", 24 Sept. 1931.

45. Protestants and Catholics had briefly united in these demonstrations, and Unionist leaders responded by guaranteeing Protestant workers positions over Catholics; Liz Curtis, *Nothing But The Same Old Story: The Roots of Anti-Irish Racism* (1985), p. 69; *Labour Party Conference Report 1932*, p. 245; *The Times*, 23 Sept. 1932; "A. M." to Mr. K. Thompson, 1976, MSS 14, RCA; quoted Hutt, *Post War History*, p. 224.

46. Kelly, *Clenched Fists*, p. 80; Hutt, *Post War History*, p. 225.

47. *The Times*, 19 Oct. 1932; 20 Oct. 1932.

48. *Daily Worker*, 28 Jan. 1932; NUWM Monthly Report Bulletin, Feb. 1931, HP/MML-AIII; C. G. Maby, Chief Constable to Town Clerk, 26 Feb. 1932, Police Records, 34908/460, Bristol Records Office (BRO).

49. *Daily Worker*, 8 Feb. 1932; *The Times*, 10 Feb. 1932; M. Bonds, CID Sergeant, "Report on Unemployed Accommodation", 20 Feb. 1932, Police Records, 34908/46d, BRO; C. G. Maby to Under Secretary of State, 24 Feb. 1932, Police Records, 34908/46d, BRO; NUWM leaflet, Police Records 34908/46d, BRO.

50. Lewis Grassic Gibbon, *Grey Granite; A Scots Quair* (1934, pub. 1946) (New York, 1977), p. 394; Statements Received in Connection with Unemployed Demonstration, Police Records, 34908/46d, BRO; Superintendent E. Burns, "Report No.203 A", 23 Feb. 1932, Police Records, 34908/46d, BRO; a host of savage implements later displayed by the police to the press as having been used by the unemployed in the fight are not mentioned in any police report; *The Times*, 24 Feb. 1932.

51. Constable G. Wakefield, "Report of NUWM meeting", 14 March 1932, Police Records, 34908/46d, BRO; Sergeant Y. Burns, "Transcript of . . . a meeting . . . of the Bristol East Labour Party", 27 Feb. 1932; C. G. Maby to Town Clerk, 26 Feb. 1932; Bristol Council Minutes, 22 Dec. 1931, BRO; "Employed and Unemployed Rally", NUWM leaflet, March 1932, Police Records, 34908/46d, BRO; Town Clerk to C. G. Maby, 8 March 1932, Police Records, 34908/46d, BRO.

52. Max Cohen, *I Was One of the Unemployed* (1945), p. 19.

53. Paynter, *My Generation*, p. 90.

54. Quoted Nigel Gray, *The Worst of Times* (1985), pp. 201, 200; Alaric Jacob, "Sharing Orwell's 'Joys'—But Not His Fears", C. Norris (ed.), *Inside The Myth. Orwell: Views From the Left* (1984), p. 74; Gibbon, *Grey Granite*, pp. 394-95; James Barke, *Major Operation* (1936), p. 399.

55. Gwyn A. Williams, *When Was Wales?* (Harmondsworth 1986), p. 264.

56. see E. Roberts, *A Woman's Place: An Oral History of Working Class Women, 1890-1940* (Oxford 1985); D. Gittins, "Marital Status, Work and Kinship, 1850-1930", J. Lewis (ed.), *Labour and Love: Women's Experience of Home and Family 1859-1960* (Oxford 1986), p. 251; "it is easier for a camel to pass through the eye of a needle than for married women to get past the above [Anomalies] regulations", Sid Elias, *A Practical Guide to the Unemployment Acts* (pamp. 1931).

57. *Islington Woman Worker*, Oct. 1927, CP papers, 9.5.78/VQ, JJ/BL; Harry Davies, *The Lean Years* (unpub. ms.), ch. 3.

58. *Blaydon Courier*, 21 Nov. 1936.

59. Branson, *CPGB, 1927-1941*, p. 231; *NUWM National Conference Report 1939*, HP/MML-AIII; Paynter, *My Generation*, p. 104; *Daily Worker*, 28 Aug. 1930; 26 Sept. 1939; 11 Dec. 1930; NUWM Reports on Branch Activities, May 1931, June 1931, Sept. 1931, HP/MML-AIII; NUWM NAC Report, 3-4 Oct. 1931, HP/MML-AII; NUWM NAC Report, 7-8 May 1932, HP/MML-AII.

60. S. Orwell and I. Angus (eds.), *The Collected Esays, Journalism and Letters of George Orwell Vol. I.* (Harmondsworth 1971), p. 207.

61. *Daily Worker*, 5 June 1930; T. A. Richardson to NUWM HQ, 23 May 1939, HP/MML-AVIII-IB; Wyncoll, *Nottingham*, p. 222.

62. A. Croft, "Introduction", Walter Brierley, *Means Test Man* (1935) (Nottingham 1983), p. xv; Lewis Jones, *We Live* (1939) (1978), p. 249.

63. Keyssar, *Unemployment*, p. 297.

Chapter 7

1. *Nottingham Guardian*, 6 Dec. 1932; 2 Nov. 1932.

2. Led by Arnold White and Powell Williams, the Central Unemployed Organisation Committee failed to gain the support of the East End unemployed for its demand to restrict alien immigration as a solution to unemployment; see Watmough, "Unemployment in London," pp. 55-57; Braddock, *Braddocks*, p. 48.

3. *The Times*, 28 Jan. 1932; the TUC-dominated *Daily Herald* made no mention of this unofficial aim in its report of the same day; the TUC seemed to take an interest in the unemployed associations only when unemployed disturbances were at their height, such as in late October 1932 when the hunger marchers were in London, see *The Times*, 27 Oct. 1932; *Labour*, Feb. 1934, p. 131; a history of the unemployed associations is given in Clinton, *Trades Councils*, pp. 160-66.

4. Oswald Mosley, *My Life* (1968), p. 278; *Blackshirt*, Feb. 1933; 20 July 1934; 21 Nov. 1936; 21 Dec. 1933; Ellen Wilkinson and Edward Lonze, *Why Fascism?* (1934), p. 60; *Blackshirt*, 16 Aug. 1935; 23 March 1934; 21 Dec. 1934.

5. *Blackshirt*, 2 March 1934; 17 Aug. 1934; 22 March 1935; 18 April 1935; 9 Oct. 1937; *Fascist Week*, 23 March 1934; the BUF called for "work not maintenance", and the abolition of the means test, *Fascism For The Millions* (BUF pamp. 1936), p. 61; *Blackshirt*, 28 Jan. 1937; 6 Feb. 1937; 16 Oct. 1937; 30 Oct. 1937; Feb. 1939; March 1939; April 1939; Leslie Paul, *Angry Young Men* (1951), p. 232; Wal Hannington to Joan Simon, 29 Dec. 1959, HP/CPA-A2c.

6. James Barke, *Major Operation* (1936), p. 135.

7. In fact the paddling pool had been made by university students, and MacDonald was rebuked upon this point, and upon the total inadequacy of voluntary service as a method of helping the unemployed by the Brynmar Council a few days later; Hannington, *Distressed Areas*, pp. 201-3.

8. *The Times*, 20 Dec. 1932.

9. NCSS Unemployment Committee, Secretary's Report, 1 March 1934, National Council for Voluntary Organisations Archive (NCVOA)/NCSS Box 5; £150,000 was received from the Ministry of Labour and £240,000 from the Commissioner for Special Areas; "Financial Statement . . . Unemployment Committee", 31 March 1937, NCVOA/NCSS Box 5; NCSS "Unemployment Committee Progress Report," June 1933, NCVOA/NCSS Box 5; Report of Public Assistance Committee, 1933, City of Liverpool, Liverpool Records Office, Liverpool Public Assistance Committee Minutes, File 1. Unless otherwise acknowledged, all documents cited in this chapter from the NCVOA are NCSS documents.

10. *Annual Report of the National Council for Voluntary Organisations 1985-86* (1986), p. 27.

11. Margaret Brasnett, *Voluntary Social Action: A History of the National Council of Social Service 1919 -1969* (1986); Ralph Hayburn, "The Voluntary Occupational Centre Movement, 1932-1939", *Journal of Contemporary History* (1971), p. 157.

12. Brasnett, *Action*, p. 15; this account of the origins of the NCSS is derived from Brasnett, *Action*, pp. 1-20; Lord Beveridge, *Voluntary Action: A Report On Methods of Social Advance* (1948), p. 149.

13. G. D. H. Cole, "A Retrospect of the History of Voluntary Social Service", A. F. C. Bourdillon (ed.), *Voluntary Social Services: Their Place in the Modern State* (1945), p. 25; Brasnett, *Action*, pp. 54-55.

14. Kingsford, *Marchers*, p. 86; "NCSS Memorandum: The Work of the NCSS in relation to unemployed people and their dependents", 1 Dec. 1937, NCVOA/NCSS Box 5; "Conference of Mayors and Chairmen and Secretaries of the Town [C.S.S.] Committees", 19-21 Jan. 1934, NCVOA/NCSS Box 5; for example, five "recreational centres" were established in Leeds, and nine "unemployment centres" in Manchester; Leeds Unemployed Social Work Committee, "Social Work Among the Unemployed", 1936, NCVOA-QGX/D; Hayburn, "Centres", p. 159.

15. Lionel Stalsey to J. H. Whitley, 13 March 1928, NCVOA/NCSS Box 5; *The Times*, 28 Jan. 1932; Brasnett, *Action*, p. 69; all nine unemployment centers in Manchester were closed in the summer of 1932 due to lack of funding; Hayburn, "Centres", p. 159; "Draft of speech made by Prince of Wales at Tyneside", April 1932, NCVOA/NCSS Box 16.

16. PRO Cab 24/233, CP 307, "Unemployment Committee Interim Report", 24 Oct. 1932.

17. Eva Hubback and Alan Collinridge, "NCSS Memorandum on a Central Body to Organise Education and Occupational Schemes for the Unemployed", 8 Nov. 1932, NCVOA/NCSS Box 5; "Voluntary Occupations for the unemployed, Confidential Minutes of a Meeting held 21 Nov. 1932", NCVOA/NCSS Box 5; J. A. Barlow, Ministry of Labour, to Secretary, NCSS, 22 Nov. 1932, NCVOA/NCSS Box 16; "Finance Sub-Committee Meeting", 16 Dec. 1932, NCVOA/NCSS Box 16; Ministry of Labour to NCSS (copy), 17 Dec. 1932, NCVOA/NCSS Box 16; *The*

Times, 20 Dec. 1932; "Finance Sub-Committee Memorandum", 12 Jan.1933, NCVOA/NCSS Box 16.

18. "Private Appeals", 27 April 1933, NCVOA/NCSS Box 16; P. W. S. Andrews and Elizabeth Brunner, *The Life of Lord Nuffield* (Oxford 1955), p. 264; "Deed of Covenant made by Sir William Morris" (copy), 1 Jan. 1933, NCVOA/NCSS Box 16.

19. *The Times*, 20 Dec. 1932; "Memorandum", 3 Nov. 1932, NCVOA/NCSS Box 16; Edward, Prince of Wales, to E. R. Peacock, NCSS, 1 Dec. 1932, NCVOA/NCSS Box 5; H.R.H. Prince of Wales, "Unemployment and Voluntary Service", text of talk broadcast by the BBC on 27 Jan. 1934, NCVOA/NCSS Box 16; Mais's talks were later published as S. P. B. Mais, *S.O.S. Talks on Unemployment* (1933).

20. "Centres for Unemployed Men", 1933, NCVOA/NCSS Box 5; NCSS, *Work with the Unemployed: An Account of Some Experiments* (1932), p. 5.

21. Mais, *S.O.S. Talks*, pp. 266-67.

22. Kathleen Jones, "Eileen Younghusband: a biography", *Occasional Papers in Social Administration* (1984), p. 34; Brasnett, *Action*, p. 62; Hayburn, "Centres", p. 157.

23. "Memorandum", 21 Nov. 1932, NCVOA/NCSS Box 5.

24. Richard Griffiths, *Fellow Travellers of the Right: British Enthusiasts for Nazi Germany 1933-1939* (Oxford 1983) p. 269; William Teeling, *The Near-by Thing or Living With Our Unemployed and How they Are Solving Their Own Problems* (1933) pp. 224; 103-4.

25. Mais, *S.O.S. Talks*, p. 149; South East Lancashire and North East Cheshire Advisory Council Annual Report, 29 June 1937, NCVOA/NCSS Box 14.

26. "Minutes of a meeting on the subject of unemployment", 5 Jan. 1933, NCVOA/NCSS Box 5; "Unemployment Committee, Progress Report", June 1933, NCVOA/NCSS Box 5; "Unemployment Committee, Secretary's Report", 22 Nov. 1934, NCVOA/NCSS Box 5 .

27. Northern Ireland Council of Social Service, Annual Report, 1940, NCVOA/NCSS Box 14; L. F. Ellis, "Private and Confidential: Paper No. 2, NCSS Unemployment Committee", 14 Feb. 1933, NCVOA/NCSS Box 5; Circular 1316, Asst. Secretary, Ministry of Health to Local Authorities, 7 March 1933, NCVOA/NCSS Box 5.

28. *Men Without Work*, p. 55; L. F. Ellis "NCSS Confidential Memorandum on Policy for 1934-35", 17 Oct. 1934, NCVOA/NCSS Box 5; Hannington, *Struggles*, p. 274.

29. A. D. Lindsay to Prime Minister, 10 May 1933, NCVOA/NCSS Box 5; J. Ramsay MacDonald to A. D. Lindsay, 22 May 1933, NCVOA/NCSS Box 5; L.F. Ellis to Sir Henry Betterton, 22 Nov. 1933, NCVOA NCSS Box 5; Noreen Branson and Margot Heinemann, *Britain in the Nineteen Thirties* (1971), p. 43, which is not to say the Ministry of Labour did not apply considerable pressure upon the unemployed to go to the training camps.

30. L. F. Ellis, "NCSS Memorandum on Policy for 1934-35", 17 Oct. 1934, NCVOA/NCSS Box 5.

31. Teeling, *Near-by*, p. 14.

32. Brighton Centre for the Unemployed, *Annual Report, 1934*, NCVOA/NCSS Box 1; Programme of Visit of HRH The Prince of Wales to Liverpool, 25 Nov. 1932, NCVOA/NCSS Box 16.

33. Constitution of the East Shropshire Association of Mutual Services Clubs, 1935, NCVOA/NCSS Box 14.

34. Teeling, *Near-by*, p. 209.

35. *Birmingham Post*, 16 May 1935.

36. Some NCSS publications cite the figure of 700 clubs in existence in 1932, but this would seem to be derived from 1 Feb. 1933 figures, as it was not until then that the NCSS Unemployment Committee conducted any surveys.

37. "Tour of the Birmingham Service Clubs by HRH Prince George, K.G.", 27 Nov. 1933, NCVOA/NCSS Box 16; "HRH The Prince George's Tour in the Midlands, Detailed Programme, 12-13 July 1934", NCVOA/NCSS Box 16; "Minutes of a meeting regarding occupation centres for the unemployed in London", 7 July 1932, NCVOA/NCSS Box 12; "London Council for Voluntary Occupation during Unemployment, Report on Work in 1933", NCVOA/NCSS Box 12; "Report on Bristol Unemployment Welfare Association", 16 May 1938, NCVOA/NCSS Box 12; "Visit of . . . Prince of Wales to Liverpool, 25 Nov. 1932", NCVOA/NCSS Box 16; Hubback and Collinridge, "Memorandum", 8 Nov. 1932.

38. Stockport People's Service Guild, Fourth Annual Report, 1937, NCVOA/NCSS Box 1; "Visit of Prince of Wales to Liverpool, 25 Nov. 1932", NCVOA/NCSS Box 16; "Unemployment Committee Progress Report", 30 Sept. 1938, NCVOA/NCSS Box 5; NCSS, *Out of Adversity: A Survey of the Clubs for Men and Women which have grown out of the Needs of Unemployment* (1939), p.62; Wilkinson, *Town That Was Murdered*, p. 232; Hannington, *Distressed*, p. 195.

39. Henry Mess, "Social Service with the Unemployed", G. Williams (ed.), *Voluntary Social Services since 1918* (1947), p. 47; *Adversity*, pp. 35-36; "Memorandum on Meeting of Advisory Officers", 27 July 1933, NCVOA/NCSS Box 14.

40. "Voluntary Occupation During Unemployment" (1933); "Agenda and Notes for NCSS Conference on Unemployment in Large Cities", Dec. 1938, NCVOA/NCSS Box 12; Sir Wyndham Deeds to the Warden of All-Souls, 7 May 1937, NCVOA/NCSS Box 16.

41. Hannington, *Distressed Areas*, p. 203; "Conference of representatives of Regional Committees and of the Unemployment Committee of the NCSS", Sept. 1935, NCVOA NCSS Box 5; Nottingham County Unemployed Workers Committee Meeting, 20 July 1934, Nottinghamshire Records Office, DD/RC/7/1.

42. Mess, "Service", p. 48; *Adversity*, p. 37; Teeling, *Near-by*, p. 111.

43. A. D. Lindsay to L. F. Ellis, 21 Feb. 1933, NCVOA/NCSS Box 5; Walter Citrine, General Secretary, TUC, to A. D. Lindsay, 15 Nov. 1937, NCVOA/NCSS Box 46; Ellis, in early 1934, wrote that the unemployed clubs enjoyed the "tacit" if not official consent of the trades councils, though this would seem more wishful thinking than actual fact, L. F. Ellis to F. Farrer, 4 Jan. 1934, NCVOA/NCSS Box

46; see Clinton, *Trades Councils*, p. 144; Leonard King to R. G. Ash Moody, NCSS, 29 April 1936, NCVOA/NCSS Box 46; Leonard King to L. F. Ellis, 8 May 1936, NCVOA/NCSS Box 46.

44. *Adversity*, p. 63; Brasnett, *Action*, p. 72; "Unemployment Committee, Secretary's Report", 22 Nov. 1934, NCVOA/NCSS Box 5; "Hand Work in Occupation Centres for Men", 1933, NCVOA-QGX/FYX/FX.

45. "Memorandum", 19 April 1933, NCVOA/NCSS Box 5; "Meeting With Advisory Officers and Area Secretaries", 6 Nov. 1934, NCVOA/NCSS Box 14; NCSS, "Conference of Unemployment Secretaries", 27-28 March 1941, NCVOA/NCSS Box 5; NCSS, "Voluntary Service and Unemployment, Summary of Progress in 1933"; NCVOA/NCSS Box 5; NCSS, "Memorandum on Meeting of Advisory Officers", 27 July 1933, NCVOA/NCSS Box 14.

46. Wilkinson, *Town*, p. 233.

47. "Unemployment and Community Service, Summary of Report, 1936", NCVOA/NCSS Box 5; "Report for NCSS on Girls Clubs and Unemployment", Jan. 1933, NCVOA/NCSS Box 8; G. H. Roberts, "Cookery and Homecraft Classes for Women", 28 Jan. 1937, NCVOA/NCSS Box 8; Brasnett, *Action*, p. 74. The Special Areas were south Wales, Cumberland, Durham, Northumberland, and west Scotland, and were so called in consequence of the Special Areas (Development and Improvement) Act of 1934, an acknowledgement, though little more than that, by the government of the plight of these areas. The act had been introduced into the Commons as the Depressed Areas Bill, but the word "Depressed" was too much for the peers of the House of Lords, who substituted "Special" for "Depressed". Notwithstanding the wise lords' polite euphemism, the areas were special primarily for the extent of economic depression and social distress.

48. "NCSS Statement to the Beveridge Committee", 27 July 1942, NCVOA/NCSS Box 5; *South East Lancashire and North East Cheshire Advisory Council (SELNEC) Second Annual Report*, 29 June 1937, NCVOA/NCSS Box 14.

49. For example, see Teeling, *Near-by*, p. 69; "NCSS Unemployment Committee Progress Report", June 1933, NCVOA/NCSS Box 5; John Newson, "To Unemployed Clubs", broadcast 2 Jan. 1935 (typescript), NCVOA/NCSS Box 16; *SELNEC Report*, 1937; Sir Percy Watkins, "The King's Visit to South Wales: Memorandum", 11 Dec. 1936, NCVOA/NCSS Box 16.

50. *A King's Story: The Memoirs of H.R.H. The Duke of Windsor* (1951), p. 244.

51. H.R.H. The Prince of Wales, "Unemployment and Voluntary Service", broadcast by BBC, 27 Jan. 1934 (typescript), NCVOA/NCSS Box 16; Teeling, *Near-by*, pp. 70, 87.

52. Some of the novels concerned with unemployment are Walter Greenwood, *Love on the Dole* (1933); Walter Brierley, *Means Test Man* (1935); Harold Heslop, *Last Cage Down* (1935); James Barke, *Major Operation* (1936); Simon Blumfield, *Jew Boy* (1936); Lewis Jones, *We Live* (1939); Lewis Grassic Gibbon, *Grey Granite* (written 1934, pub. 1946). Lionel Millard, "NCSS Report on Drama in Unemployed Clubs", 1938, NCVOA/NCSS Box 14.

53. "Meeting on Physical Training, Leeds", 13 Oct. 1933, NCVOA/NCSS Box 5; "Carnegie Physical Training College: Short Course for the NCSS Syllabus", Sept. 1933, NCVOA/NCSS Box 5.

54. "Physical Education", Jan. 1934, NCVOA/NCSS Box 5; "Physical Training among the Unemployed", 14 June 1935, NCVOA/NCSS Box 5; *Co-operative News*, 14 Nov. 1936; "NCSS Estimates 1939/40", NCVOA/NCSS Box 5; "NCSS Unemployment Committee, Memorandum on Progress and Policy", 31 March 1938, NCVOA/NCSS Box 5.

55. NUWM NAC Report, 25-26 Feb. 1933, HP/MML-AI and AII; Wilkinson, *Town*, p. 227.

56. Y. G. Evans to Oliver Harris, 16 April 1937, NUM/SWMF/F.42, SWCA.

57. Mess, "Social Service", p. 50.

Conclusion

1.Meeting of Subsidies Committee of FBI, 5 May 1925, Confederation of British Industries, MSS 200/F/3/51/17/1, Modern Records Centre; *Labour Leader*, 18 Aug. 1905.

2. *Pall Mall Gazette*, 11 Feb. 1886, Kingsford, *Hunger Marchers*, p. 70.

Bibliographical Essay

I have drawn heavily upon some sources that are sometimes considered unimportant, and paid less heed to other sources that are more often consulted. This was partly because the breadth of the subject of the book made a selective reading of sources imperative, and partly because the sources deemed unimportant proved to be central to exploring the subject of the book. This is not to demean the importance of traditional sources, particularly the voluminous reports of various government enquiries, but only to acknowledge that the gargantuan nature of mass unemployment had one corollary in the gargantuan mass of material produced about it, and that for a historian to be familiar with anything more than a minuscule fraction of that vast corpus is no more possible than it was to know personally each and every unemployed worker. This book is simply the following of one rarely travelled, somewhat overgrown path through that vast wilderness.

I have relied upon contemporary socialist and Marxist newspapers, journals, pamphlets, and leaflets to flesh out the world of the politically active unemployed. Of particular interest for 1884-1910 is the SDF's *Justice* and, from the 1890s, the ILP's *Labour Leader* and Blatchford's *Clarion.* The Socialist League's *Commonweal* is interesting in presenting the ultra-left position on the politics of the unemployed, and serves as a useful counterpoint, ideologically and organizationally, to those socialists who did work with the unemployed. The *Daily Herald* is invaluable for the early 1920s, but following its incorporation into the Labour machine in 1929 is of little interest for the 1930s. *The Ex-Service Man*, *The Fighter*, and the *Territorial Service Gazette* are useful on ex-service men's organizations, while *The Socialist*, *Solidarity*, *The Vanguard*, *Workers' Dreadnought*, and *The Worker* convey the vitality and plurality of socialist activity and thought in the immediate post-war period. *The Worker*, in its later incarnation as the paper of the National Minority

Movement, published "The Unemployed Worker" as a one-page supplement for the NUWCM between 1929 and 1931. The unemployed produced a number of their own papers during the inter-war period: *Out of Work* (1921-1923), *Unemployed Special* (1932), and the *Unemployed Leader* (1932-1935). *Out of Work* is as wild and fascinating as the movement that produced it. The latter two papers are less lively and less interesting. The CPGB's various papers-*The Communist*, the *Workers Weekly*, *Workers' Life*, and the *Sunday Worker* (for the 1920s), and the *Daily Worker* (for the 1930s), are useful for their recording of the various minor struggles of local groups of unemployed, but often more revealing are articles in such journals as *Labour Monthly*, *RILU Magazine*, and *International Press Correspondence* (*Inprecorr*). The latter two are important as guides to the serpentine route that the Comintern line towards the unemployed took during the inter-war period, but being international journals of the global Communist movement's activities, they were also organs in which the truth about the unemployed's activity did not loom large, with achievements being greatly exaggerated and the role of the NUWM distorted, while the setbacks and failures of the unemployed in Britain were only rarely acknowledged, and then only as a stick with which to beat the NUWM. *Blackshirt* and *Fascist Week* are important and neglected sources for BUF attitudes to the unemployed. And, much more useful than might be supposed, *The Times* is excellent both as a source of received conservative opinion about the activity of the unemployed and as a chronicle of unemployed activity. Numerous pamphlets and leaflets were consulted, housed variously at the Bodleian Library, the Working Class Movement Library, and the Communist Party Archives. The Working Class Movement Library, the Marx Memorial Library, and the G. D. H. Cole collection in the library of Nuffield College, Oxford, contain important collections of contemporary socialist literature that were of considerable use.

These sources, from CPGB pamphlets through to *The Times*, are not without dangers of overemphasis and the ideological restructuring of reality to serve their own varied political ends, but then there are no sources not similarly affected. What these sources offer that other sources lack is both an interest (often hostile) in the activity of the unemployed, a sense of the world of the unemployed as being politically and socially constructed, rather than naturally given and preordained, and an awareness of the activity of the unemployed as being ongoing, organized insofar as it was invariably focused upon immediately realizable objectives, and subject to both defeat and success in attempting to realize these objectives. In other words, a sense of the politics of the unemployed as a historical phenomenon, of the unemployed as people who make their own history, and not as other sources would have them, passive and inert, apart from the odd occasion when they rise for no good reason beyond excessive suffering.

On the inter-war period Wal Hannington's various books—*Unemployed Struggles 1919-1936* (1936, repub. 1977), *The Problem of the Distressed Areas* (1937), *A Short History of the Unemployed* (1938), *Ten Lean Years* (1940), and *Never on our Knees* (1967)—and some of his pamphlets, particularly *Black Coffins* (1939), remain the authoritative, although, as I have suggested problematic, accounts of the politics of the inter-war unemployed. Harry McShane's *No Mean Fighter* (1980) offers an invaluable account of the NUWM by one of its outstanding leaders, which serves as a reflective counterpoint to Hannington's more celebratory writings.

A wealth of information upon the politics of unemployed ex-service men and later the early post-World War I unemployed organizations is contained in Cabinet Papers 24: 1918-1923. Of particular importance are the Directorate of Intelligence's fortnightly "Report on Revolutionary organizations", which, whereever I have been able to corroborate them, were highly accurate in their factual detail and in their general sense of revolutionary ferment, though somewhat off the mark in attributing such global ferment to the conventional bogey of an international Jewish conspiracy. There is also much of worth contained in the Ministry of Labour's Cabinet papers. Cabinet Papers for the 1930s are less interesting.

Upon the NUWCM/NUWM the most important collections of papers are the NUWM collection held by the marvelous Working Class Movement Library (Manchester) created and run by a leader of the famous Salford 1932 NUWM demonstration (later made legendary through its fictional portrayal in Walter Greenwood's novel *Love on the Dole*) Eddy Frow, and his wife Ruth. Eddy Frow along with John Mahon has co-authored a very useful bibliography of the NUWCM and NUWM, copies of which can be purchased from the Working Class Movement Library. The Working Class Movement Library also houses numerous pamphlets and leaflets important to any study of the politics of the unemployed. The Marx Memorial Library has one part of the Wal Hannington papers, mainly ephemera from the NUWM in the 1930s. The other, more important part of the Wal Hannington papers is held by the Communist Party in its archives, and contains, in addition to much NUWM ephemera, Hannington's scrapbooks and personal papers. Also held by the Communist Party Archives are the Tom Mann papers, of some interest, particularly in Mann's detailing of his reaction to his imprisonment in 1932 as treasurer of the NUWM.

The Pollard papers, John Johnson collection, Bodleian Library, contains much useful and hitherto unused ephemera from the CPGB in the 1920s, and a fascinating study upon the lost world of early British Communism could be made by examining these papers. Scattered through the various collections held by the South Wales Coalfield Archive (University College, Swansea) is much about the inter-war unemployed movements. Obvious starting points are the NUM/SWMF papers and the Mardy Lodge papers, but individuals' papers such as those of Glyn Evans, Eddy Jones (Cwmbran), and J. S. Williams are also of note. Local records offices sometimes (though not always) possess interesting material upon the activity of the unemployed, contained in council minutes, police records, and PAC minutes. Of note are the Bristol Council minutes, 1932-1933, and the Bristol Police records, 1932, held by the Bristol Records Office; Liverpool PAC minutes, 1930-1933, and Liverpool Watch Committee minutes, 1932, held by the Liverpool Records Office. The National Council of Social Service collection held by the National Council of Voluntary Organisations Archive is the major source for the history of the unemployed club movement.

Rich both creatively and historically are the novels concerned with the unemployed produced by working class writers during the 1930s, such as Walter Greenwood, *Love on the Dole* (1933), Walter Brierley, *Means Test Man* (1935), Harold Heslop, *Last Cage Down* (1935), James Barke, *Major Operation* (1936), Simon Blumfield, *Jew Boy* (1936), Lewis Jones, *We Live* (1939), and Lewis Grassic Gibbon, *Grey Granite* (written 1934, pub. 1946). Written later, and as yet unpublished (apart from some extracts), is Harry Davies, *The Lean Years* (unpub. ms. in possession of its author).

An overlooked yet rich source are the many working class memoirs, biographies, and local histories now coming out of the community publishing movement in Britain, such as Wilf Gray, Mick Jenkins, and Eddie and Ruth Frow, *Unemployed Demonstrations, Salford and Manchester: October 1931* (Manchester 1981), Stephen "Johnny" Hicks, *Sparring For Luck. Autobiography of the East End Boxer-Poet* (1982), Jane Bellamy et al., *Who was Harry Cowley?* (Brighton 1984), Brian Lewis and Bill Gledhill, *Tommy James: A Lion of a Man* (Yorkshire 1985), and Ernie Benson, *To Struggle Is to Live Vol. 2.* (Newcastle 1980). Though not cited in the text John Taylor Caldwell, *The Red Evangel * A Life of Guy A. Aldred * Boy Preacher * Humanist * Anarchist-Communist* (unpub. ms., Mitchell Library, Glasgow 1980), a lengthy account of an important figure in Glaswegian radical history, has some interesting detail about Aldred's involvement and differences with the inter-war unemployed movements. In the course of researching this book I made a number of interviews, the tapes of which are in my possession, with Harry Davies (23 January 1986); Bob Edwards (4 February 1986); Tony Gilbert (11 February 1986); Finlay Hart (30 July 1986); C. L. R. James (11 February 1986); Rose Kerrigan (17 June 1986); Harry McShane (30 July 1986); and Alfred Salisbury, (4 February 1986).

With regard to secondary authorities there is no work of British history upon the unemployed of comparable ambition and achievement to Alexander Keyssar's masterly study of the jobless in Massachusetts, *Out of Work. The First Century of Unemployment in Massachusetts* (Cambridge 1986). On the social origins of the unemployed written as Marx put it, "in the annals of mankind in letters of blood and fire", no account has yet surpassed that given by him in *Capital, Vol. I*, chapters 26 to 28, although numerous more recent works inform it. Useful background to the history of the politics of the unemployed in the late Victorian and Edwardian periods is contained in José Harris's worthy though turgid *Unemployment and Politics 1886-1914* (Oxford 1972). More insightful on the Edwardian era is K. D. Brown's scholarly *Labour and Unemployment, 1900-1914* (Newton Abbot 1971). For the inter-war period Peter Kingsford, *The Hunger Marchers in Britain 1920-1940* (1982), has much of interest, but is restricted by its deliberately narrow focus upon hunger marches. For a general overview of socialist politics through the era covered in this book, James Hinton, *Labour and Socialism. A History of the British Labour Movement, 1867-1974* (Brighton 1983) is a masterly and much underrated summary. For the period up until 1914 the various essays of Eric Hobsbawm, particularly those contained in the volumes *Labouring Men* (1964) and *Worlds of Labour*

(1984), and his major works on the nineteenth century, *The Age of Revolution* (1962); *The Age of Capital* (1975); and *The Age of Empire* (1987); remain unsurpassed as a guide to the changing nature of economy, society and politics. There is nothing approaching the power and insight of Hobsbawm's work for the period from 1918 to 1939. Sean Glynn and Alan Booth (eds.) *The Road To Full Employment* (1987) does provide a useful summary of the state of present scholarship on the study of unemployment in the inter-war period. Noreen Branson and Margot Heinemann, *Britain in the Nineteen Thirties* (1971), though now dated, still provides the best guide to this decade, in part dealing with the social costs that others would prefer to forget, while Claud Cockburn's personal and personable *The Devil's Decade* (1973) succeeds better than nearly all in conveying much of the feeling of the 1930s. As good an introduction as any to the inter-war era remains Allen Hutt's *The Post-War History of the British Working Class* (1937), which will perhaps one day be republished.

Index

In some cases my research has not turned up the first name of certain unemployed activists. In such cases only the surname has been indexed.

About the Author

RICHARD FLANAGAN holds an M.Litt. in History from Oxford University and presently resides in Hobart, Tasmania, Australia.

www.ingramcontent.com/pod-product-compliance
Ingram Content Group UK Ltd.
Pitfield, Milton Keynes, MK11 3LW, UK
UKHW041130071026
15587UKWH00009B/400

9 780313 274398